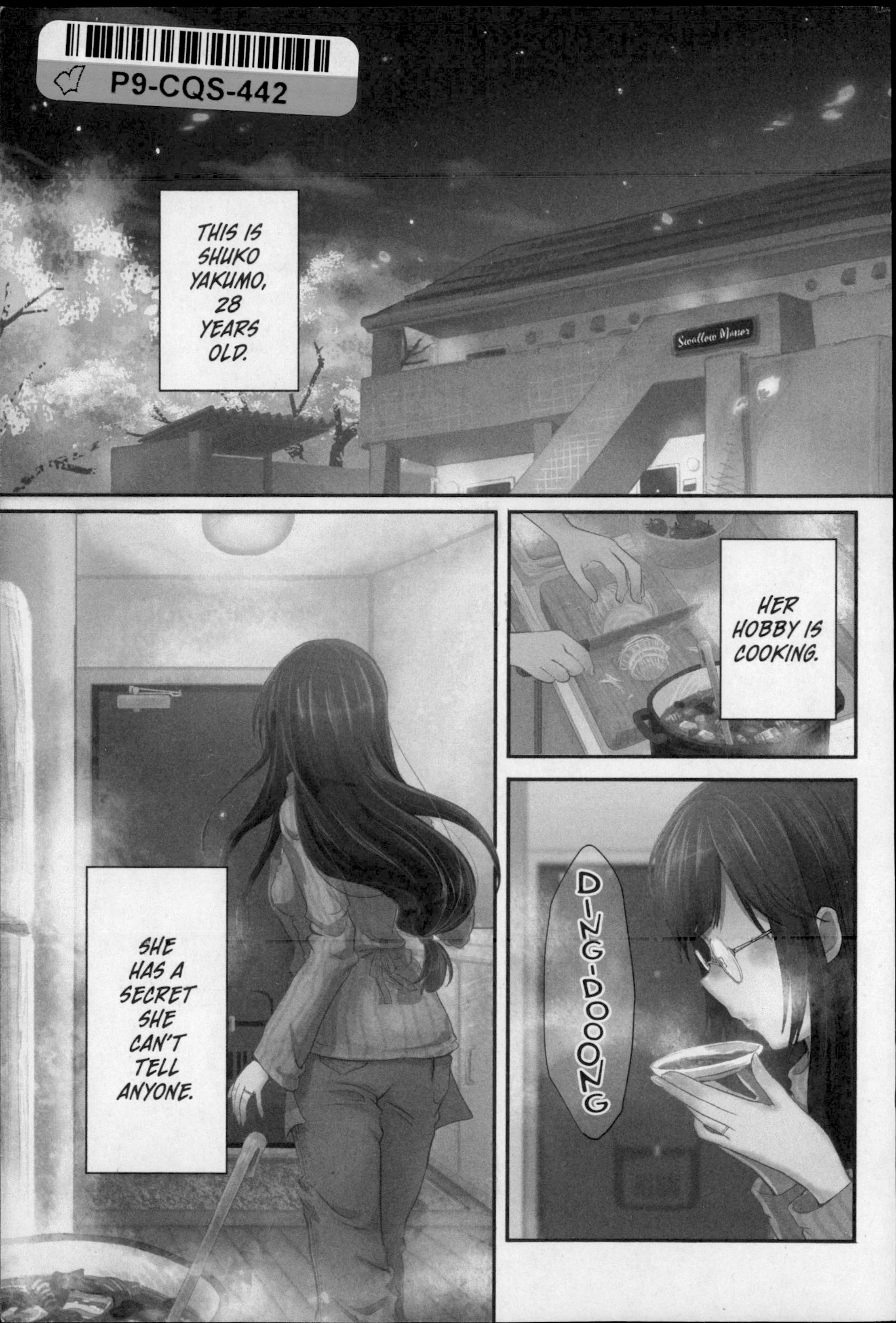
THIS IS SHUKO YAKUMO, 28 YEARS OLD.
Swallow Manor
HER HOBBY IS COOKING.
DING-DOOONG
SHE HAS A SECRET SHE CAN'T TELL ANYONE.

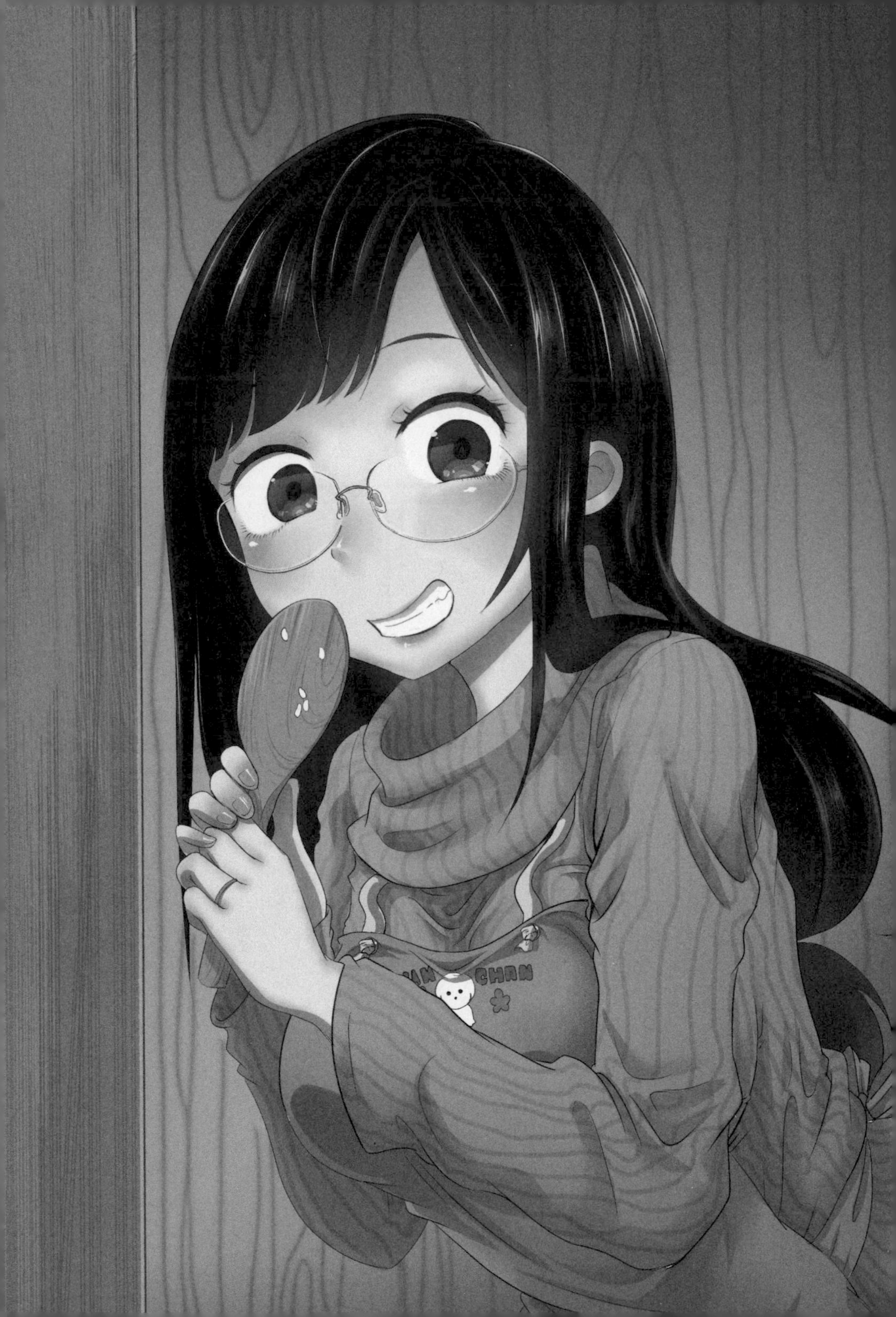
CHAN

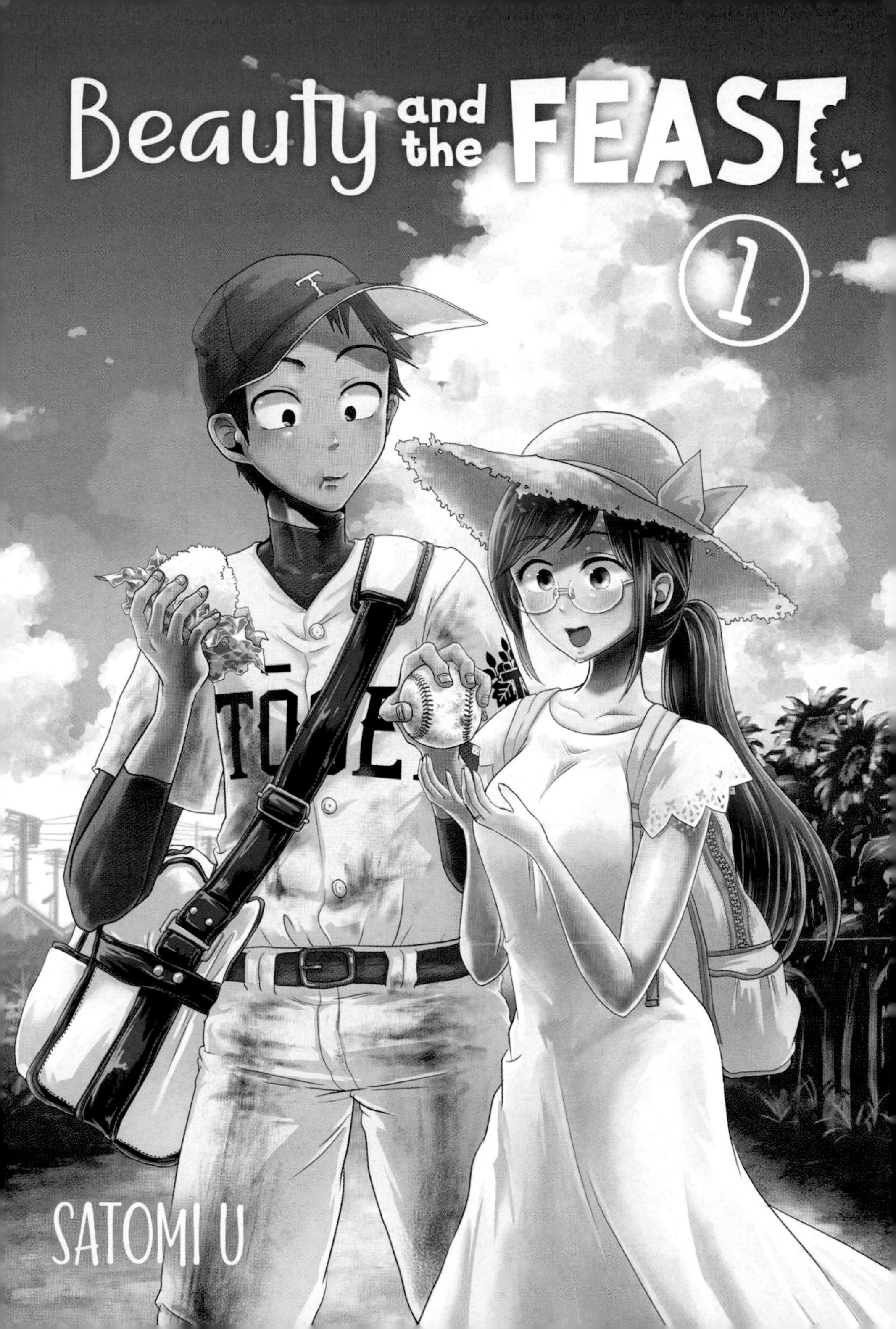
Beauty and the FEAST
1
SATOMI U

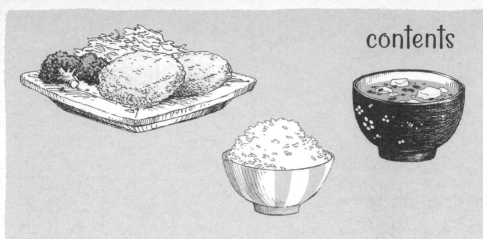

contents

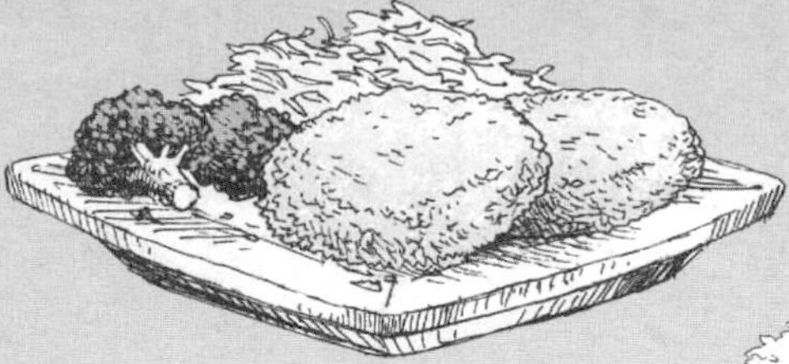
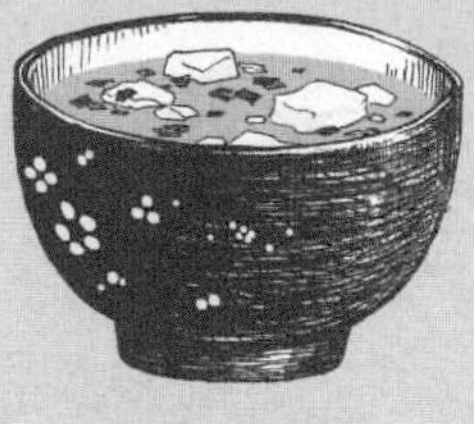
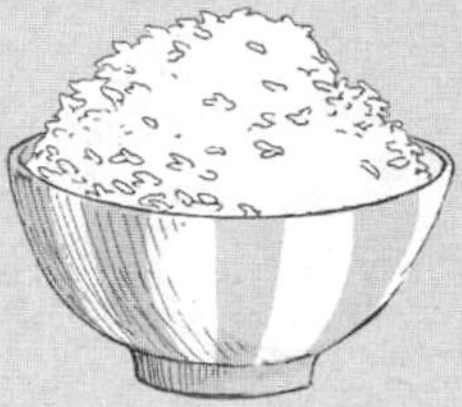

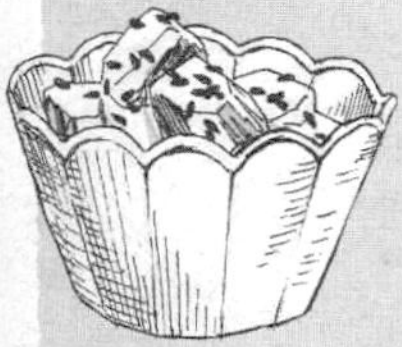
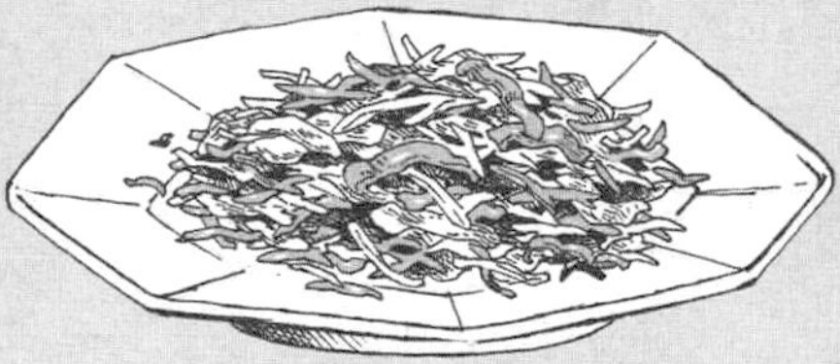
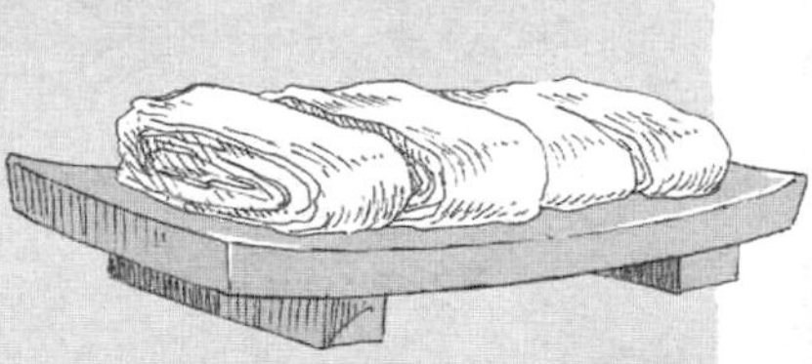
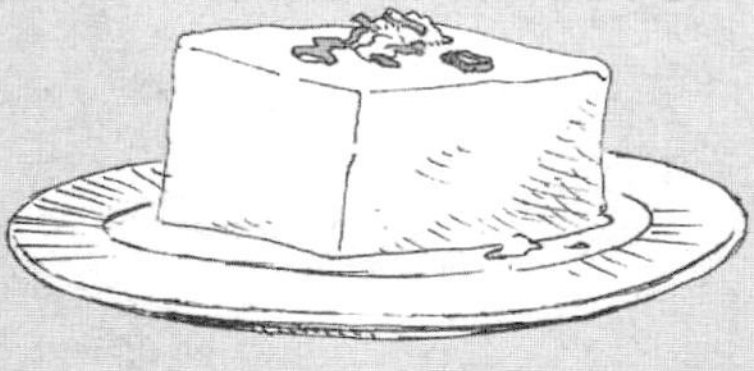
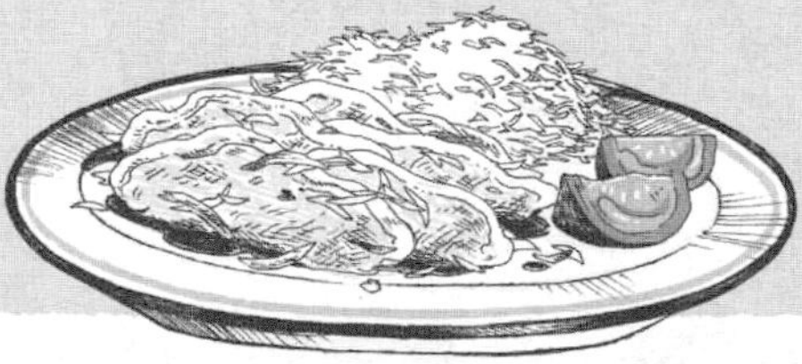

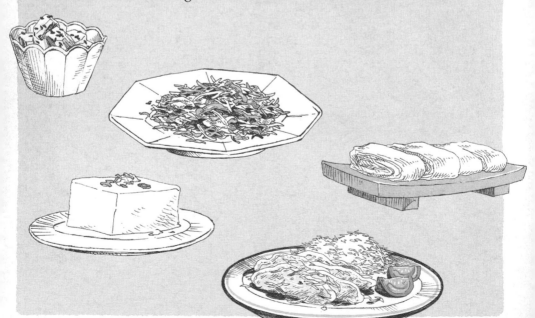

Meal 1: Yakumo-san Wants to Feed You!

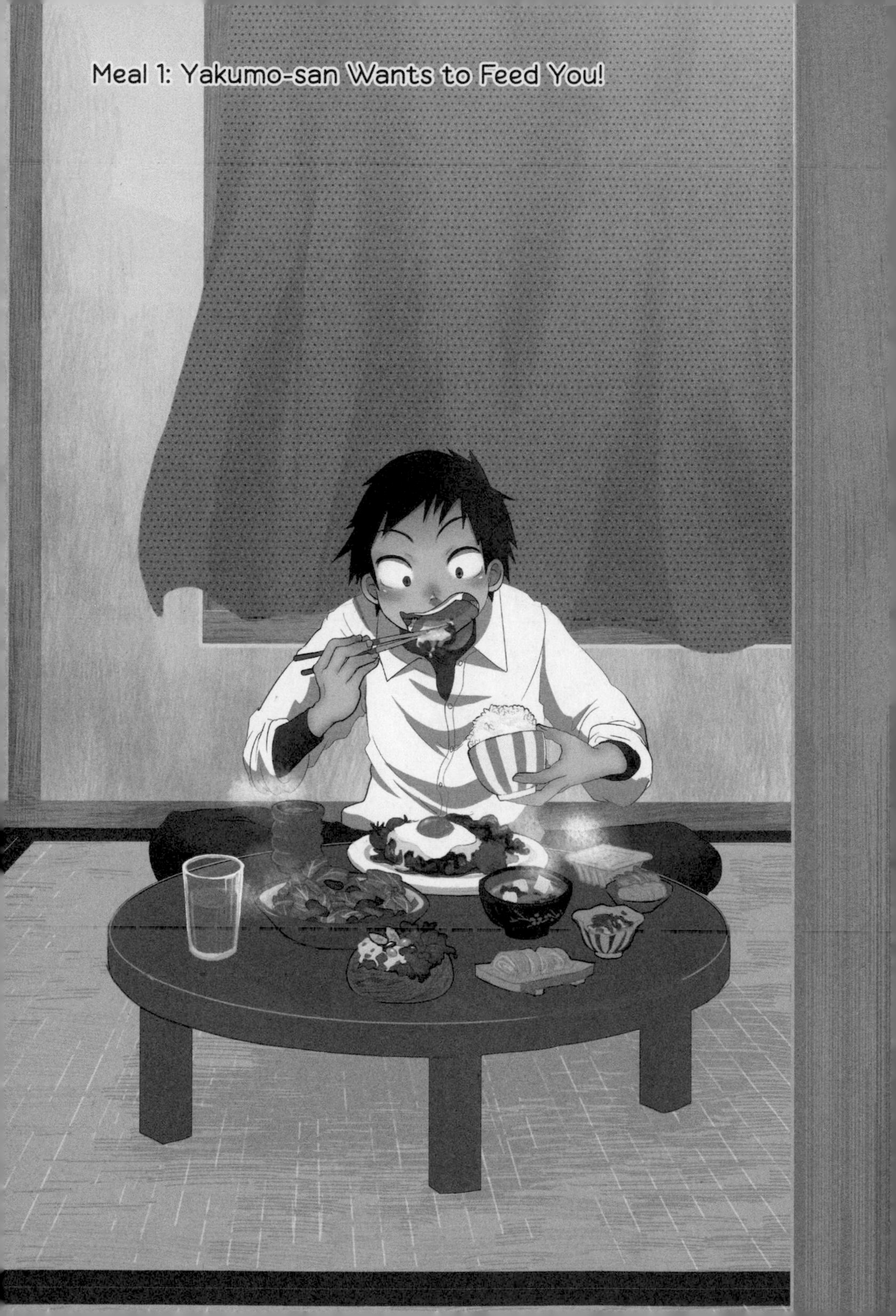

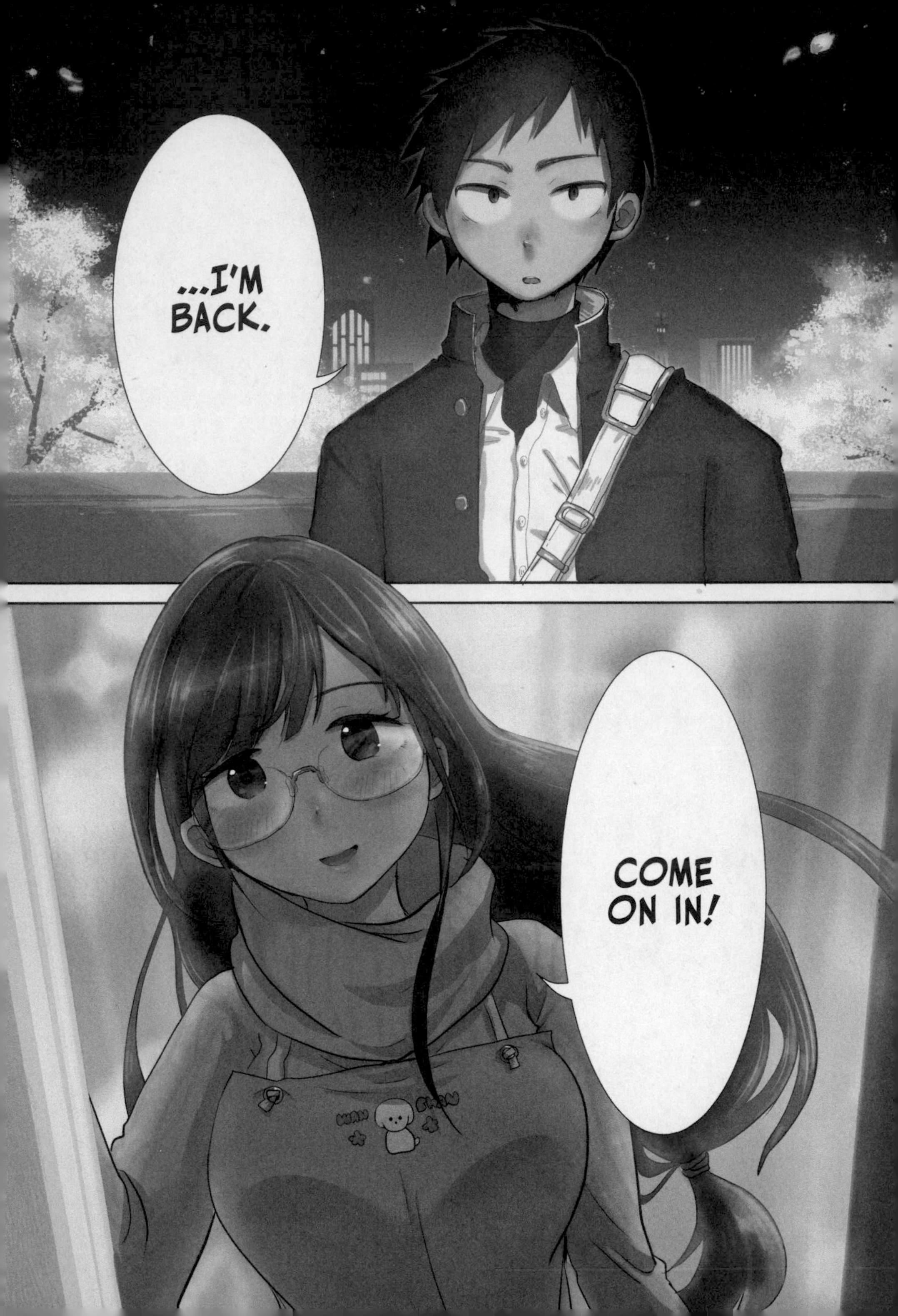
...I'M BACK.
COME ON IN!

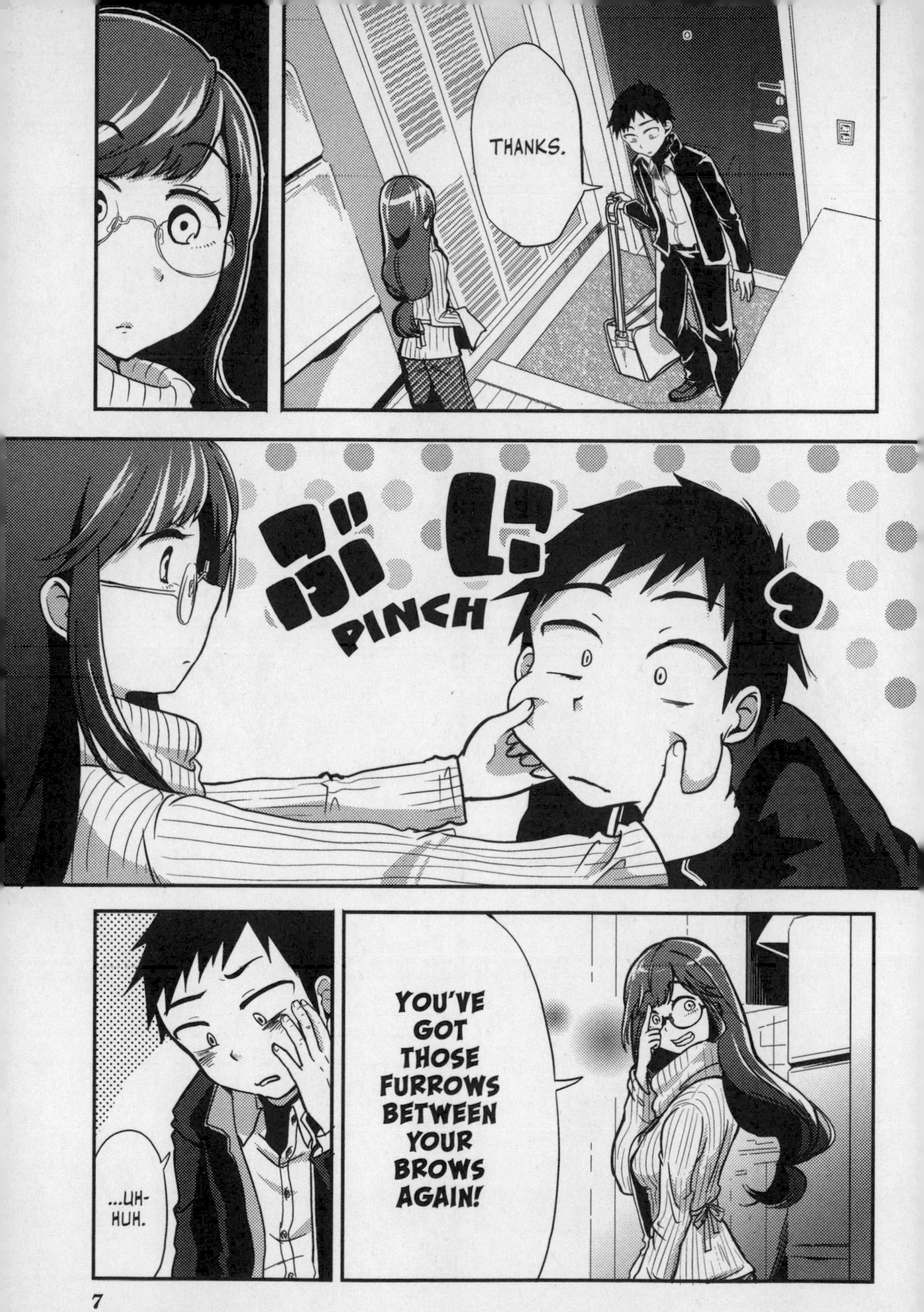
THANKS.
PINCH
YOU'VE GOT THOSE FURROWS BETWEEN YOUR BROWS AGAIN!
...UH-HUH.

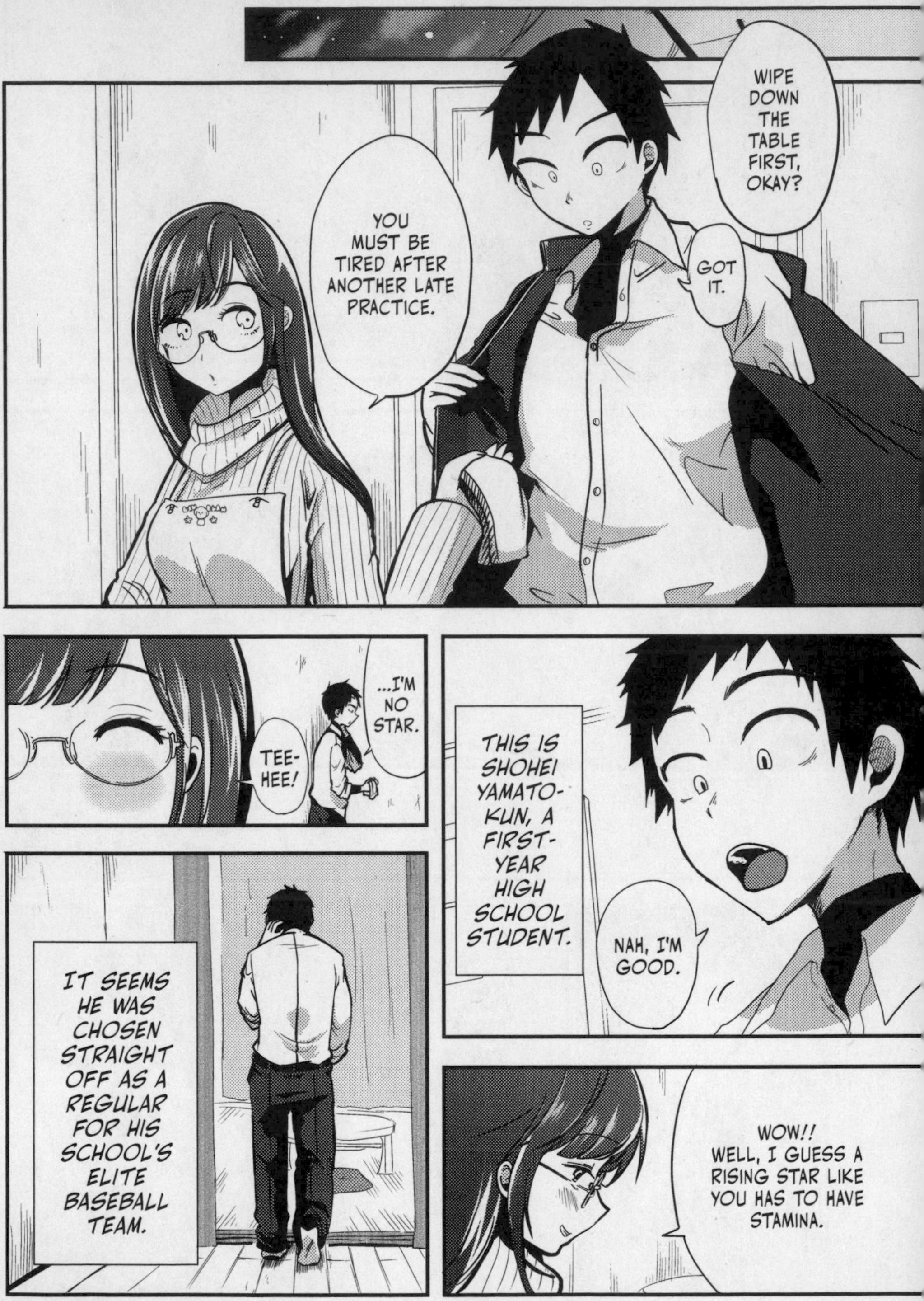
WIPE DOWN THE TABLE FIRST, OKAY?
GOT IT.
YOU MUST BE TIRED AFTER ANOTHER LATE PRACTICE.
THIS IS SHOHEI YAMATO-KUN, A FIRST-YEAR HIGH SCHOOL STUDENT.
NAH, I'M GOOD.
WOW!! WELL, I GUESS A RISING STAR LIKE YOU HAS TO HAVE STAMINA.
...I'M NO STAR.
TEE-HEE!
IT SEEMS HE WAS CHOSEN STRAIGHT OFF AS A REGULAR FOR HIS SCHOOL'S ELITE BASEBALL TEAM.

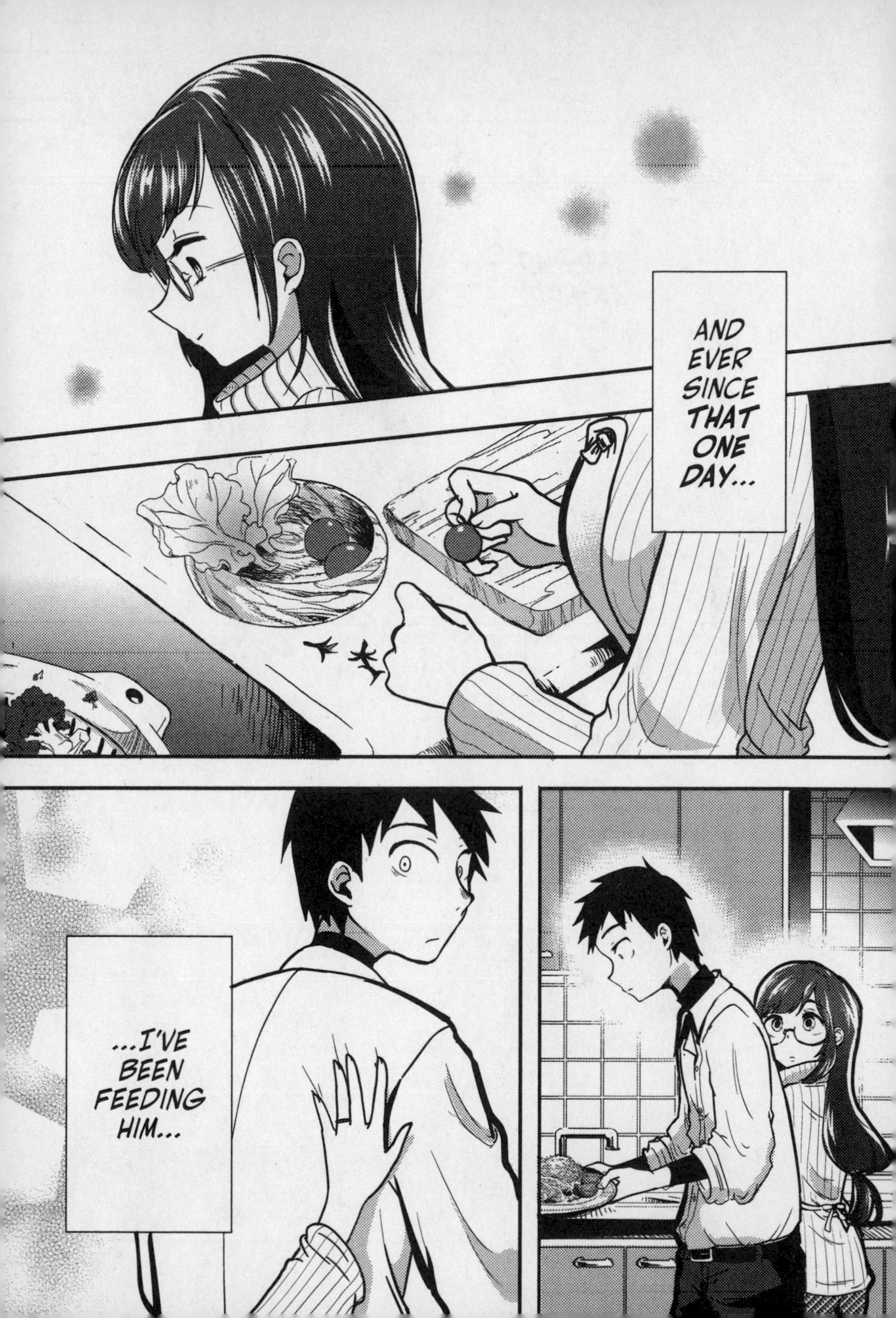
AND EVER SINCE THAT ONE DAY...
...I'VE BEEN FEEDING HIM...

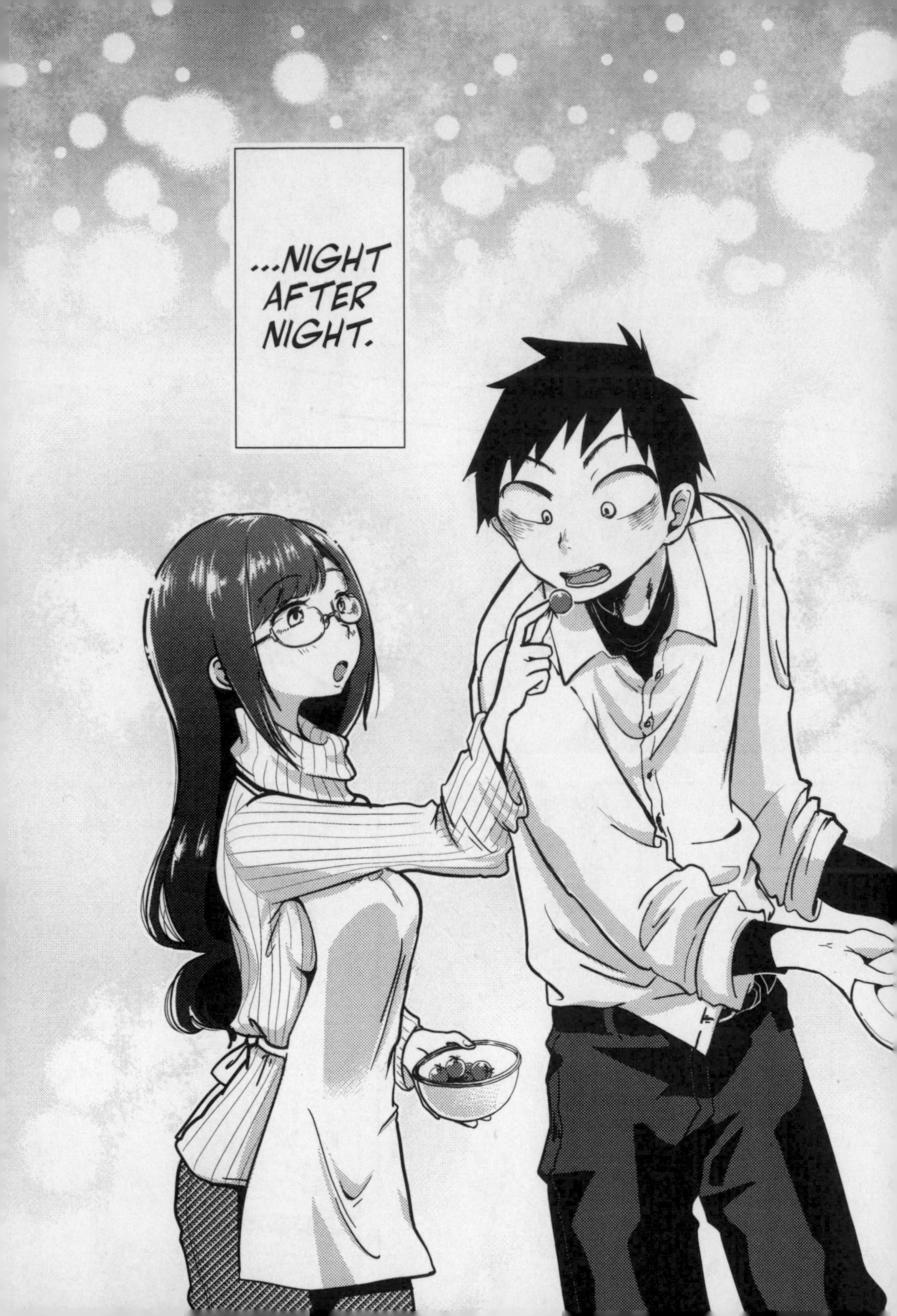
...NIGHT AFTER NIGHT.

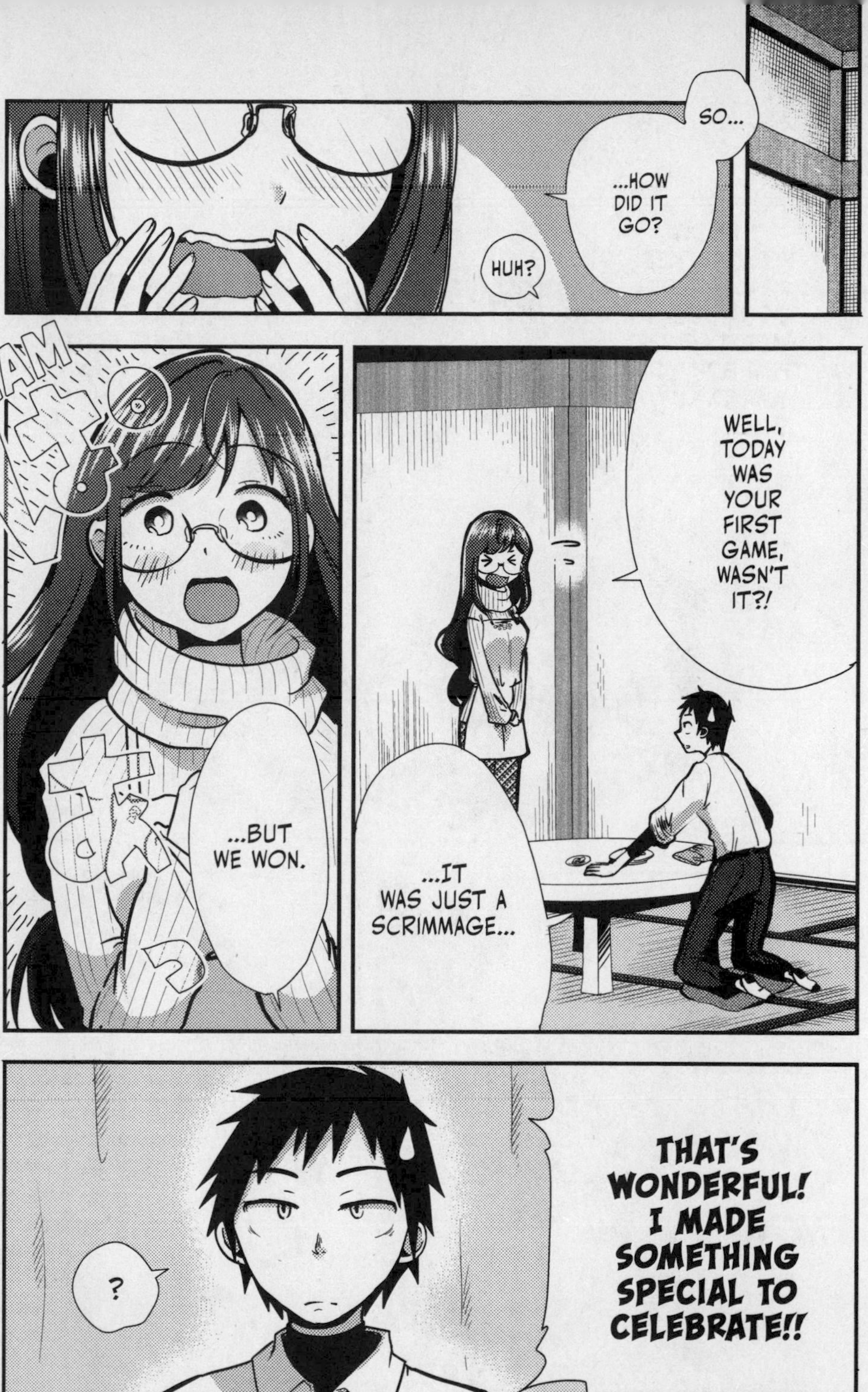
SO...
...HOW DID IT GO?
HUH?
WELL, TODAY WAS YOUR FIRST GAME, WASN'T IT?!
...IT WAS JUST A SCRIMMAGE...
BEAM
...BUT WE WON.
THAT'S WONDERFUL! I MADE SOMETHING SPECIAL TO CELEBRATE!!
?

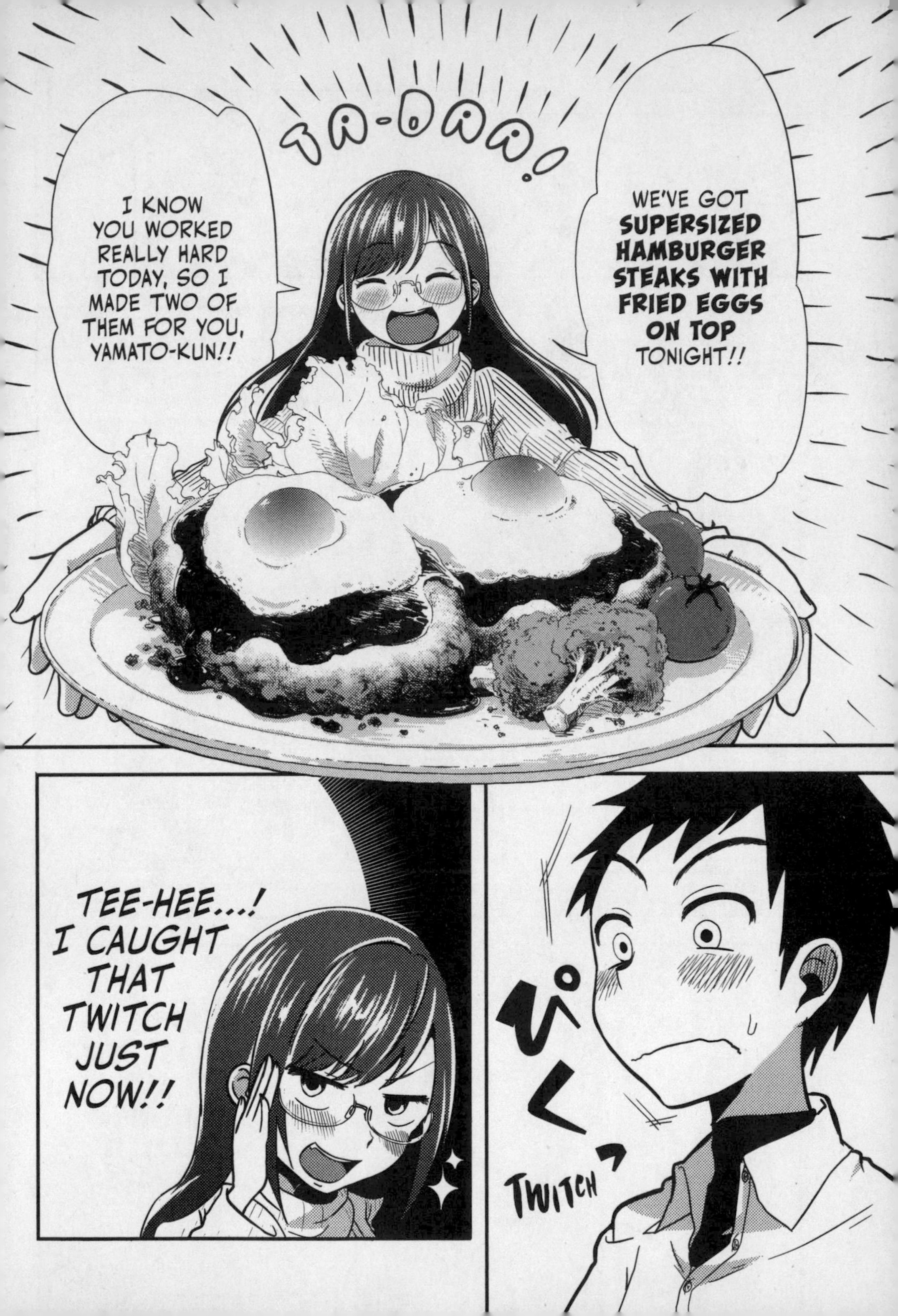
WE'VE GOT **SUPERSIZED HAMBURGER STEAKS WITH FRIED EGGS ON TOP** TONIGHT!!
TA-DAA!
I KNOW YOU WORKED REALLY HARD TODAY, SO I MADE TWO OF THEM FOR YOU, YAMATO-KUN!!
ぴく
TWITCH
TEE-HEE...! I CAUGHT THAT TWITCH JUST NOW!!

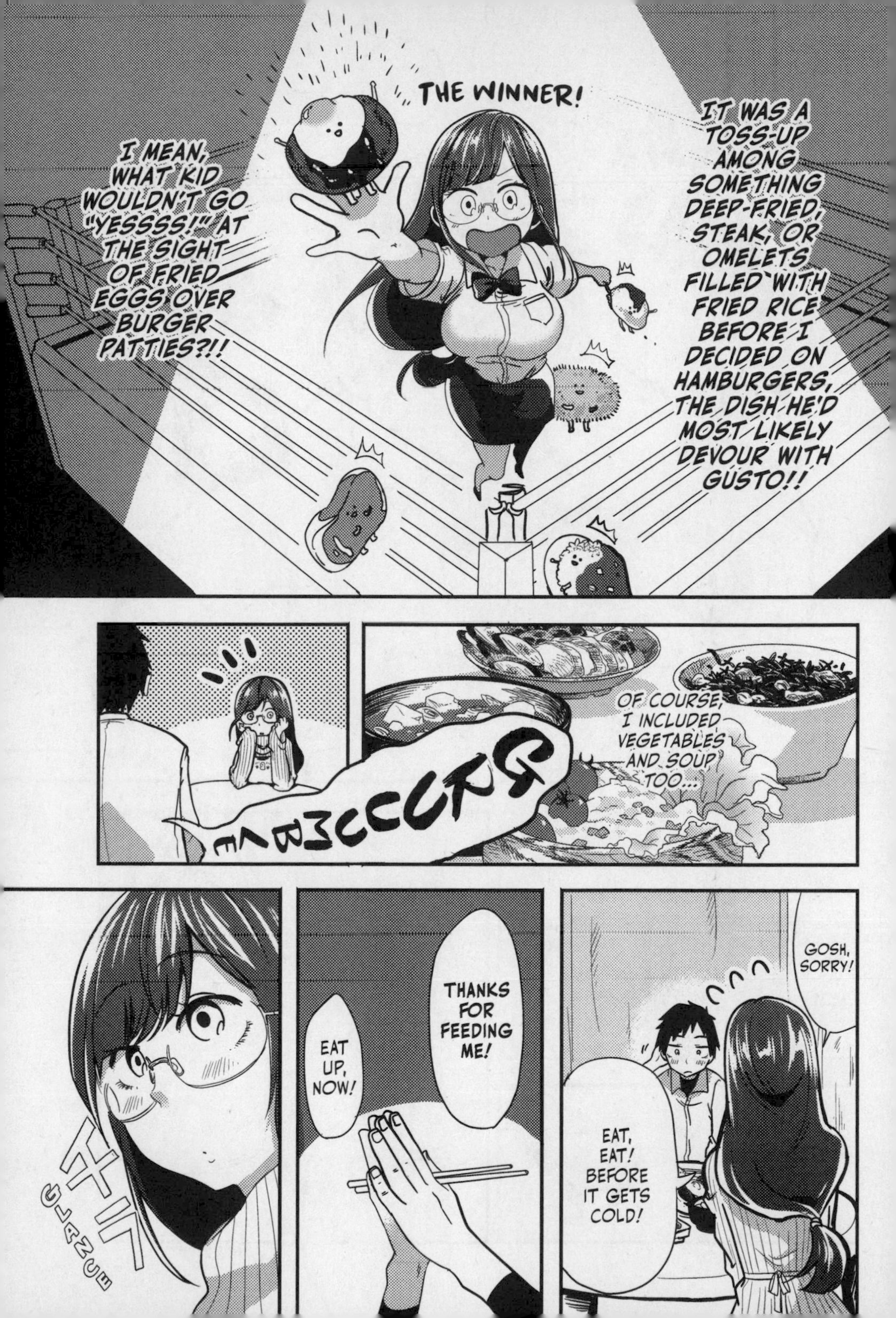
IT WAS A TOSS-UP AMONG SOMETHING DEEP-FRIED, STEAK, OR OMELETS FILLED WITH FRIED RICE BEFORE I DECIDED ON HAMBURGERS, THE DISH HE'D MOST LIKELY DEVOUR WITH GUSTO!!
THE WINNER!
I MEAN, WHAT KID WOULDN'T GO "YESSSS!" AT THE SIGHT OF FRIED EGGS OVER BURGER PATTIES?!!
OF COURSE, I INCLUDED VEGETABLES AND SOUP TOO...
GOSH, SORRY!
EAT, EAT! BEFORE IT GETS COLD!
THANKS FOR FEEDING ME!
EAT UP, NOW!
GLANCE

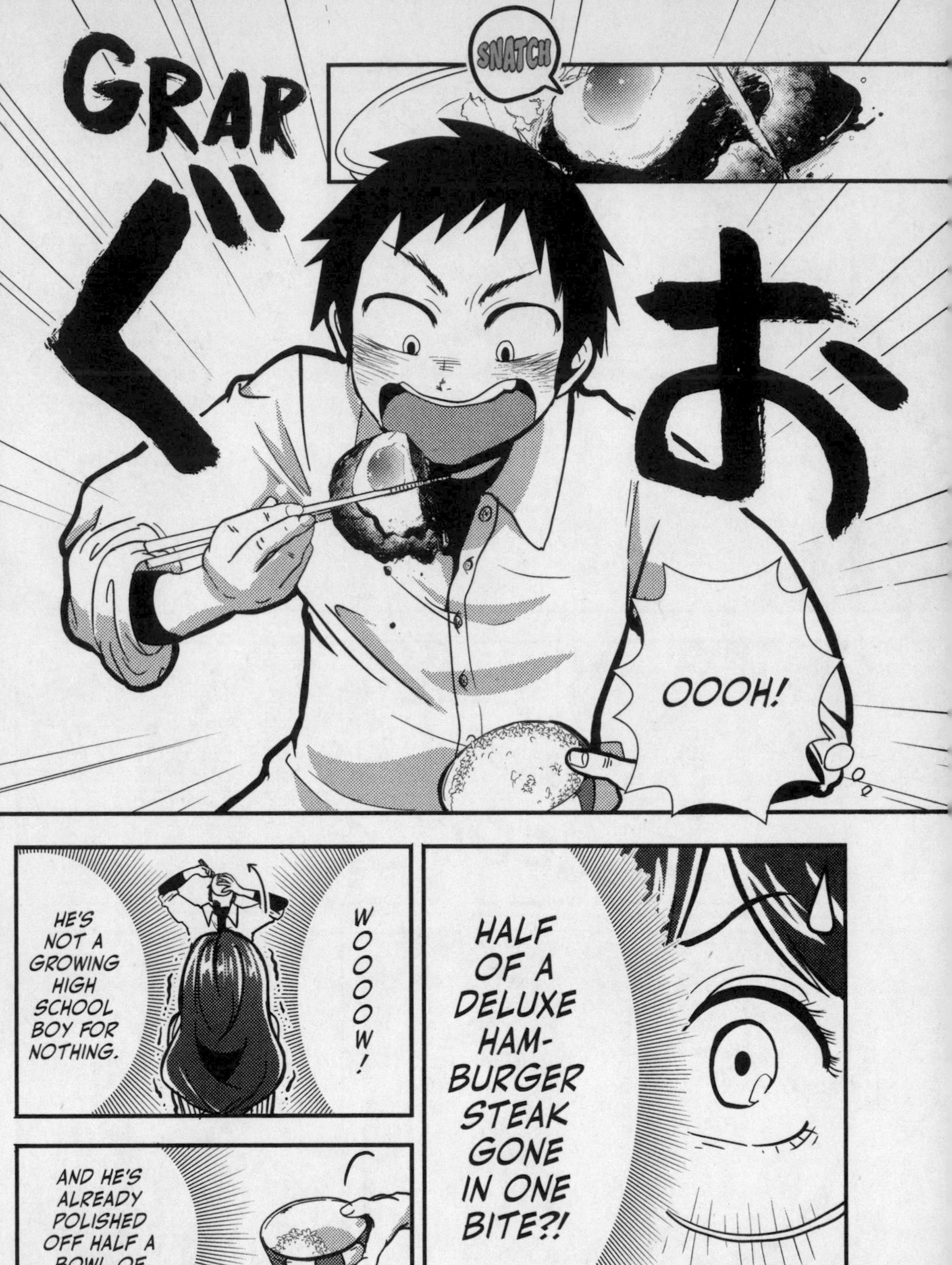
SNATCH
GRAR
ぐお
OOOH!
HALF OF A DELUXE HAMBURGER STEAK GONE IN ONE BITE?!
WOOOOOW!
HE'S NOT A GROWING HIGH SCHOOL BOY FOR NOTHING.
AND HE'S ALREADY POLISHED OFF HALF A BOWL OF RICE!!

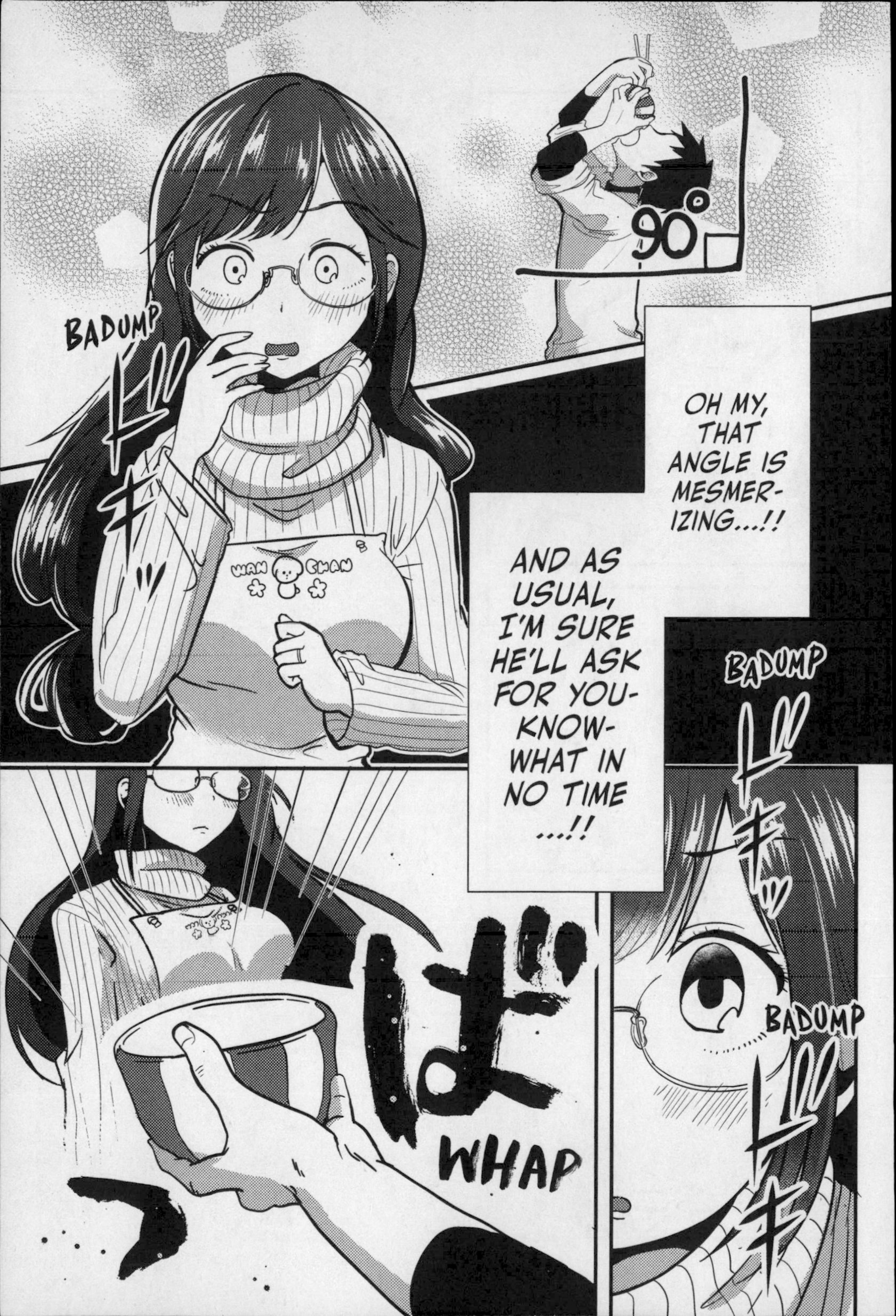
90°
BADUMP
OH MY, THAT ANGLE IS MESMER-IZING...!!
AND AS USUAL, I'M SURE HE'LL ASK FOR YOU-KNOW-WHAT IN NO TIME ...!!
BADUMP
BADUMP
WHAP

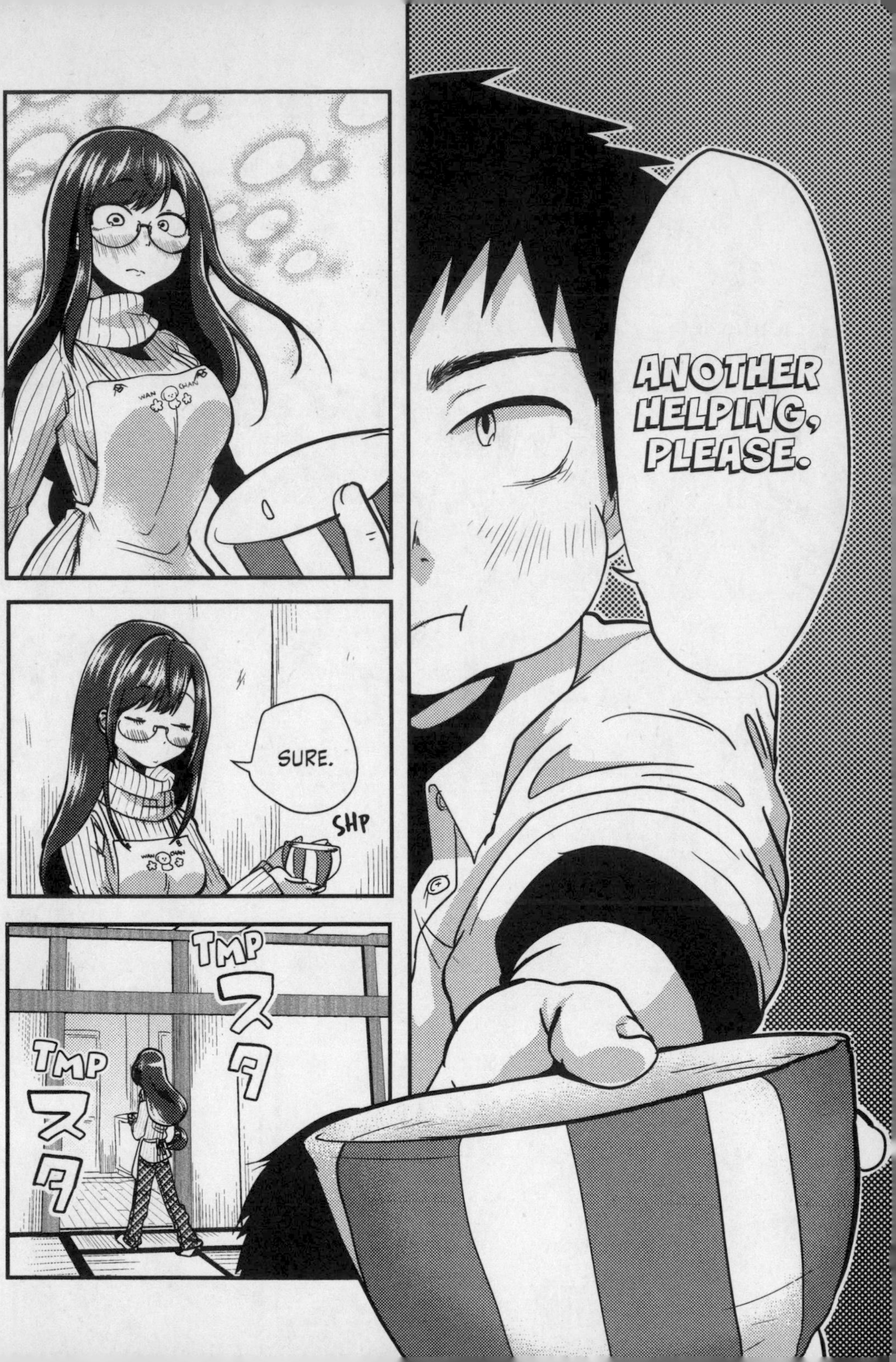
ANOTHER HELPING, PLEASE.
SURE.
SHP
TMP
スタ
TMP
スタ

MOVED

ANOTHER
HELPING...
♡

MUSIC
TO MY
EARS
...!!

KACHAK

MEAT
REALLY
BRINGS
OUT THE
BEAST IN
BOYS!!

THAT MUST
BE A NEW
RECORD
FOR THE
FASTEST
SECONDS
REQUEST
!!

AND
TONIGHT...

FWOOO

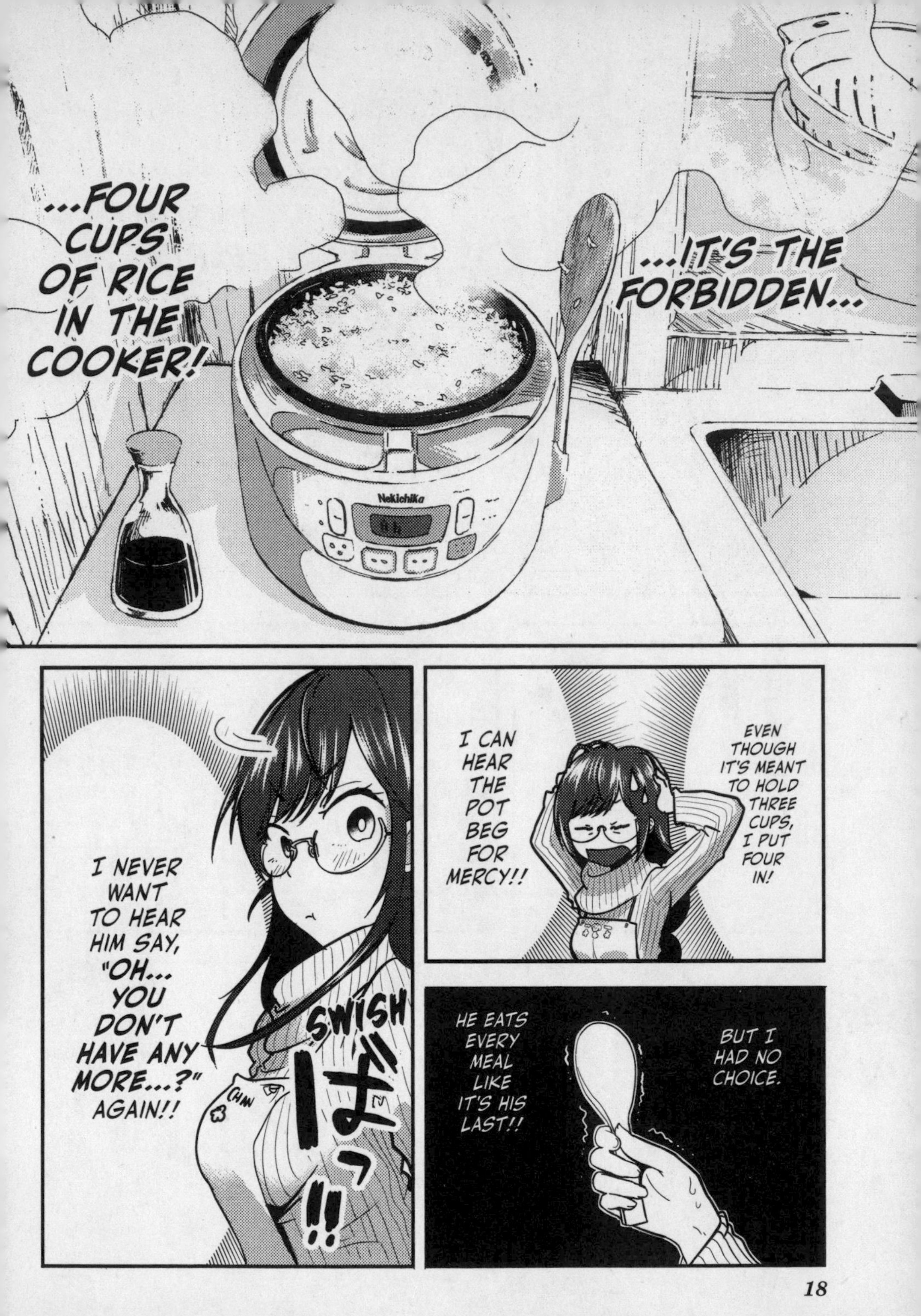

...IT'S THE FORBIDDEN...
...FOUR CUPS OF RICE IN THE COOKER!
Nekichika
EVEN THOUGH IT'S MEANT TO HOLD THREE CUPS, I PUT FOUR IN!
I CAN HEAR THE POT BEG FOR MERCY!!
BUT I HAD NO CHOICE.
HE EATS EVERY MEAL LIKE IT'S HIS LAST!!
I NEVER WANT TO HEAR HIM SAY, "OH... YOU DON'T HAVE ANY MORE...?" AGAIN!!
SWISH
ばっ!!

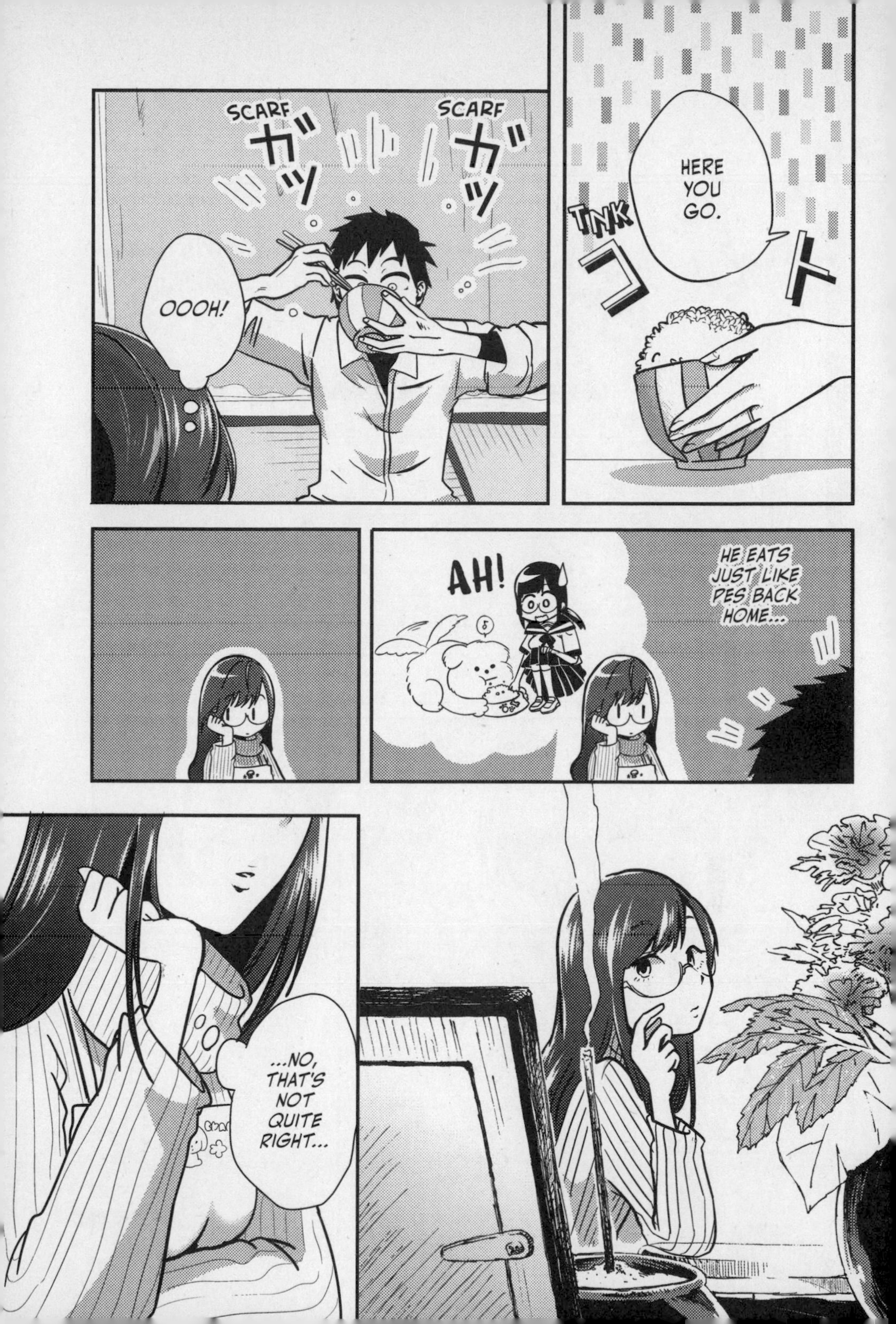
TNK
コト
HERE YOU GO.
SCARF
ガツ
SCARF
ガツ
OOOH!
AH!
HE EATS JUST LIKE PES BACK HOME...
...NO, THAT'S NOT QUITE RIGHT...

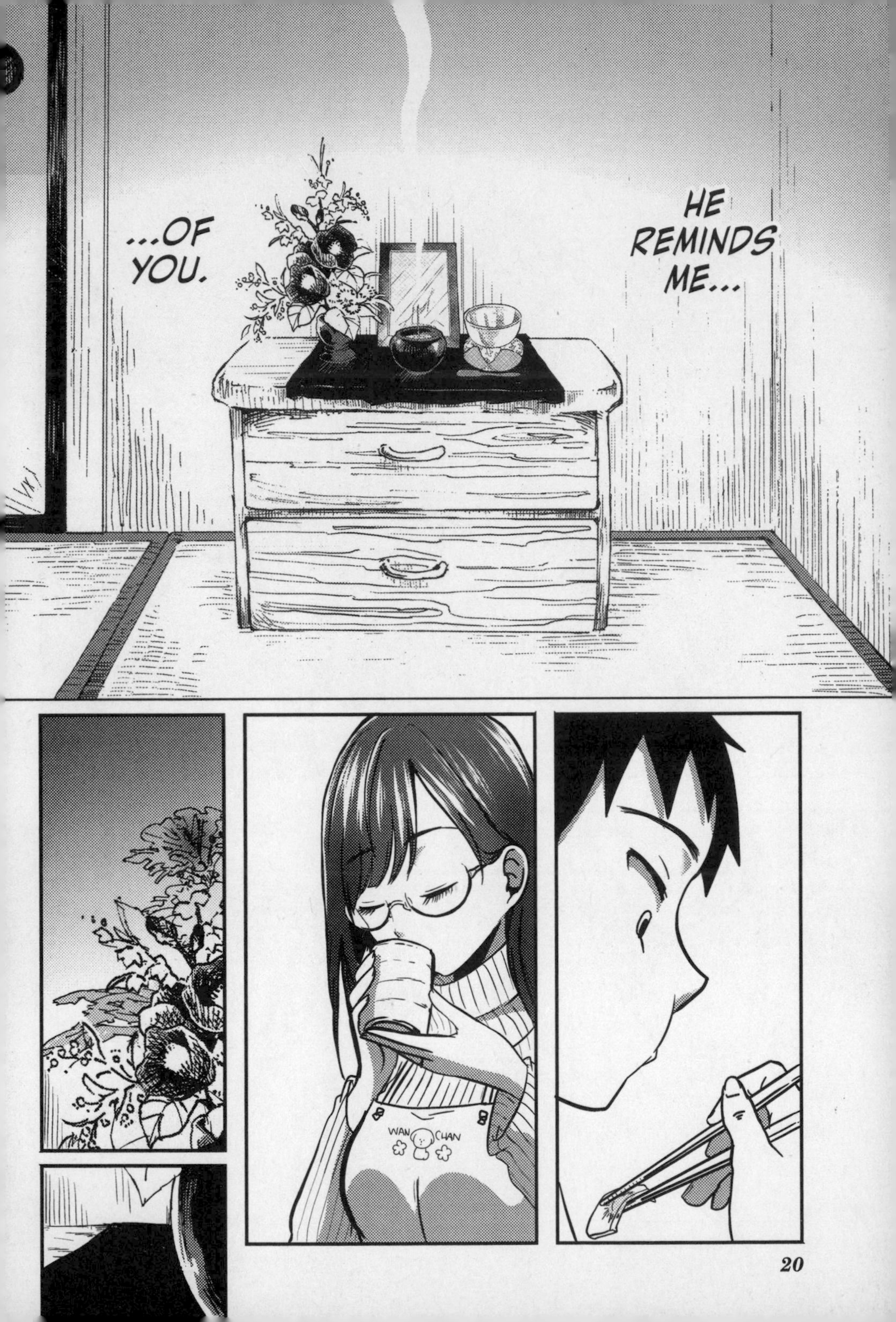
HE REMINDS ME...
...OF YOU.
WAN CHAN

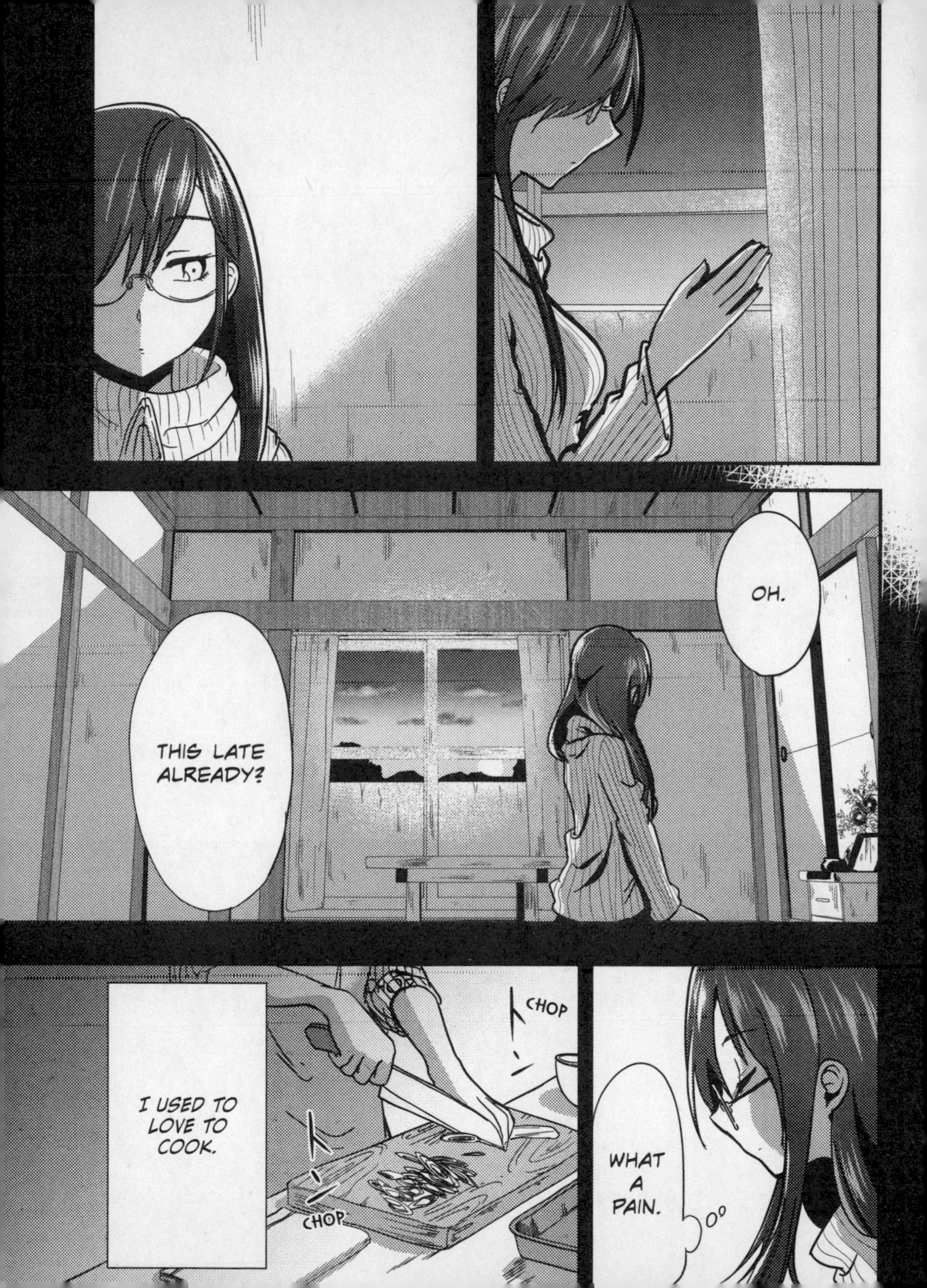
OH.
THIS LATE ALREADY?
WHAT A PAIN.
CHOP
I USED TO LOVE TO COOK.
CHOP

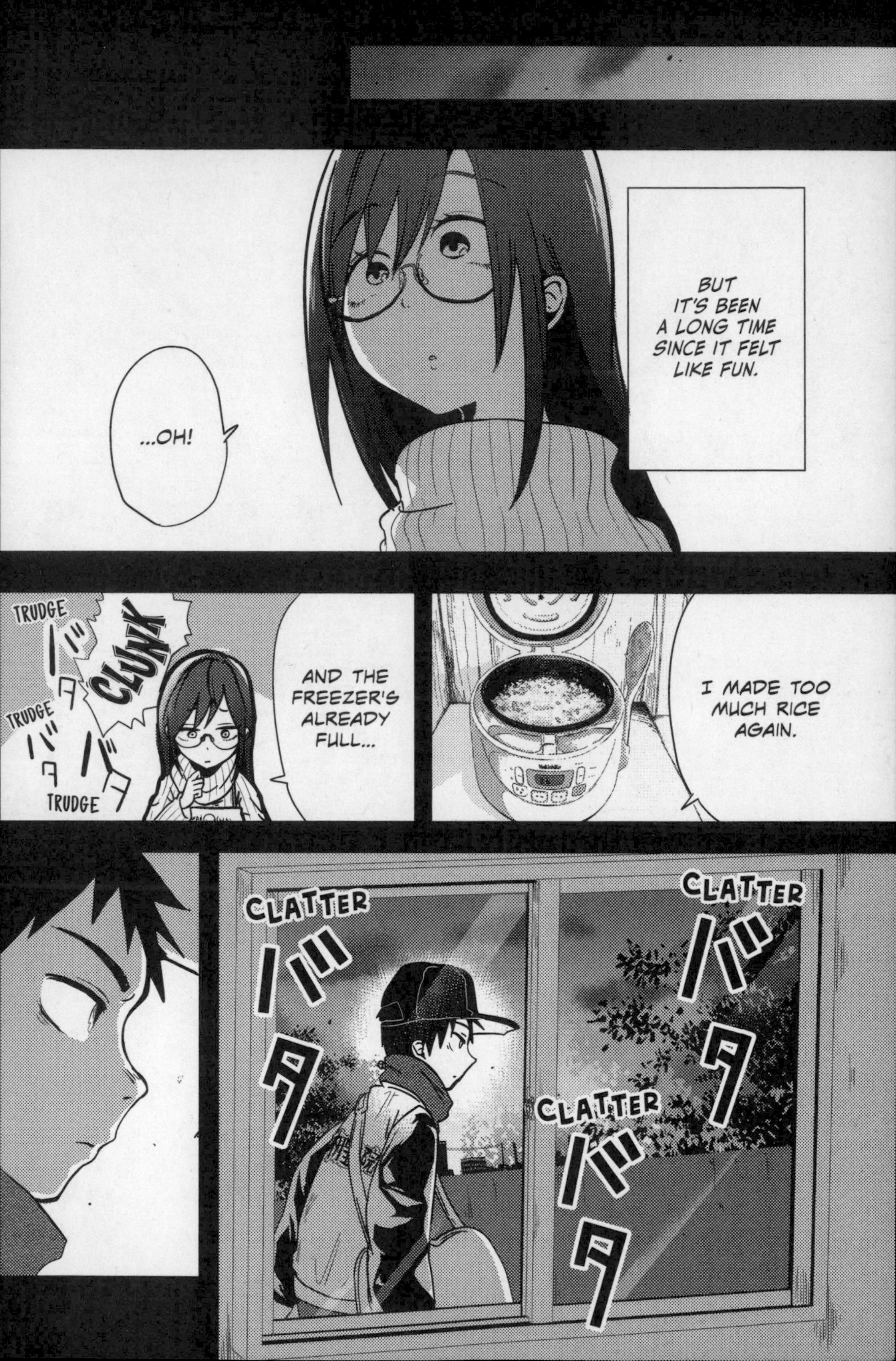
BUT IT'S BEEN A LONG TIME SINCE IT FELT LIKE FUN.
...OH!
I MADE TOO MUCH RICE AGAIN.
AND THE FREEZER'S ALREADY FULL...
CLUNK
TRUDGE
TRUDGE
TRUDGE
CLATTER
CLATTER
CLATTER

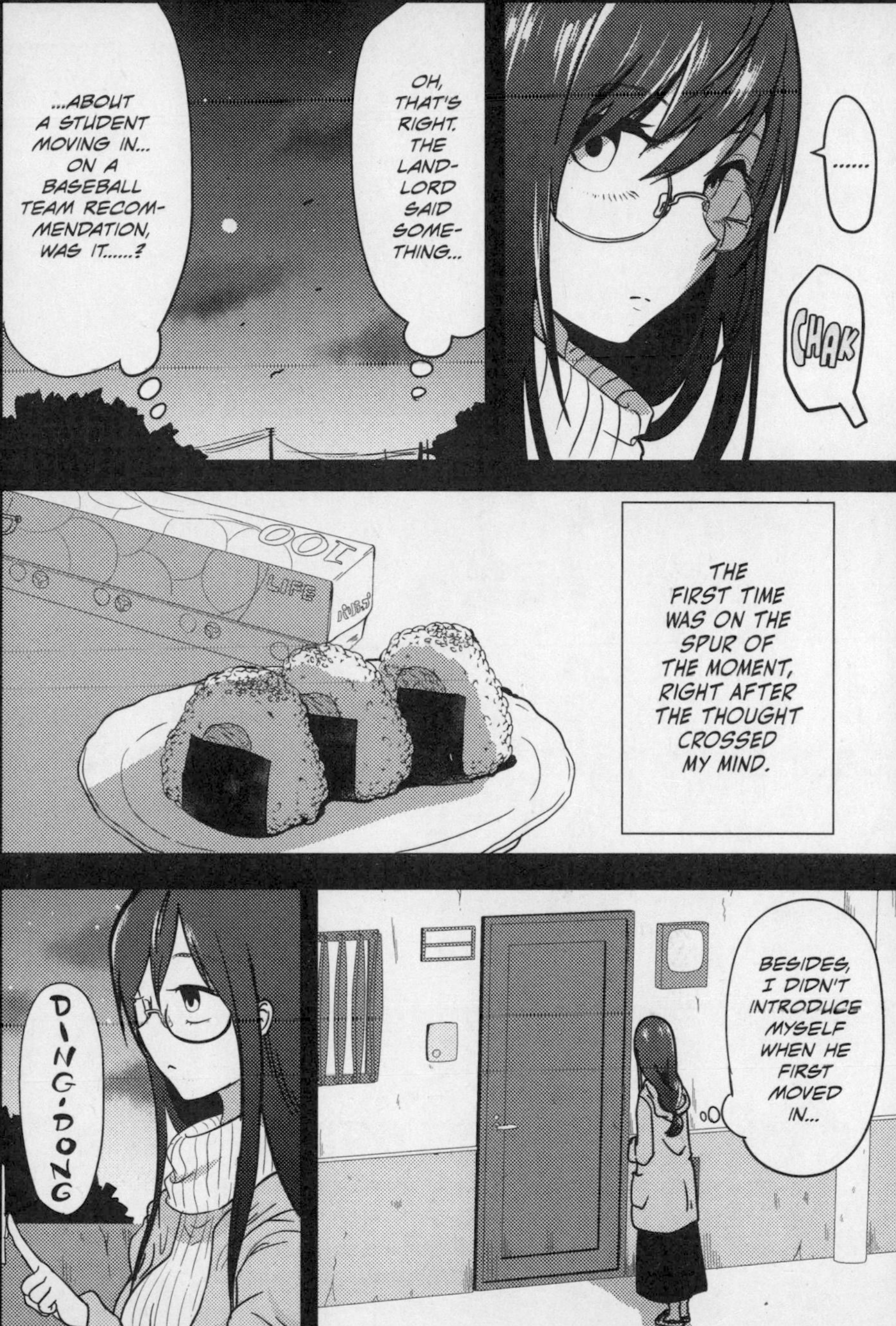
......
CHAK
OH, THAT'S RIGHT. THE LANDLORD SAID SOMETHING...
...ABOUT A STUDENT MOVING IN... ON A BASEBALL TEAM RECOMMENDATION, WAS IT......?
THE FIRST TIME WAS ON THE SPUR OF THE MOMENT, RIGHT AFTER THE THOUGHT CROSSED MY MIND.
BESIDES, I DIDN'T INTRODUCE MYSELF WHEN HE FIRST MOVED IN...
DING-DONG

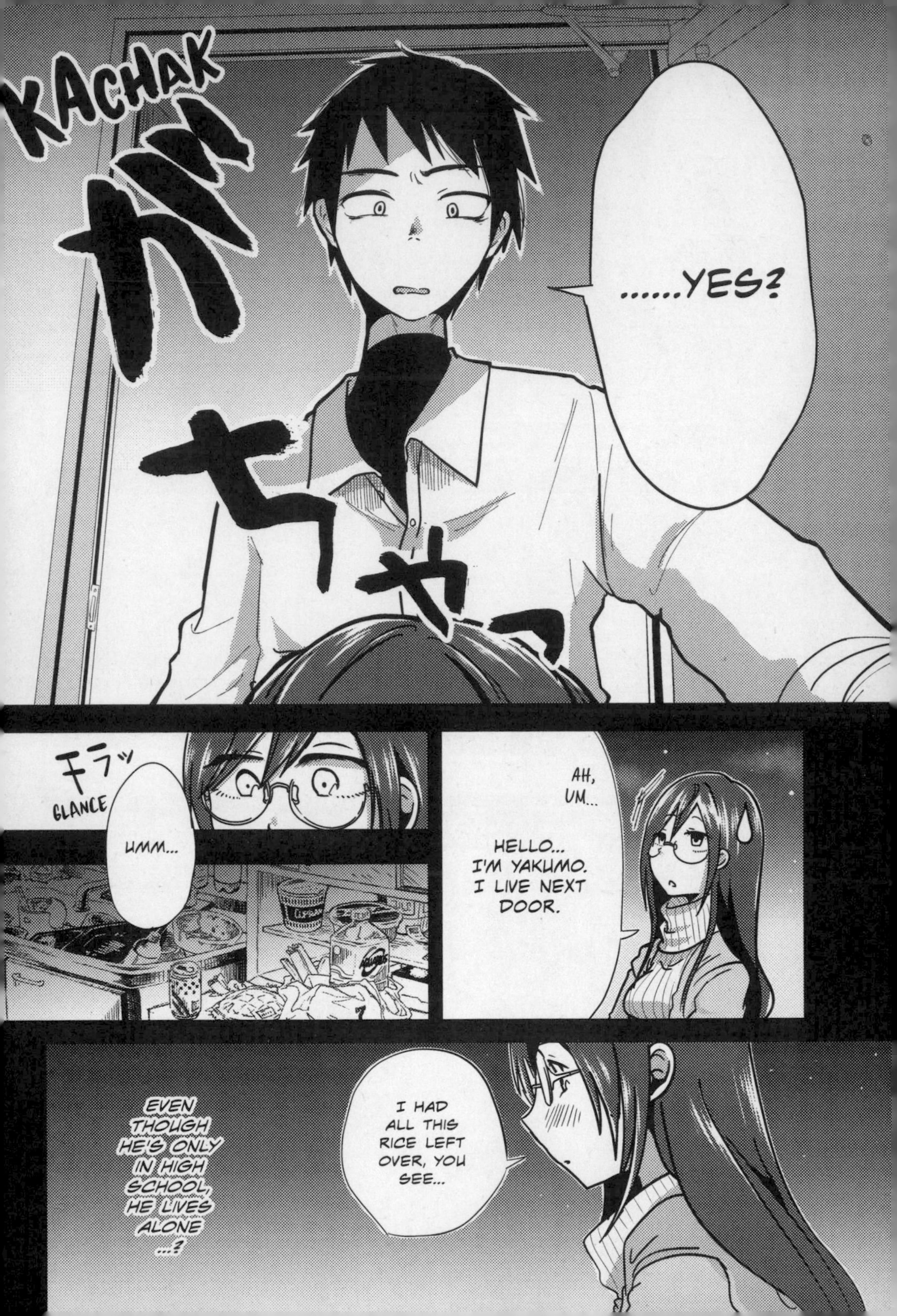
KACHAK
......YES?
AH, UM...
HELLO... I'M YAKUMO. I LIVE NEXT DOOR.
チラッ
GLANCE
UMM...
I HAD ALL THIS RICE LEFT OVER, YOU SEE...
EVEN THOUGH HE'S ONLY IN HIGH SCHOOL, HE LIVES ALONE ...?

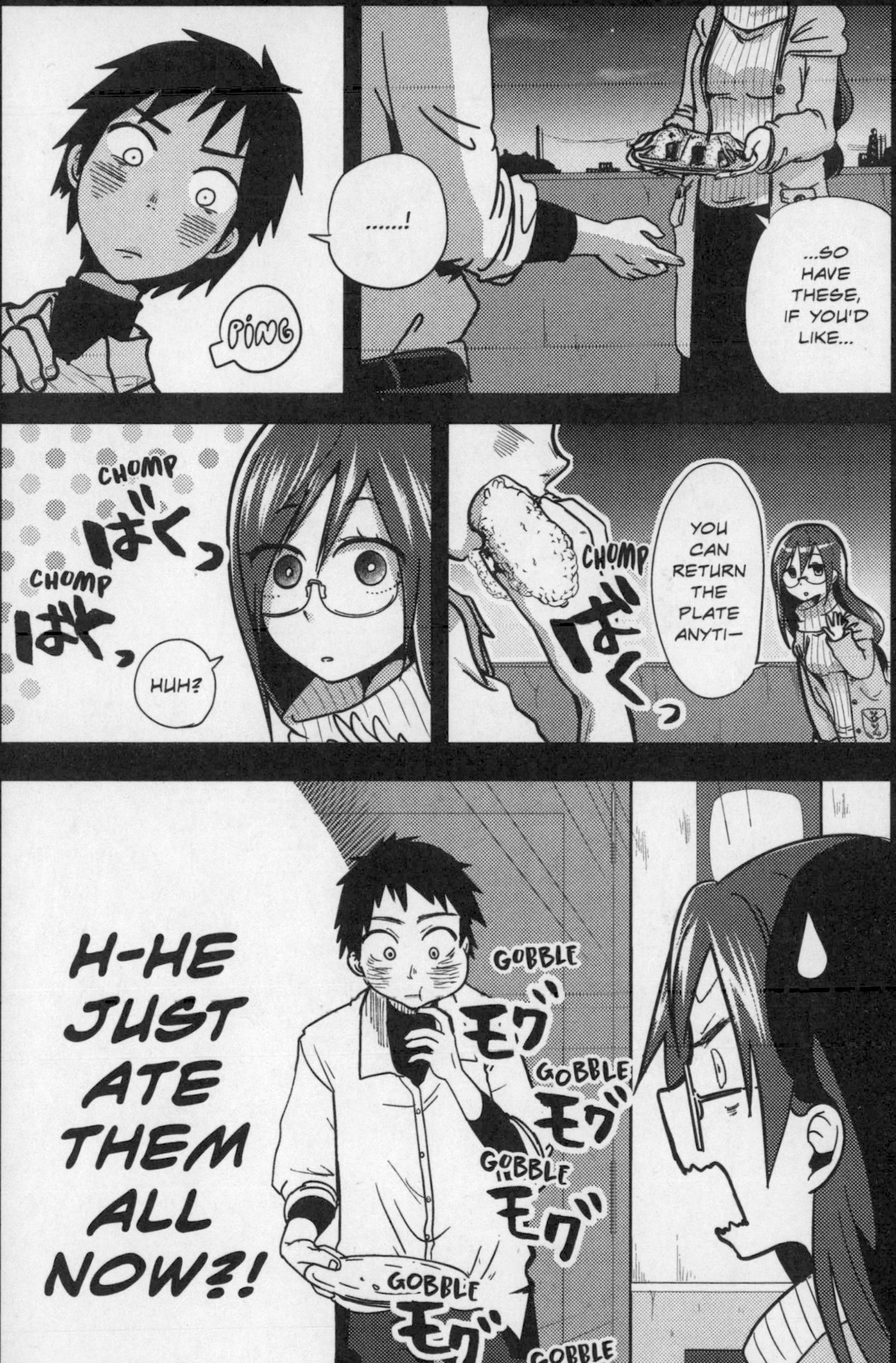
...SO HAVE THESE, IF YOU'D LIKE...
......!
PING
YOU CAN RETURN THE PLATE ANYTI—
CHOMP
ぱくっ
CHOMP
ぱくっ
CHOMP
ぱくっ
HUH?
GOBBLE
モグ
GOBBLE
モグ
GOBBLE
モグ
GOBBLE
モグ
GOBBLE
モグ
H-HE JUST ATE THEM ALL NOW?!

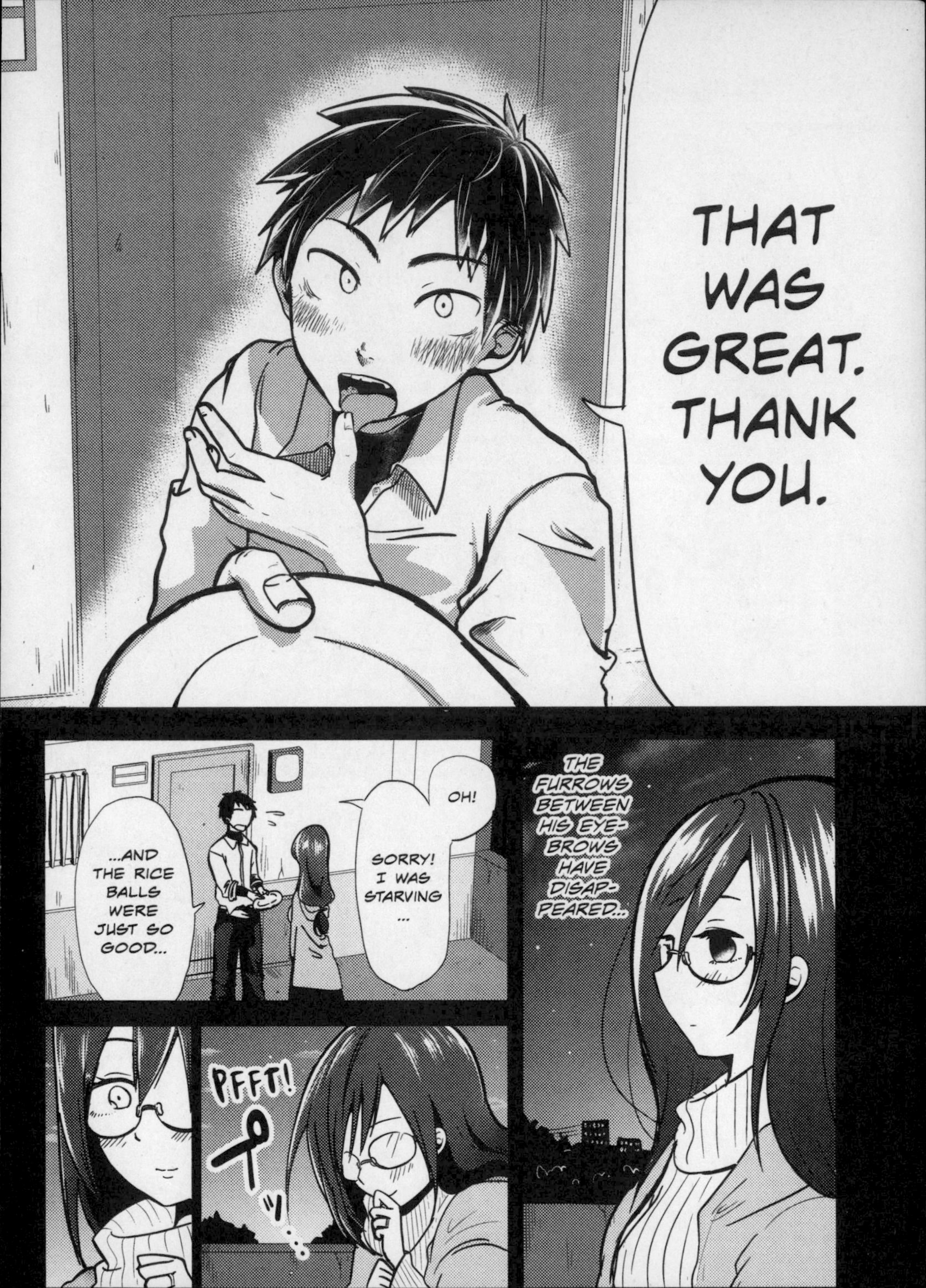
THAT WAS GREAT. THANK YOU.
THE FURROWS BETWEEN HIS EYE-BROWS HAVE DISAP-PEARED...
OH!
SORRY! I WAS STARVING ...
...AND THE RICE BALLS WERE JUST SO GOOD...
PFFT!

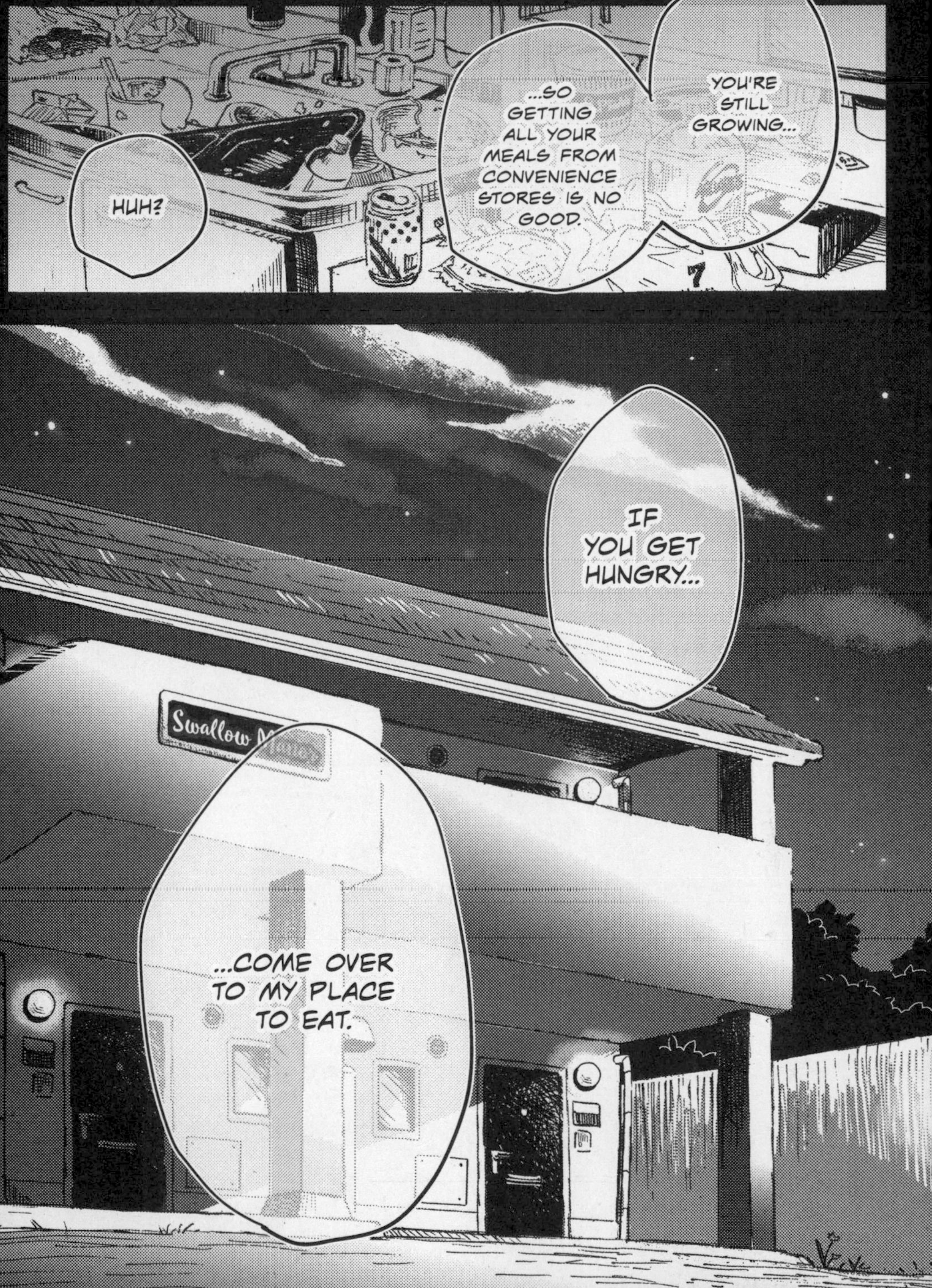
YOU'RE STILL GROWING...
...SO GETTING ALL YOUR MEALS FROM CONVENIENCE STORES IS NO GOOD.
HUH?
IF YOU GET HUNGRY...
Swallow
...COME OVER TO MY PLACE TO EAT.

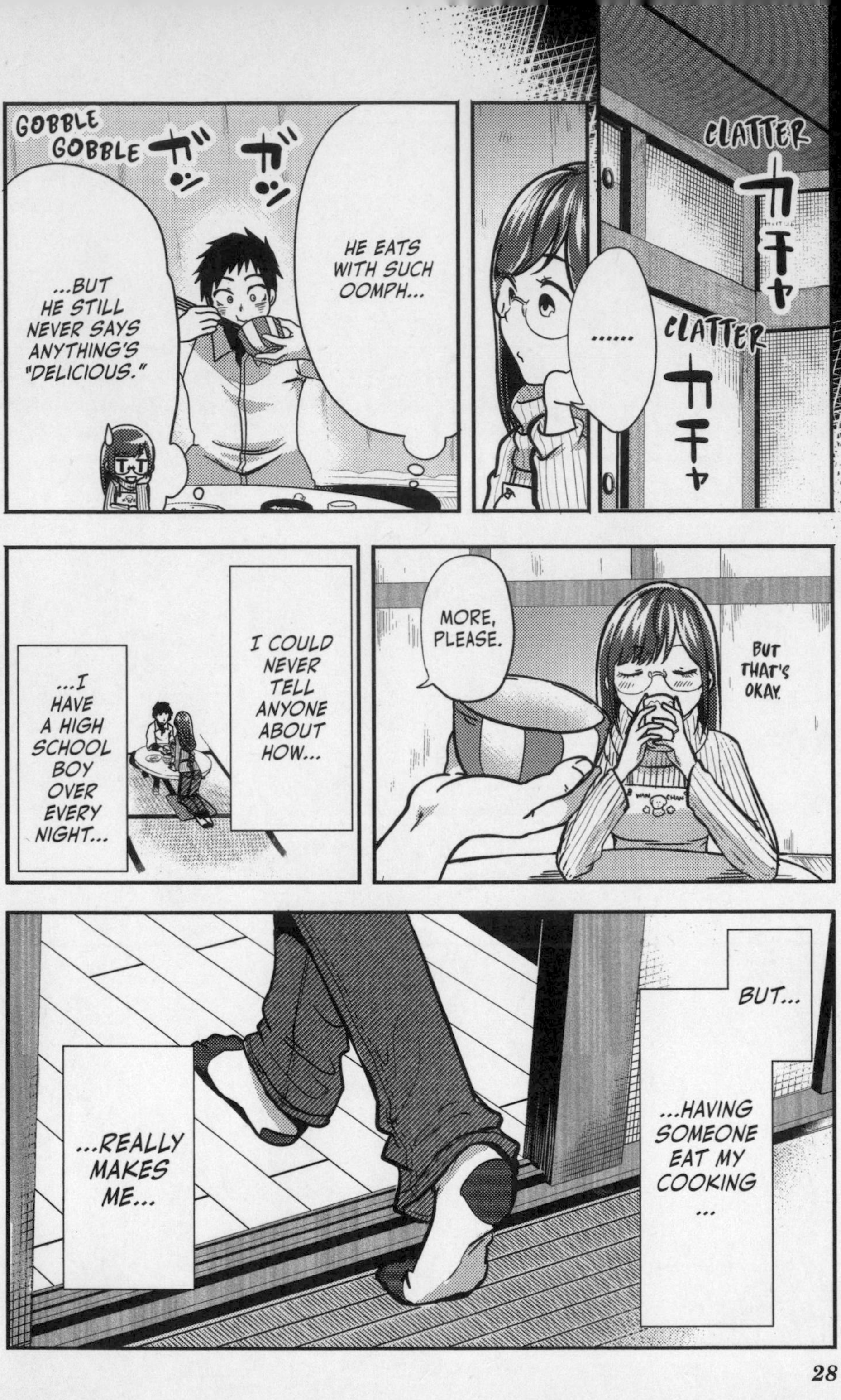
CLATTER
カチャ
CLATTER
カチャ
......
GOBBLE GOBBLE
ガツガツ
HE EATS WITH SUCH OOMPH...
...BUT HE STILL NEVER SAYS ANYTHING'S "DELICIOUS."
MORE, PLEASE.
BUT THAT'S OKAY.
I COULD NEVER TELL ANYONE ABOUT HOW...
...I HAVE A HIGH SCHOOL BOY OVER EVERY NIGHT...
BUT...
...HAVING SOMEONE EAT MY COOKING...
...REALLY MAKES ME...

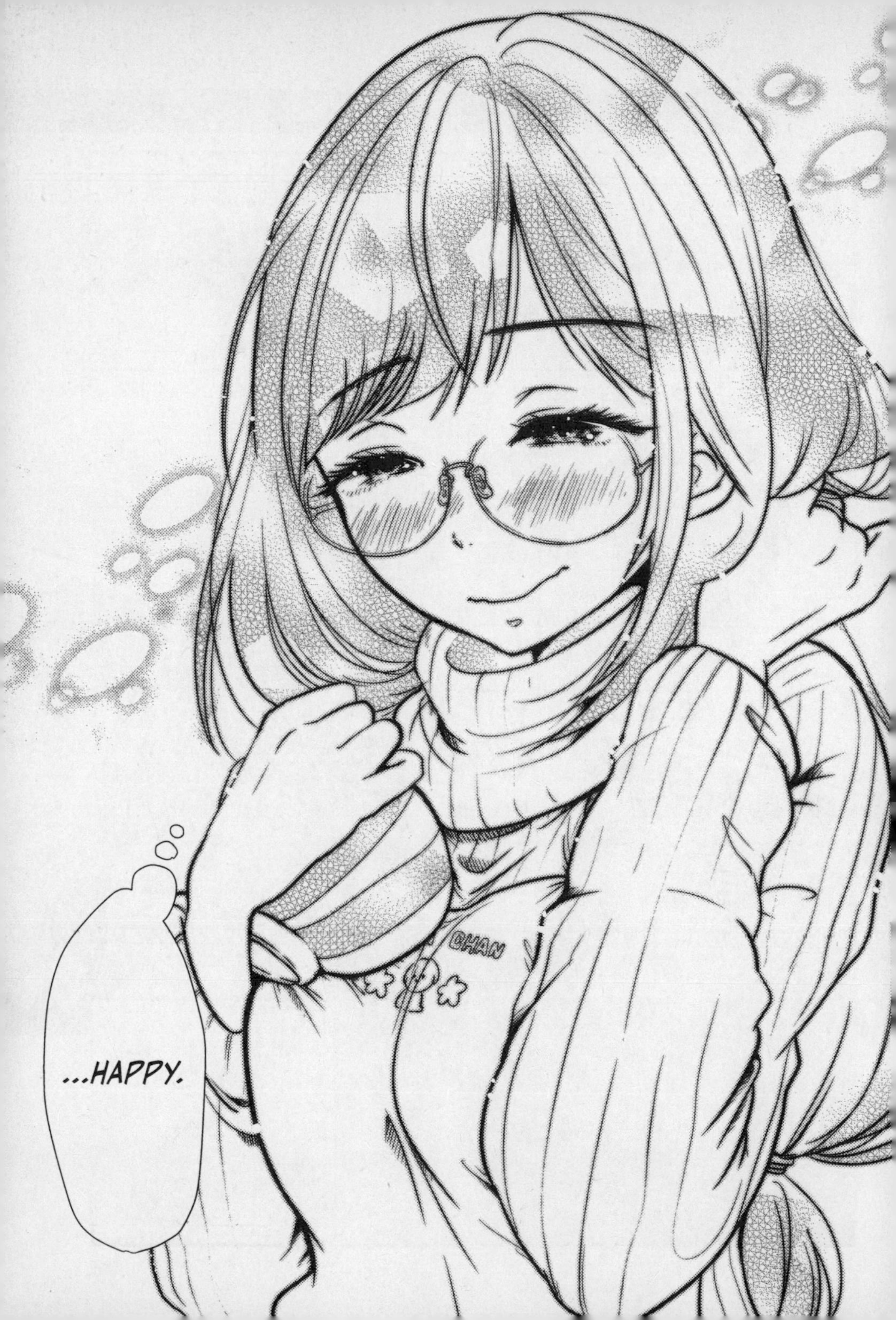
...HAPPY.
CHAN

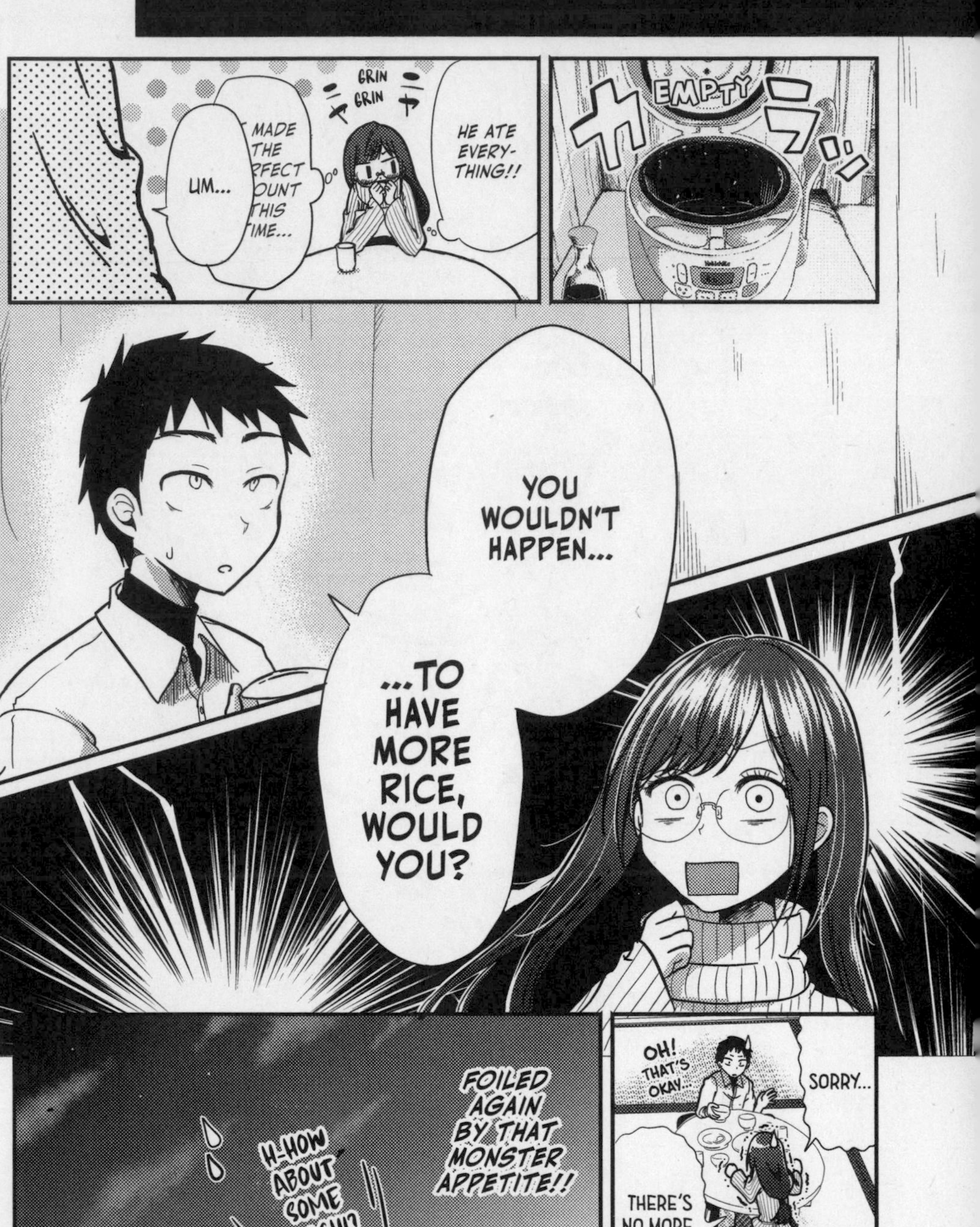
EMPTY
HE ATE EVERYTHING!!
GRIN GRIN
MADE THE RFECT OUNT THIS IME...
UM...
YOU WOULDN'T HAPPEN...
...TO HAVE MORE RICE, WOULD YOU?
SORRY...
OH! THAT'S OKAY...
THERE'S NO MORE.
FOILED AGAIN BY THAT MONSTER APPETITE!!
H-HOW ABOUT SOME MOCHI?

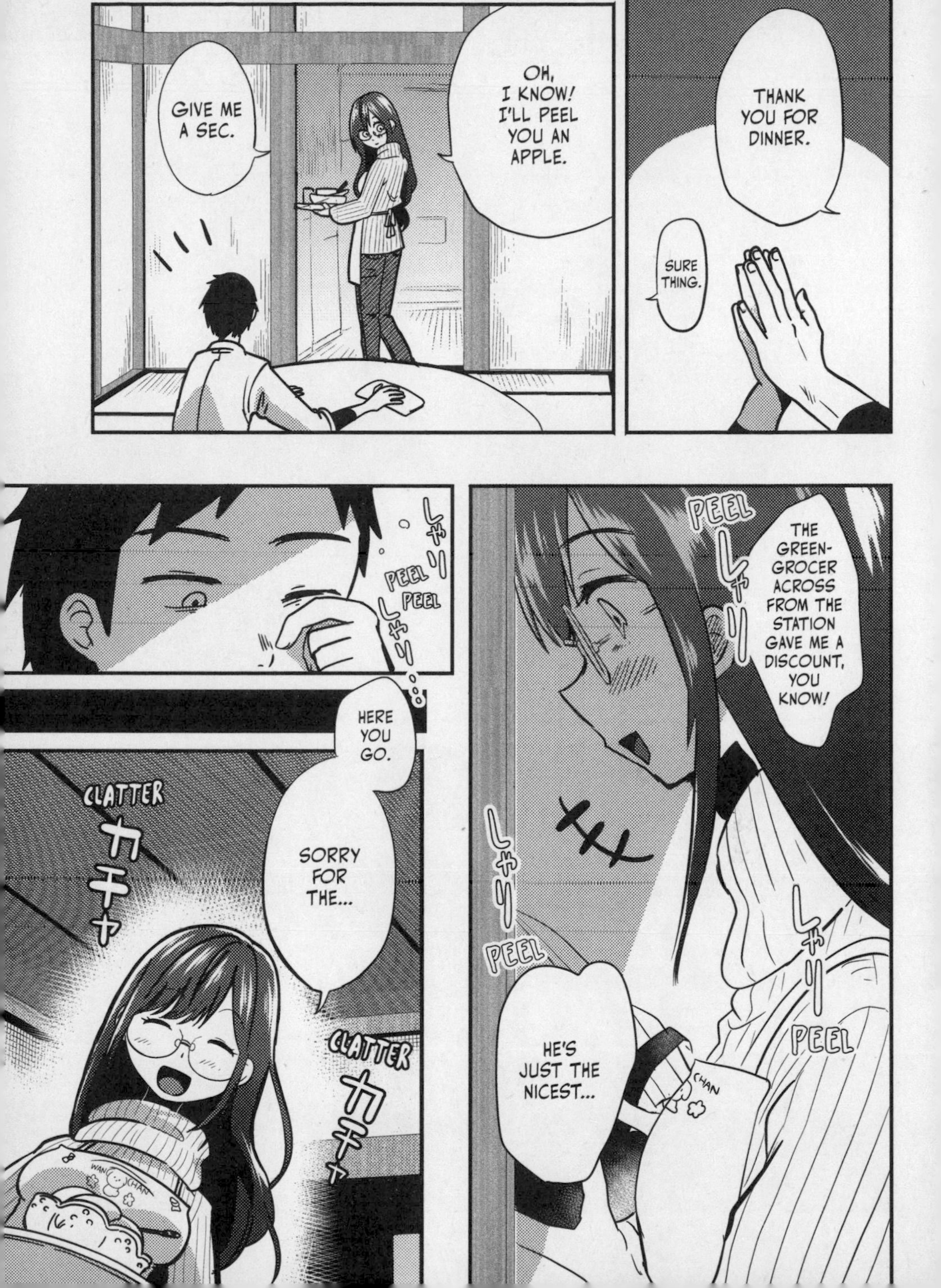
THANK YOU FOR DINNER.
SURE THING.
OH, I KNOW! I'LL PEEL YOU AN APPLE.
GIVE ME A SEC.
PEEL
しゃり
THE GREEN-GROCER ACROSS FROM THE STATION GAVE ME A DISCOUNT, YOU KNOW!
しゃり
PEEL
しゃり
PEEL
HE'S JUST THE NICEST...
CHAN
しゃり
PEEL
PEEL
しゃり...
HERE YOU GO.
SORRY FOR THE...
CLATTER
カチャ
CLATTER
カチャ
WAN CHAN

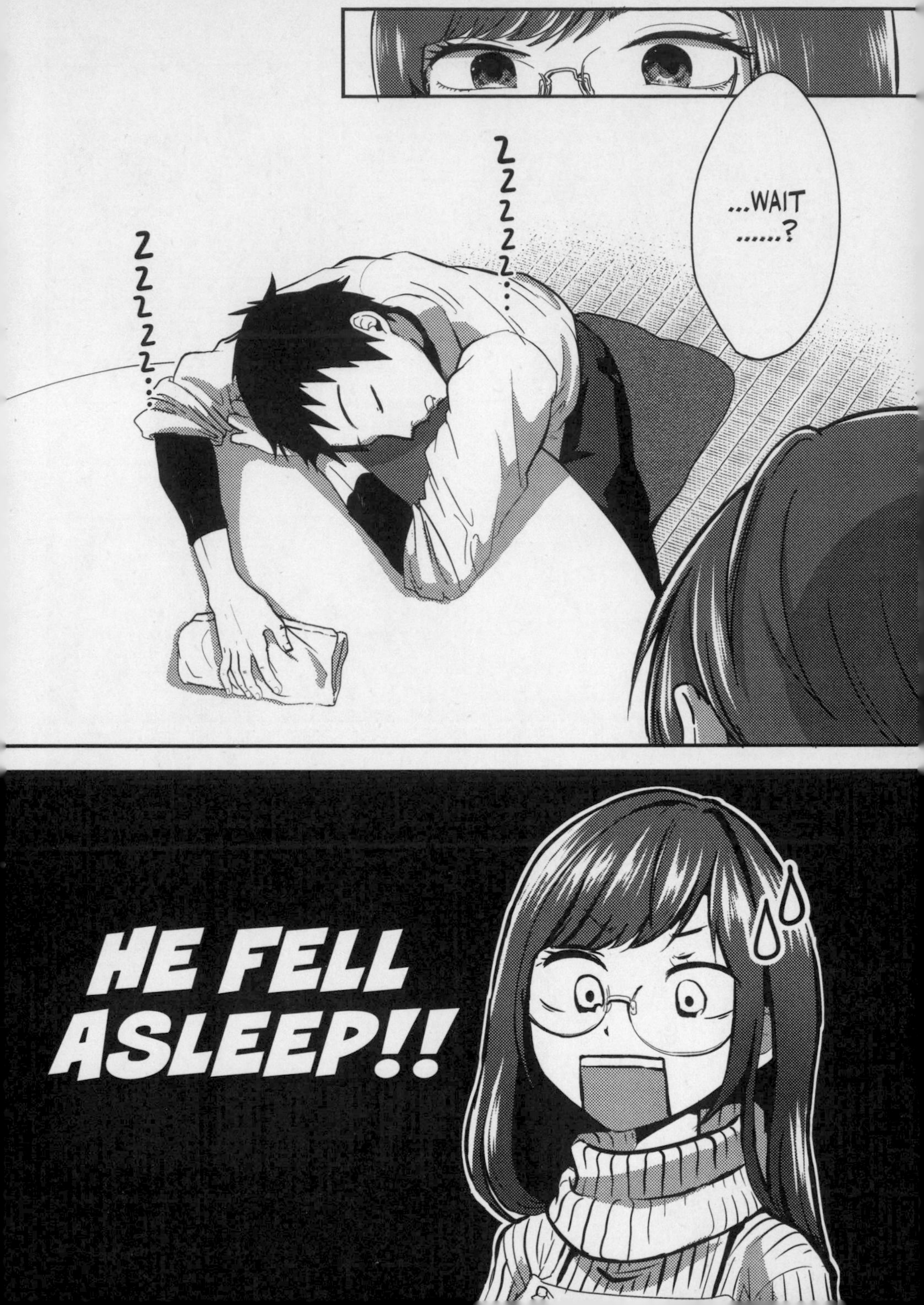
...WAIT ......?
ZZZZZZ...
ZZZZZZ...
HE FELL ASLEEP!!

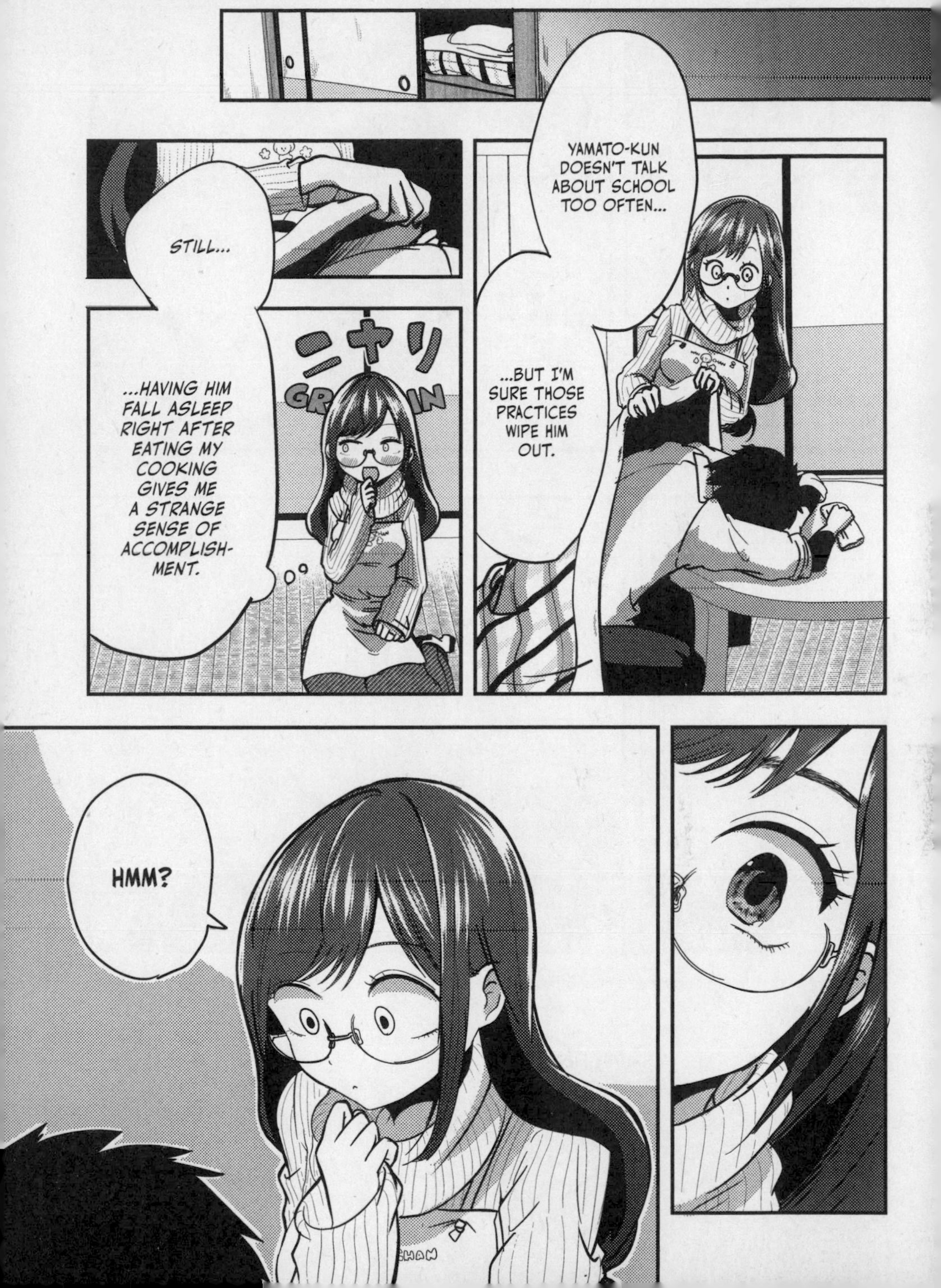
YAMATO-KUN DOESN'T TALK ABOUT SCHOOL TOO OFTEN...
...BUT I'M SURE THOSE PRACTICES WIPE HIM OUT.
STILL...
ニヤリ
...HAVING HIM FALL ASLEEP RIGHT AFTER EATING MY COOKING GIVES ME A STRANGE SENSE OF ACCOMPLISHMENT.
HMM?

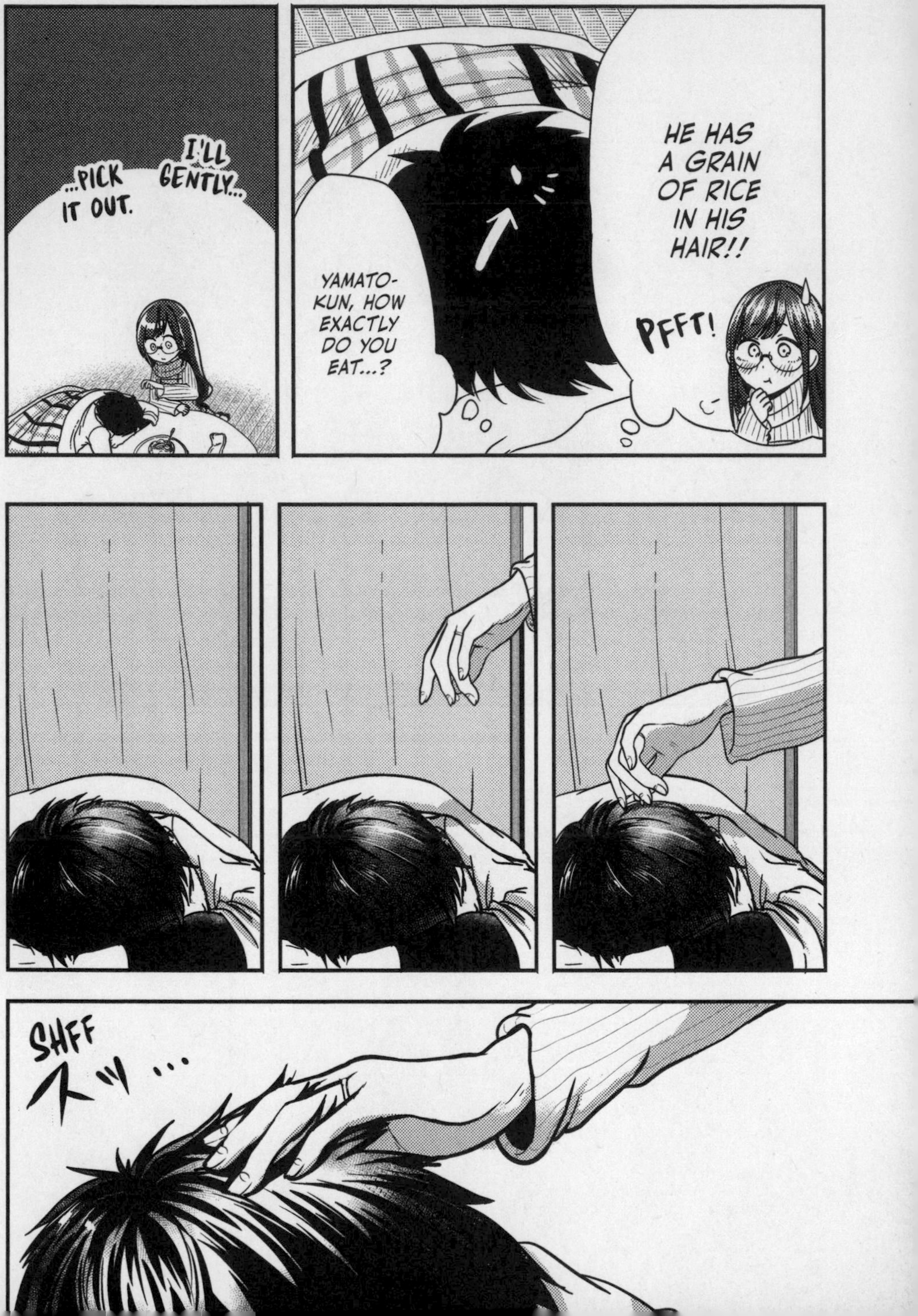
HE HAS A GRAIN OF RICE IN HIS HAIR!!
PFFT!
YAMATO-KUN, HOW EXACTLY DO YOU EAT...?
I'LL GENTLY...
...PICK IT OUT.
SHFF
スッ...

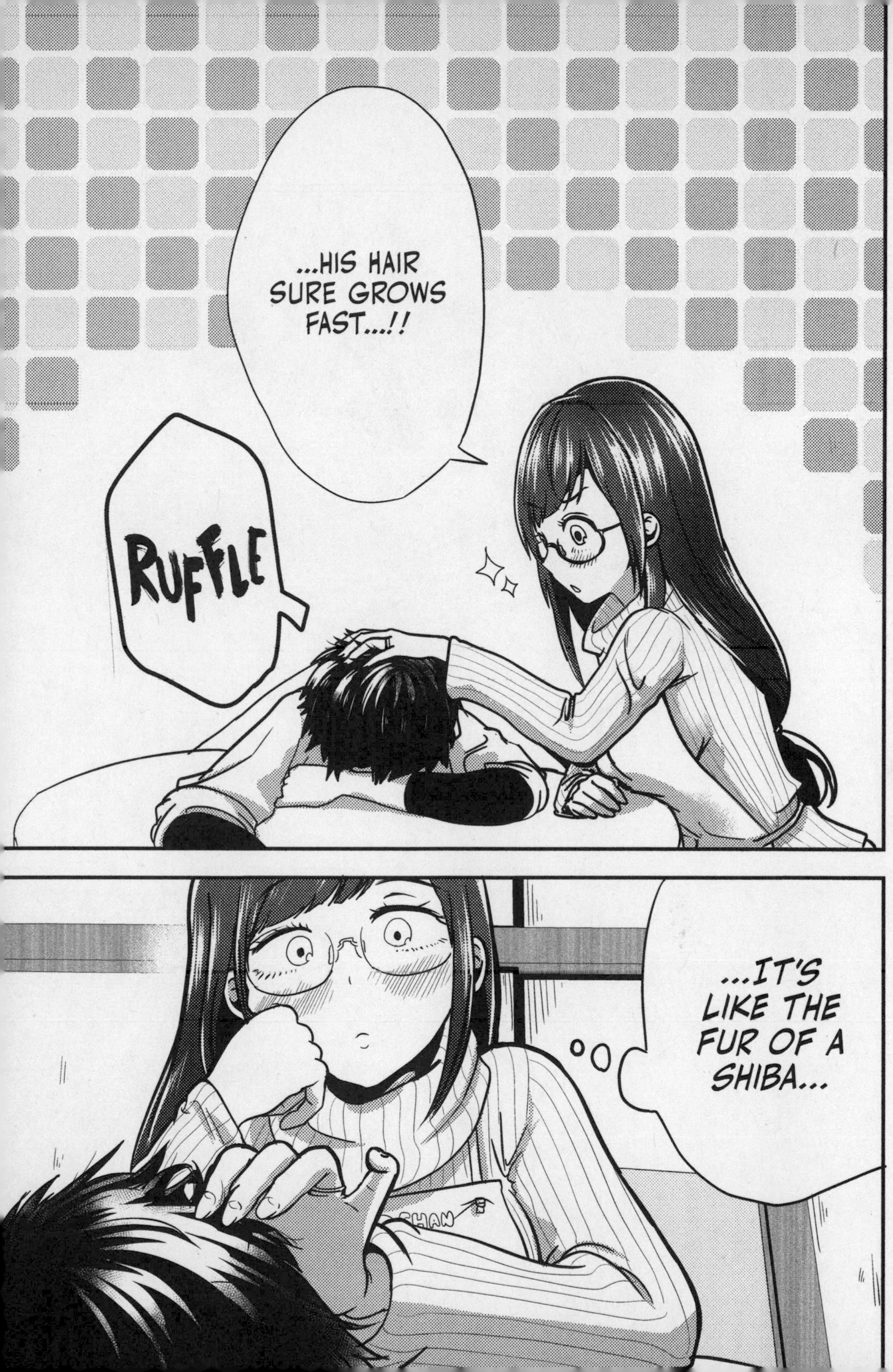
...HIS HAIR SURE GROWS FAST...!!
RUFFLE
...IT'S LIKE THE FUR OF A SHIBA...
CHAN

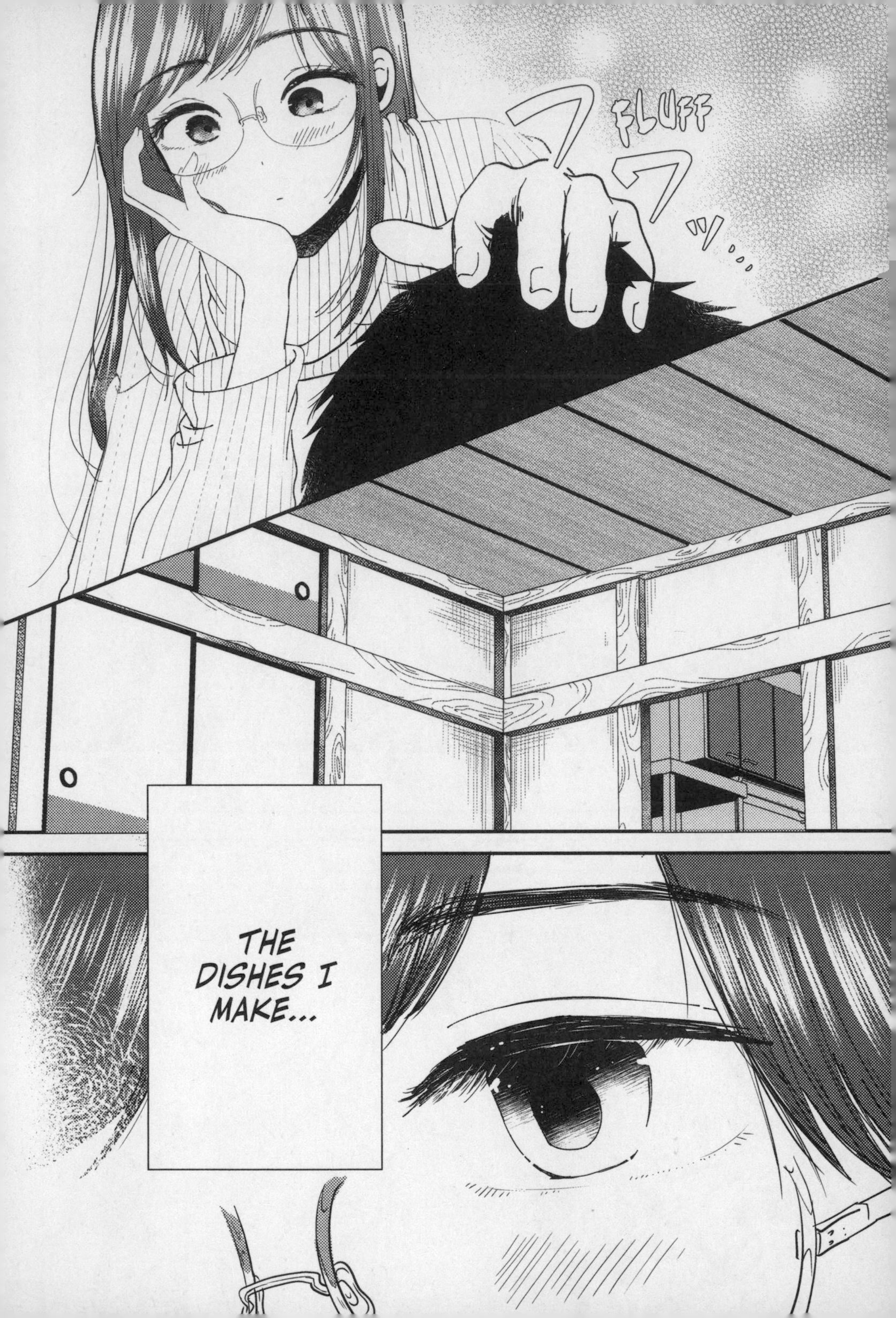
FLUFF
THE DISHES I MAKE...

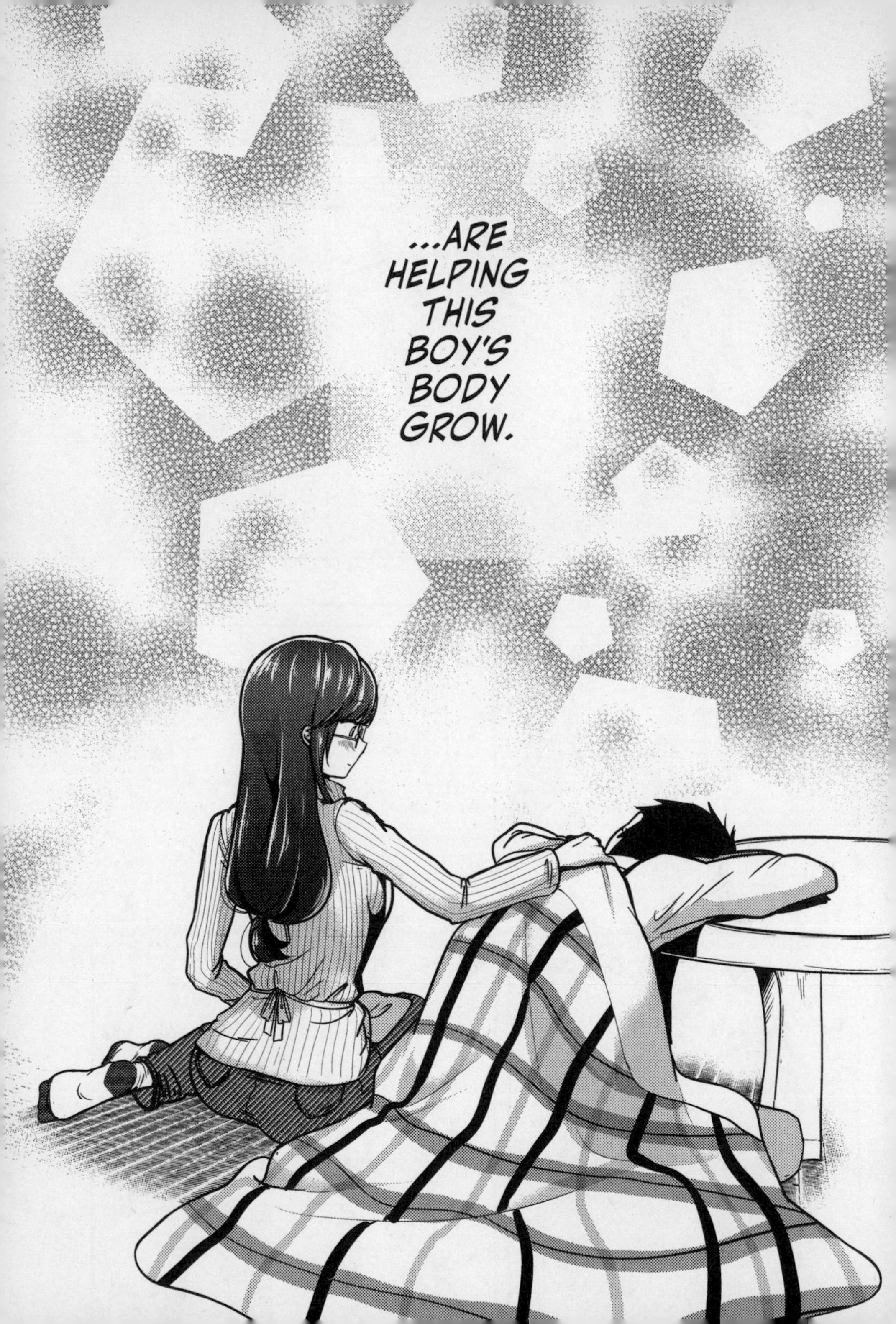
...ARE HELPING THIS BOY'S BODY GROW.

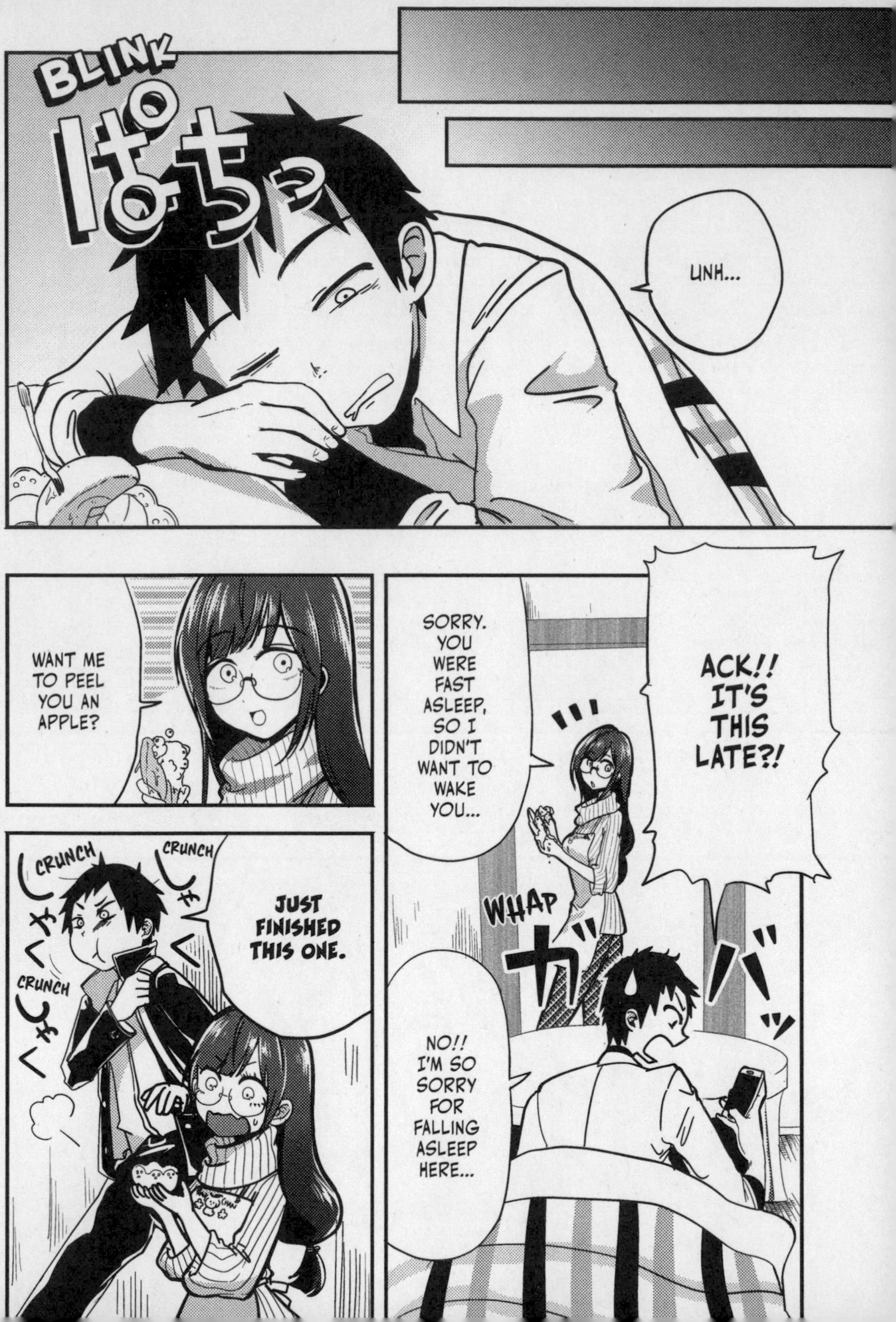
BLINK
ぱちっ
UNH...
ACK!! IT'S THIS LATE?!
SORRY. YOU WERE FAST ASLEEP, SO I DIDN'T WANT TO WAKE YOU...
WHAP
ガバッ
NO!! I'M SO SORRY FOR FALLING ASLEEP HERE...
WANT ME TO PEEL YOU AN APPLE?
CRUNCH
しゃく
CRUNCH
しゃく
CRUNCH
しゃく
JUST FINISHED THIS ONE.

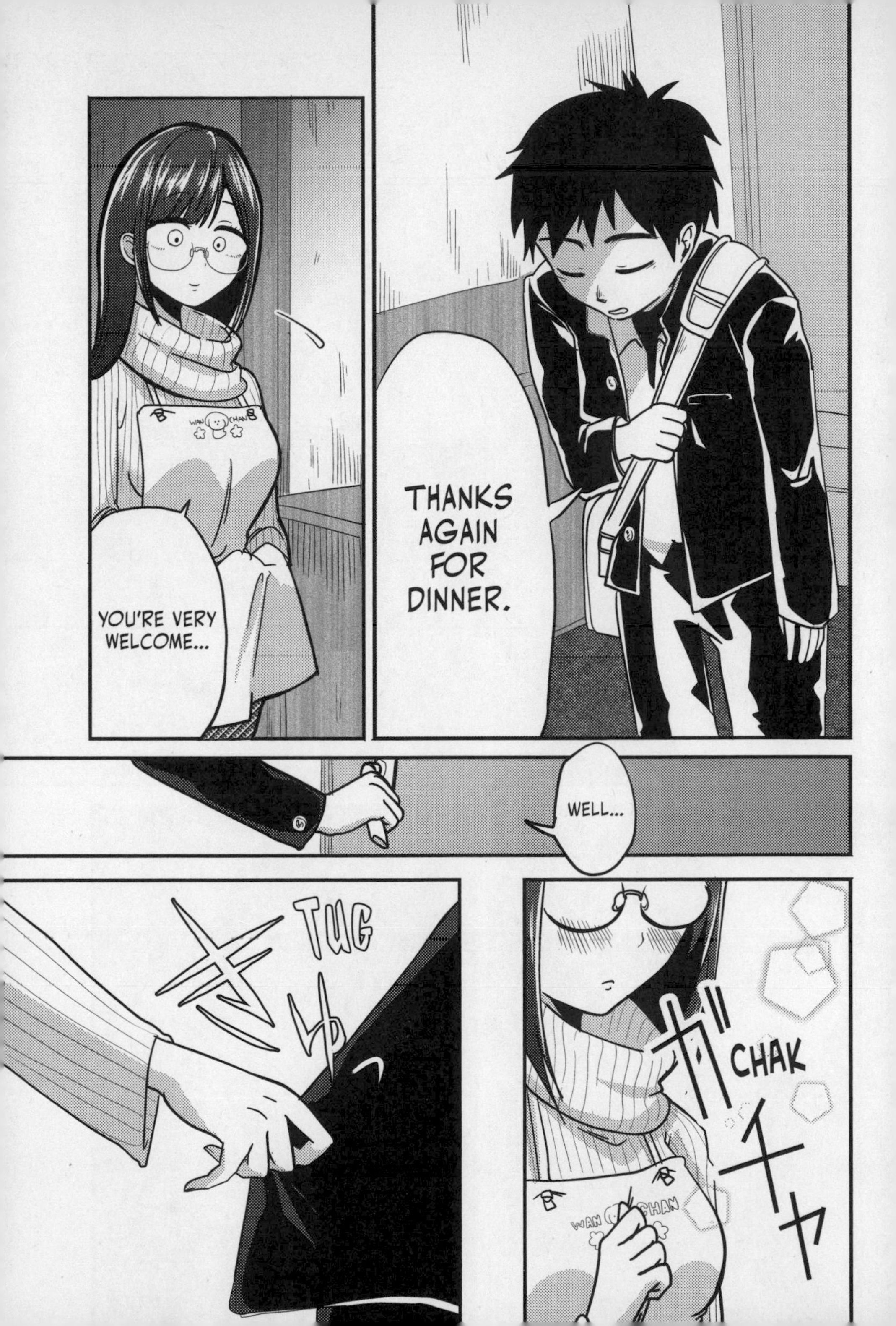
THANKS AGAIN FOR DINNER.
YOU'RE VERY WELCOME...
WELL...
CHAK
TUG

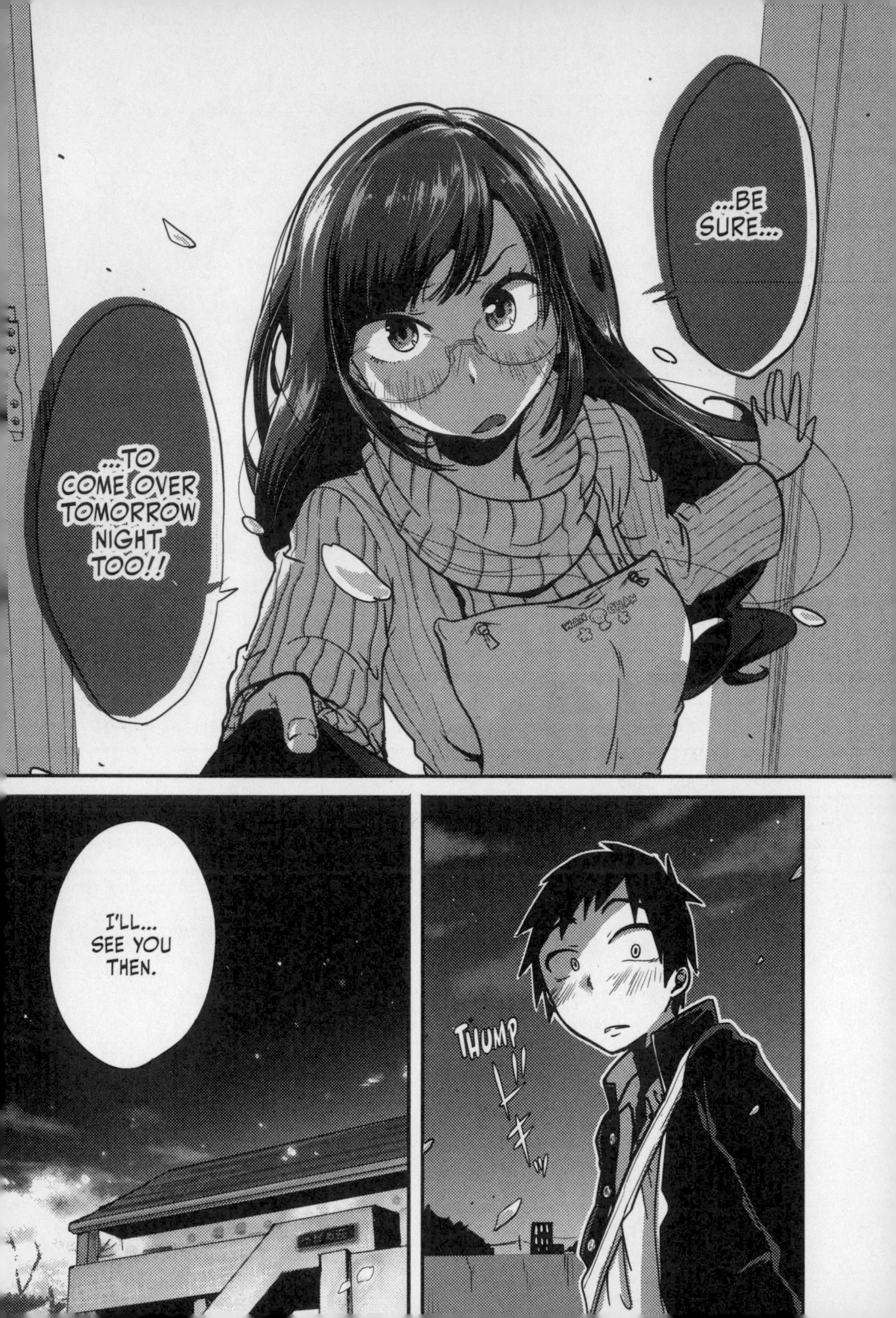
...BE SURE...
...TO COME OVER TOMORROW NIGHT TOO!!
THUMP
I'LL... SEE YOU THEN.

Beauty and the **FEAST**

Beauty and the FEAST

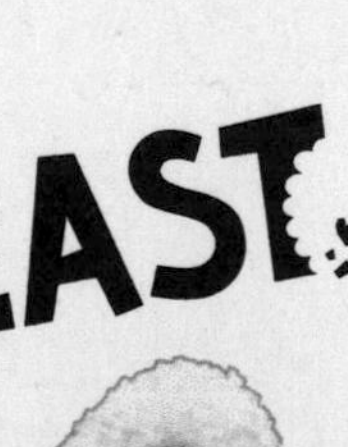

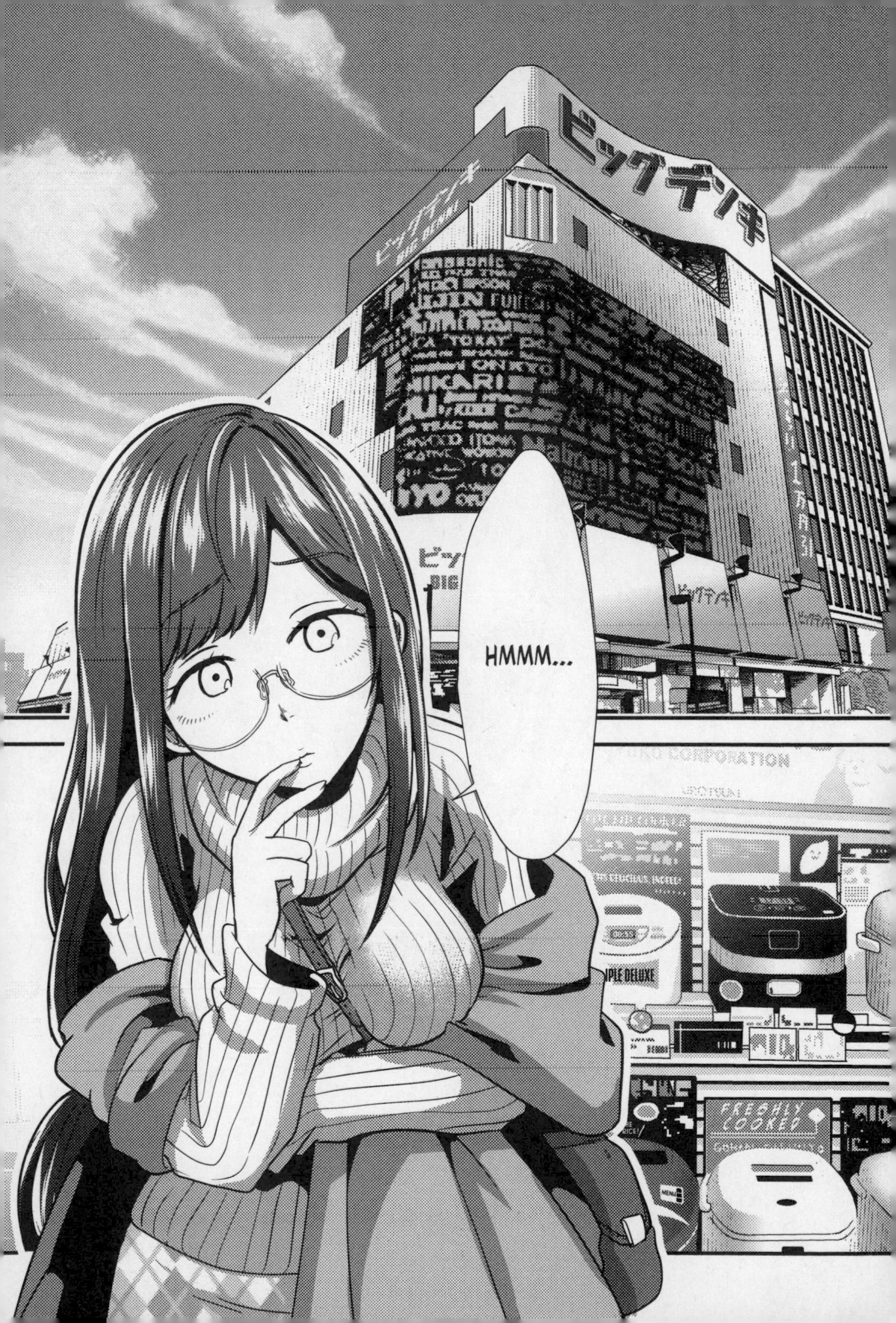
ビッグデンキ
HMMM...
FRESHLY COOKED

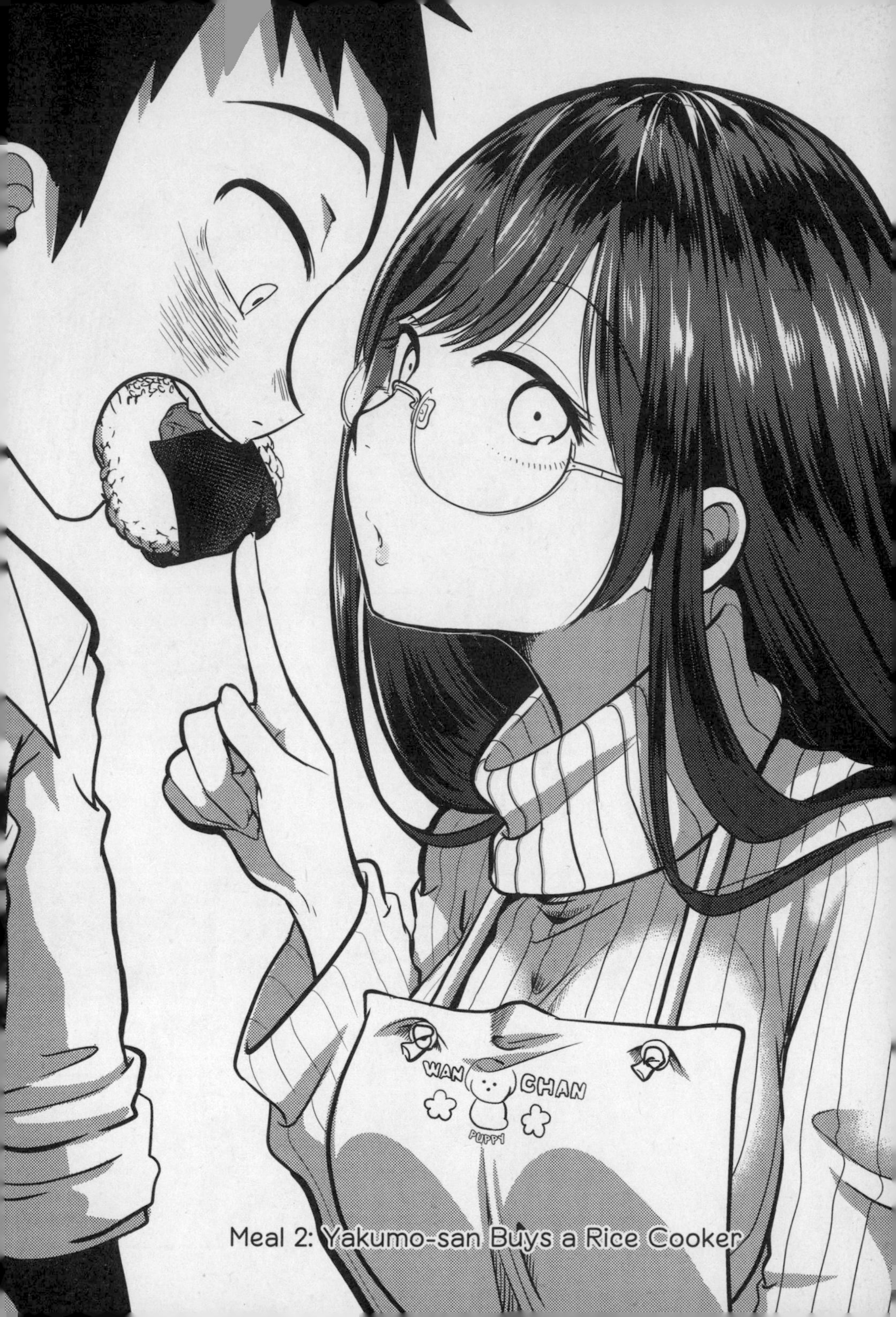
WAN CHAN
PUPPY

Meal 2: Yakumo-san Buys a Rice Cooker

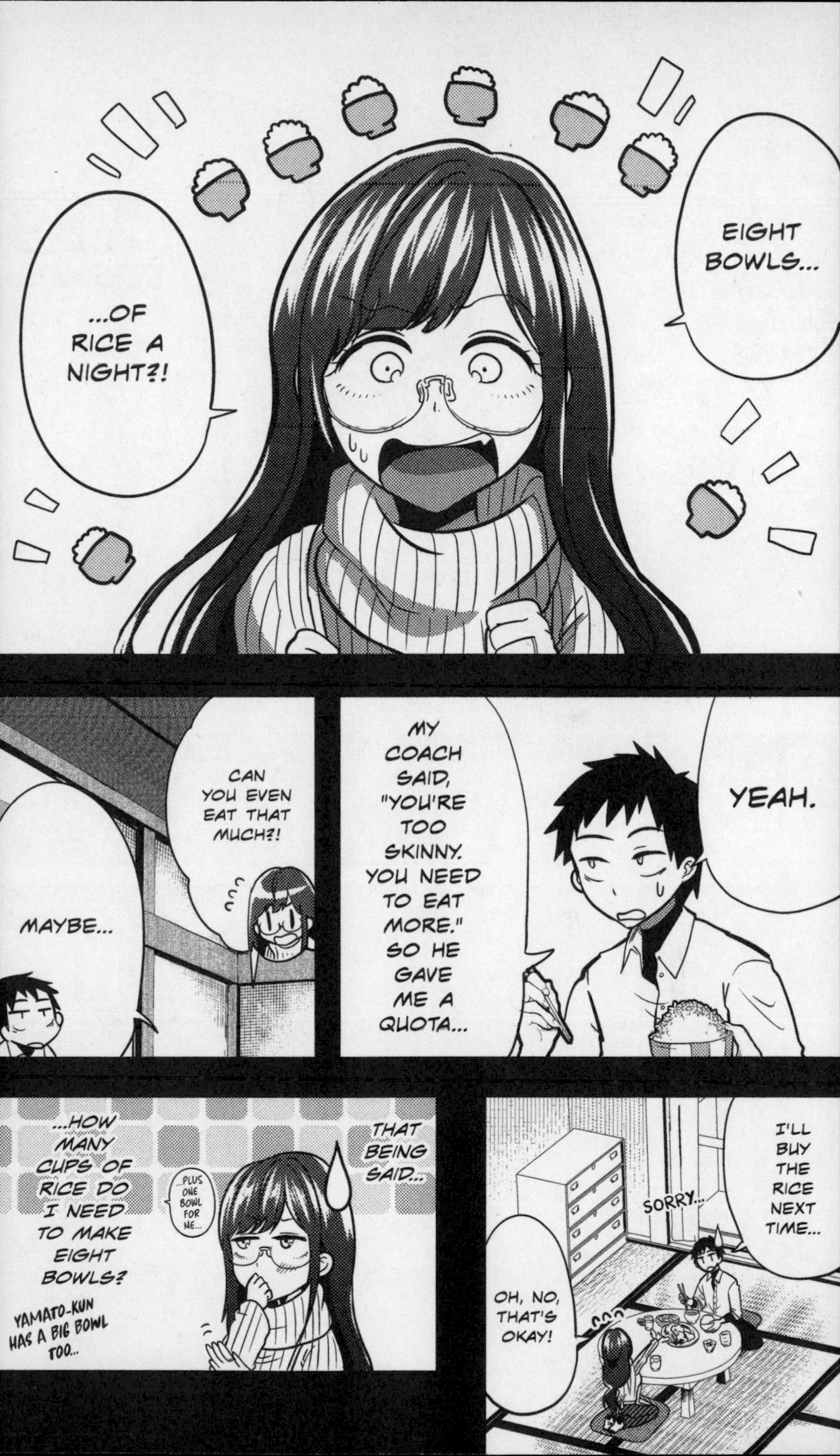
EIGHT BOWLS...
...OF RICE A NIGHT?!
YEAH.
MY COACH SAID, "YOU'RE TOO SKINNY. YOU NEED TO EAT MORE." SO HE GAVE ME A QUOTA...
CAN YOU EVEN EAT THAT MUCH?!
MAYBE...
I'LL BUY THE RICE NEXT TIME...
SORRY...
OH, NO, THAT'S OKAY!
THAT BEING SAID...
...PLUS ONE BOWL FOR ME...
...HOW MANY CUPS OF RICE DO I NEED TO MAKE EIGHT BOWLS?
YAMATO-KUN HAS A BIG BOWL TOO...

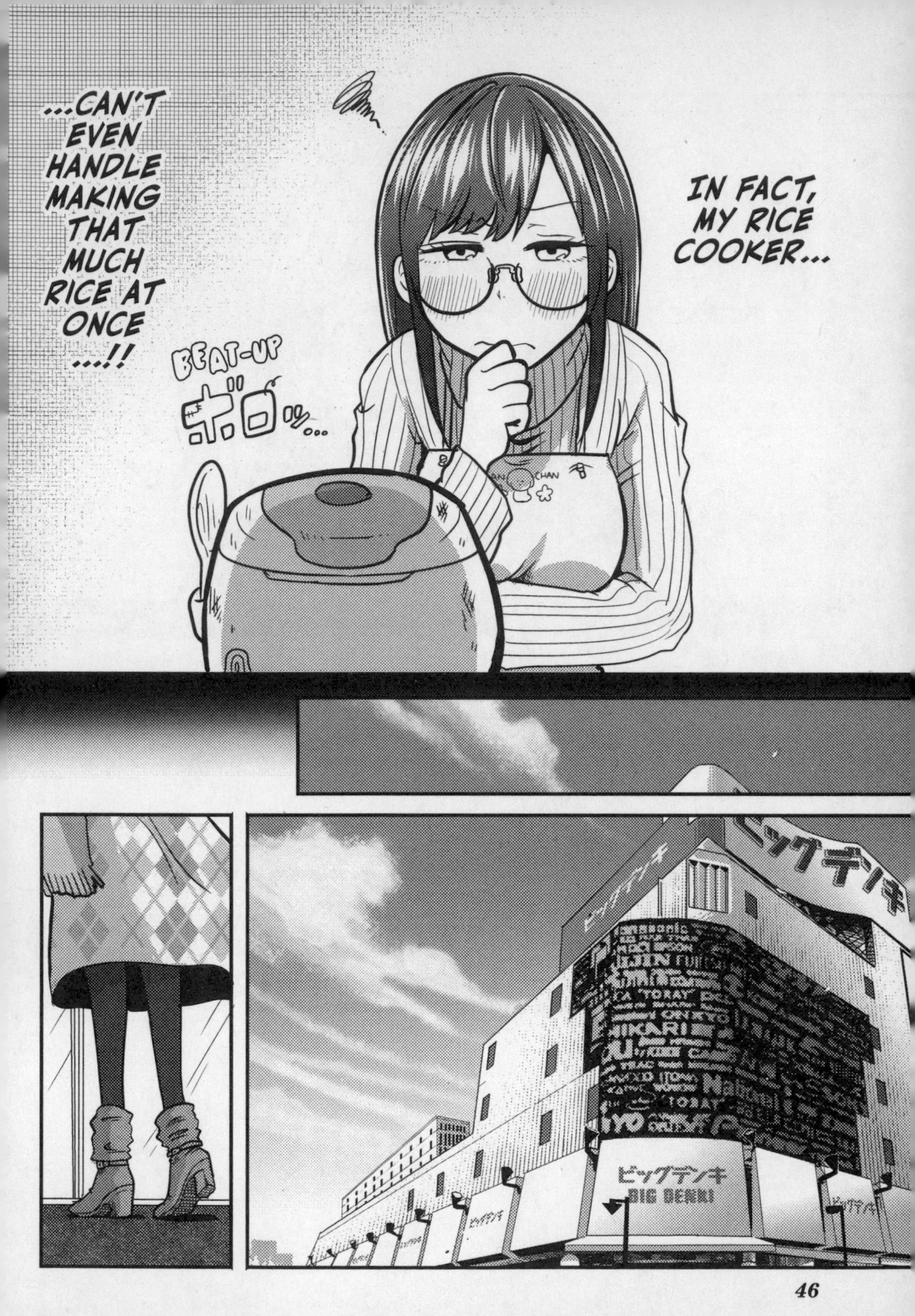
IN FACT, MY RICE COOKER...
...CAN'T EVEN HANDLE MAKING THAT MUCH RICE AT ONCE ....!!
BEAT-UP
ボロッ...
ビッグデンキ
ビッグデンキ
ビッグデンキ
BIG DENKI

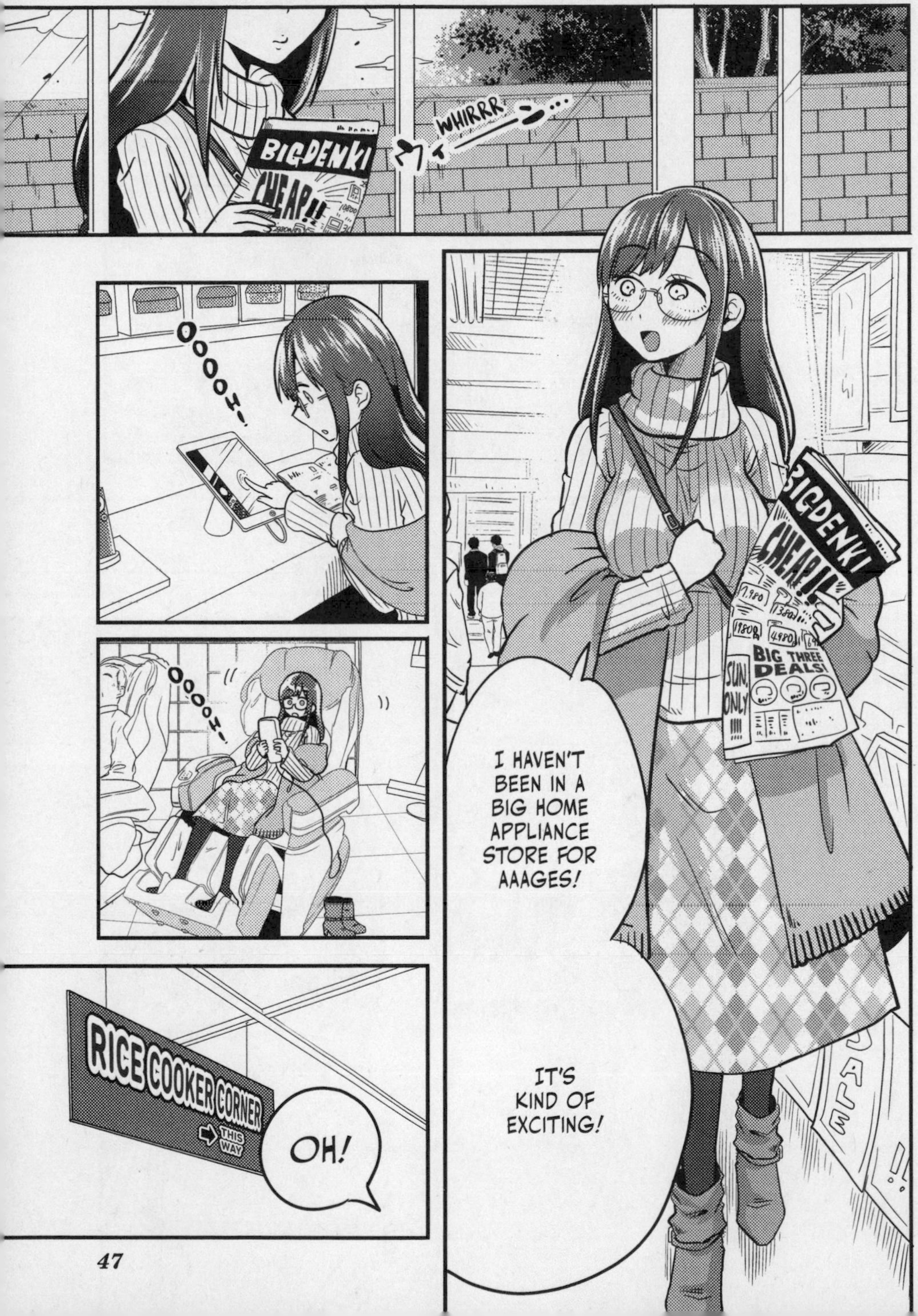
BIGDENKI
CHEAP!!
WHIRRR
BIGDENKI
CHEAP!!
BIG THREE DEALS!
SUN. ONLY !!!!
I HAVEN'T BEEN IN A BIG HOME APPLIANCE STORE FOR AAAGES!
IT'S KIND OF EXCITING!
OOOOOH!
OOOOH!
RICE COOKER CORNER
THIS WAY
OH!

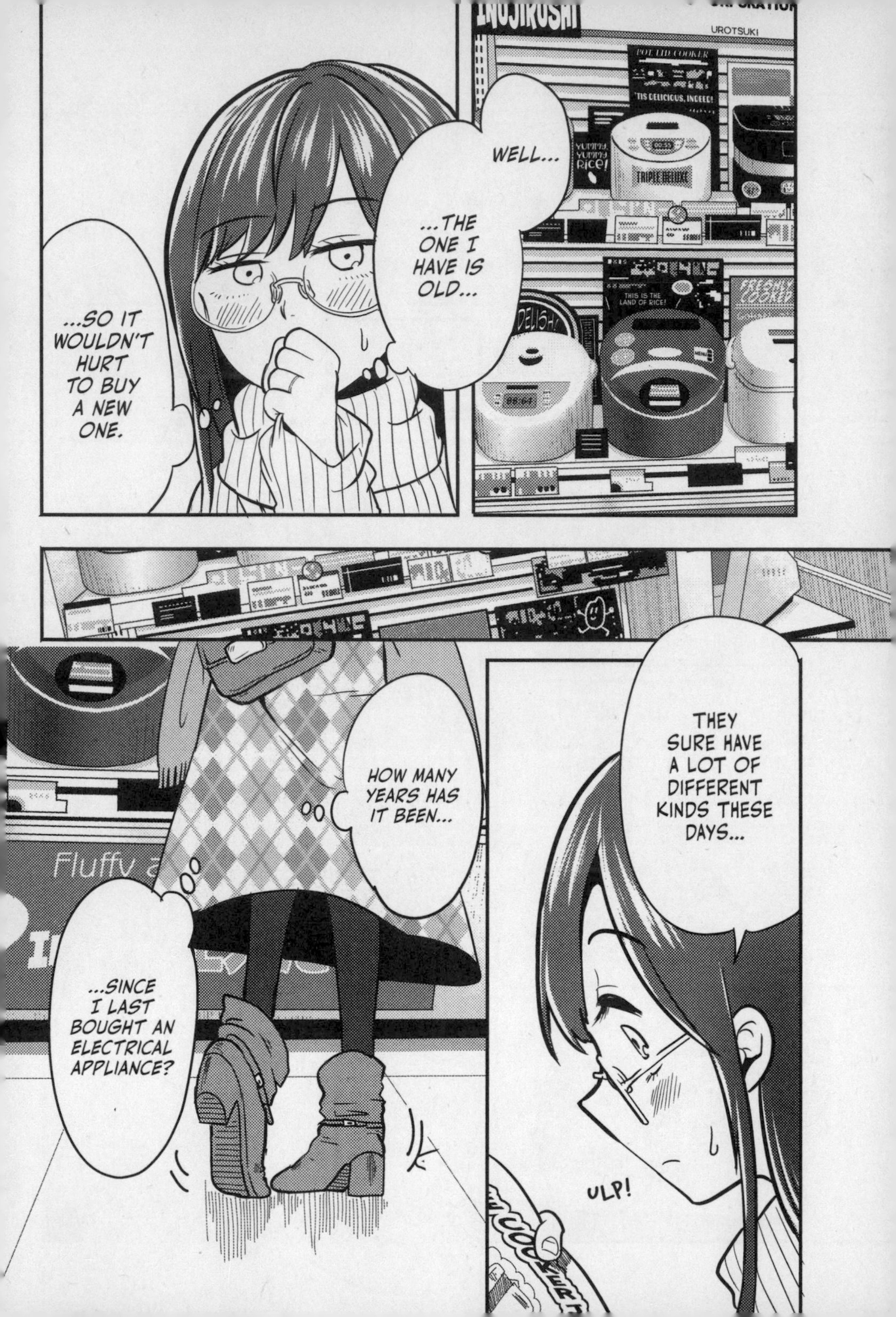
INUJIROSHI
UROTSUKI
POTTED COOKER
'TIS DELICIOUS, INDEED!
YUMMY, YUMMY RICE!
TRIPLE DELUXE
THIS IS THE LAND OF RICE!
DELISH!
FRESHLY COOKED
WELL...
...THE ONE I HAVE IS OLD...
...SO IT WOULDN'T HURT TO BUY A NEW ONE.
THEY SURE HAVE A LOT OF DIFFERENT KINDS THESE DAYS...
ULP!
HOW MANY YEARS HAS IT BEEN...
...SINCE I LAST BOUGHT AN ELECTRICAL APPLIANCE?

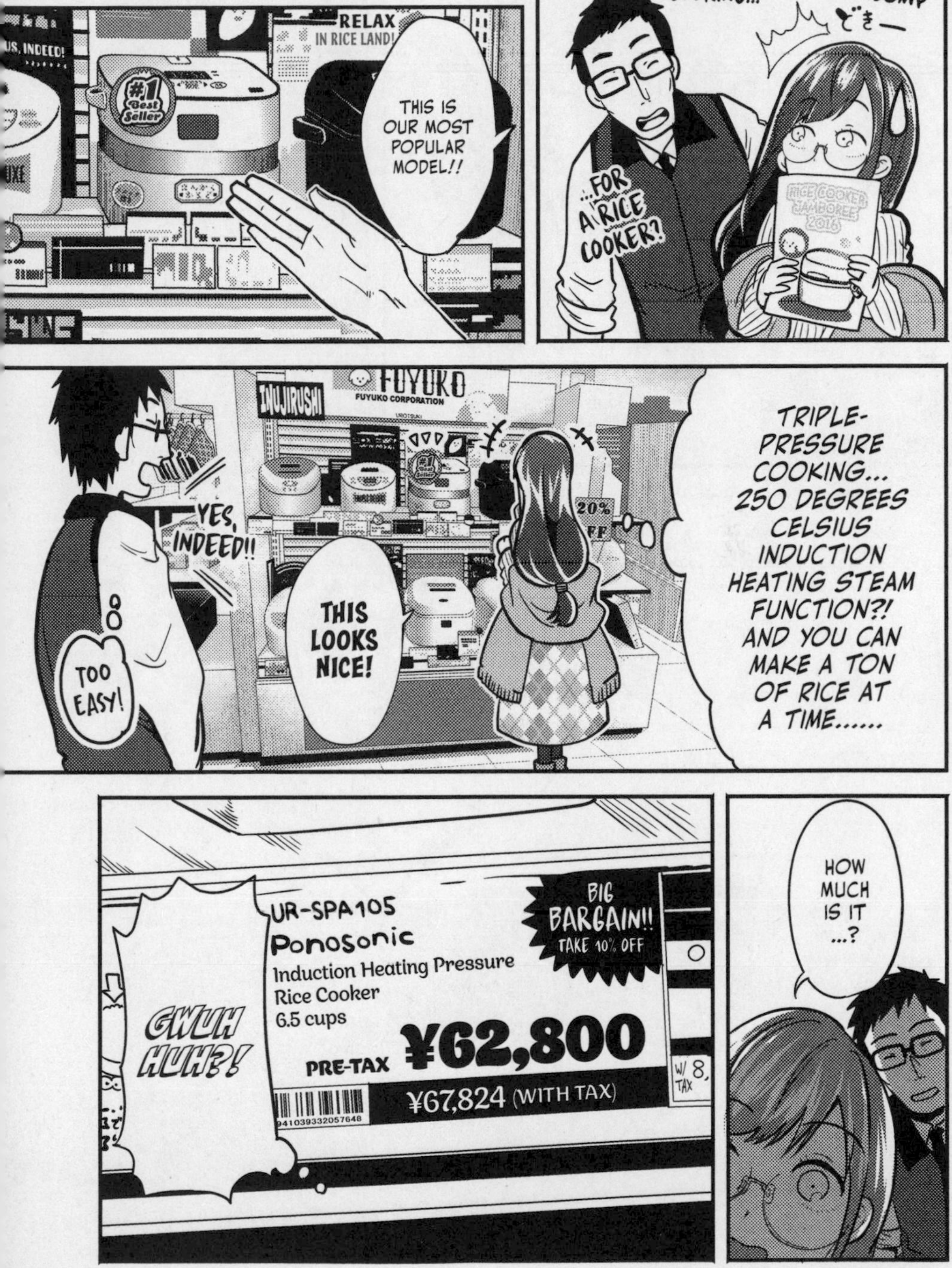
ARE YOU LOOKING...
BADUMP
どきー
...FOR A RICE COOKER?
RICE COOKER JAMBOREE 2016
RELAX IN RICE LAND!
US, INDEED!
#1 Best Seller
THIS IS OUR MOST POPULAR MODEL!!
TRIPLE-PRESSURE COOKING... 250 DEGREES CELSIUS INDUCTION HEATING STEAM FUNCTION?! AND YOU CAN MAKE A TON OF RICE AT A TIME......
FUYUKO
FUYUKO CORPORATION
INUJIRUSHI
20% OFF
THIS LOOKS NICE!
YES, INDEED!!
TOO EASY!
HOW MUCH IS IT ...?
BIG BARGAIN!! TAKE 10% OFF
UR-SPA105
Ponosonic
Induction Heating Pressure Rice Cooker
6.5 cups
PRE-TAX ¥62,800
¥67,824 (WITH TAX)
W/ 8, TAX
GWUH HUH?!

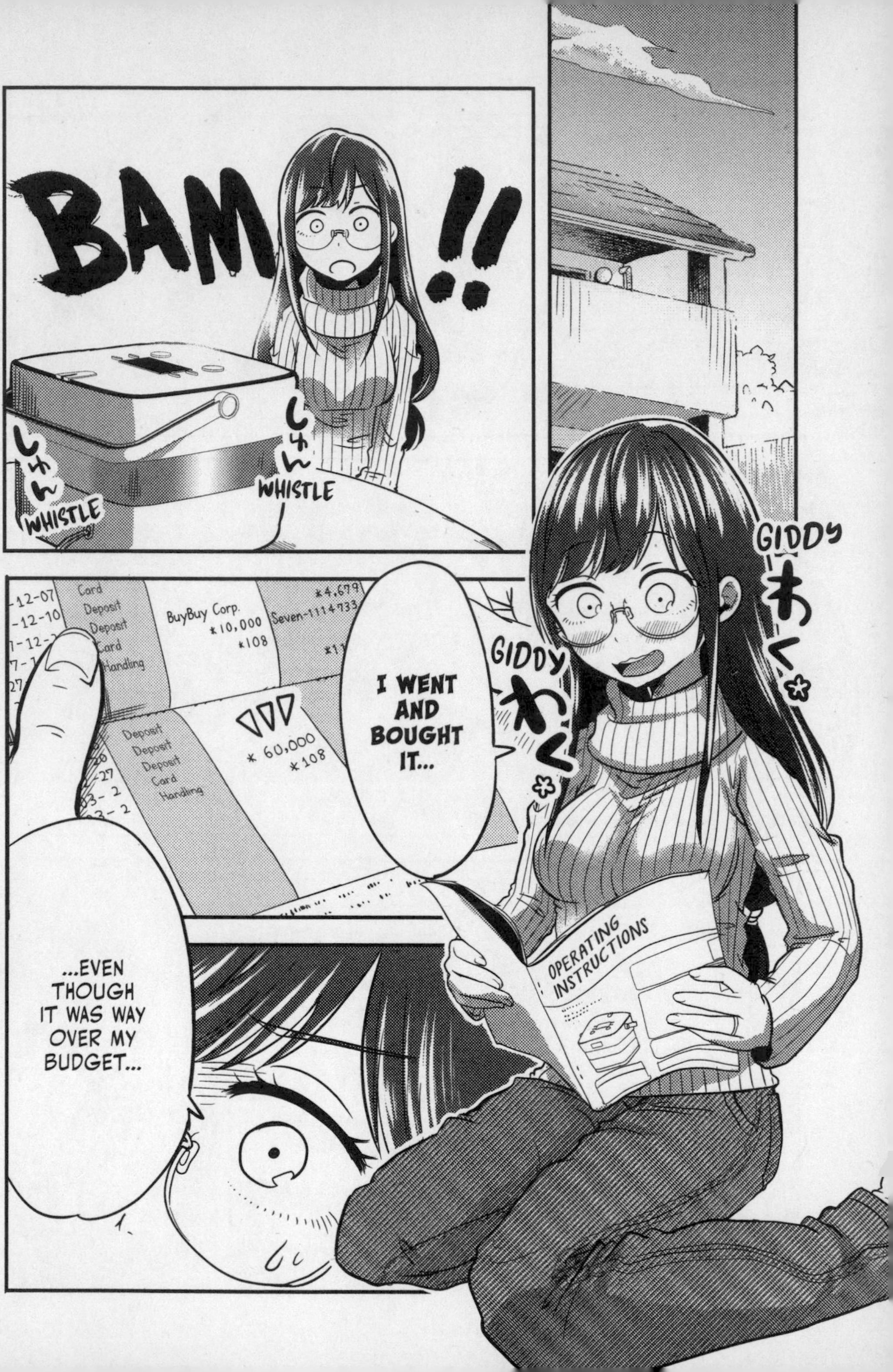
BAM!!
しゅん
WHISTLE
しゅん
WHISTLE
GIDDY
わく
GIDDY
わく
I WENT AND BOUGHT IT...
-12-07 Card ¥4,679
-12-10 Deposit BuyBuy Corp. ¥10,000 Seven-1114733
Deposit
Card ¥108
Handling
Deposit
Deposit
Deposit ¥60,000
Card ¥108
Handling
...EVEN THOUGH IT WAS WAY OVER MY BUDGET...
OPERATING INSTRUCTIONS

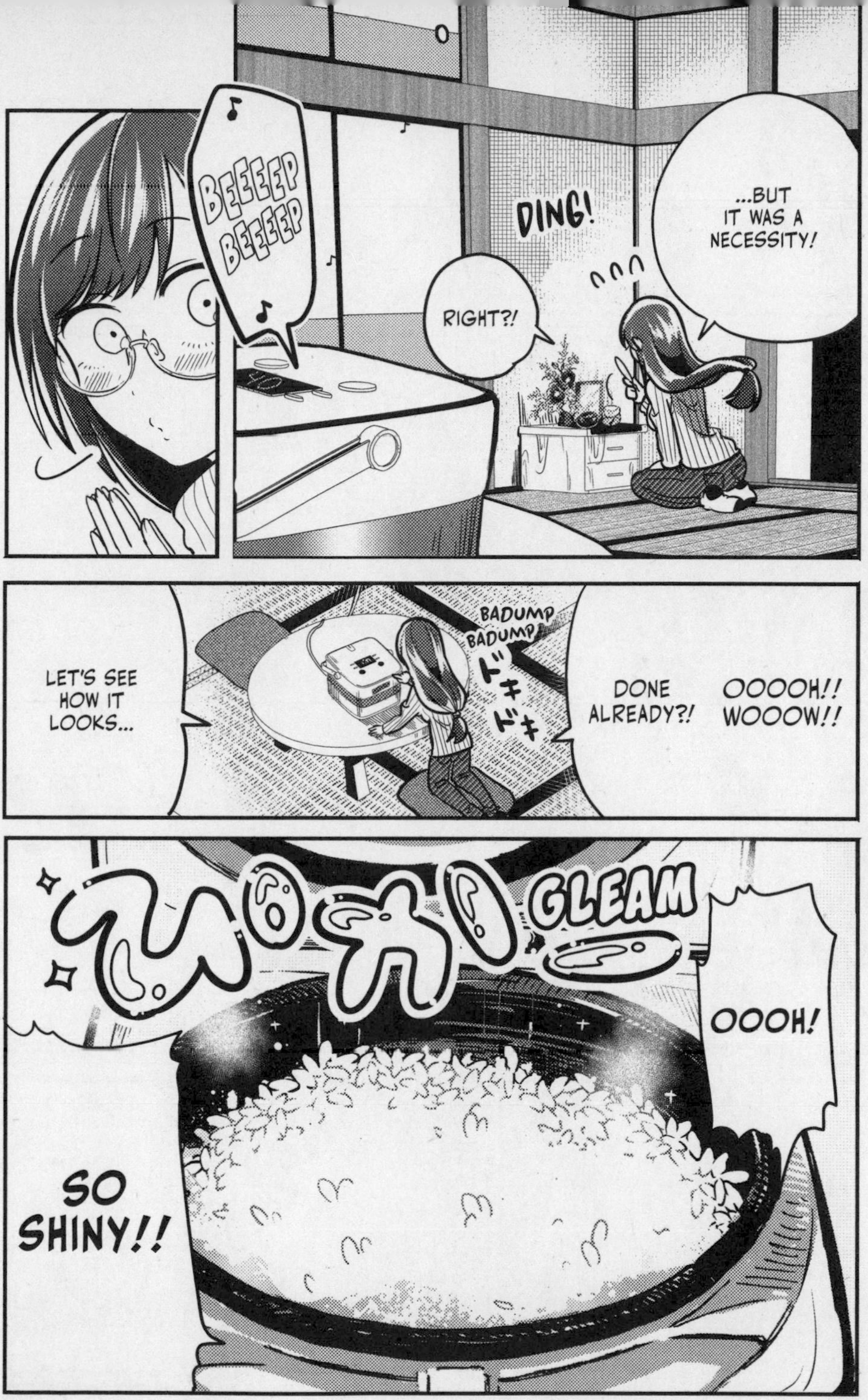
...BUT IT WAS A NECESSITY!
RIGHT?!
DING!
BEEEEP BEEEEP
OOOOH!! WOOOW!!
DONE ALREADY?!
BADUMP BADUMP
ドキドキ
LET'S SEE HOW IT LOOKS...
OOOH!
GLEAM
SO SHINY!!

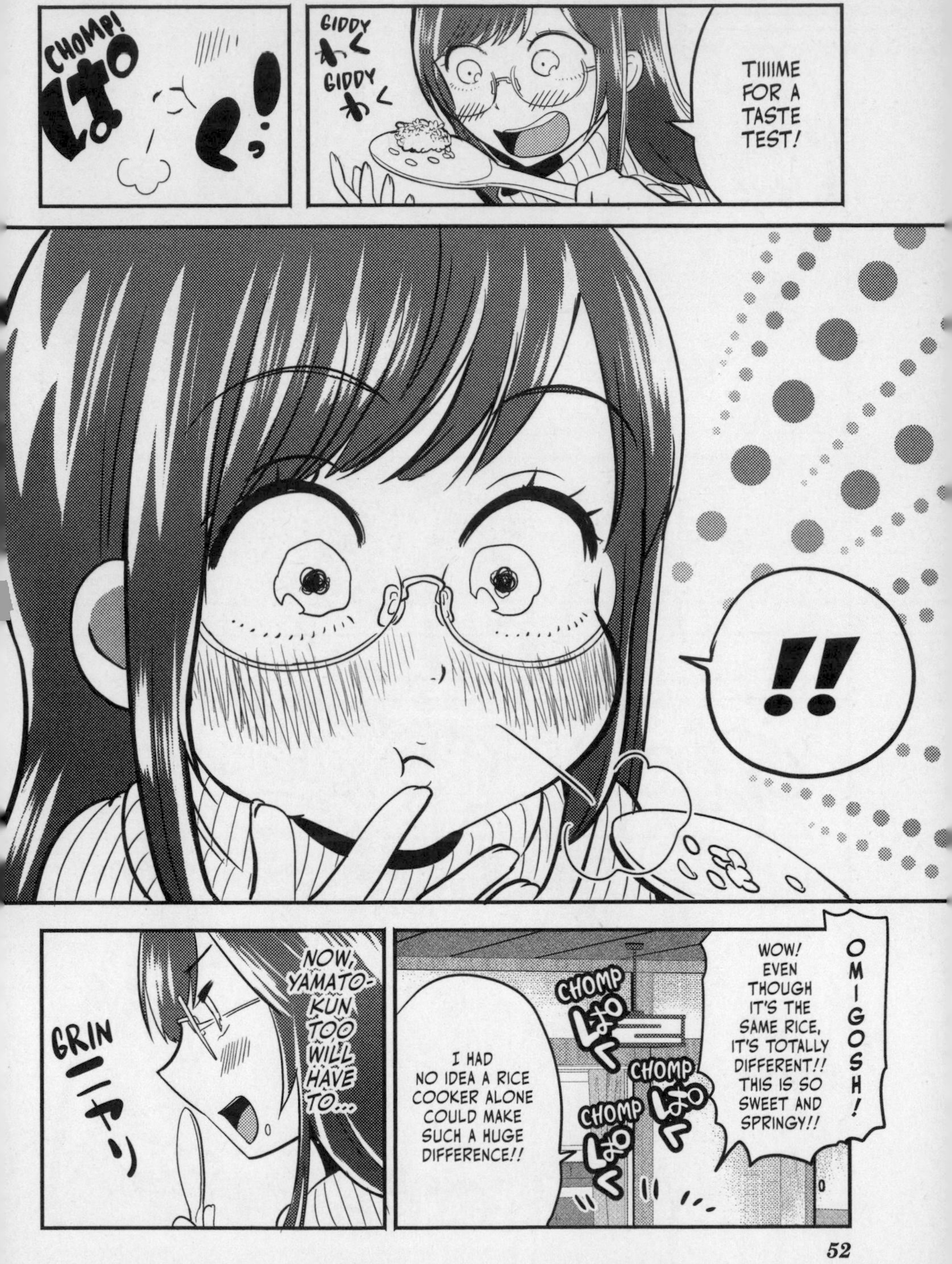

GIDDY わく
GIDDY わく
TIIIIME FOR A TASTE TEST!
CHOMP! ぱくっ!
!!
OMIGOSH!
WOW! EVEN THOUGH IT'S THE SAME RICE, IT'S TOTALLY DIFFERENT!! THIS IS SO SWEET AND SPRINGY!!
CHOMP
CHOMP
CHOMP
I HAD NO IDEA A RICE COOKER ALONE COULD MAKE SUCH A HUGE DIFFERENCE!!
NOW, YAMATO-KUN TOO WILL HAVE TO...
GRIN ニヤリ

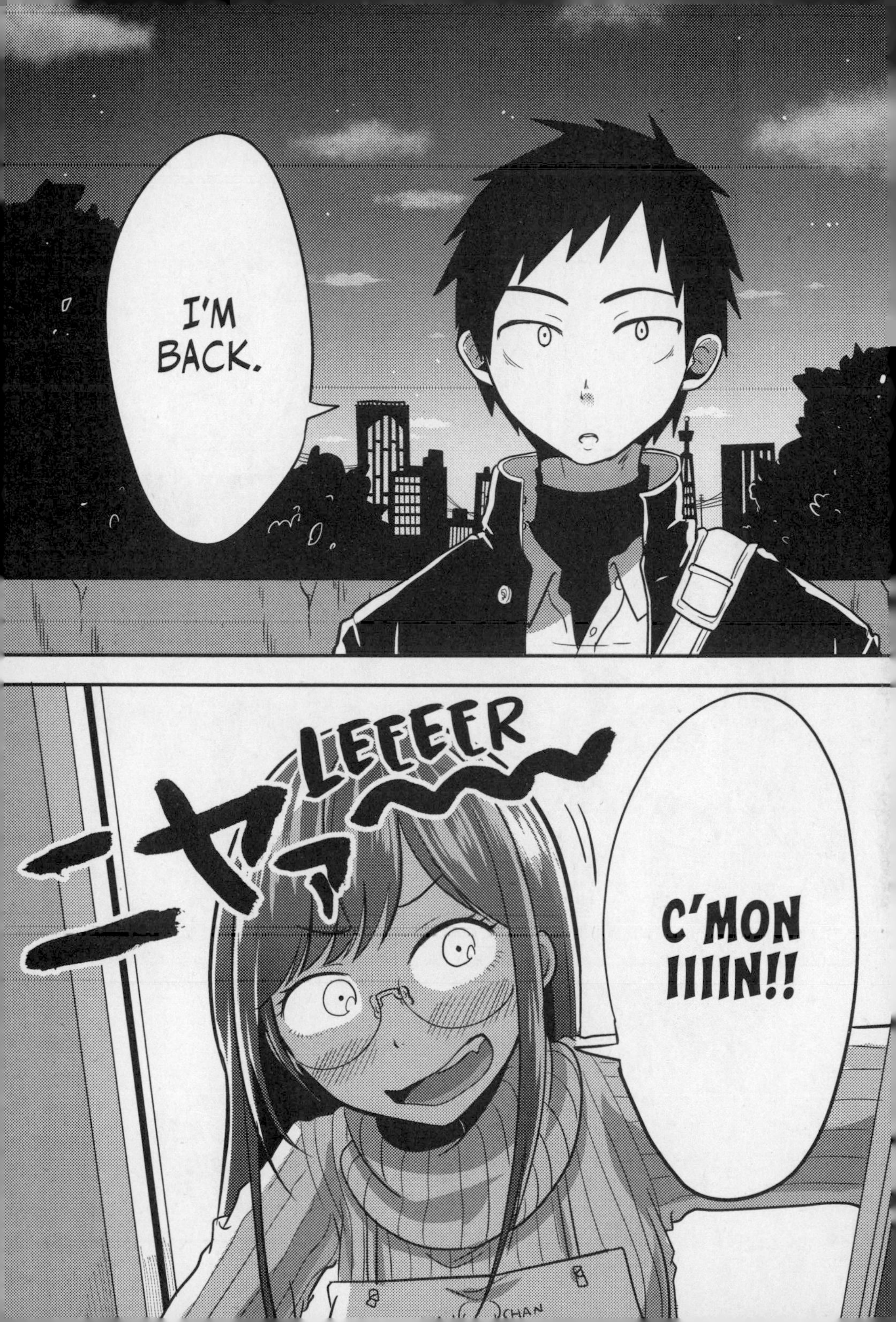
I'M BACK.
C'MON IIIIN!!
LEEEER

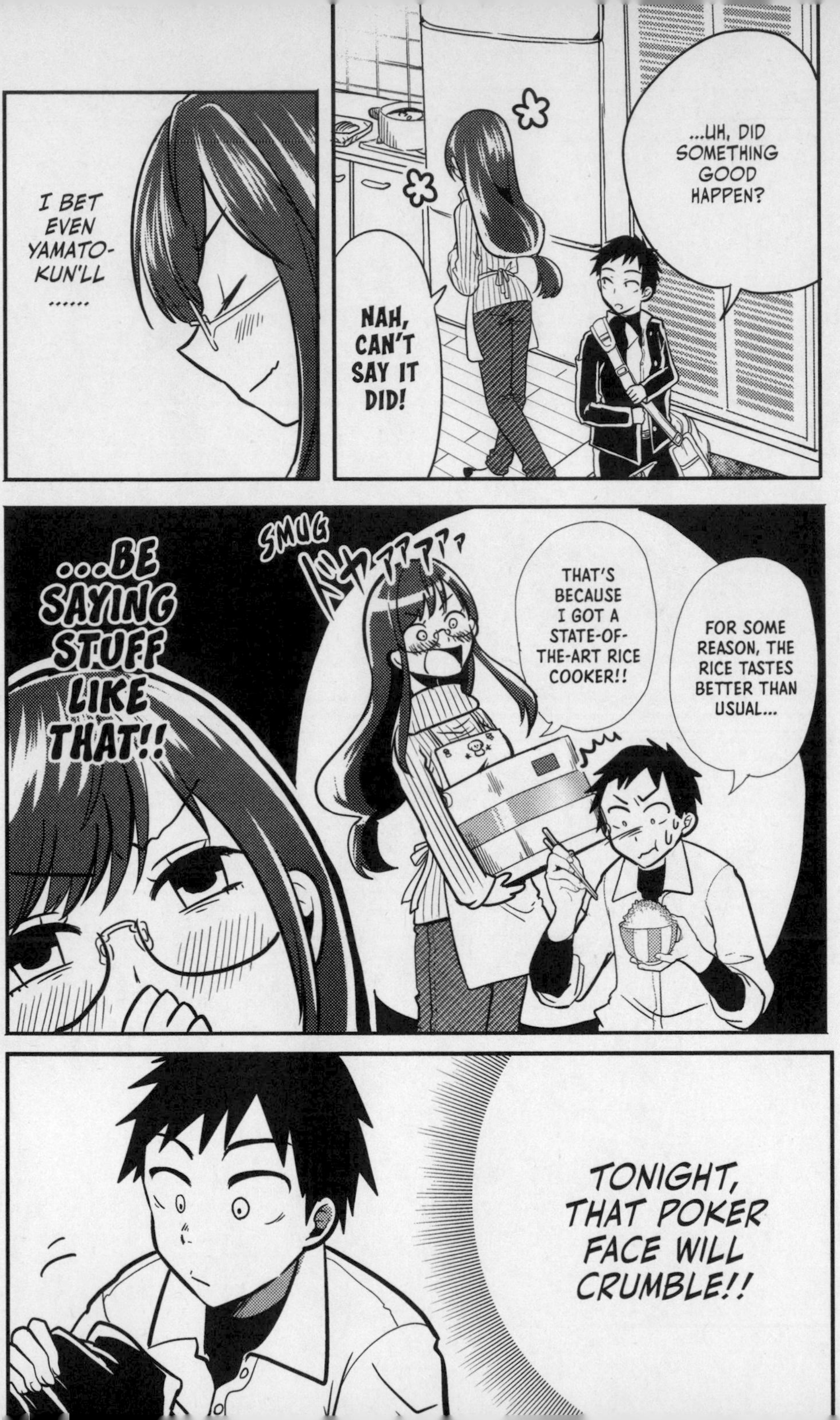
...UH, DID SOMETHING GOOD HAPPEN?
NAH, CAN'T SAY IT DID!
I BET EVEN YAMATO-KUN'LL ......
SMUG
FOR SOME REASON, THE RICE TASTES BETTER THAN USUAL...
THAT'S BECAUSE I GOT A STATE-OF-THE-ART RICE COOKER!!
...BE SAYING STUFF LIKE THAT!!
TONIGHT, THAT POKER FACE WILL CRUMBLE!!

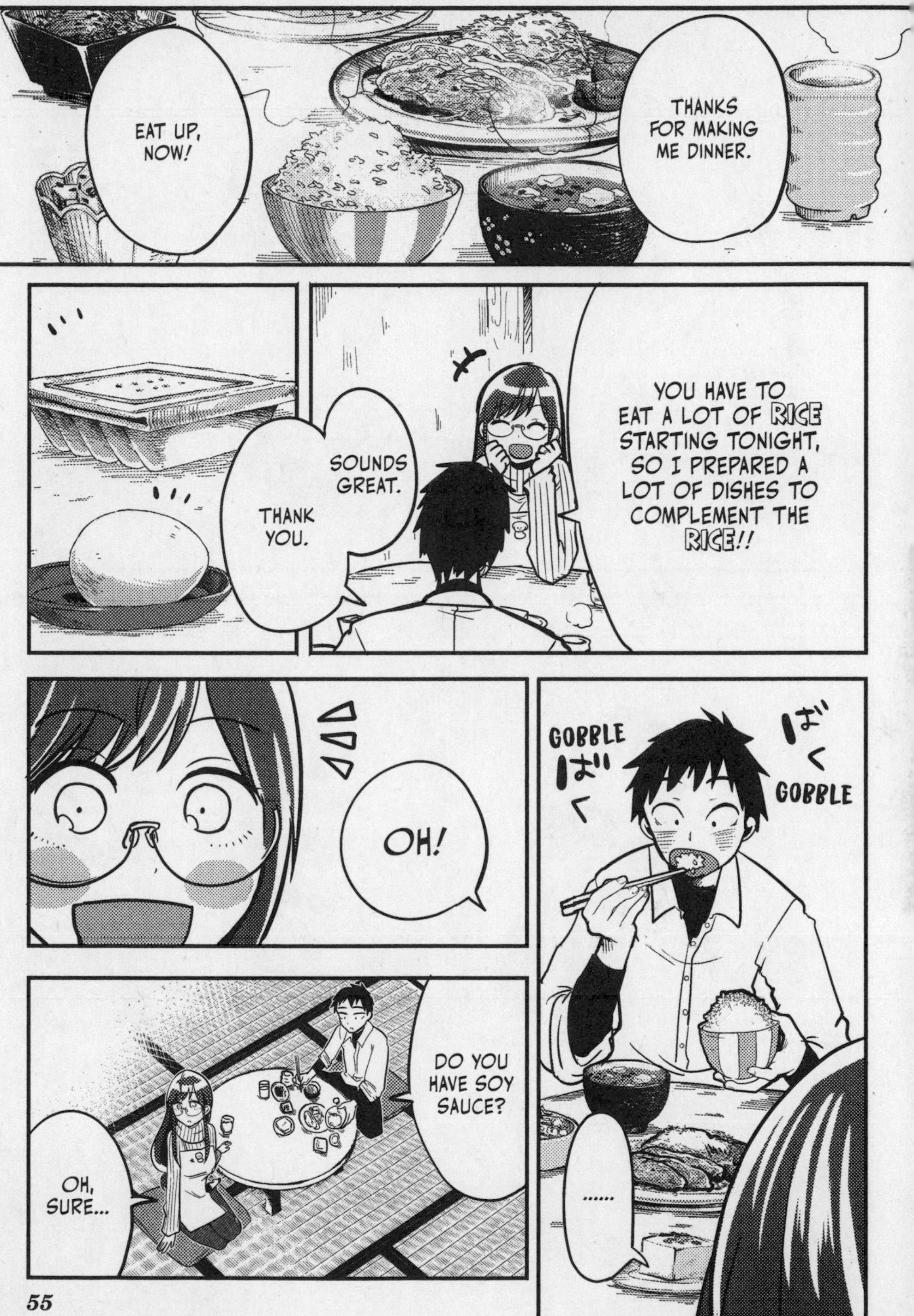
THANKS FOR MAKING ME DINNER.
EAT UP, NOW!
YOU HAVE TO EAT A LOT OF RICE STARTING TONIGHT, SO I PREPARED A LOT OF DISHES TO COMPLEMENT THE RICE!!
SOUNDS GREAT.
THANK YOU.
ばく
GOBBLE
ばく
GOBBLE
......
OH!
DO YOU HAVE SOY SAUCE?
OH, SURE...

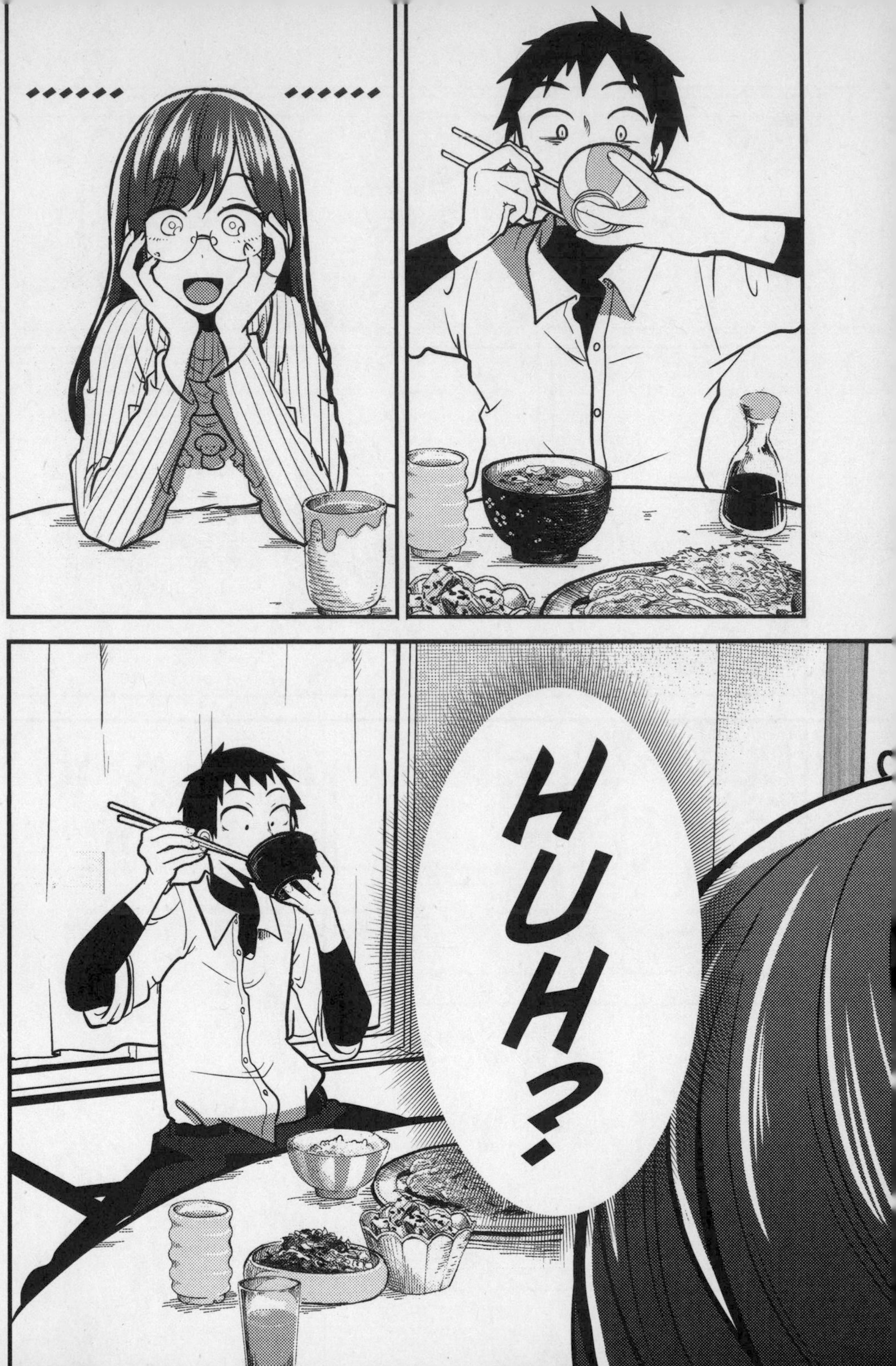
......
......
HUH?!

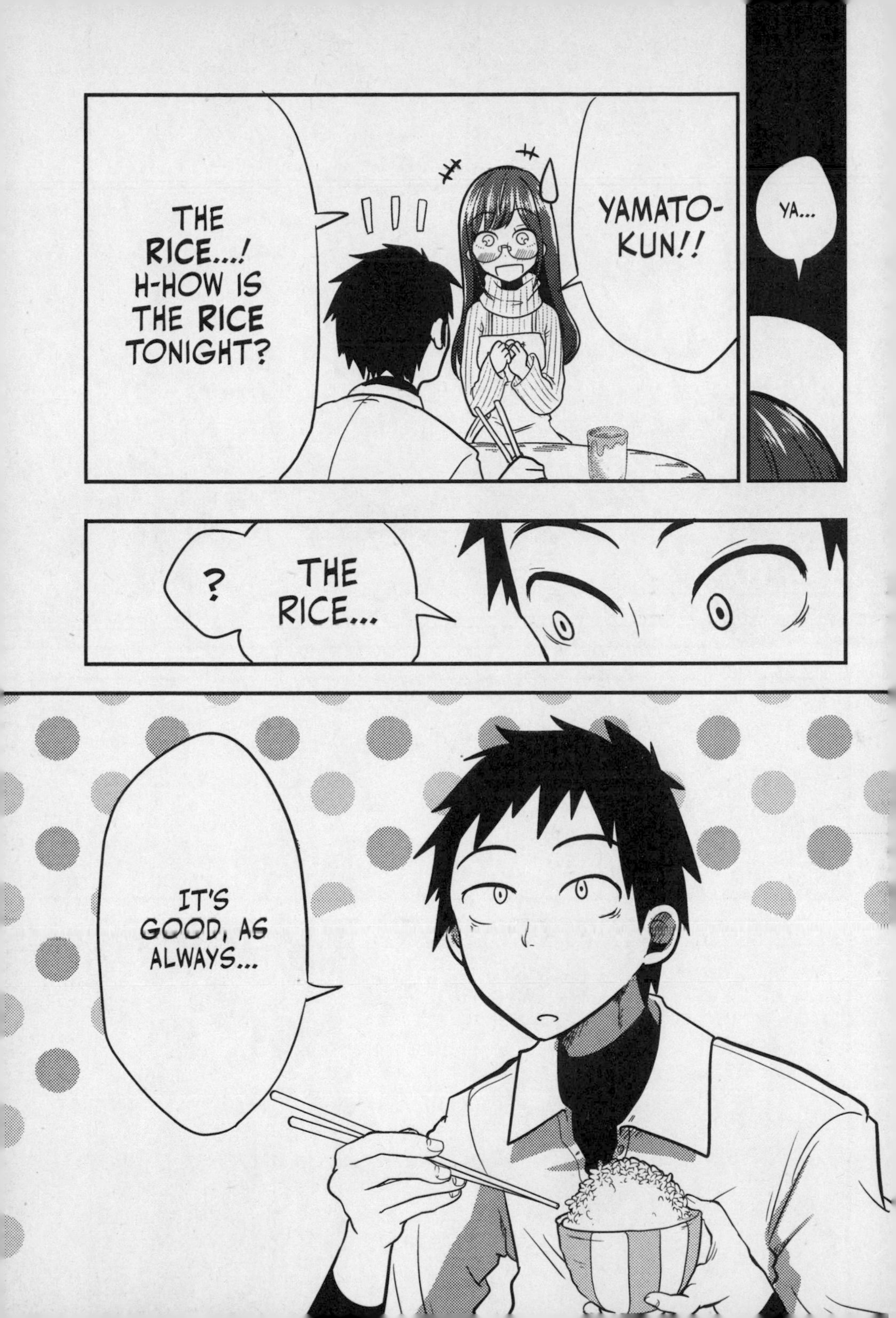
YA...
YAMATO-KUN!!
THE RICE...! H-HOW IS THE RICE TONIGHT?
? THE RICE...
IT'S GOOD, AS ALWAYS...

A-AS ALWAYS?!!

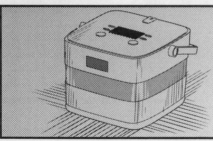

WELL...

HE'S CHOWING DOWN, SO I CAN'T COMPLAIN, BUT......!!

Y-YAMATO-KUN, ARE YOU DOING OKAY?

YOU'RE ON YOUR SIXTH BOWL ALREADY...

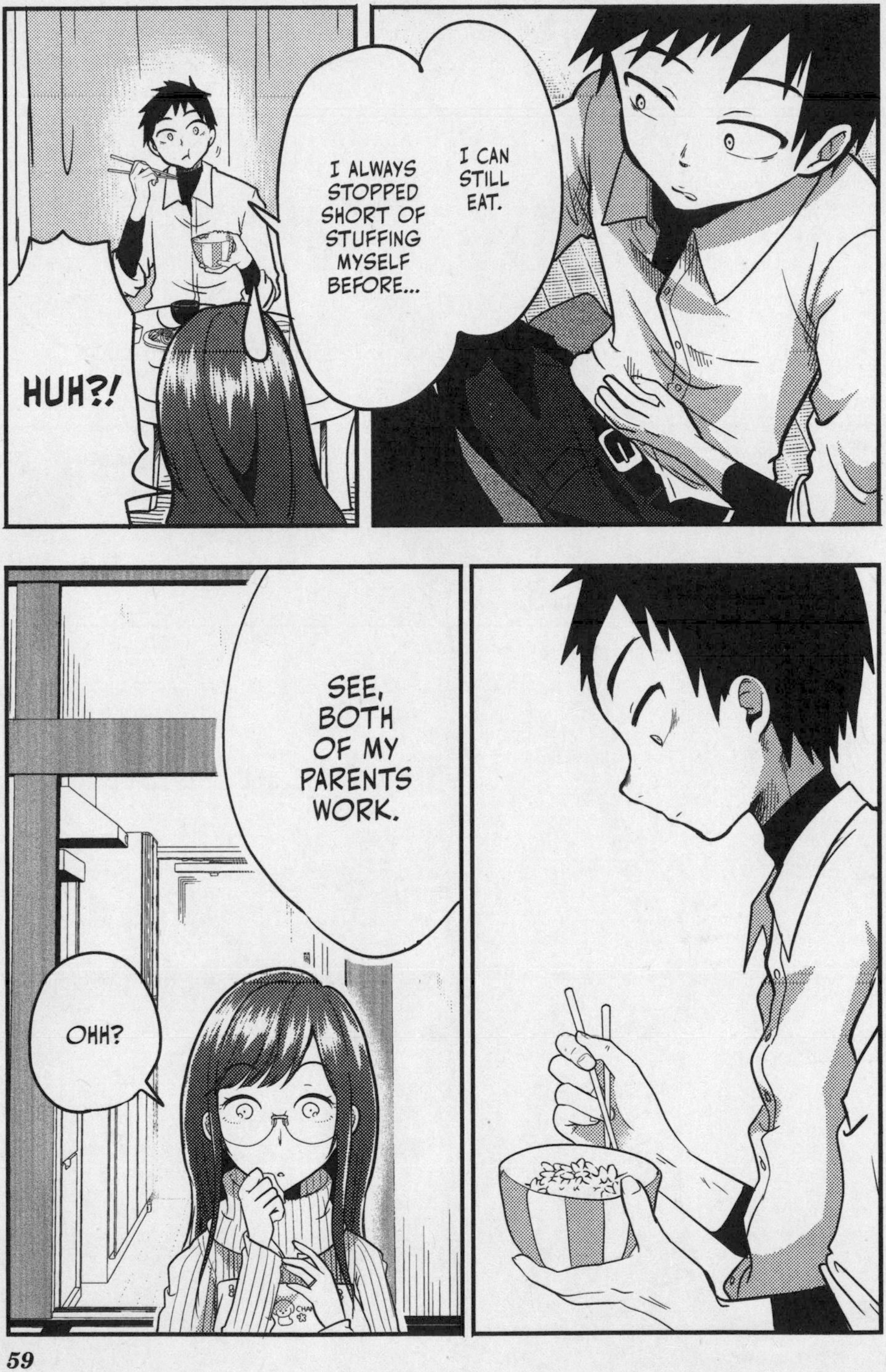
I CAN STILL EAT.
I ALWAYS STOPPED SHORT OF STUFFING MYSELF BEFORE...
HUH?!
SEE, BOTH OF MY PARENTS WORK.
OHH?

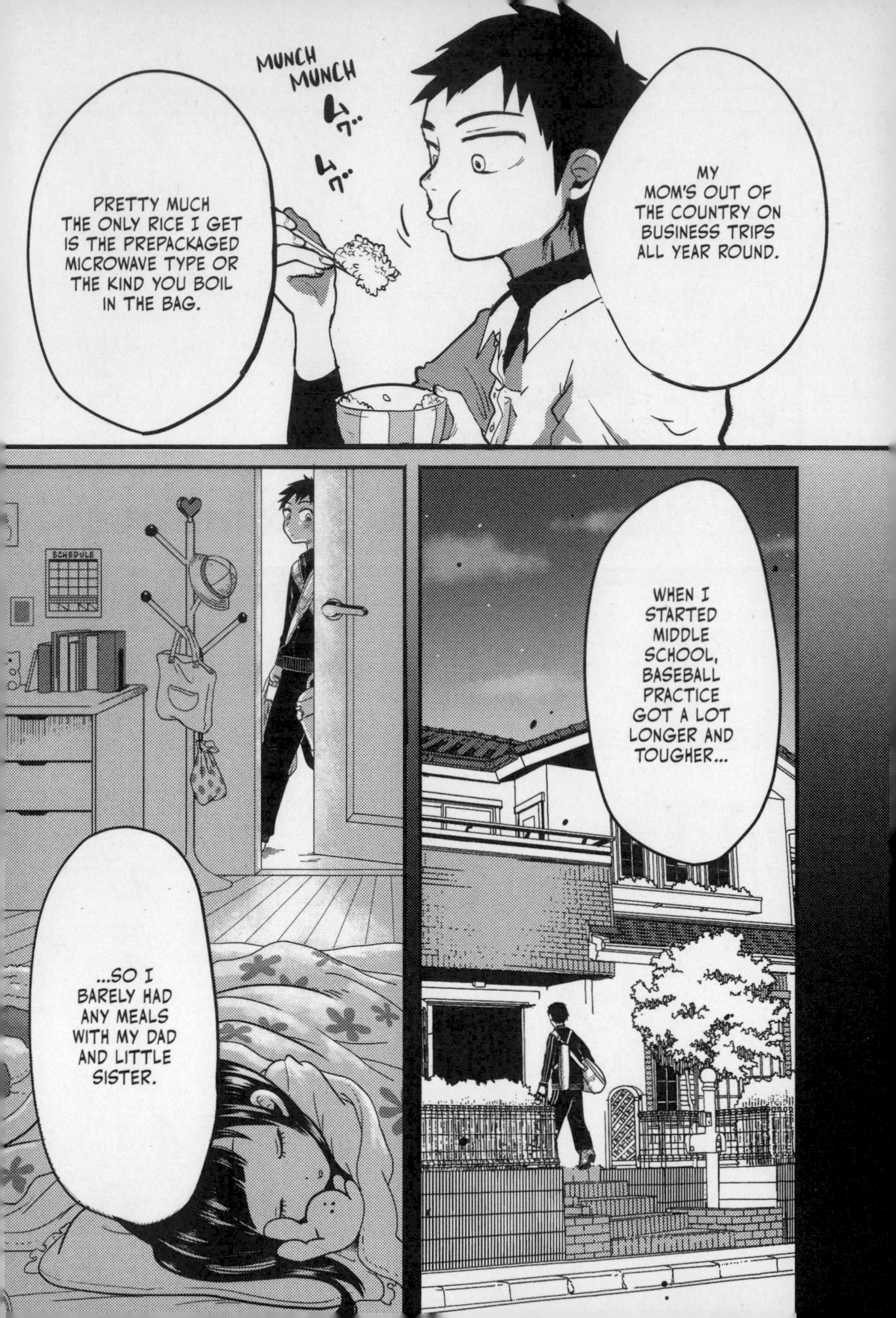
MY MOM'S OUT OF THE COUNTRY ON BUSINESS TRIPS ALL YEAR ROUND.
MUNCH MUNCH
ムグ ムグ
PRETTY MUCH THE ONLY RICE I GET IS THE PREPACKAGED MICROWAVE TYPE OR THE KIND YOU BOIL IN THE BAG.
WHEN I STARTED MIDDLE SCHOOL, BASEBALL PRACTICE GOT A LOT LONGER AND TOUGHER...
...SO I BARELY HAD ANY MEALS WITH MY DAD AND LITTLE SISTER.

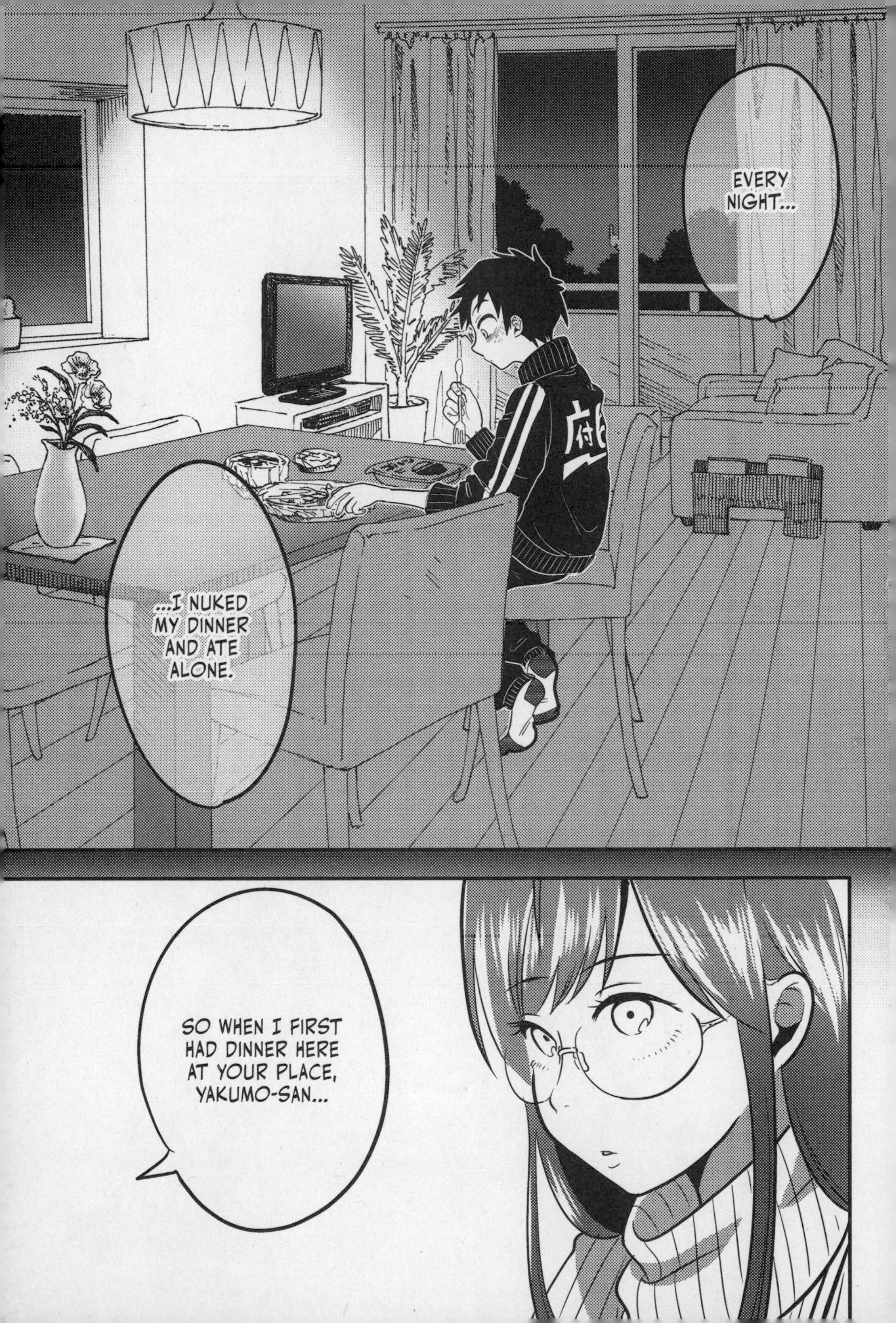
EVERY NIGHT...
...I NUKED MY DINNER AND ATE ALONE.
SO WHEN I FIRST HAD DINNER HERE AT YOUR PLACE, YAKUMO-SAN...

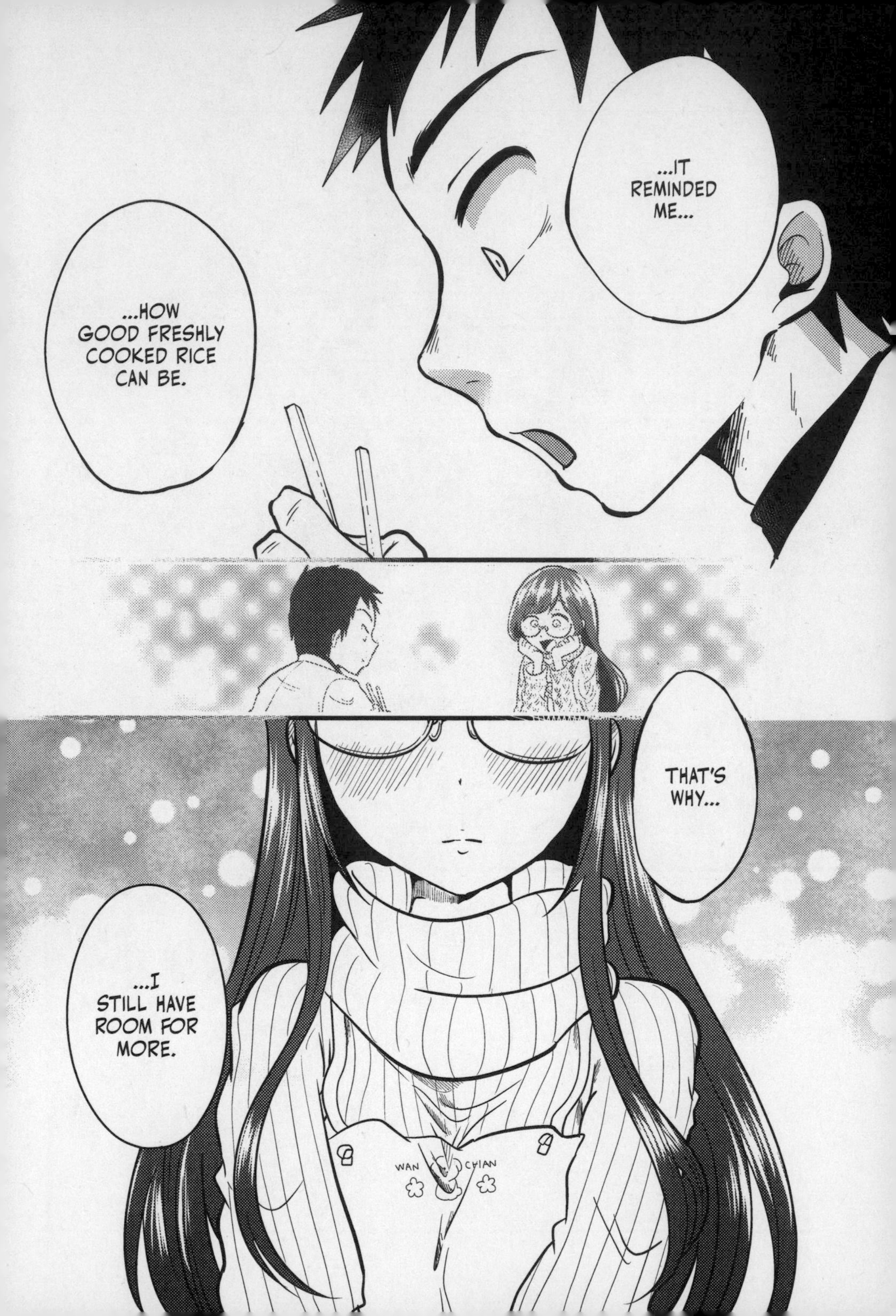
...IT REMINDED ME...
...HOW GOOD FRESHLY COOKED RICE CAN BE.
THAT'S WHY...
...I STILL HAVE ROOM FOR MORE.
WAN
CHAN

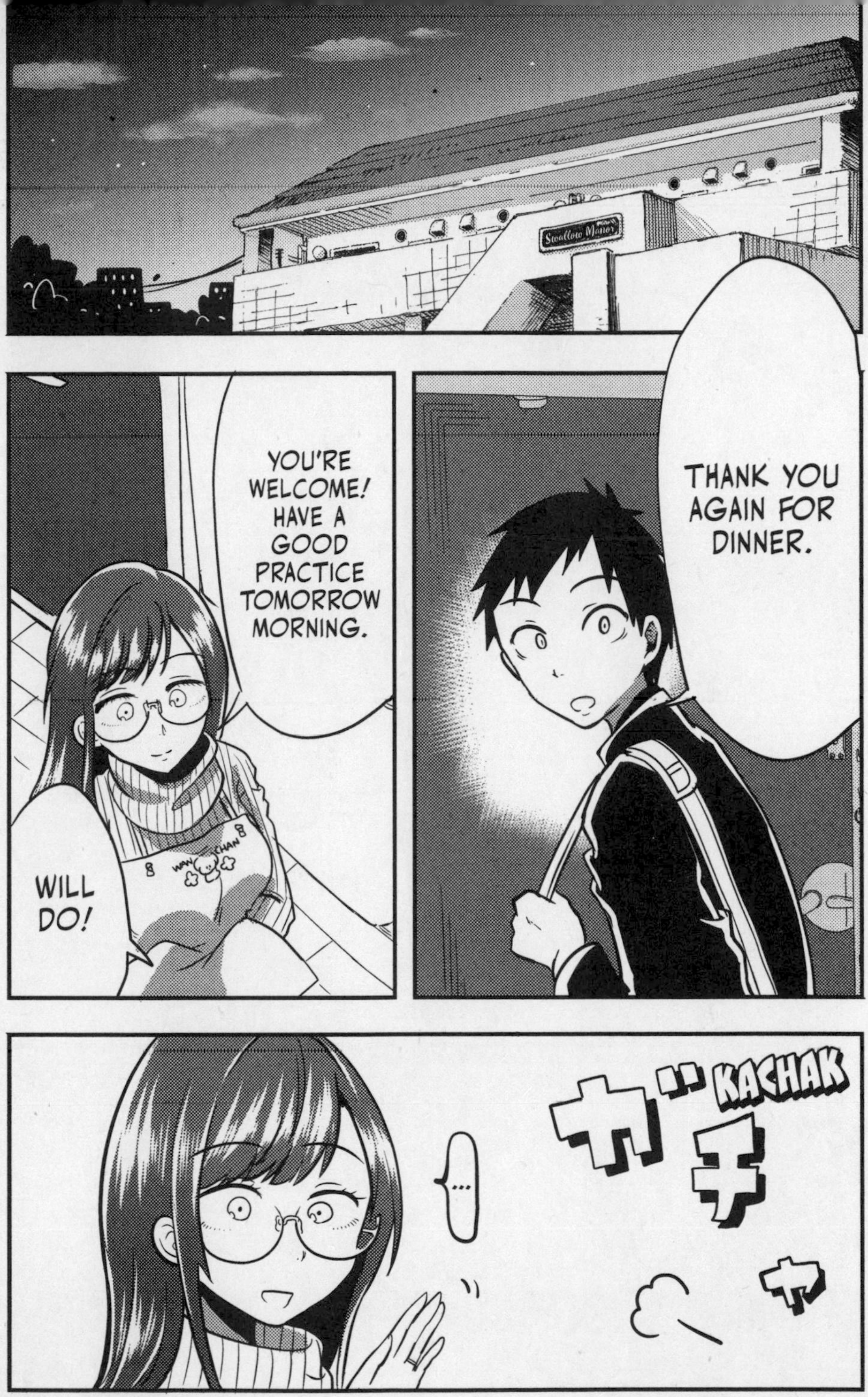
Swallow Manor
THANK YOU AGAIN FOR DINNER.
YOU'RE WELCOME! HAVE A GOOD PRACTICE TOMORROW MORNING.
WILL DO!
KACHAK
...

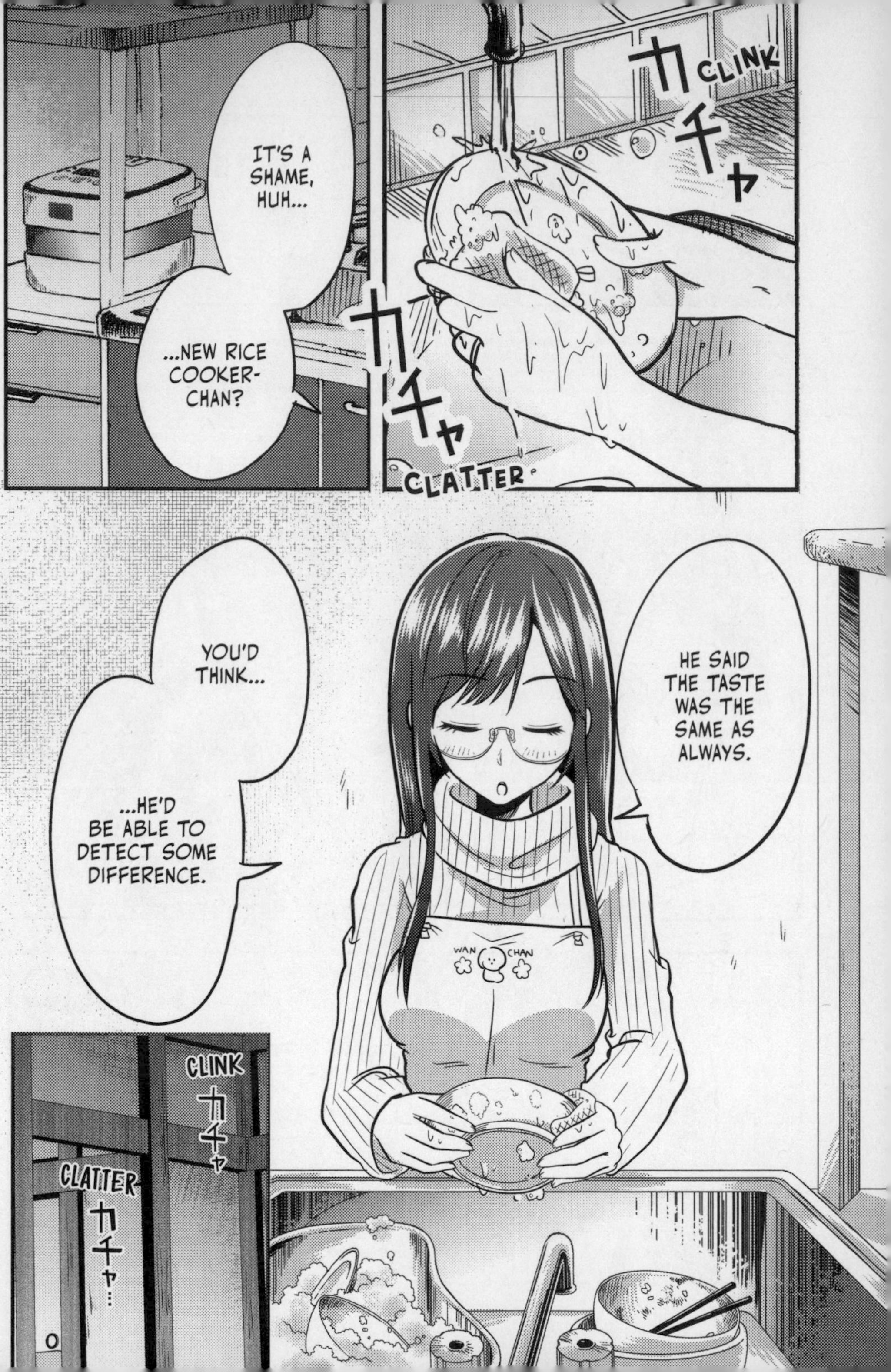
カチャ
CLINK
カチャ
CLATTER
IT'S A SHAME, HUH...
...NEW RICE COOKER-CHAN?
HE SAID THE TASTE WAS THE SAME AS ALWAYS.
YOU'D THINK...
...HE'D BE ABLE TO DETECT SOME DIFFERENCE.
WAN CHAN
CLINK
カチャ
CLATTER
カチャ...

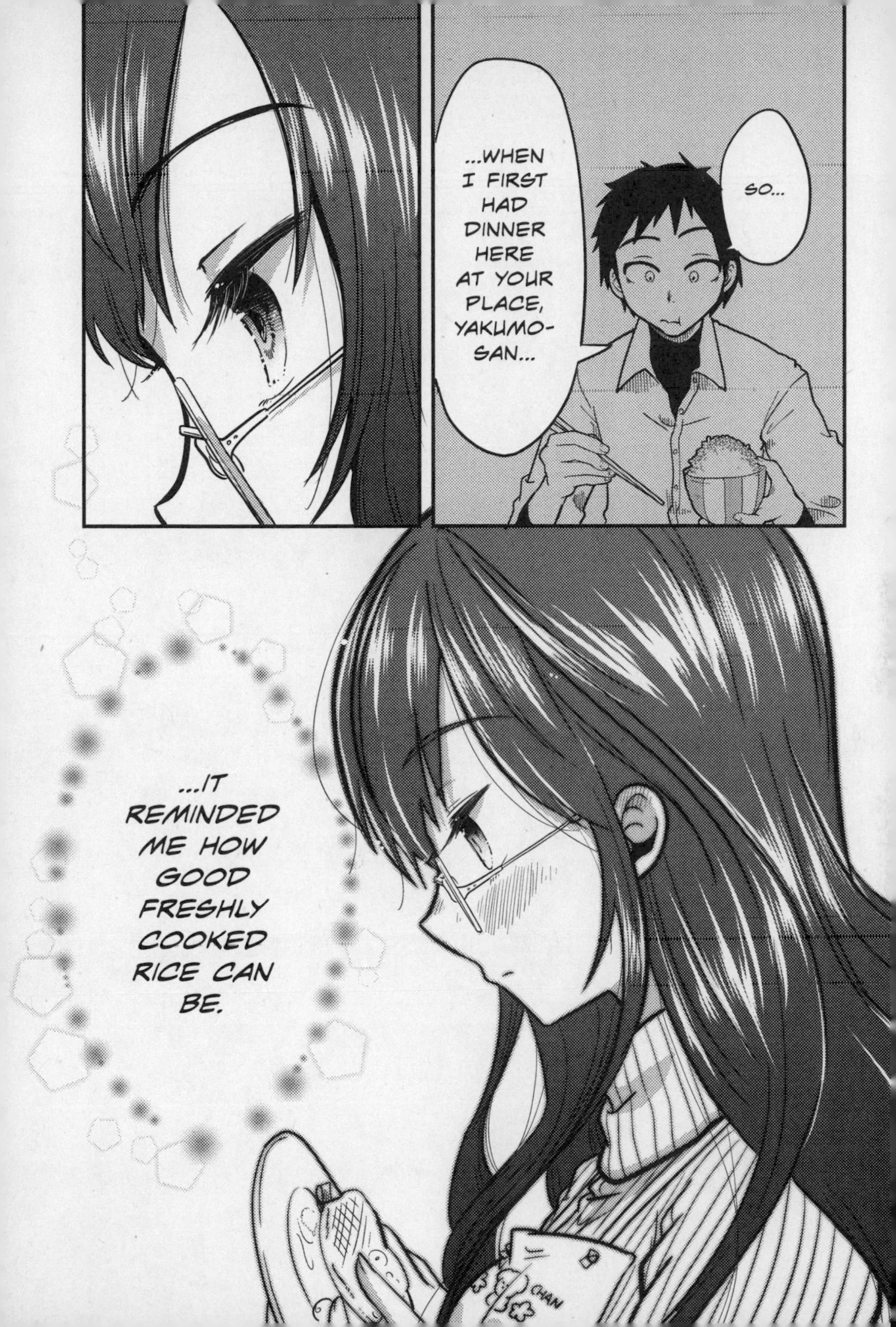
SO...
...WHEN I FIRST HAD DINNER HERE AT YOUR PLACE, YAKUMO-SAN...
...IT REMINDED ME HOW GOOD FRESHLY COOKED RICE CAN BE.
CHAN

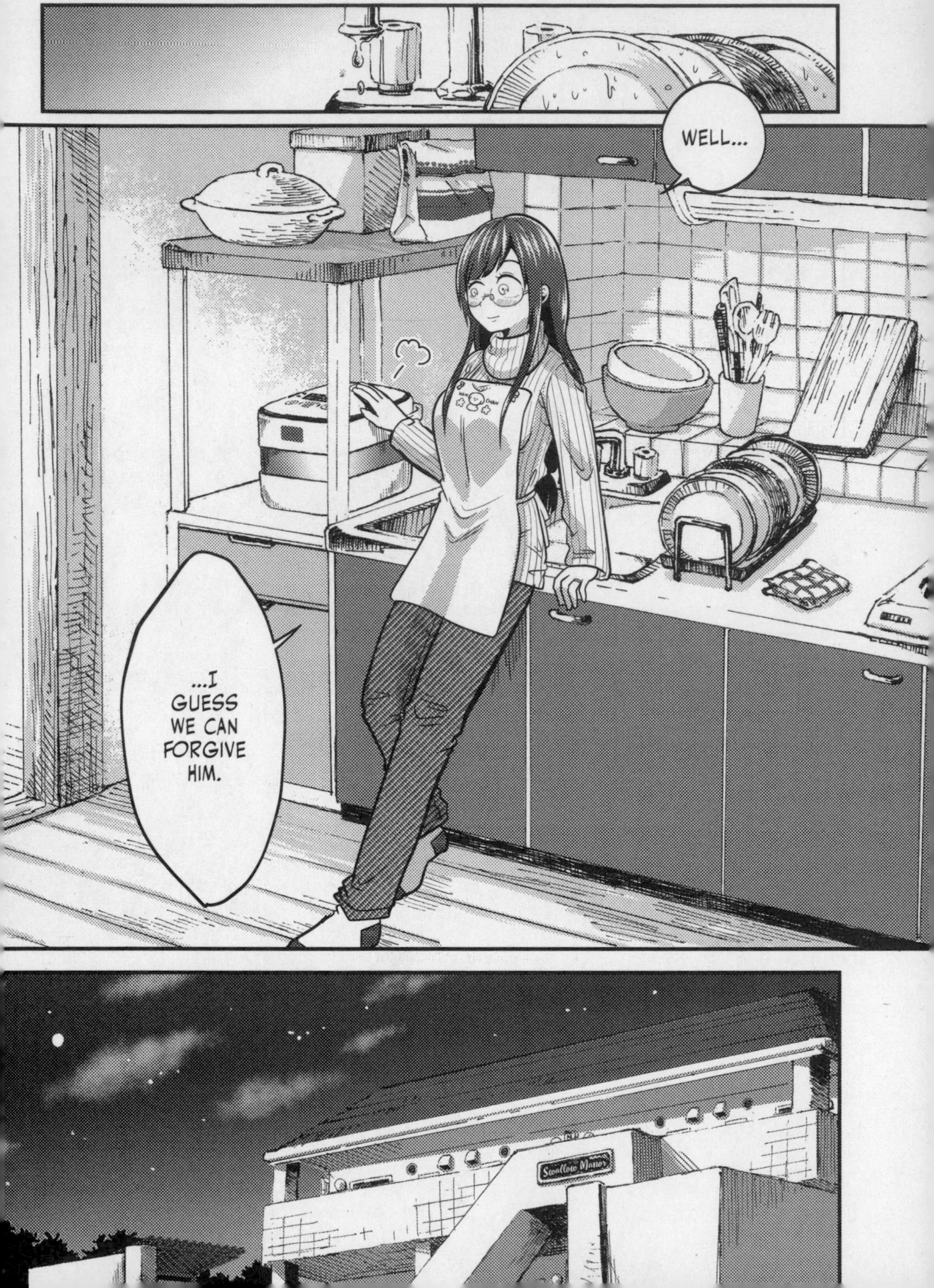
WELL...
...I GUESS WE CAN FORGIVE HIM.
Swallow Manor

Beauty and the FEAST.

Beauty and the FEAST

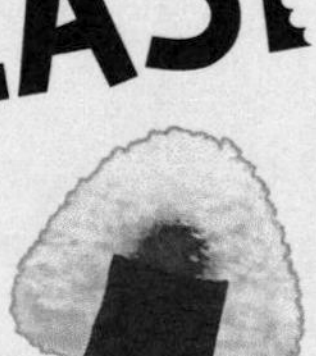

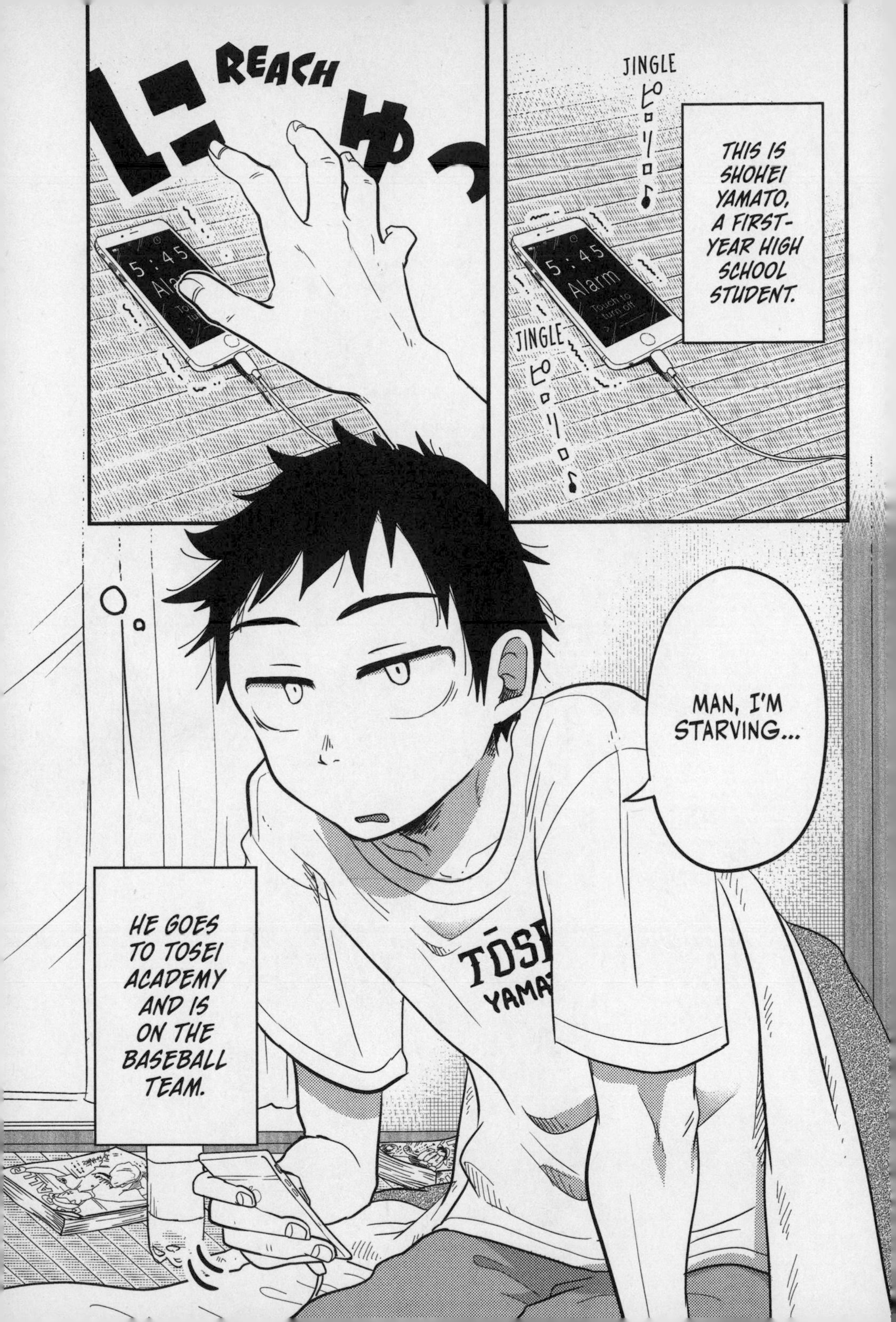
JINGLE
ピロリロ♪
5:45
Alarm
Touch to turn off
JINGLE
ピロリロ♪
THIS IS SHOHEI YAMATO, A FIRST-YEAR HIGH SCHOOL STUDENT.
REACH
にゅっ
MAN, I'M STARVING...
HE GOES TO TOSEI ACADEMY AND IS ON THE BASEBALL TEAM.

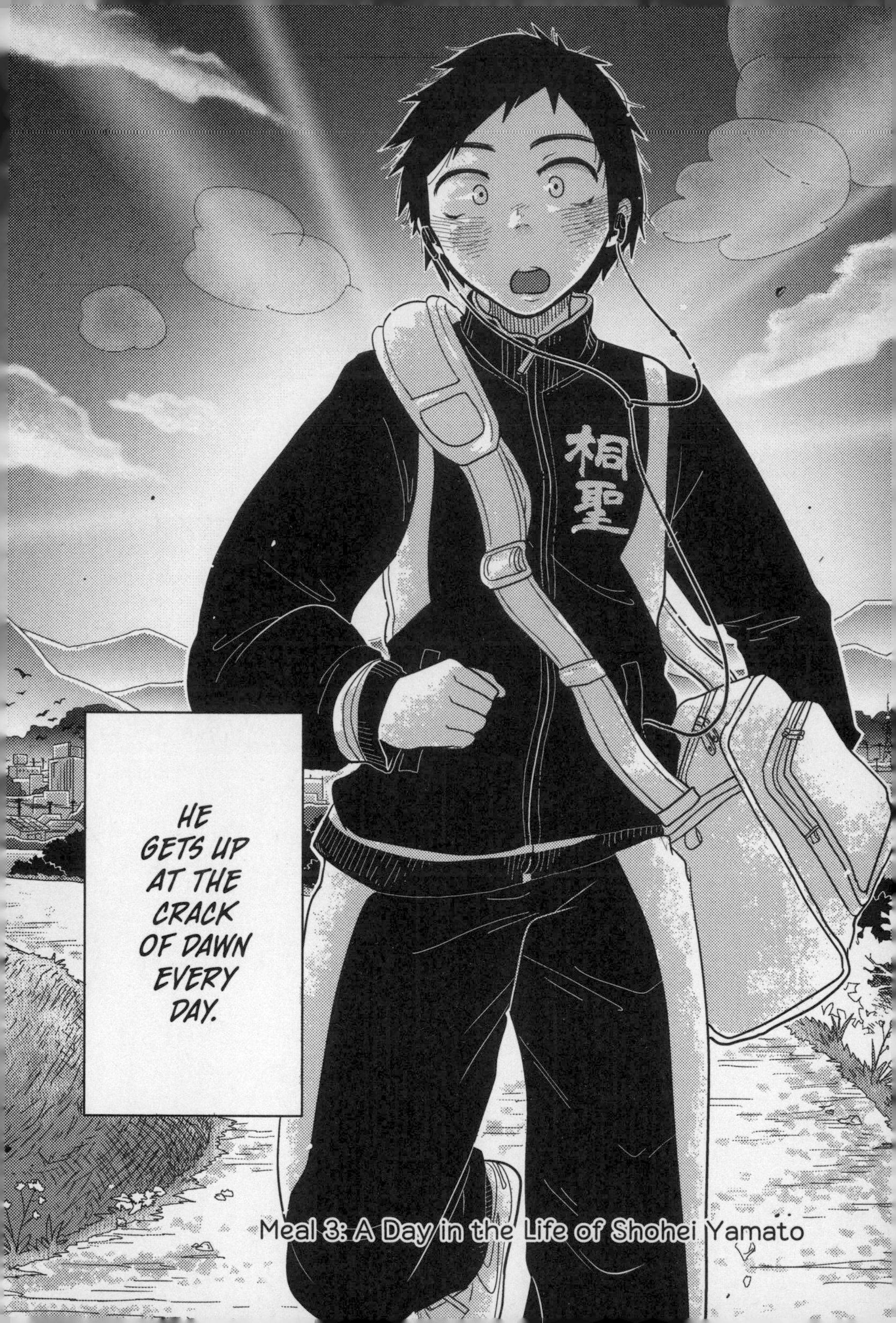
HE GETS UP AT THE CRACK OF DAWN EVERY DAY.
相聖
Meal 3: A Day in the Life of Shohei Yamato

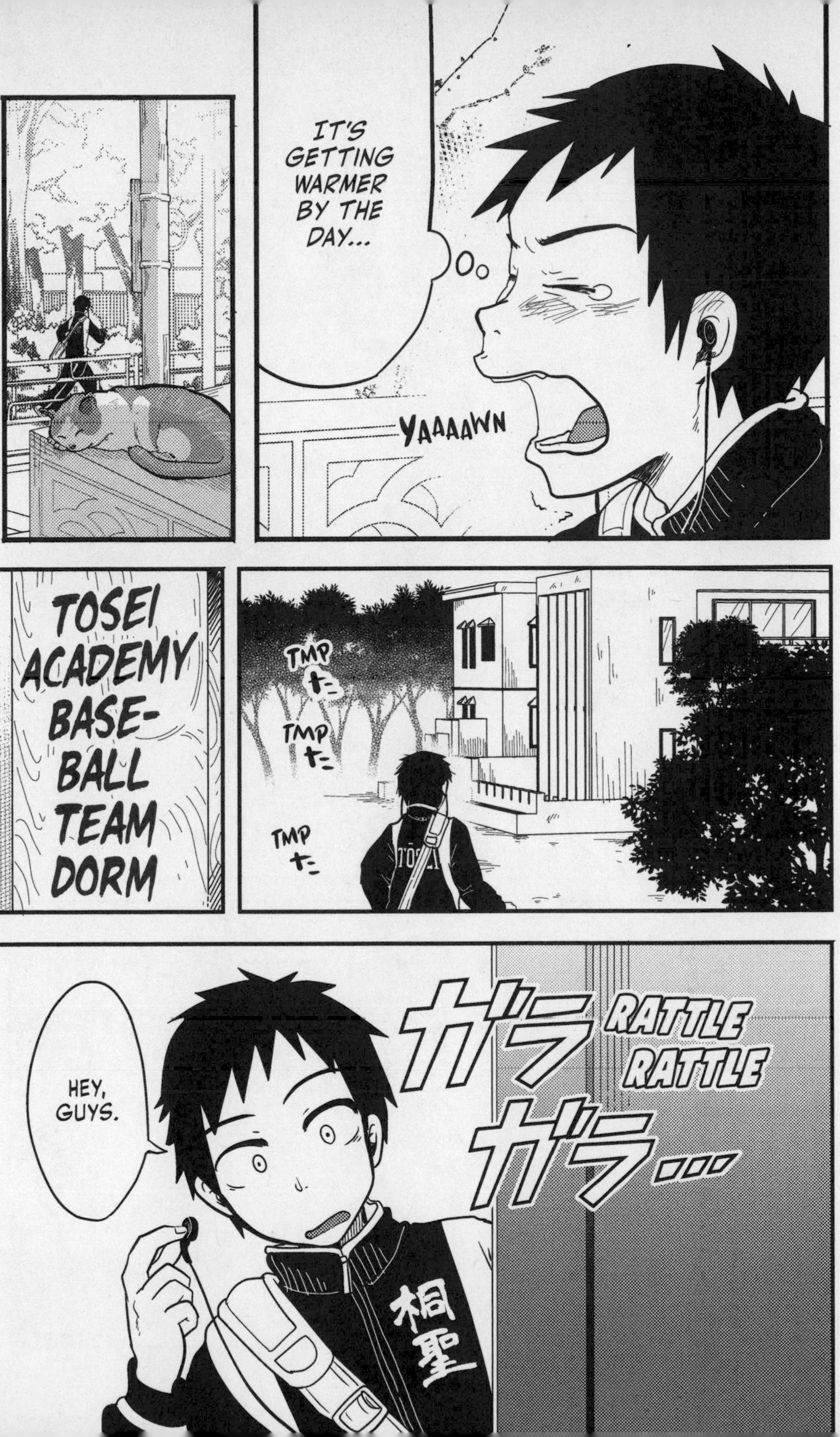
IT'S GETTING WARMER BY THE DAY...
YAAAAWN
TMP た
TMP た
TMP た
TOSEI
TOSEI ACADEMY BASE-BALL TEAM DORM
ガラ
RATTLE RATTLE
ガラ...
HEY, GUYS.
桐聖

I'M SLEEPY-YYYYY.

MORNIN', YAMATO.

MORNIN'!

RIGHT.

LET'S HUSTLE.

IF WE DON'T FINISH SETTING THE TABLES BY THE TIME THE THIRD-YEARS GET THERE...

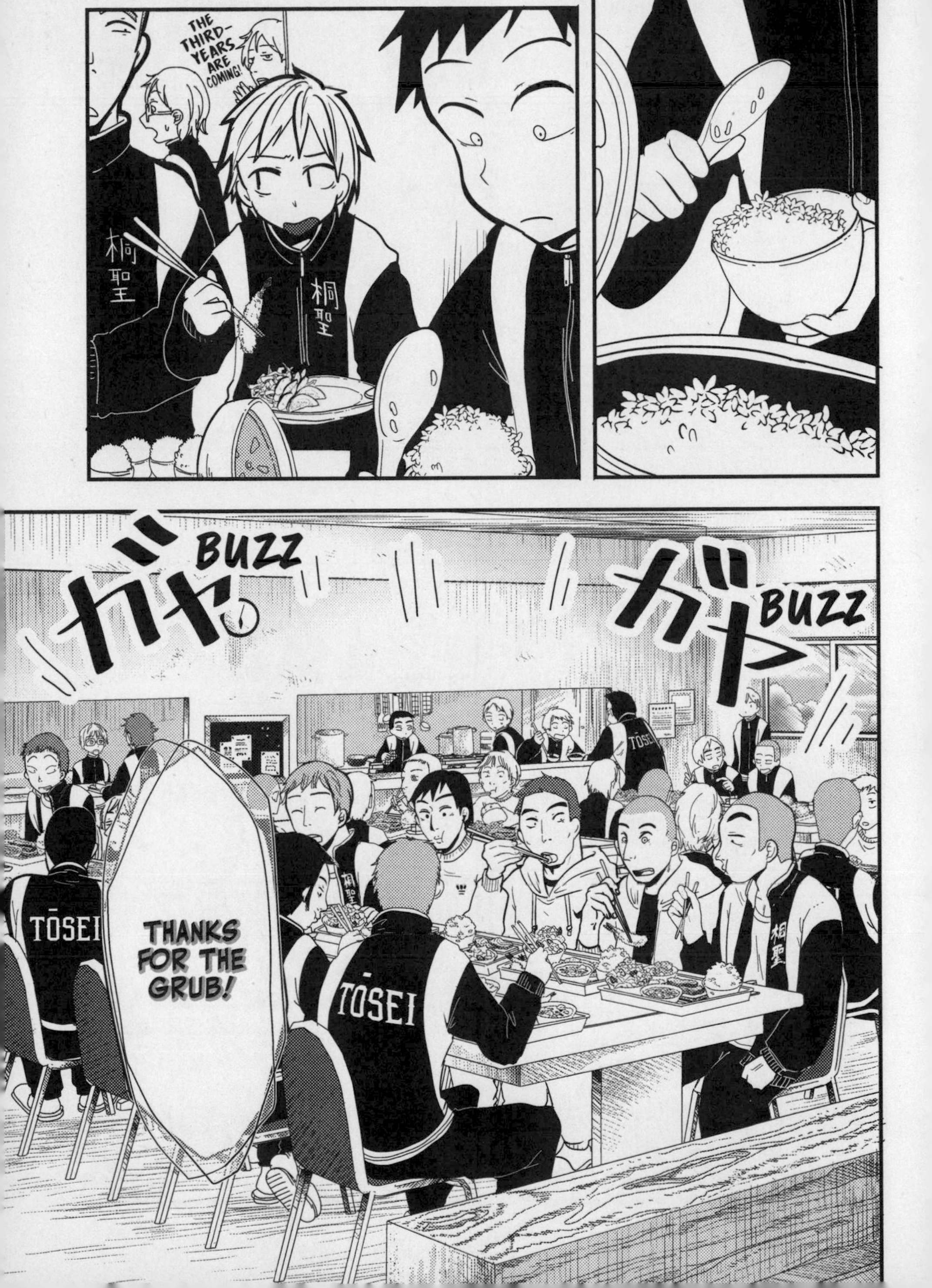
THE THIRD-YEARS ARE COMING!
ガヤ
BUZZ
ガヤ
BUZZ
THANKS FOR THE GRUB!

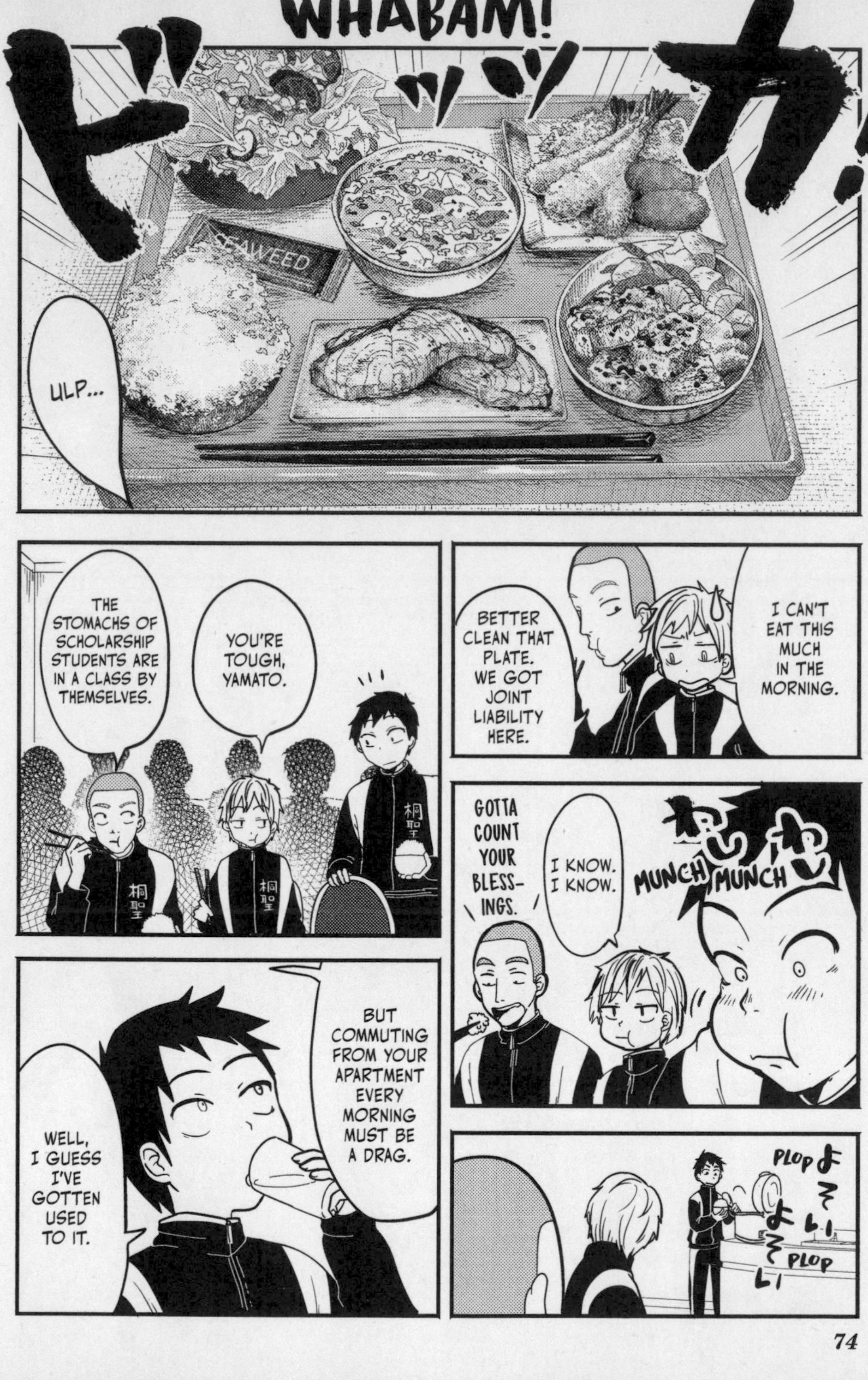
WHABAM!
ULP...
I CAN'T EAT THIS MUCH IN THE MORNING.
BETTER CLEAN THAT PLATE. WE GOT JOINT LIABILITY HERE.
YOU'RE TOUGH, YAMATO.
THE STOMACHS OF SCHOLARSHIP STUDENTS ARE IN A CLASS BY THEMSELVES.
MUNCH MUNCH
I KNOW. I KNOW.
GOTTA COUNT YOUR BLESS-INGS.
BUT COMMUTING FROM YOUR APARTMENT EVERY MORNING MUST BE A DRAG.
WELL, I GUESS I'VE GOTTEN USED TO IT.
PLOP
PLOP

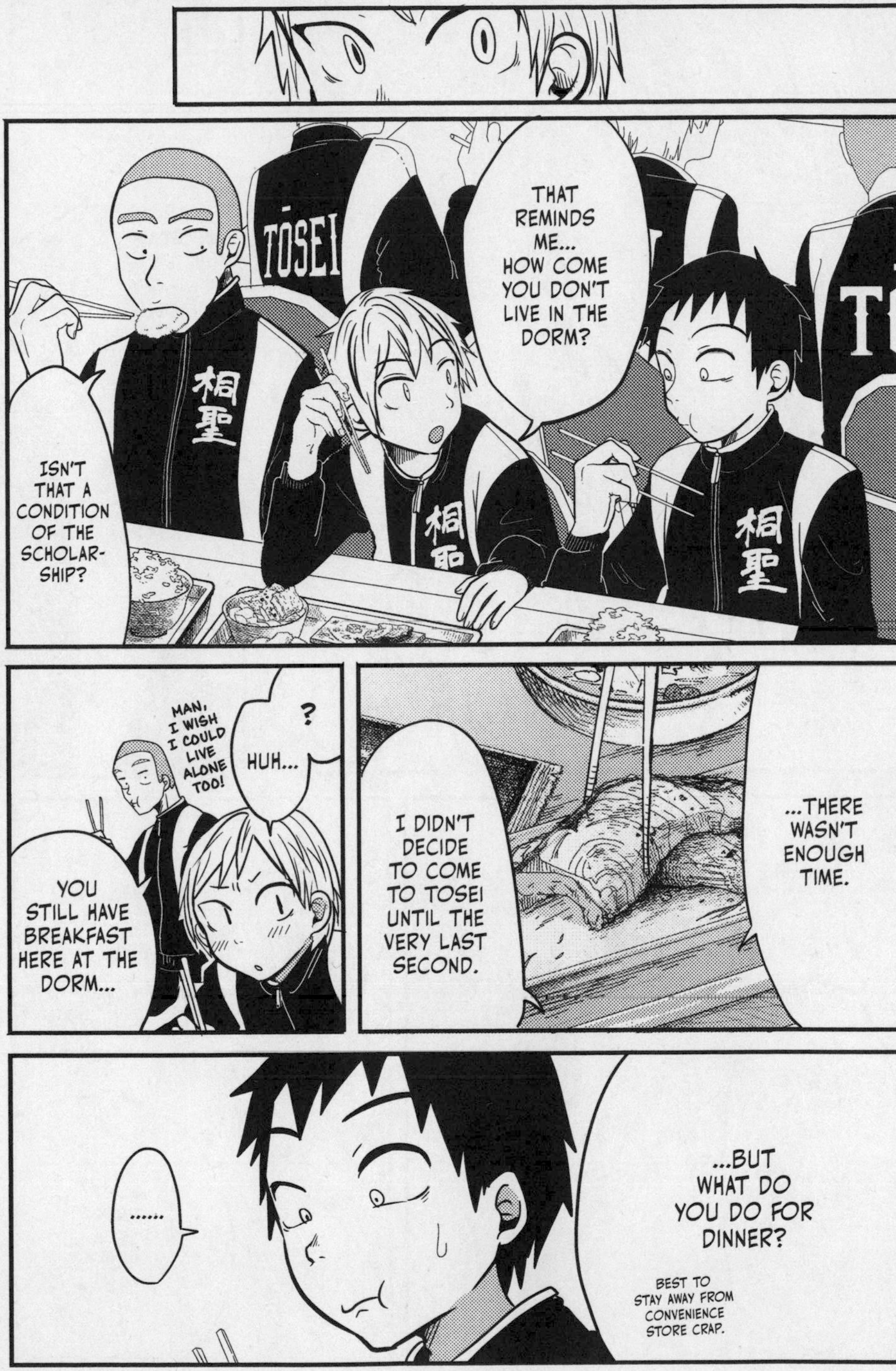
TŌSEI
THAT REMINDS ME... HOW COME YOU DON'T LIVE IN THE DORM?
ISN'T THAT A CONDITION OF THE SCHOLAR-SHIP?
...THERE WASN'T ENOUGH TIME.
I DIDN'T DECIDE TO COME TO TOSEI UNTIL THE VERY LAST SECOND.
?
HUH...
MAN, I WISH I COULD LIVE ALONE TOO!
YOU STILL HAVE BREAKFAST HERE AT THE DORM...
...BUT WHAT DO YOU DO FOR DINNER?
BEST TO STAY AWAY FROM CONVENIENCE STORE CRAP.
......

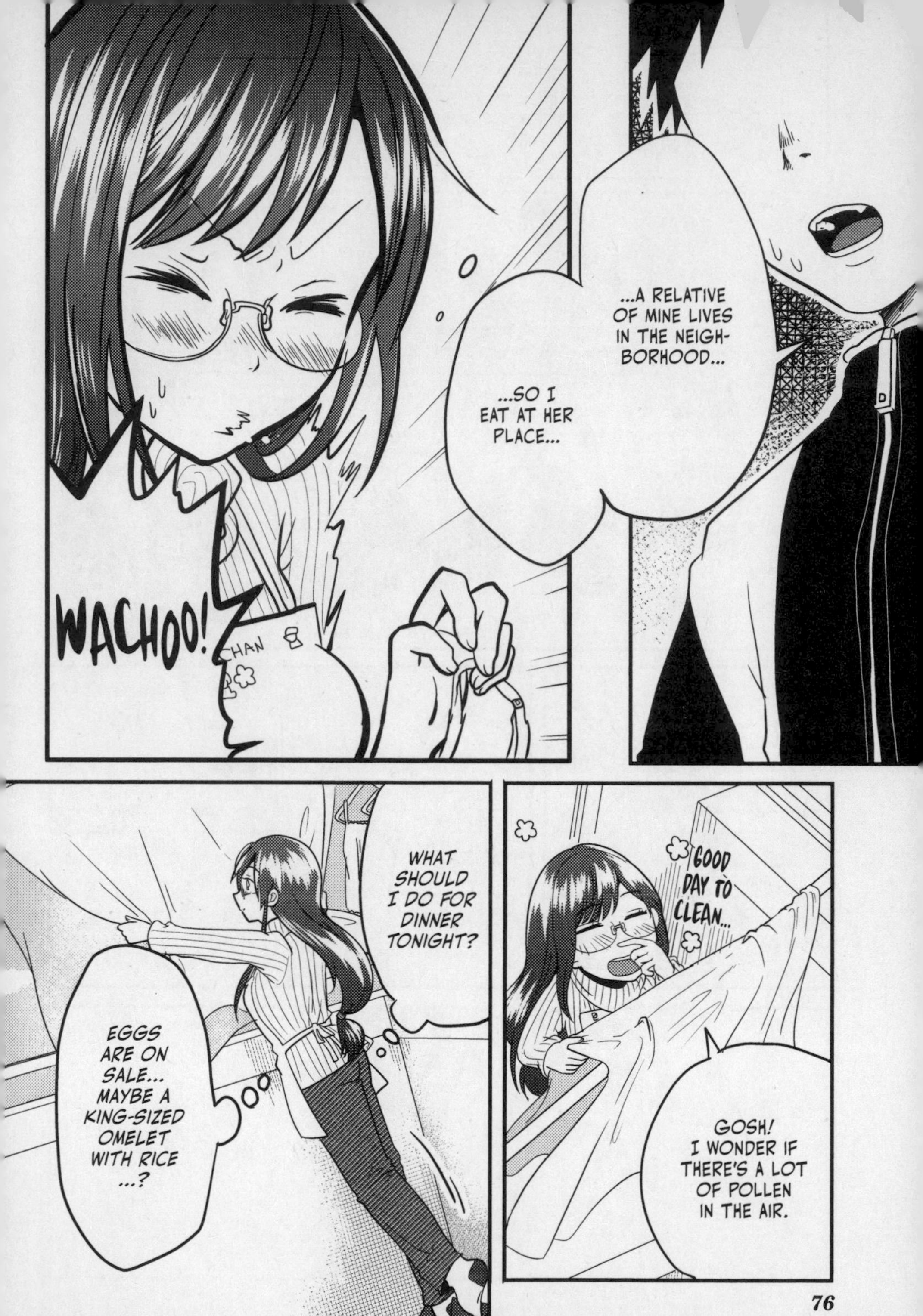
...A RELATIVE OF MINE LIVES IN THE NEIGHBORHOOD...
...SO I EAT AT HER PLACE...
WACHOO!
CHAN
GOOD DAY TO CLEAN...
GOSH! I WONDER IF THERE'S A LOT OF POLLEN IN THE AIR.
WHAT SHOULD I DO FOR DINNER TONIGHT?
EGGS ARE ON SALE... MAYBE A KING-SIZED OMELET WITH RICE ...?

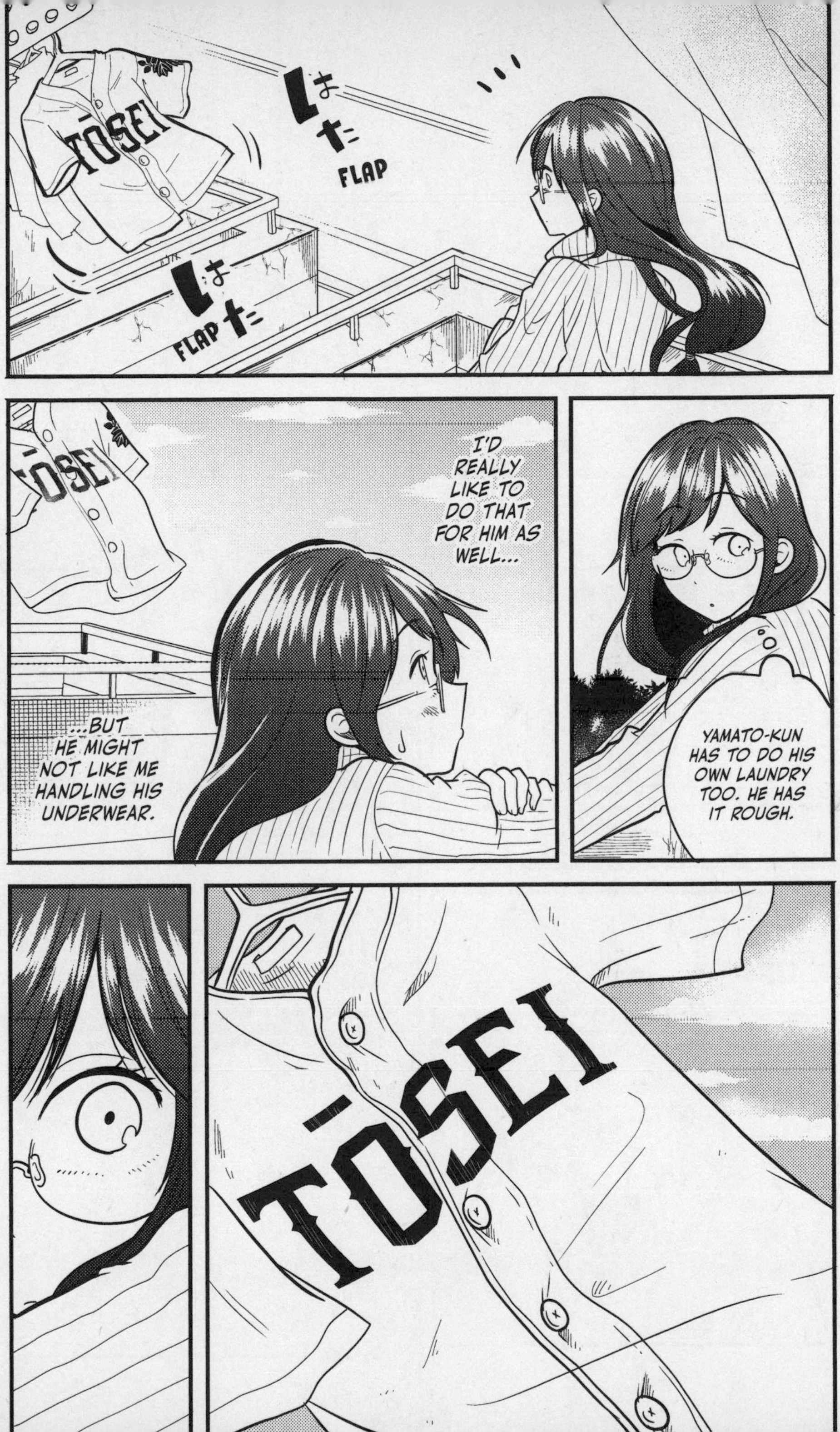
TŌSEI
ぱた
FLAP
ぱた
FLAP
...
YAMATO-KUN HAS TO DO HIS OWN LAUNDRY TOO. HE HAS IT ROUGH.
TŌSEI
I'D REALLY LIKE TO DO THAT FOR HIM AS WELL...
...BUT HE MIGHT NOT LIKE ME HANDLING HIS UNDERWEAR.
TŌSEI
......

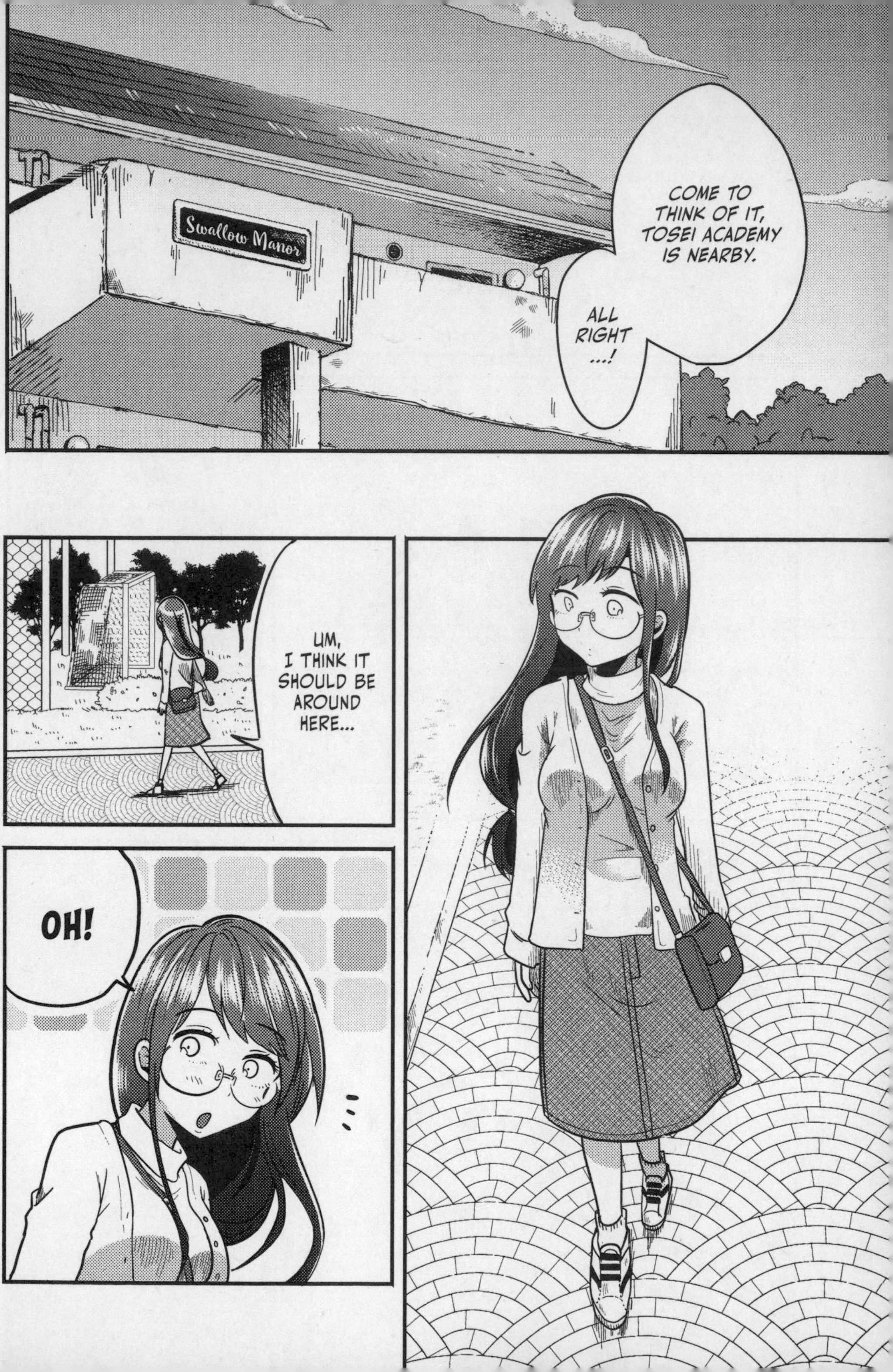
COME TO THINK OF IT, TOSEI ACADEMY IS NEARBY.
ALL RIGHT ...!
Swallow Manor
UM, I THINK IT SHOULD BE AROUND HERE...
OH!

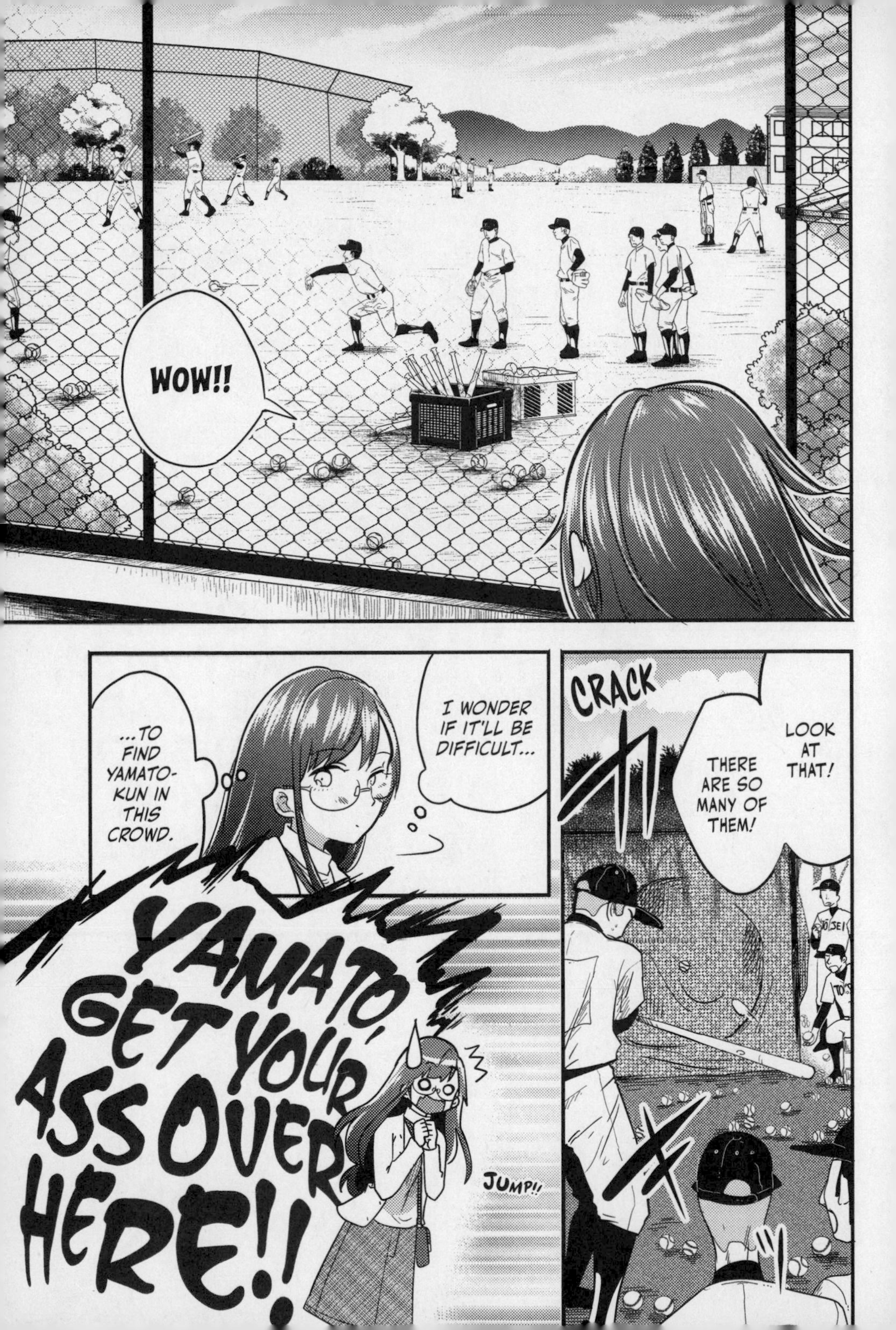
WOW!!
CRACK
LOOK AT THAT!
THERE ARE SO MANY OF THEM!
I WONDER IF IT'LL BE DIFFICULT...
...TO FIND YAMATO-KUN IN THIS CROWD.
YAMATO, GET YOUR ASS OVER HERE!!
JUMP!!

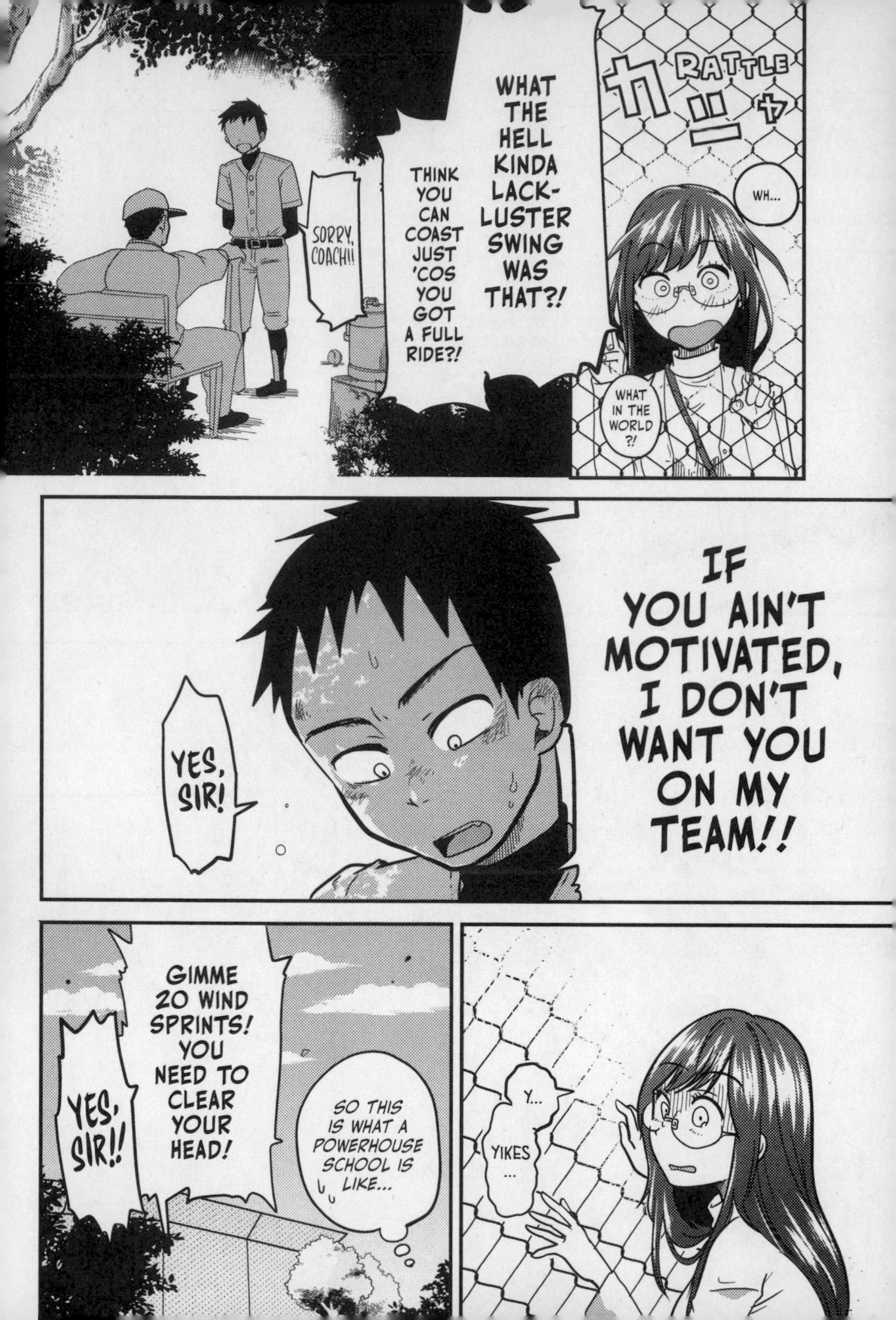
カ RATTLE ニー ャ
WH...
WHAT IN THE WORLD ?!
WHAT THE HELL KINDA LACK-LUSTER SWING WAS THAT?!
THINK YOU CAN COAST JUST 'COS YOU GOT A FULL RIDE?!
SORRY, COACH!!
IF YOU AIN'T MOTIVATED, I DON'T WANT YOU ON MY TEAM!!
YES, SIR!
Y...
YIKES ...
SO THIS IS WHAT A POWERHOUSE SCHOOL IS LIKE...
GIMME 20 WIND SPRINTS! YOU NEED TO CLEAR YOUR HEAD!
YES, SIR!!

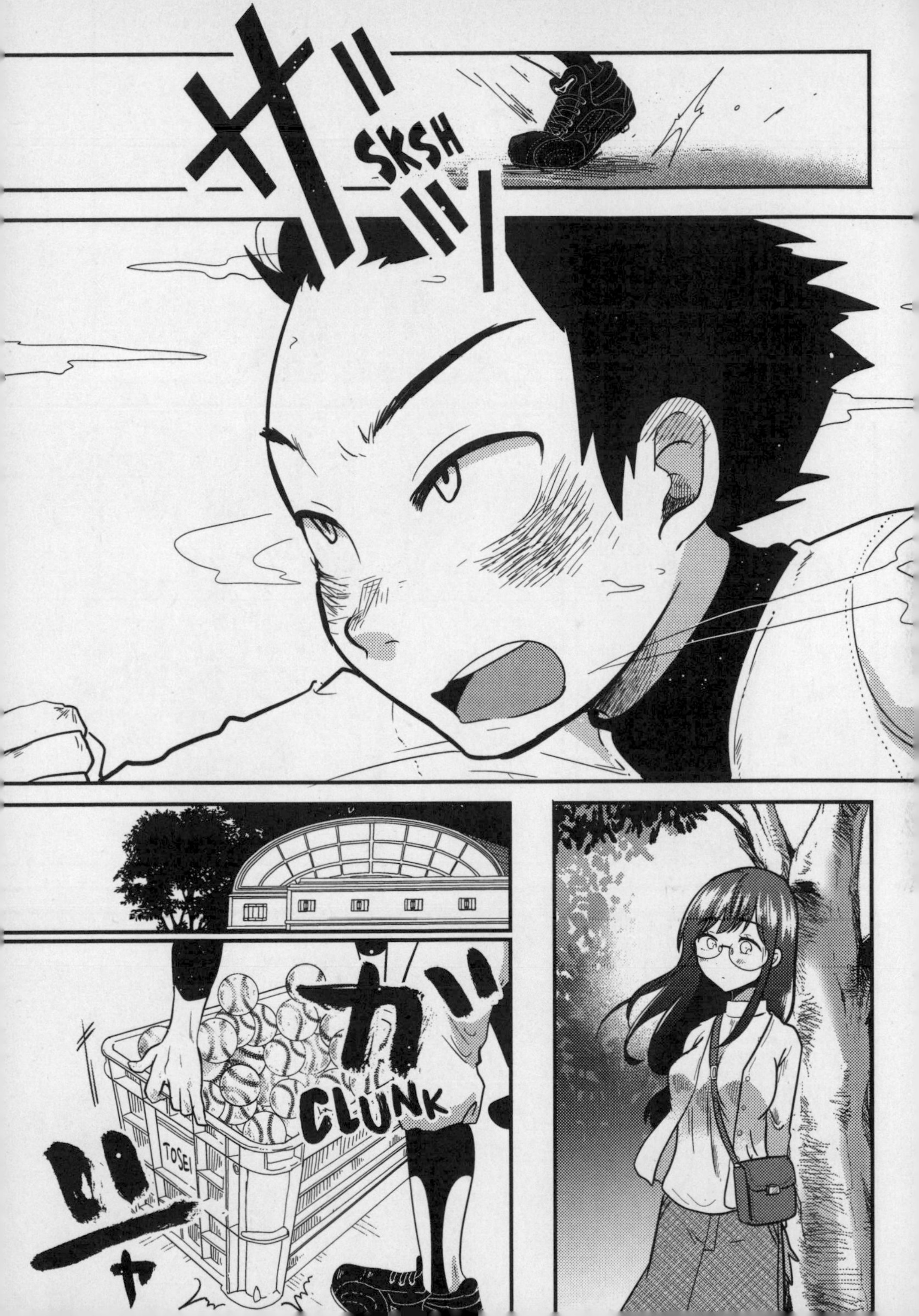
SKSH
CLUNK
TOSEI

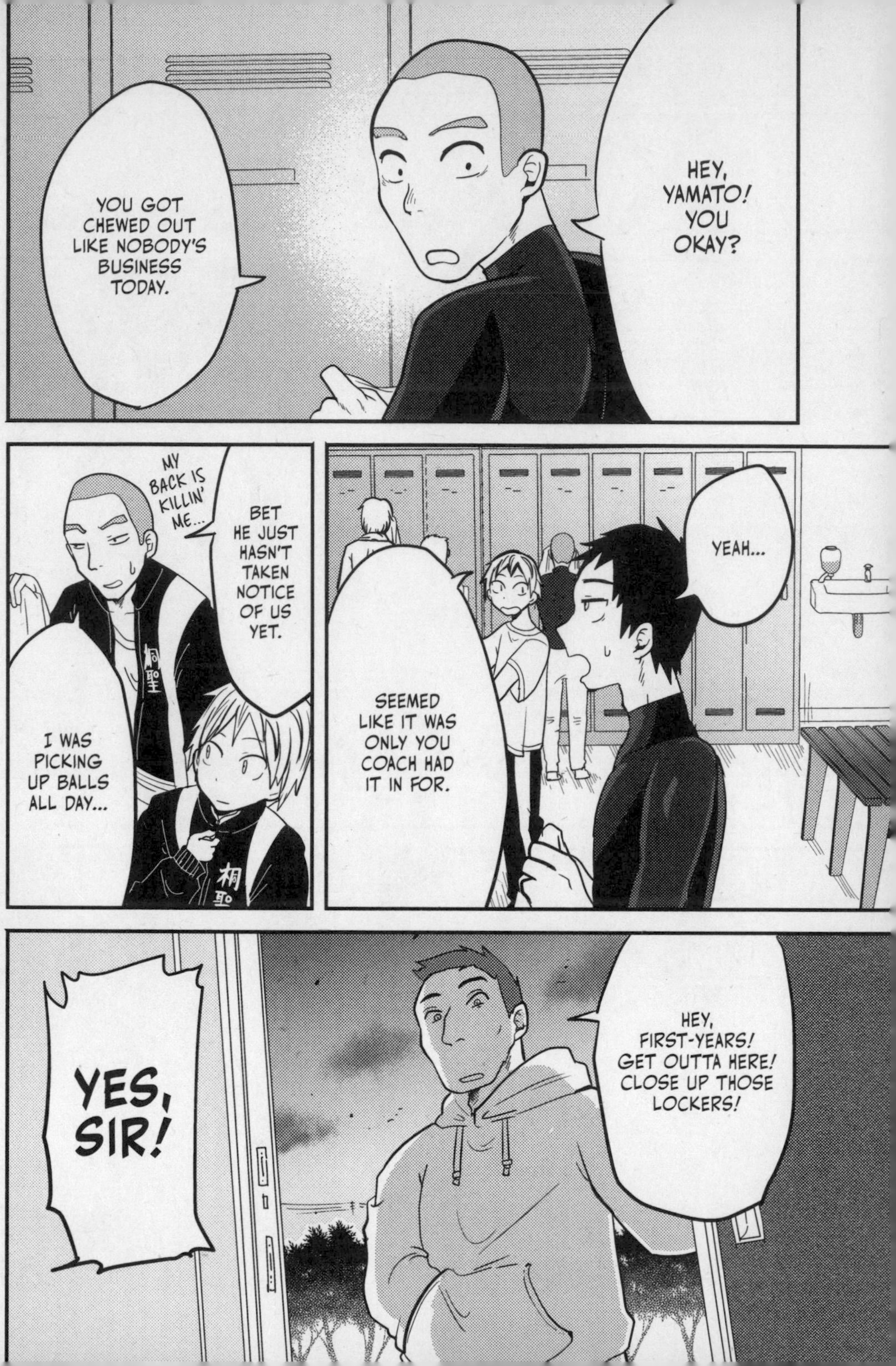
HEY, YAMATO! YOU OKAY?
YOU GOT CHEWED OUT LIKE NOBODY'S BUSINESS TODAY.
YEAH...
SEEMED LIKE IT WAS ONLY YOU COACH HAD IT IN FOR.
BET HE JUST HASN'T TAKEN NOTICE OF US YET.
MY BACK IS KILLIN' ME...
I WAS PICKING UP BALLS ALL DAY...
HEY, FIRST-YEARS! GET OUTTA HERE! CLOSE UP THOSE LOCKERS!
YES, SIR!

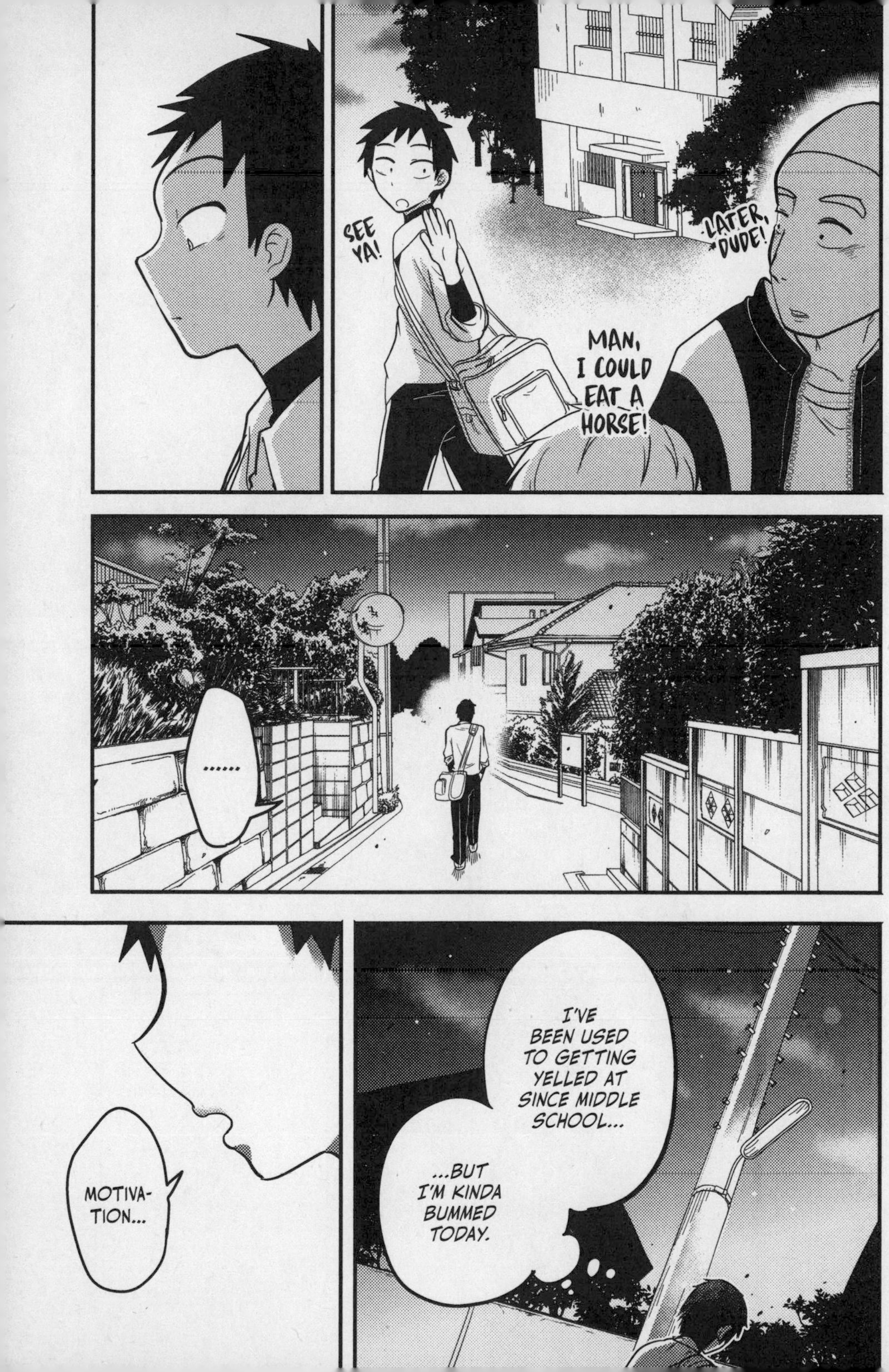
LATER, DUDE!
SEE YA!
MAN, I COULD EAT A HORSE!
......
I'VE BEEN USED TO GETTING YELLED AT SINCE MIDDLE SCHOOL...
...BUT I'M KINDA BUMMED TODAY.
MOTIVA-TION...

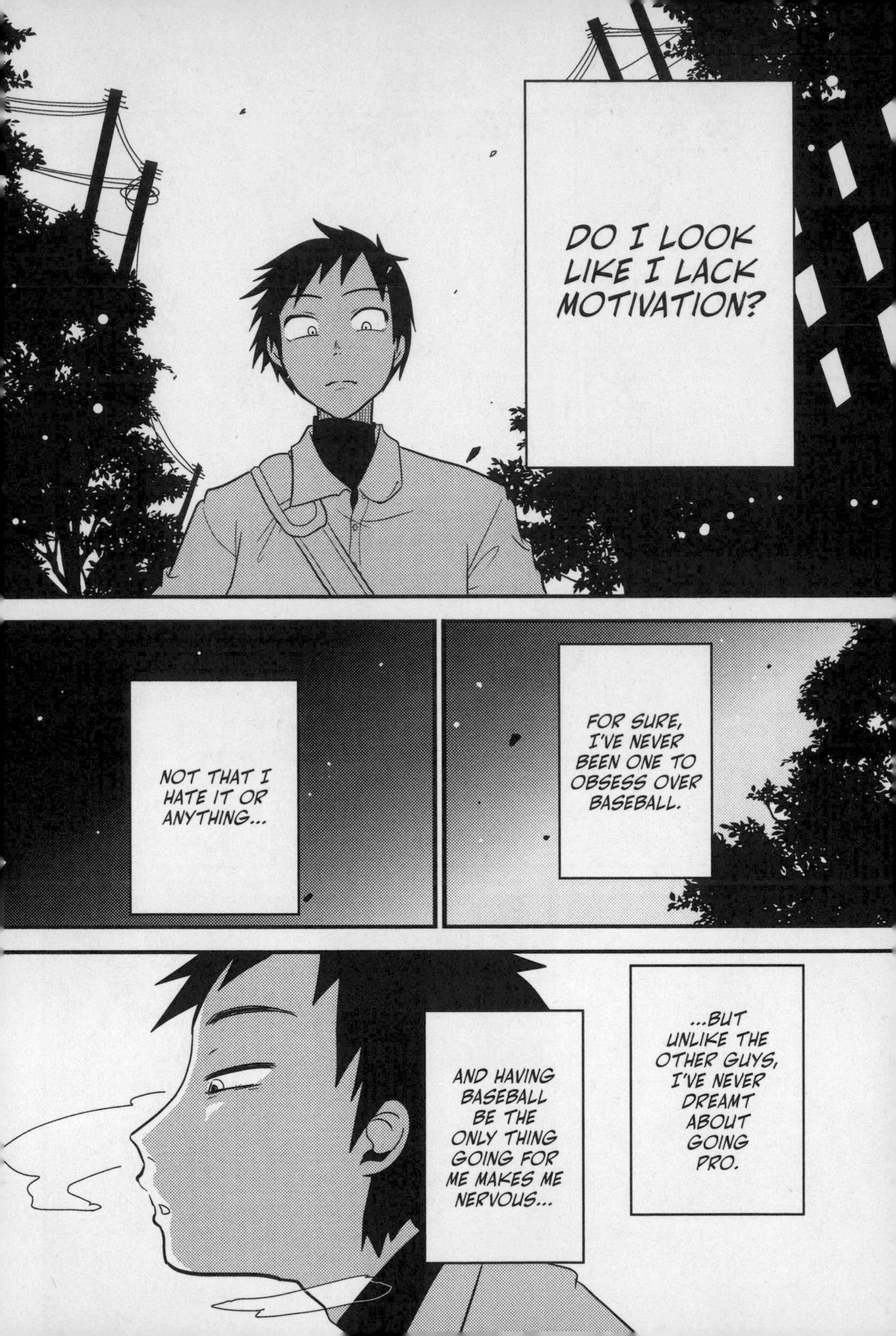
DO I LOOK LIKE I LACK MOTIVATION?
FOR SURE, I'VE NEVER BEEN ONE TO OBSESS OVER BASEBALL.
NOT THAT I HATE IT OR ANYTHING...
...BUT UNLIKE THE OTHER GUYS, I'VE NEVER DREAMT ABOUT GOING PRO.
AND HAVING BASEBALL BE THE ONLY THING GOING FOR ME MAKES ME NERVOUS...

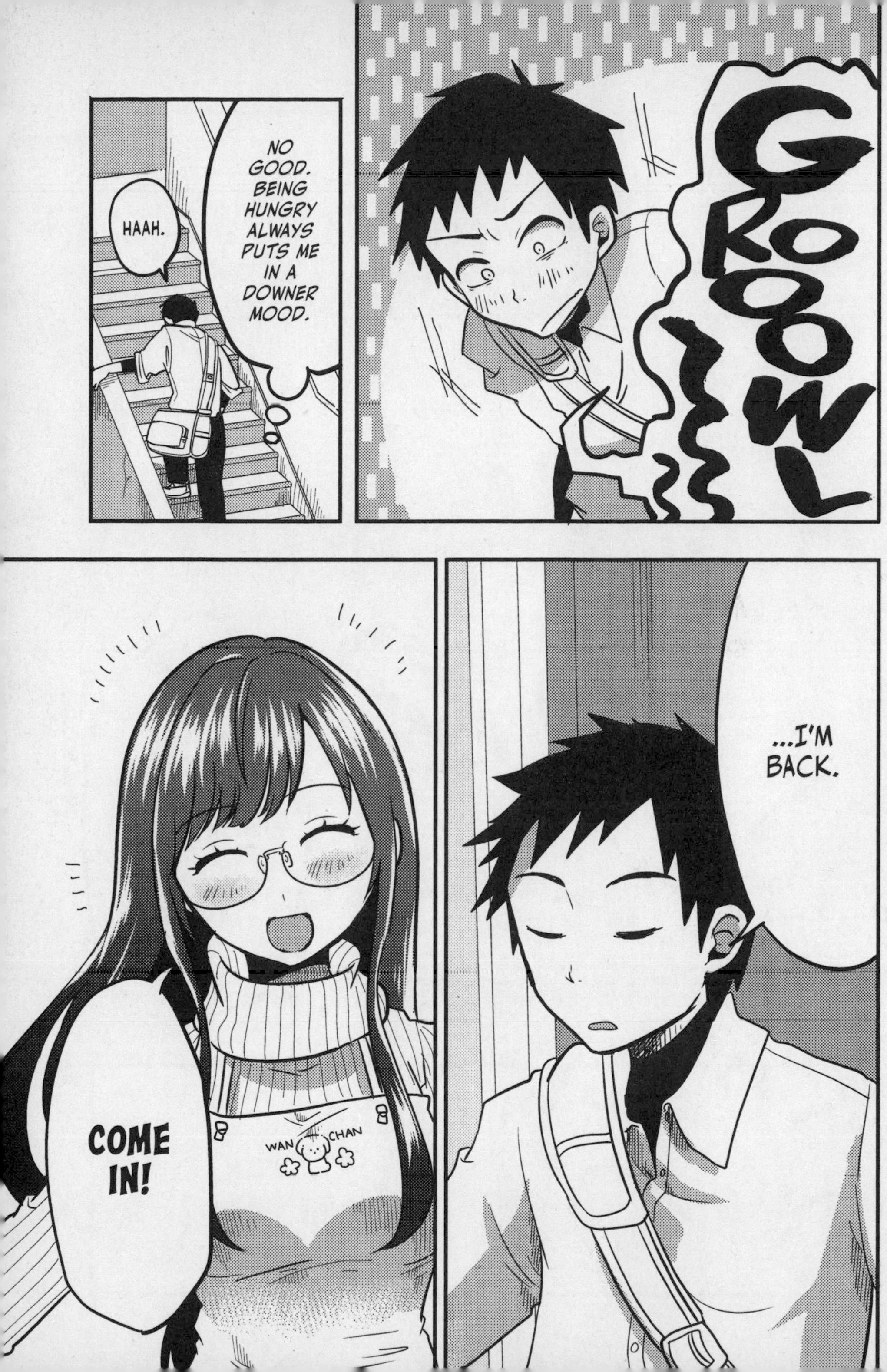
GROOWL
NO GOOD. BEING HUNGRY ALWAYS PUTS ME IN A DOWNER MOOD.
HAAH.
...I'M BACK.
COME IN!
WAN CHAN

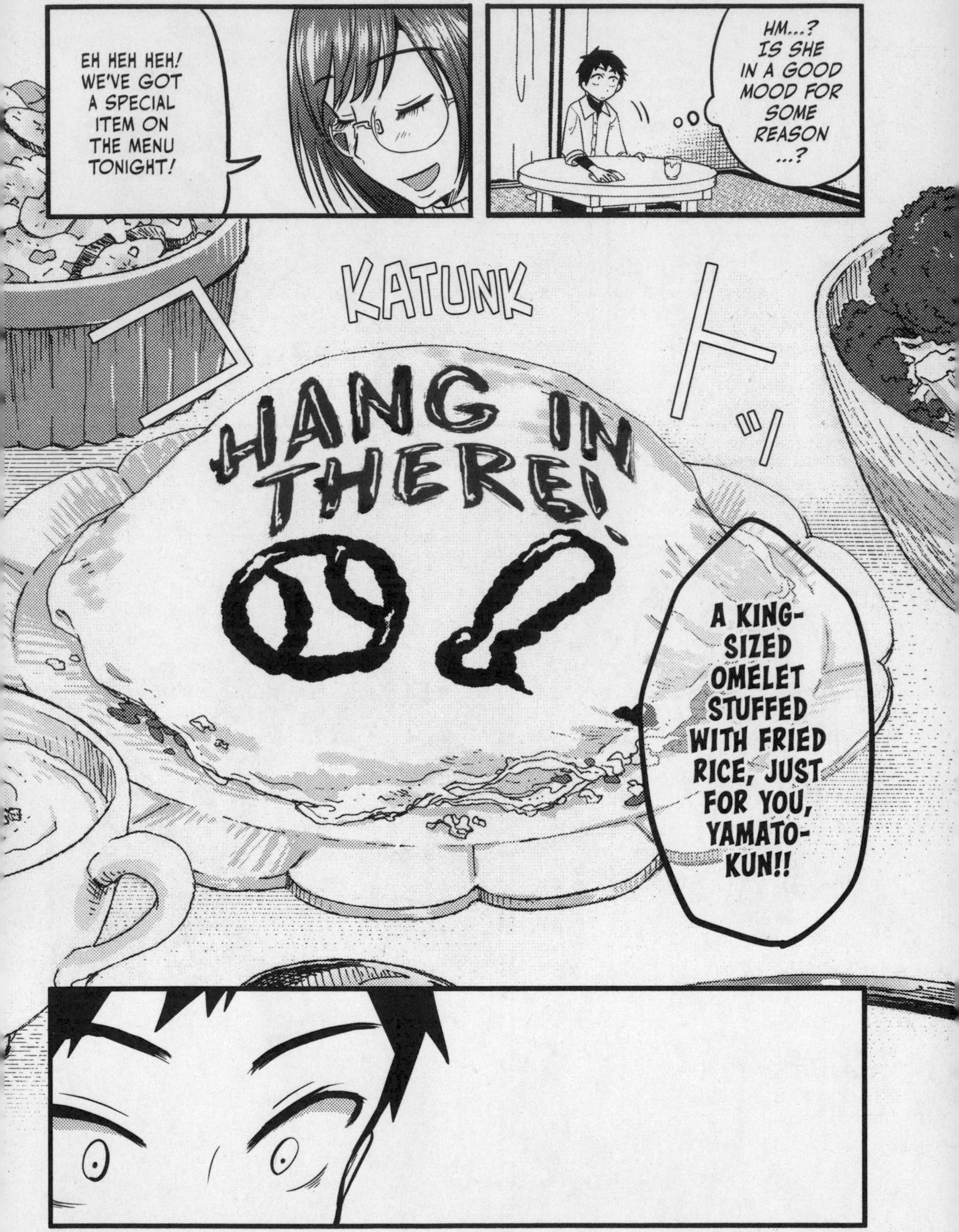
HM...? IS SHE IN A GOOD MOOD FOR SOME REASON ...?
EH HEH HEH! WE'VE GOT A SPECIAL ITEM ON THE MENU TONIGHT!
KATUNK
HANG IN THERE!
A KING-SIZED OMELET STUFFED WITH FRIED RICE, JUST FOR YOU, YAMATO-KUN!!

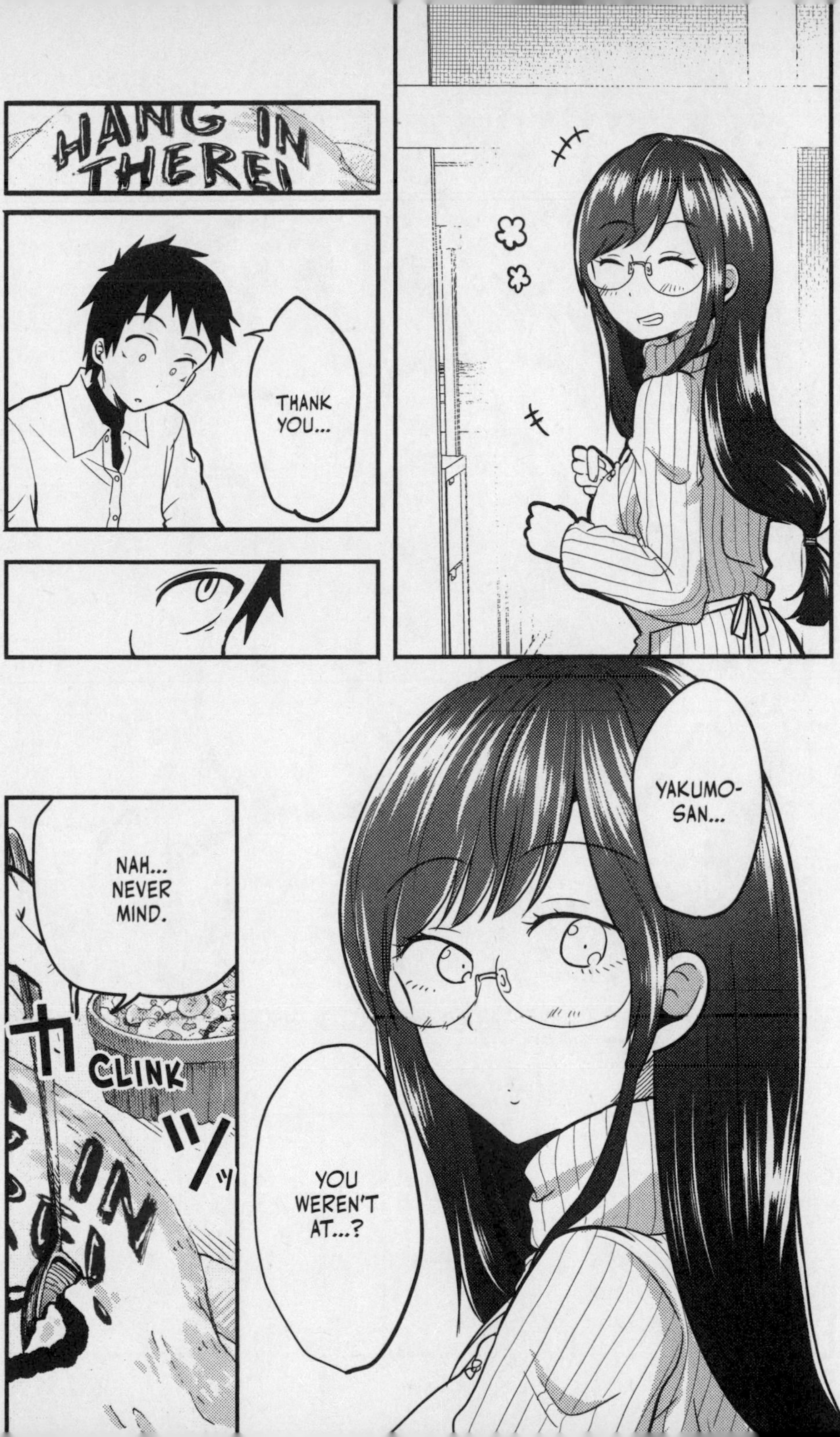
HANG IN THERE!
THANK YOU...
YAKUMO-SAN...
YOU WEREN'T AT...?
NAH... NEVER MIND.
CLINK

YUM.

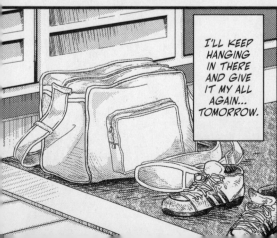

I'LL KEEP HANGING IN THERE AND GIVE IT MY ALL AGAIN... TOMORROW.

HANG IN THERE

Beauty and the FEAST.

Beauty and the FEAST.

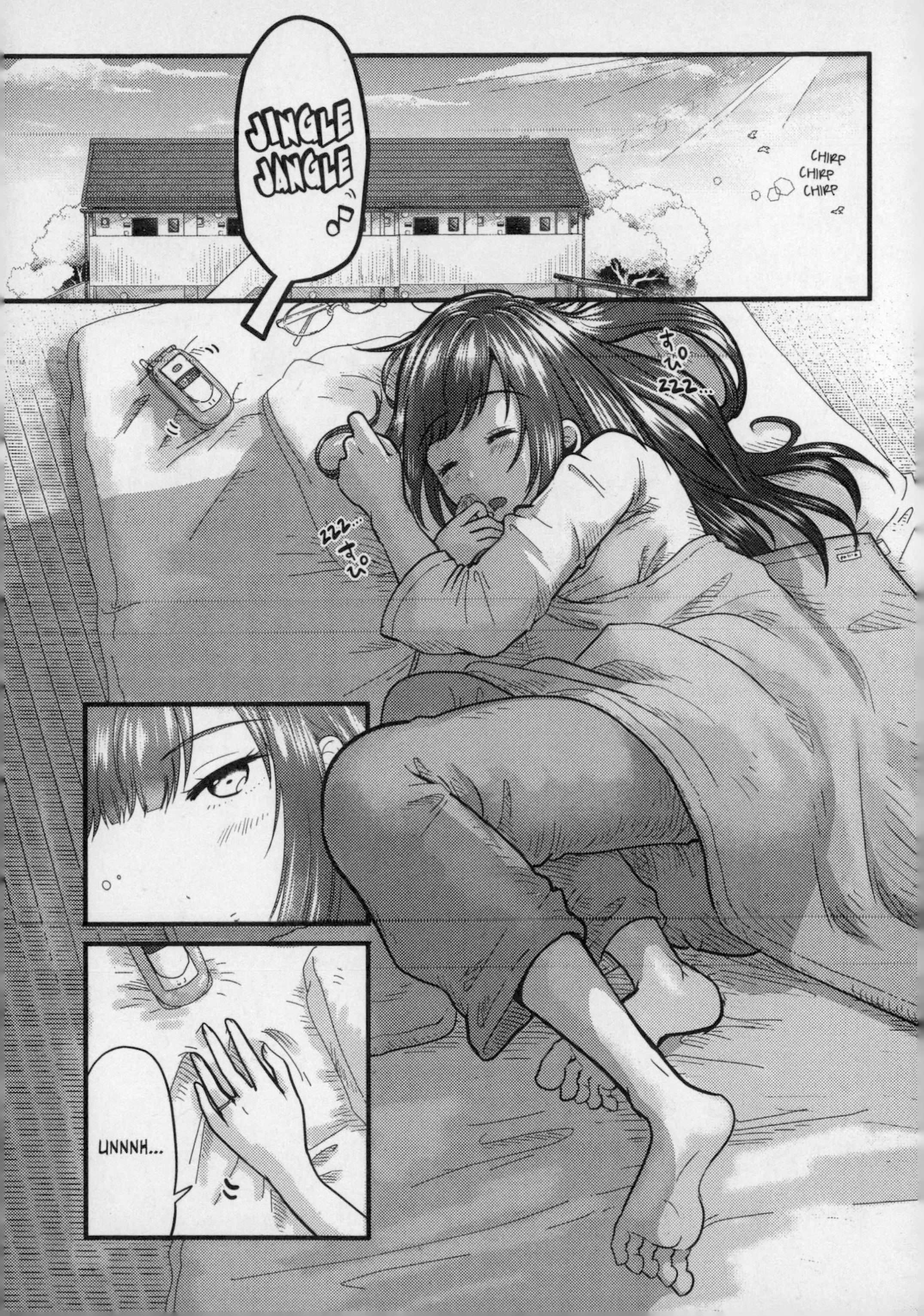
CHIRP CHIRP CHIRP
JINGLE JANGLE
すぴ zzz...
zzz... すぴ
UNNNH...

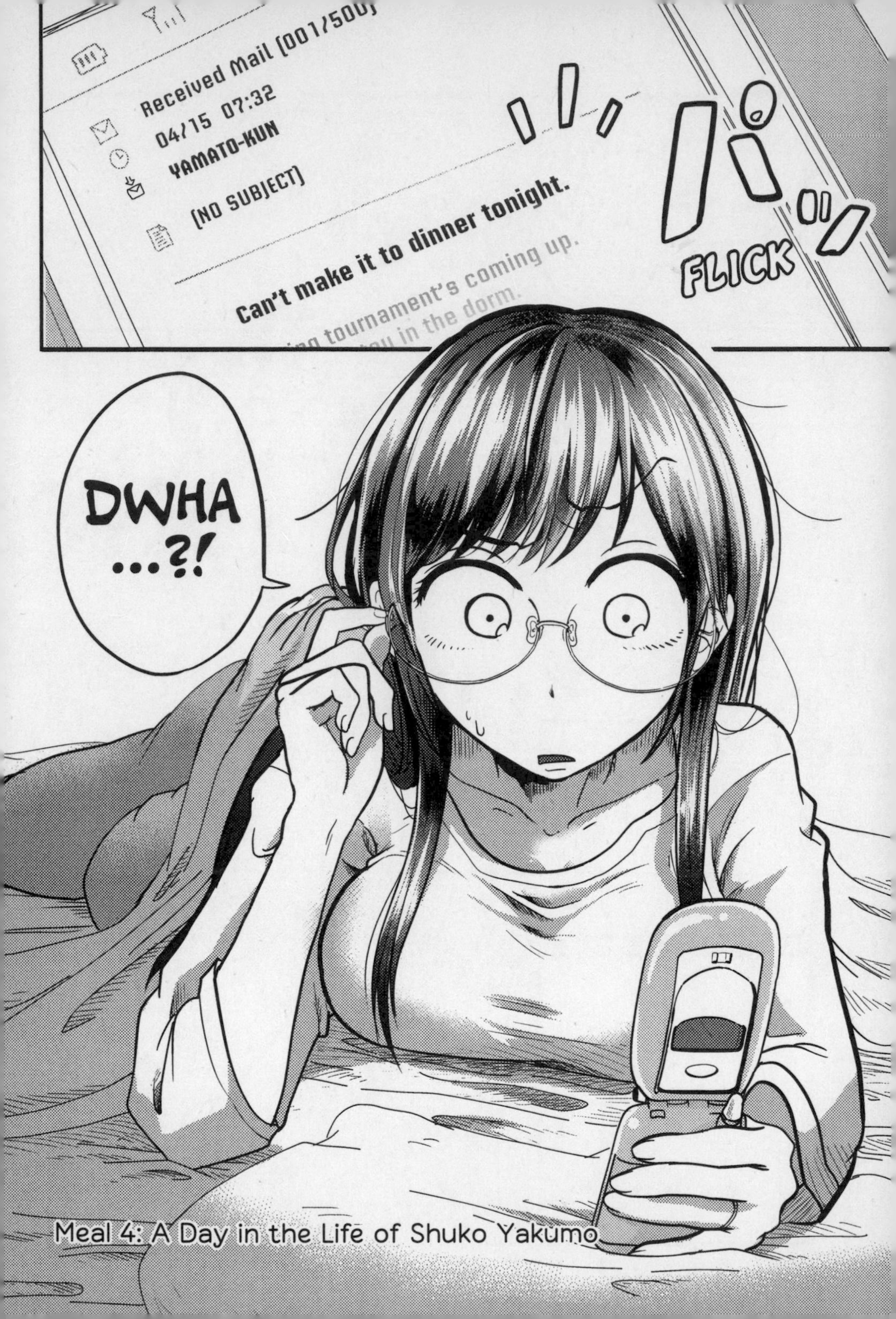
Received Mail (001/500)
04/15 07:32
YAMATO-KUN
[NO SUBJECT]
Can't make it to dinner tonight.
FLICK
DWHA ...?!

Meal 4: A Day in the Life of Shuko Yakumo

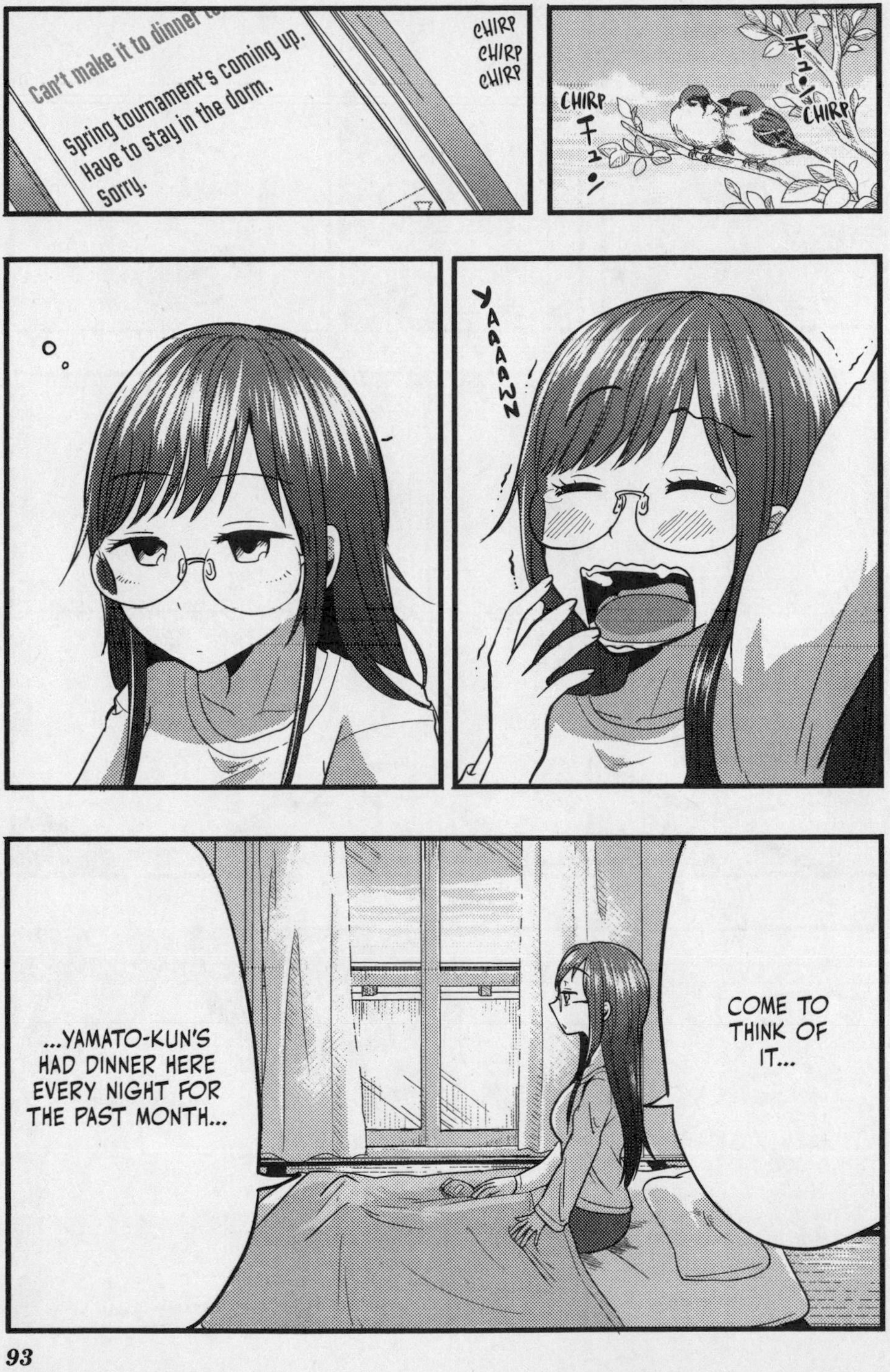
チュン
CHIRP
CHIRP
チュン
CHIRP CHIRP CHIRP
Can't make it to dinner
Spring tournament's coming up. Have to stay in the dorm. Sorry.
YAAAAAWN
COME TO THINK OF IT...
...YAMATO-KUN'S HAD DINNER HERE EVERY NIGHT FOR THE PAST MONTH...

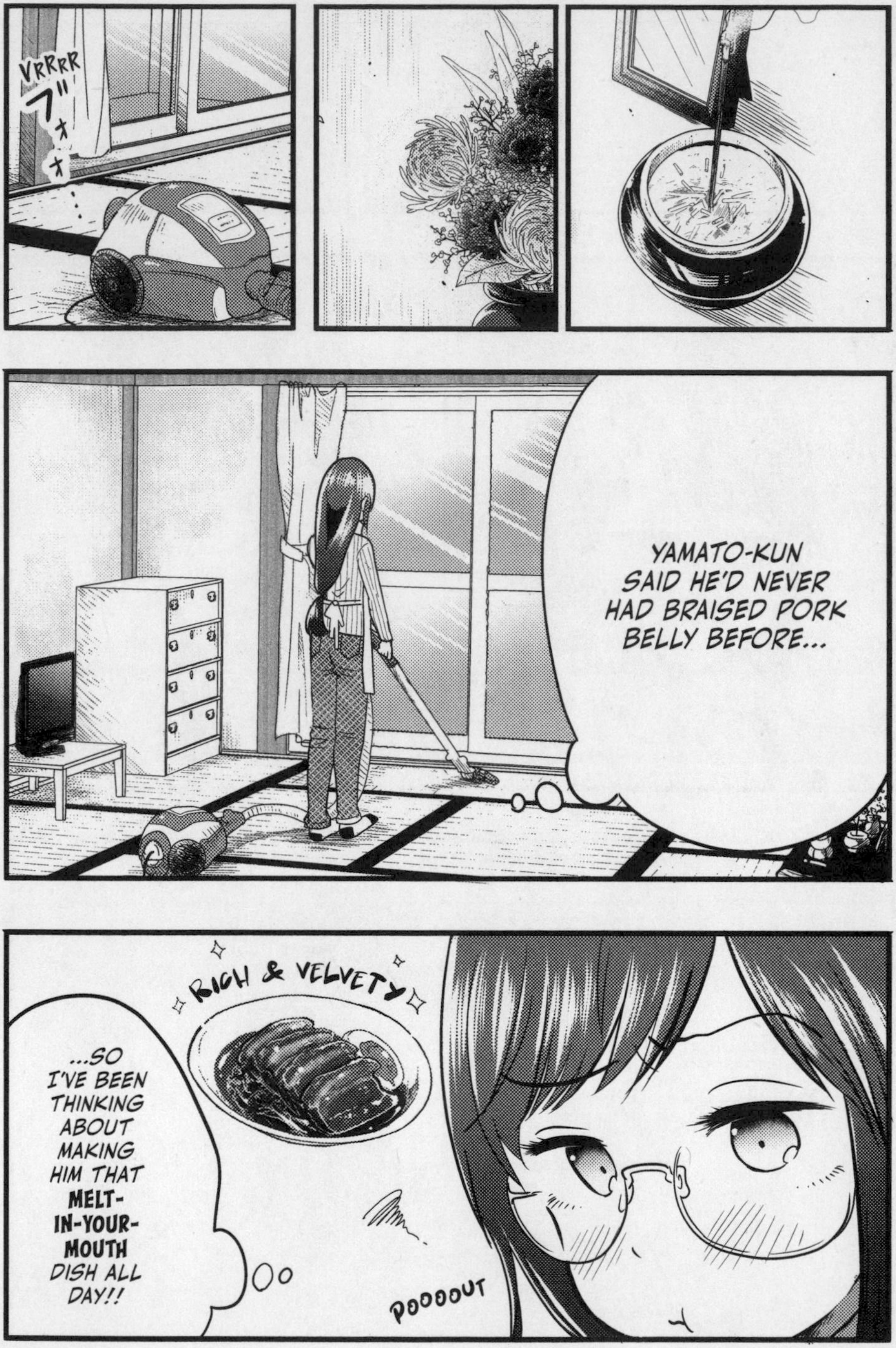
VRRRR
ブォォ…
YAMATO-KUN SAID HE'D NEVER HAD BRAISED PORK BELLY BEFORE...
RICH & VELVETY
...SO I'VE BEEN THINKING ABOUT MAKING HIM THAT MELT-IN-YOUR-MOUTH DISH ALL DAY!!
POOOOUT

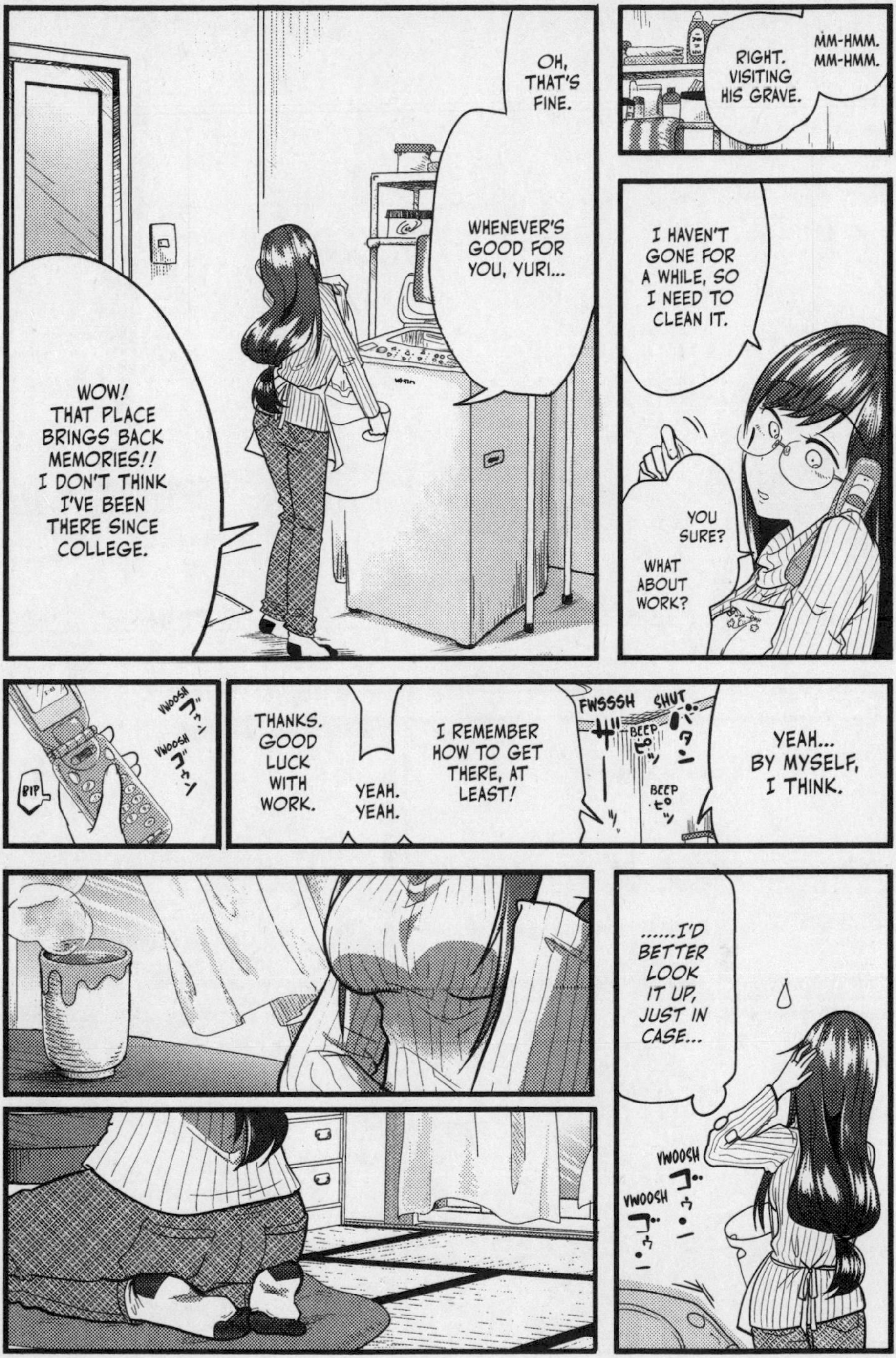
MM-HMM. MM-HMM.
RIGHT. VISITING HIS GRAVE.
I HAVEN'T GONE FOR A WHILE, SO I NEED TO CLEAN IT.
YOU SURE?
WHAT ABOUT WORK?
OH, THAT'S FINE.
WHENEVER'S GOOD FOR YOU, YURI...
WOW! THAT PLACE BRINGS BACK MEMORIES!! I DON'T THINK I'VE BEEN THERE SINCE COLLEGE.
YEAH... BY MYSELF, I THINK.
SHUT
FWSSSH
BEEP
BEEP
I REMEMBER HOW TO GET THERE, AT LEAST!
YEAH. YEAH.
THANKS. GOOD LUCK WITH WORK.
VWOOSH
VWOOSH
BIP
......I'D BETTER LOOK IT UP, JUST IN CASE...
VWOOSH
VWOOSH

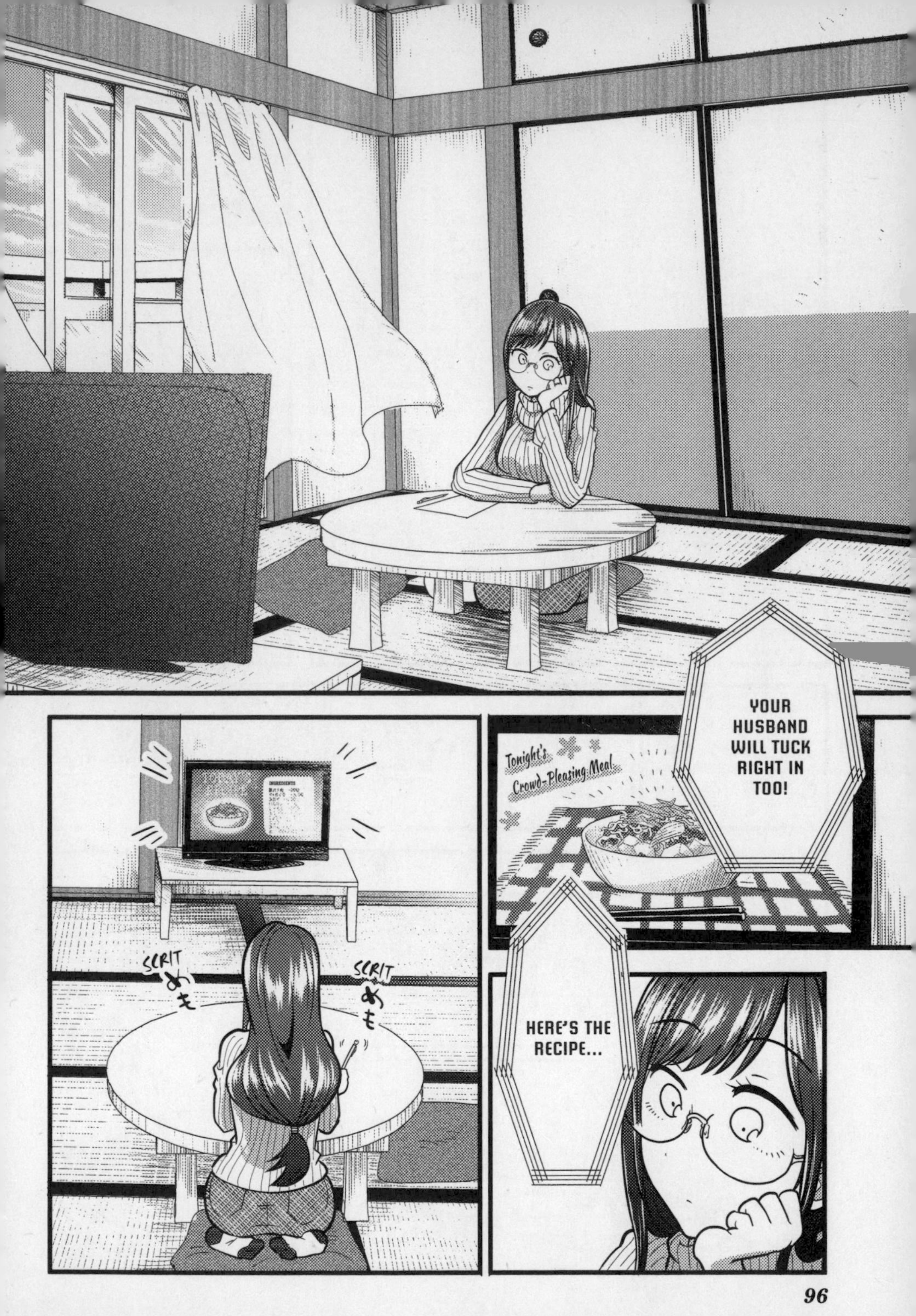
Tonight's Crowd-Pleasing Meal
YOUR HUSBAND WILL TUCK RIGHT IN TOO!
HERE'S THE RECIPE...
SCRIT めも
SCRIT めも

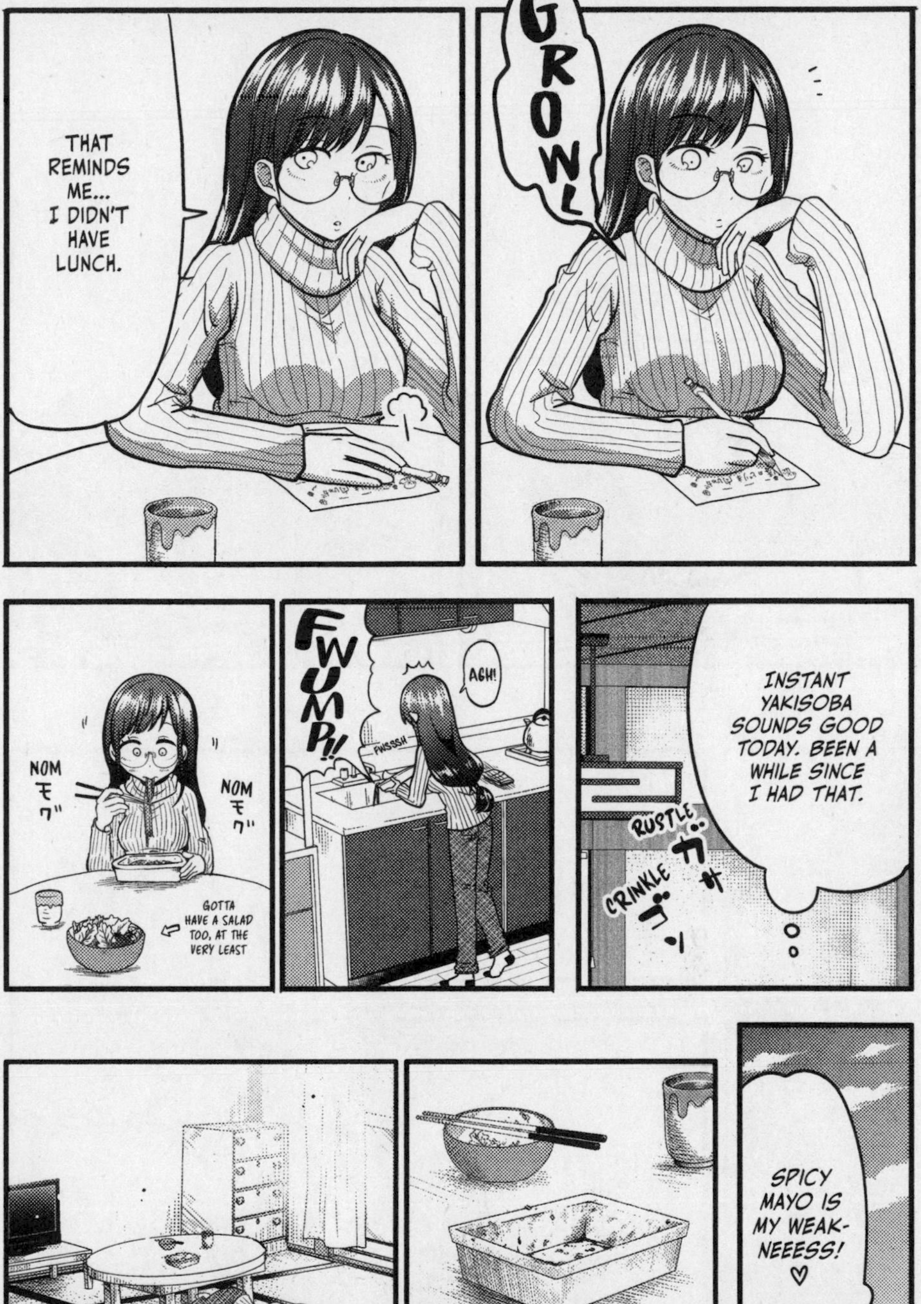
GROWL
THAT REMINDS ME... I DIDN'T HAVE LUNCH.
INSTANT YAKISOBA SOUNDS GOOD TODAY. BEEN A WHILE SINCE I HAD THAT.
RUSTLE ガサ
CRINKLE ゴソ
FWUMP!!
AGH!
FWSSSH
NOM モグ
NOM モグ
GOTTA HAVE A SALAD TOO, AT THE VERY LEAST
SPICY MAYO IS MY WEAK-NEEESS! ♡

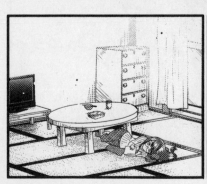

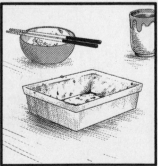

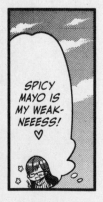

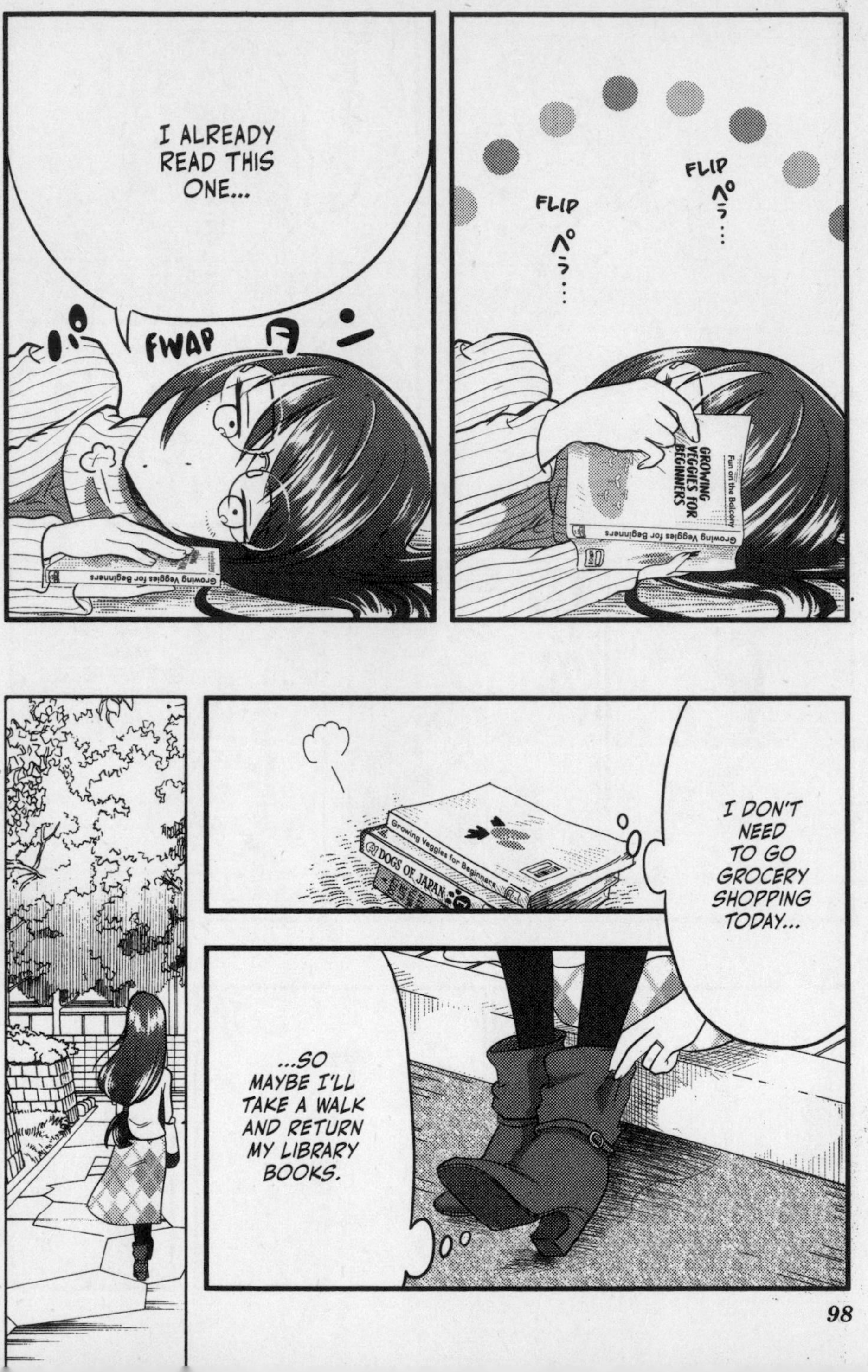
FLIP ぺら…
FLIP ぺら…
GROWING VEGGIES FOR BEGINNERS
Fun on the Balcony
Growing Veggies for Beginners
I ALREADY READ THIS ONE...
FWAP
Growing Veggies for Beginners
I DON'T NEED TO GO GROCERY SHOPPING TODAY...
Growing Veggies for Beginners
DOGS OF JAPAN
...SO MAYBE I'LL TAKE A WALK AND RETURN MY LIBRARY BOOKS.

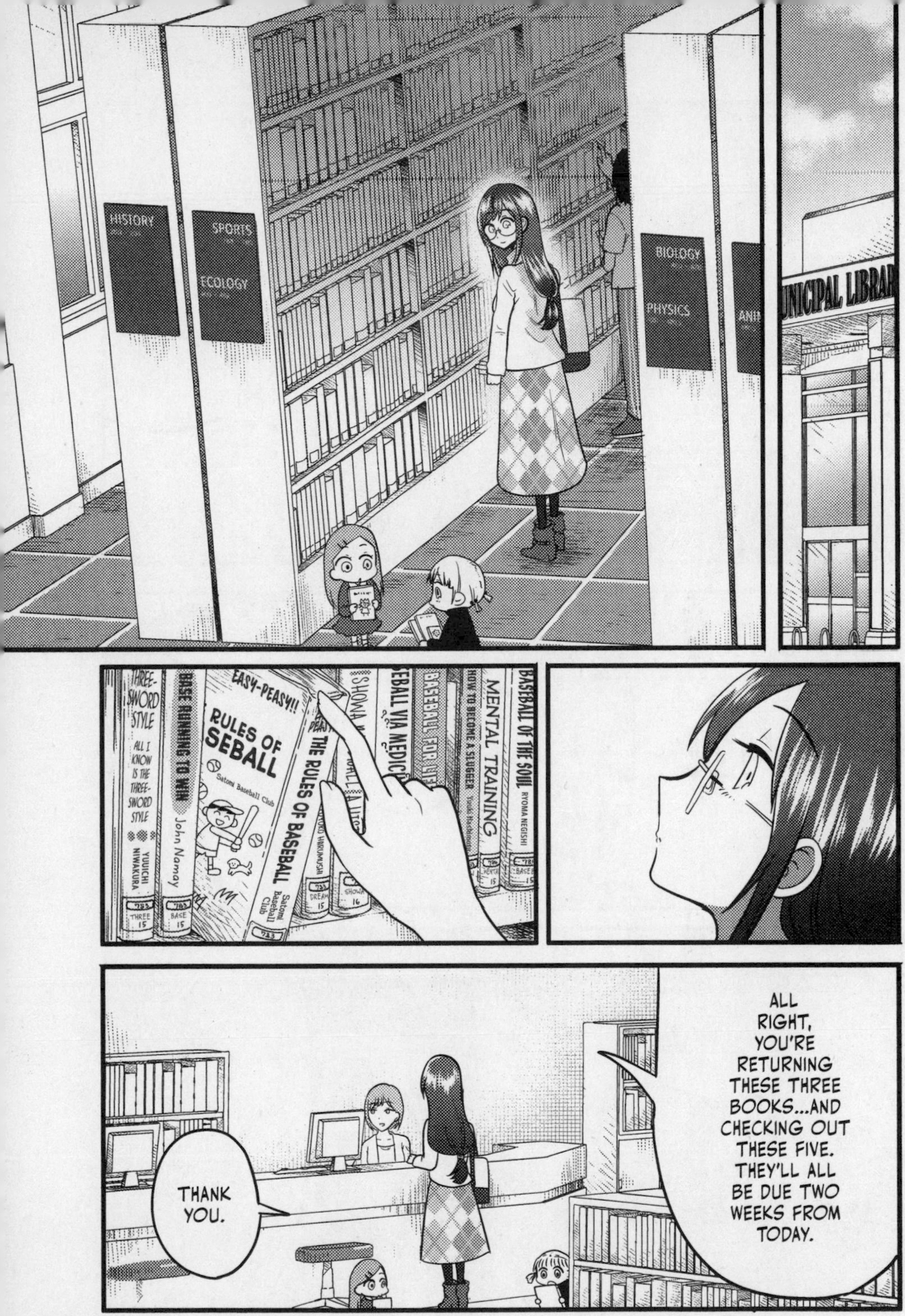
UNICIPAL LIBRAR
HISTORY
SPORTS
ECOLOGY
BIOLOGY
PHYSICS
THREE-SWORD STYLE
ALL I KNOW IS THE THREE-SWORD STYLE
YUUICHI NIWAKURA
BASE RUNNING TO WIN
John Namay
EASY-PEASY!!
RULES OF SEBALL
Satomi Baseball Club
THE RULES OF BASEBALL
Satomi Baseball Club
HOW TO BECOME A SLUGGER
MENTAL TRAINING
BASEBALL OF THE SOUL
RYOMA NEGISHI
ALL RIGHT, YOU'RE RETURNING THESE THREE BOOKS...AND CHECKING OUT THESE FIVE. THEY'LL ALL BE DUE TWO WEEKS FROM TODAY.
THANK YOU.

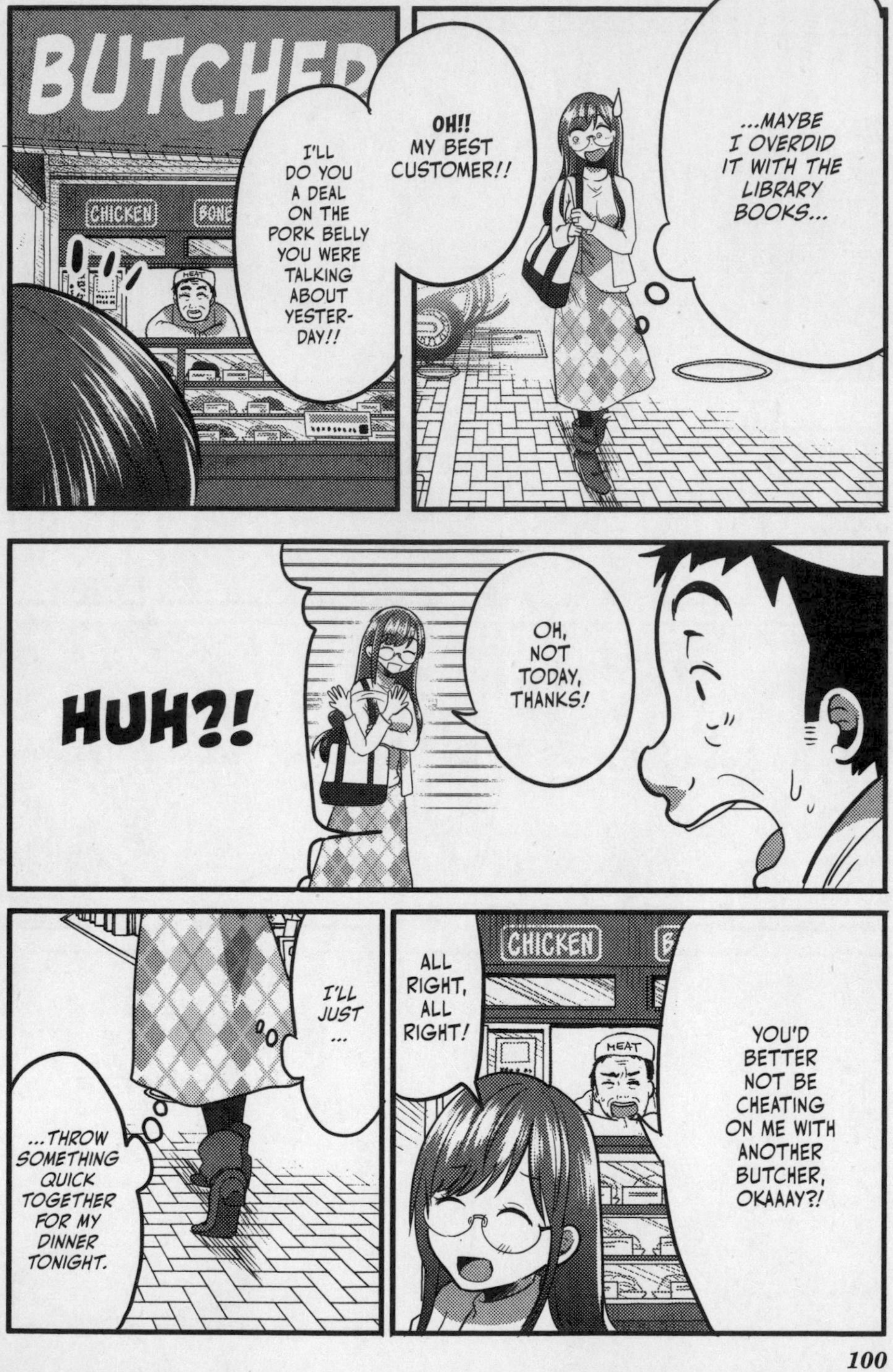
...MAYBE I OVERDID IT WITH THE LIBRARY BOOKS...
BUTCHER
OH!! MY BEST CUSTOMER!!
I'LL DO YOU A DEAL ON THE PORK BELLY YOU WERE TALKING ABOUT YESTER-DAY!!
CHICKEN
MEAT
OH, NOT TODAY, THANKS!
HUH?!
CHICKEN
MEAT
YOU'D BETTER NOT BE CHEATING ON ME WITH ANOTHER BUTCHER, OKAAAY?!
ALL RIGHT, ALL RIGHT!
I'LL JUST ...
...THROW SOMETHING QUICK TOGETHER FOR MY DINNER TONIGHT.

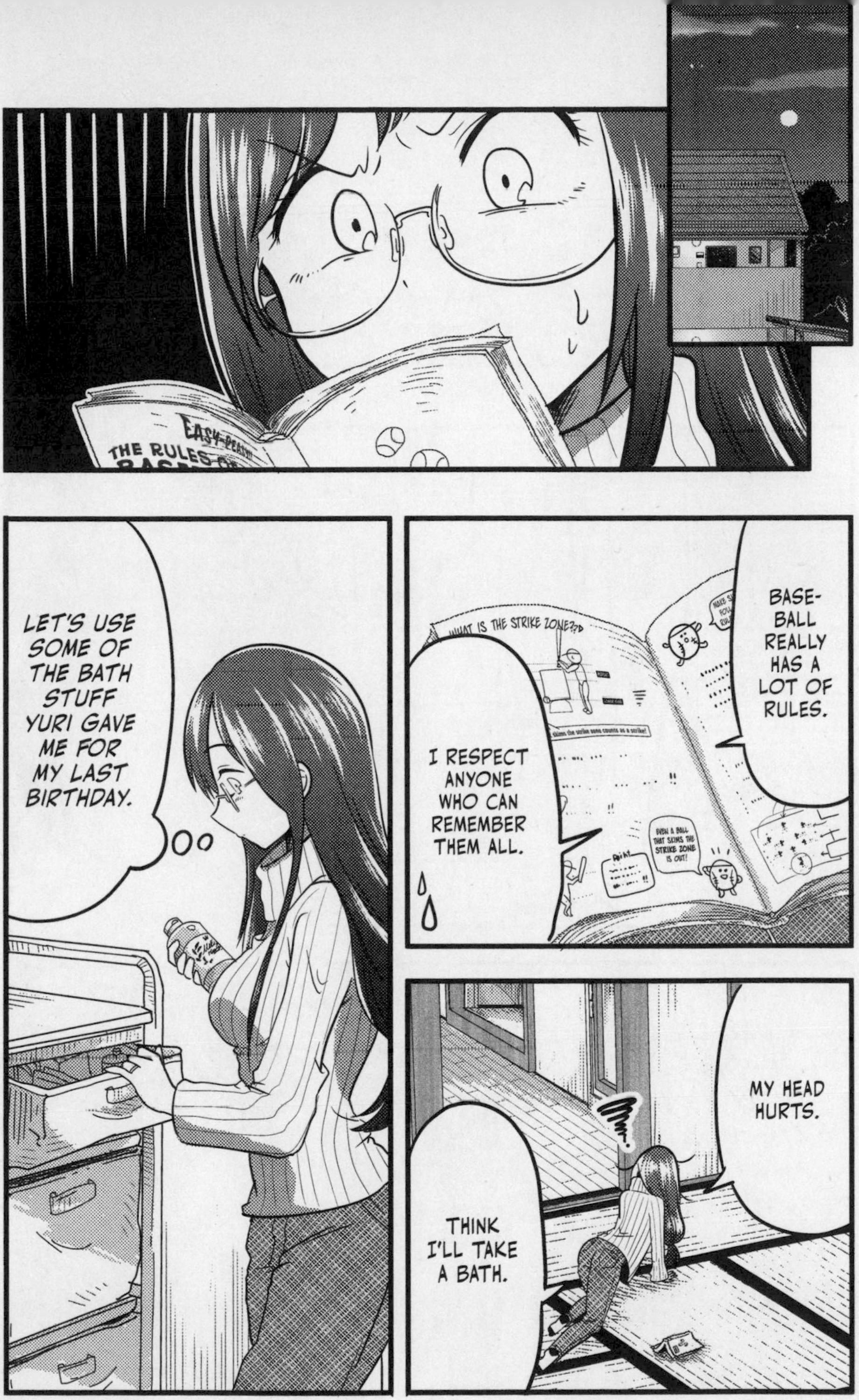
BASE-BALL REALLY HAS A LOT OF RULES.
I RESPECT ANYONE WHO CAN REMEMBER THEM ALL.
MY HEAD HURTS.
THINK I'LL TAKE A BATH.
LET'S USE SOME OF THE BATH STUFF YURI GAVE ME FOR MY LAST BIRTHDAY.

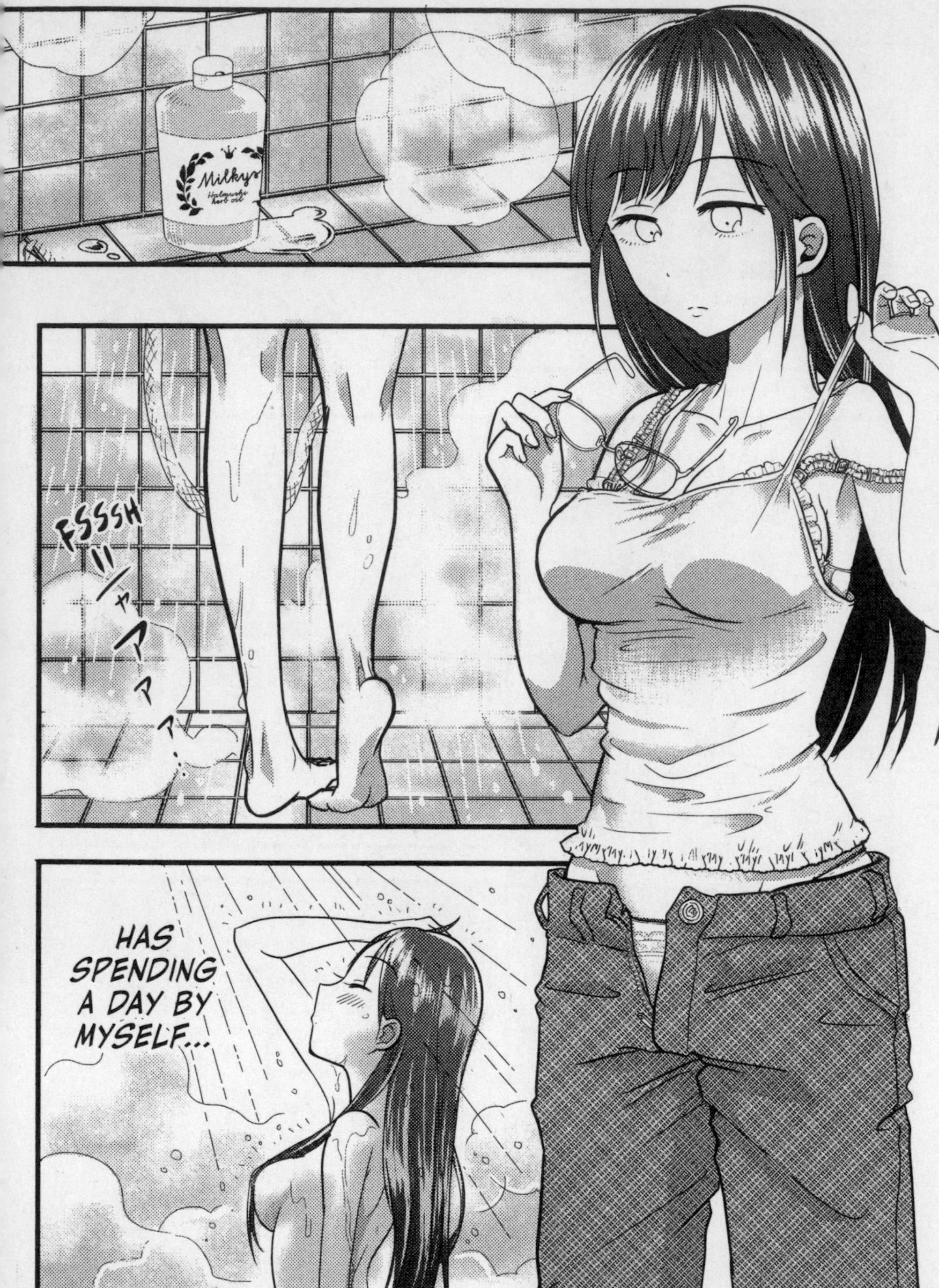
Milky
FSSSH
HAS SPENDING A DAY BY MYSELF...

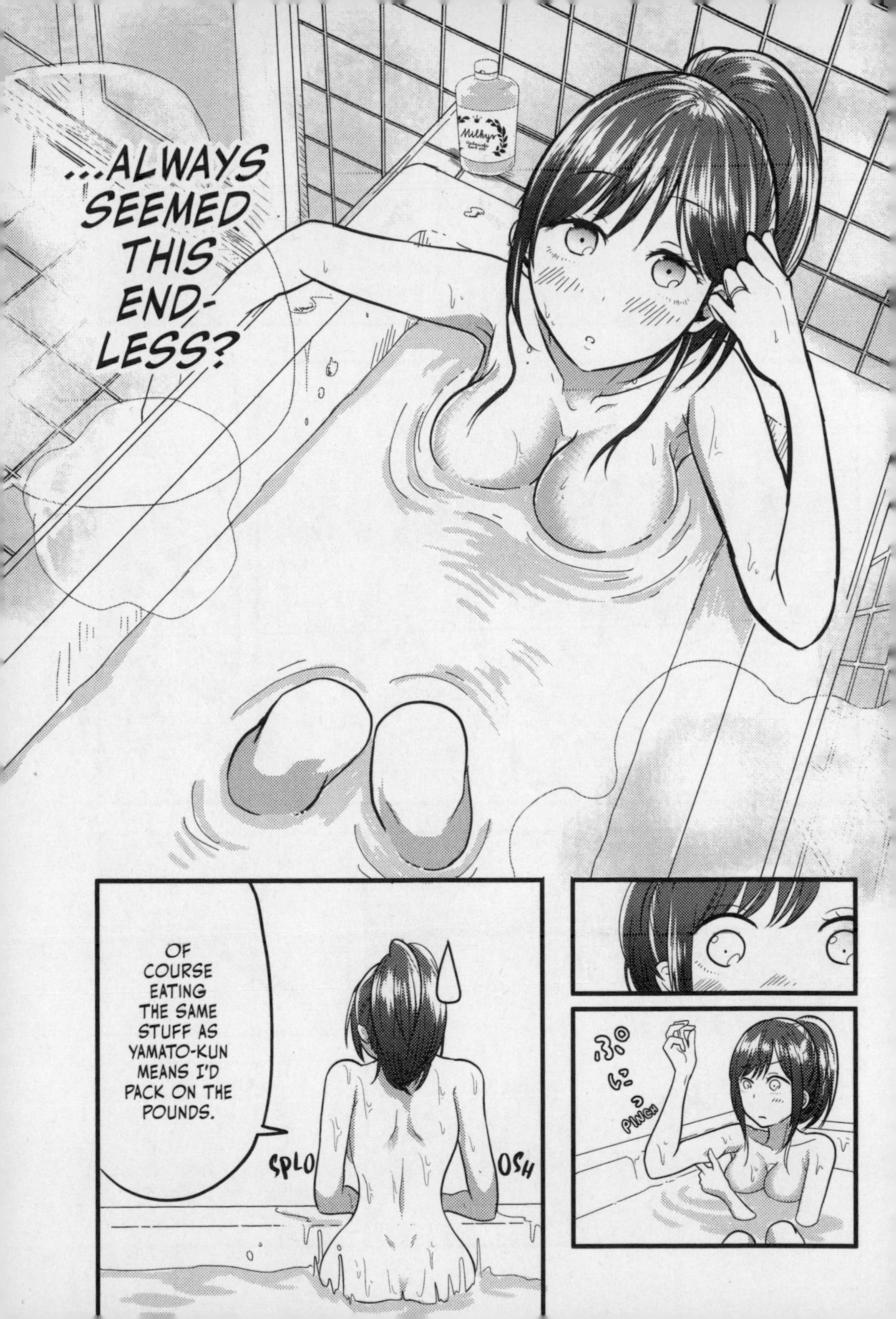
...ALWAYS SEEMED THIS END-LESS?
PINCH
OF COURSE EATING THE SAME STUFF AS YAMATO-KUN MEANS I'D PACK ON THE POUNDS.
SPLOOSH

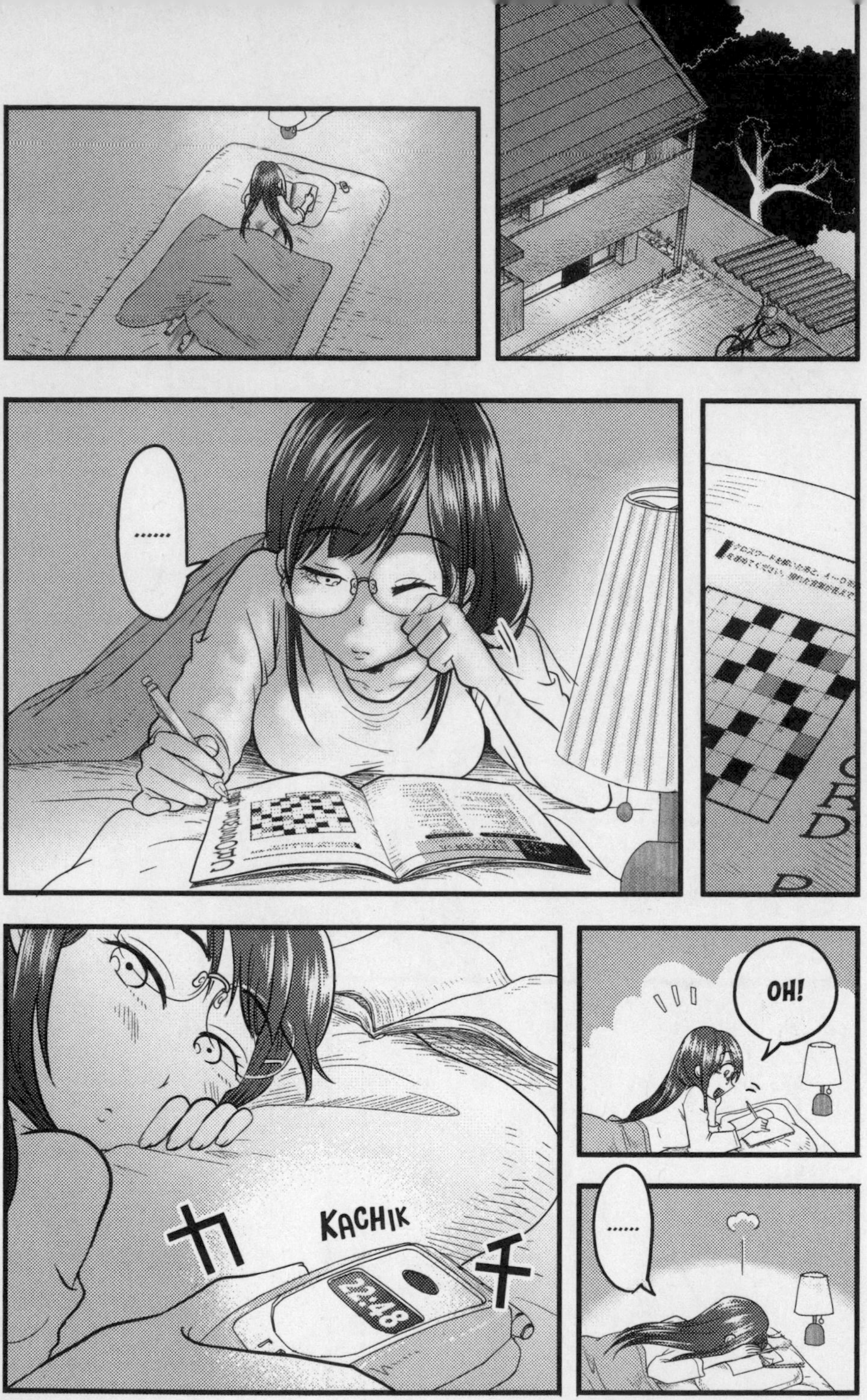
......
OH!
......
カ
KACHIK
チ

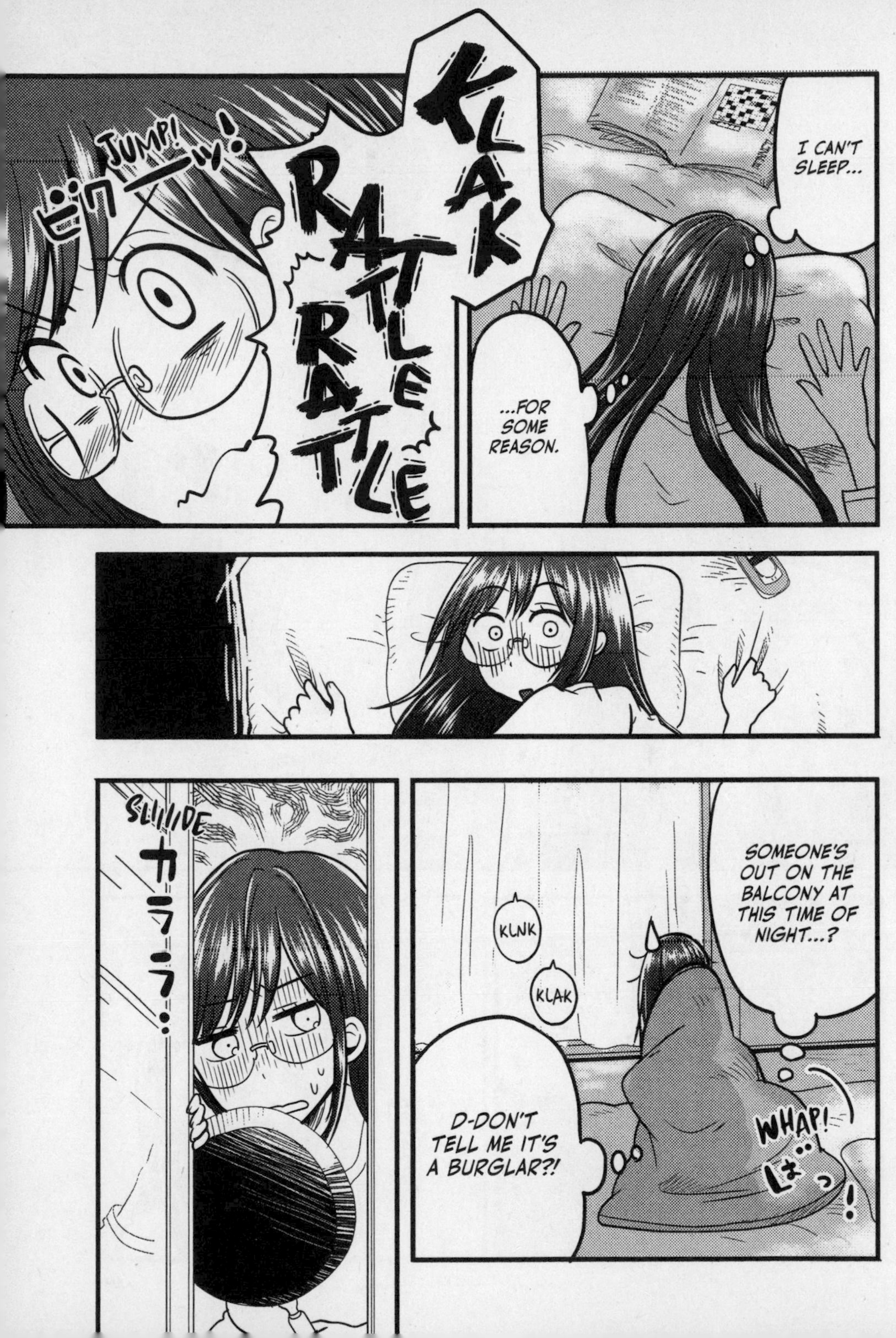
I CAN'T SLEEP...
...FOR SOME REASON.
KLAK
RATTLE RATTLE
JUMP!
ビクーッ!
SOMEONE'S OUT ON THE BALCONY AT THIS TIME OF NIGHT...?
KLNK
KLAK
D-DON'T TELL ME IT'S A BURGLAR?!
WHAP!
SLIIIIDE
カララ…

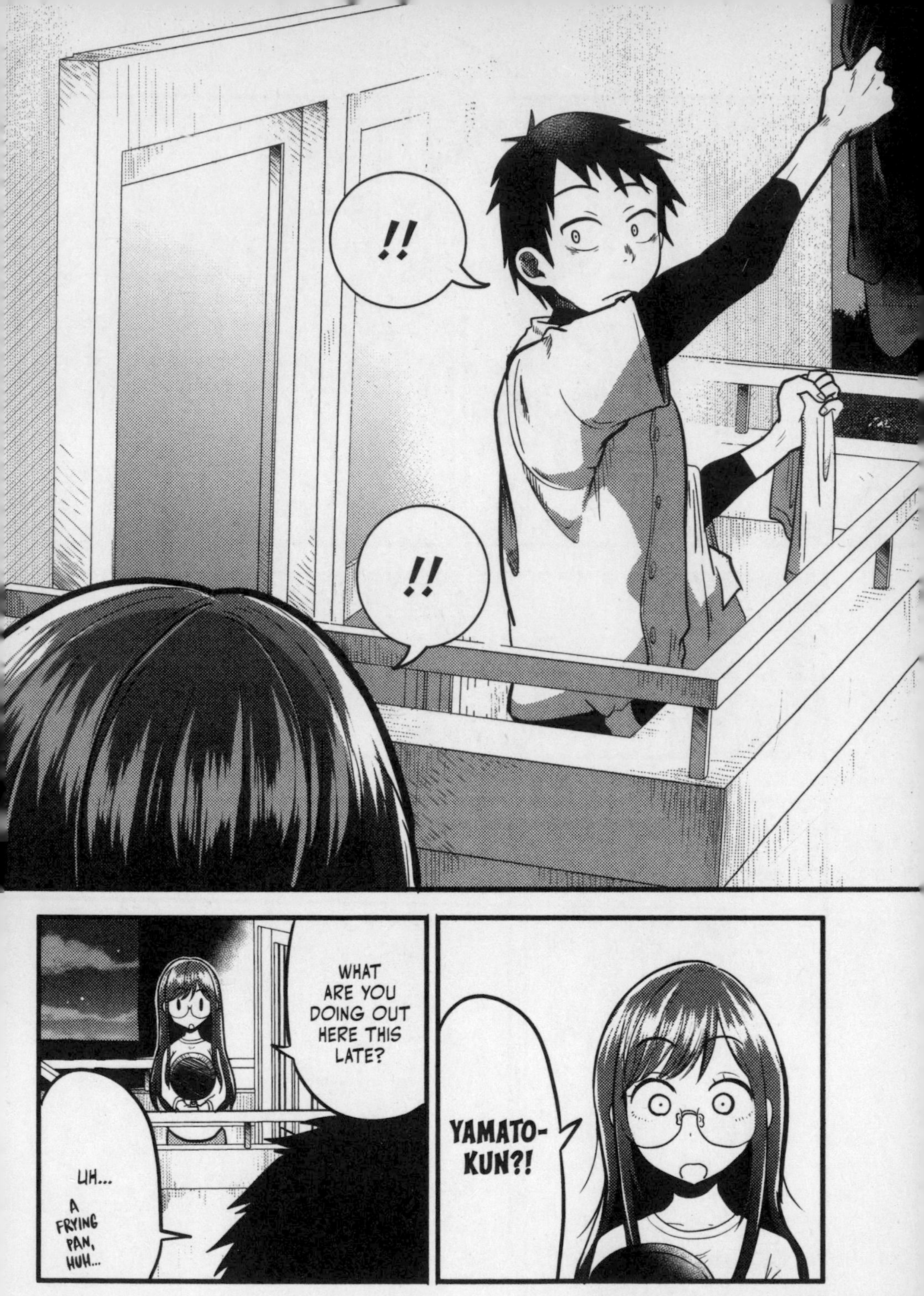
!!
!!
YAMATO-KUN?!
WHAT ARE YOU DOING OUT HERE THIS LATE?
UH...
A FRYING PAN, HUH...

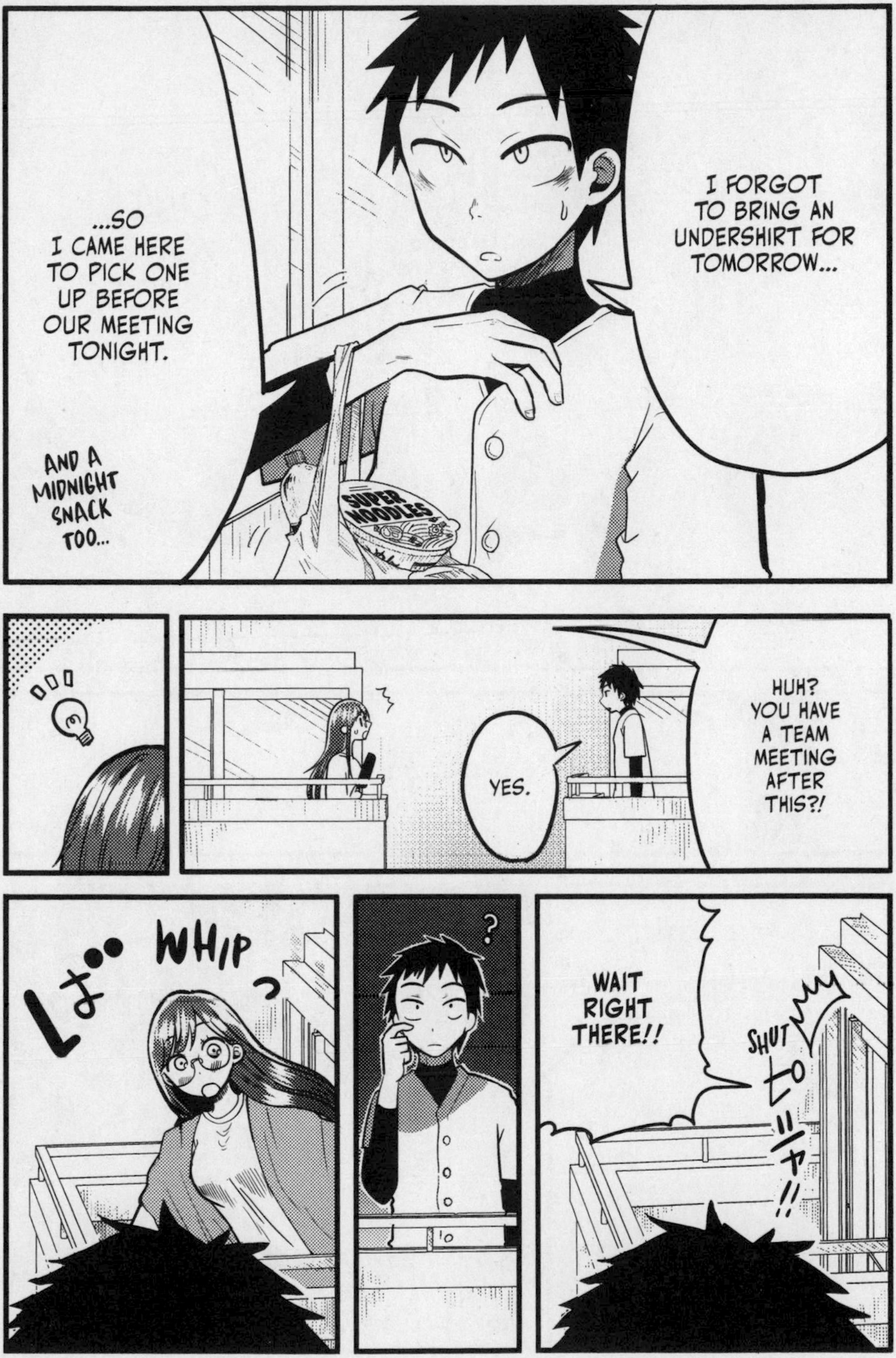
I FORGOT TO BRING AN UNDERSHIRT FOR TOMORROW...
...SO I CAME HERE TO PICK ONE UP BEFORE OUR MEETING TONIGHT.
AND A MIDNIGHT SNACK TOO...
SUPER NOODLES
HUH? YOU HAVE A TEAM MEETING AFTER THIS?!
YES.
WAIT RIGHT THERE!!
SHUT
?
WHIP

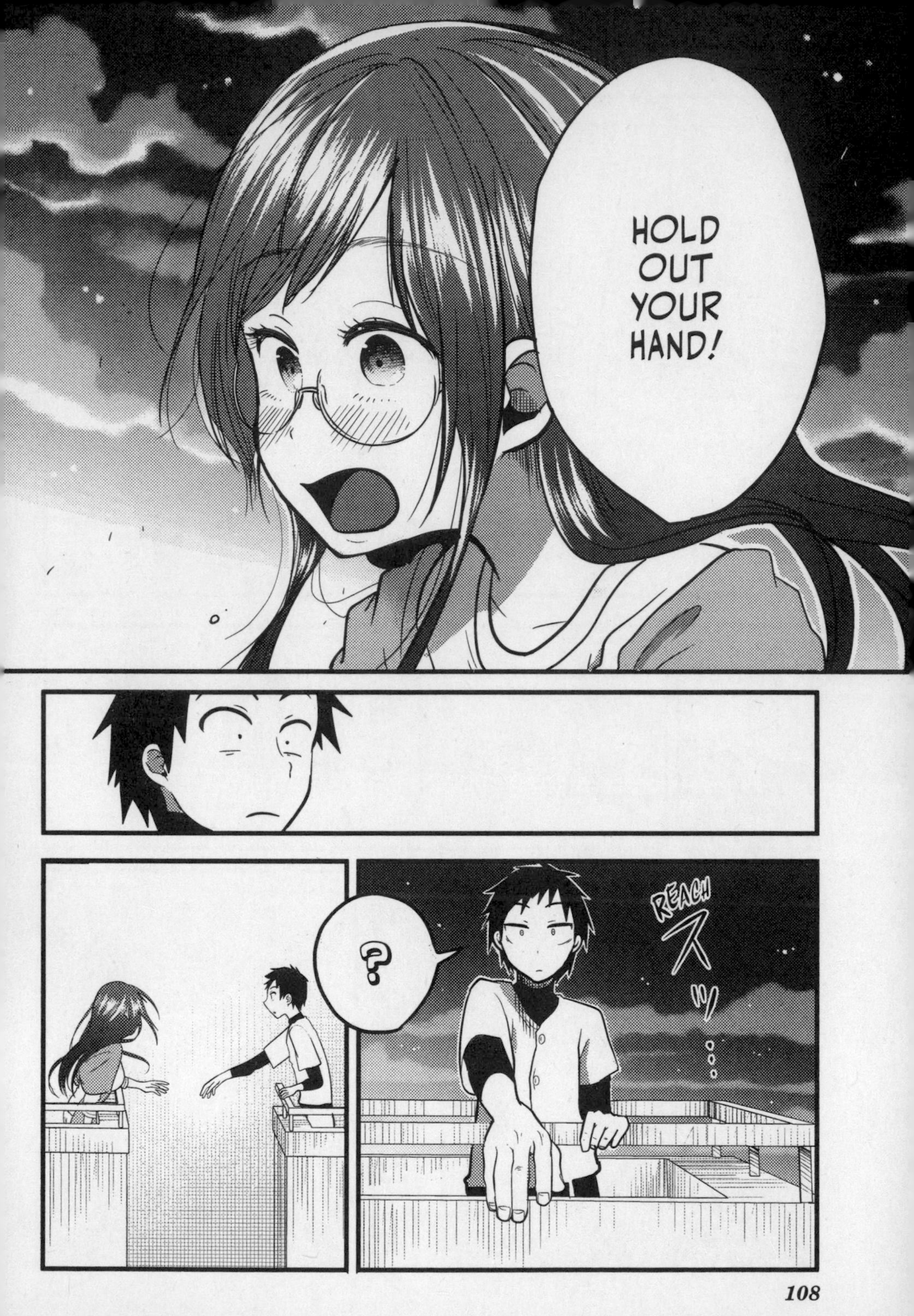
HOLD OUT YOUR HAND!
REACH
ス
?

CLUTCH
BABUMP
TRY NOT TO DROP IT!
PLOP

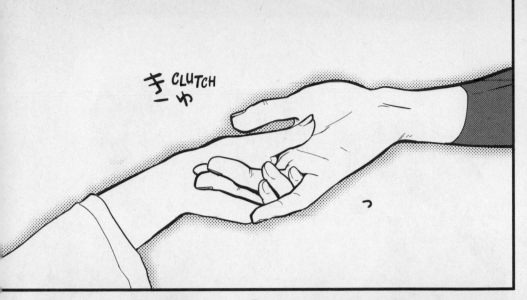

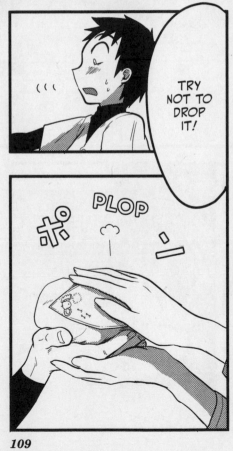

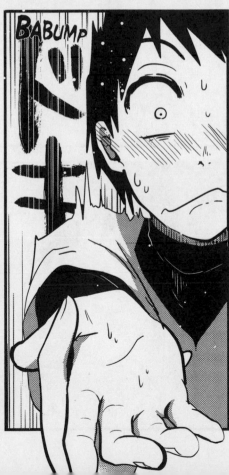

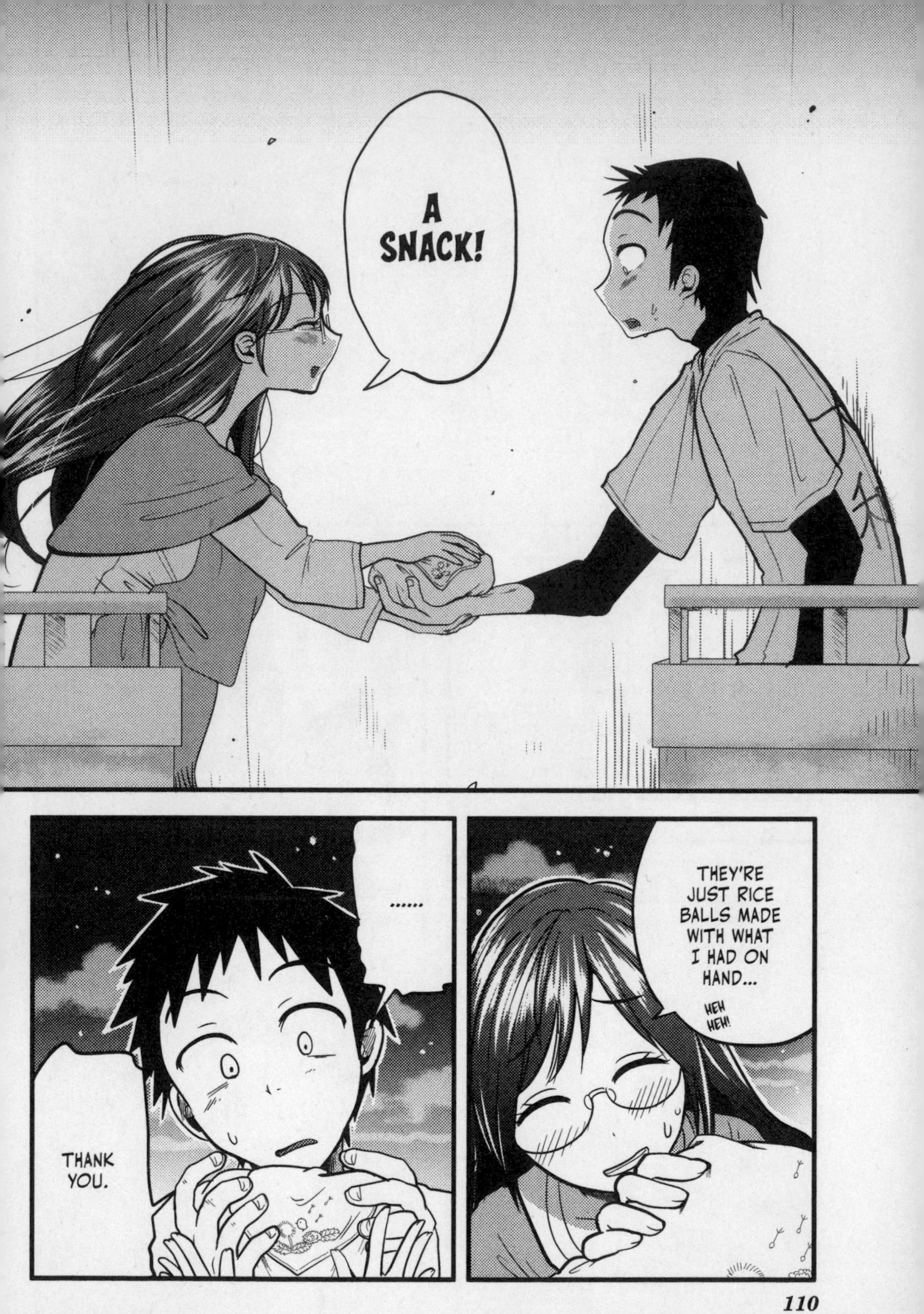
A SNACK!
THEY'RE JUST RICE BALLS MADE WITH WHAT I HAD ON HAND...
HEH HEH!
......
THANK YOU.

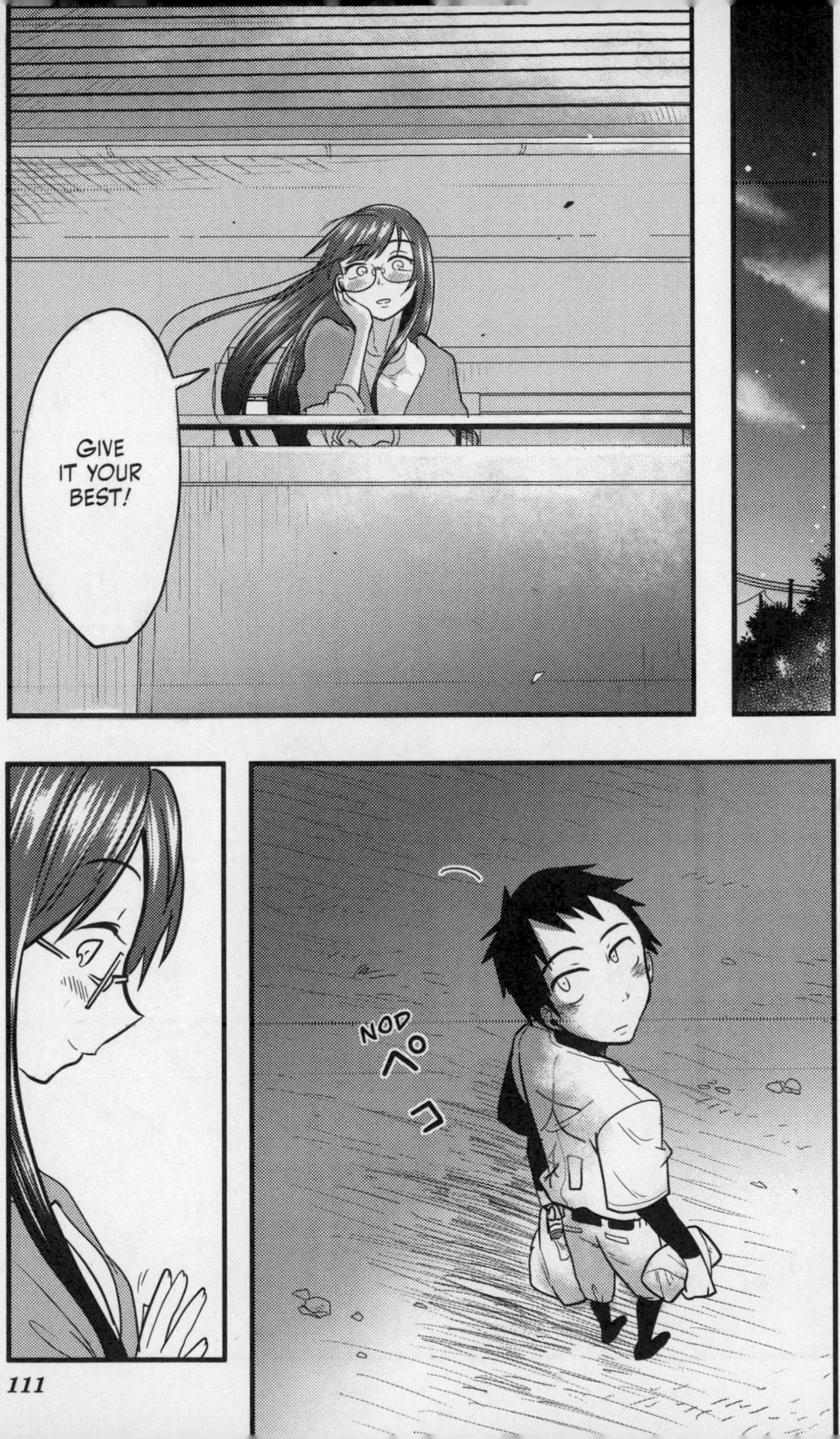
GIVE IT YOUR BEST!
NOD
へこ

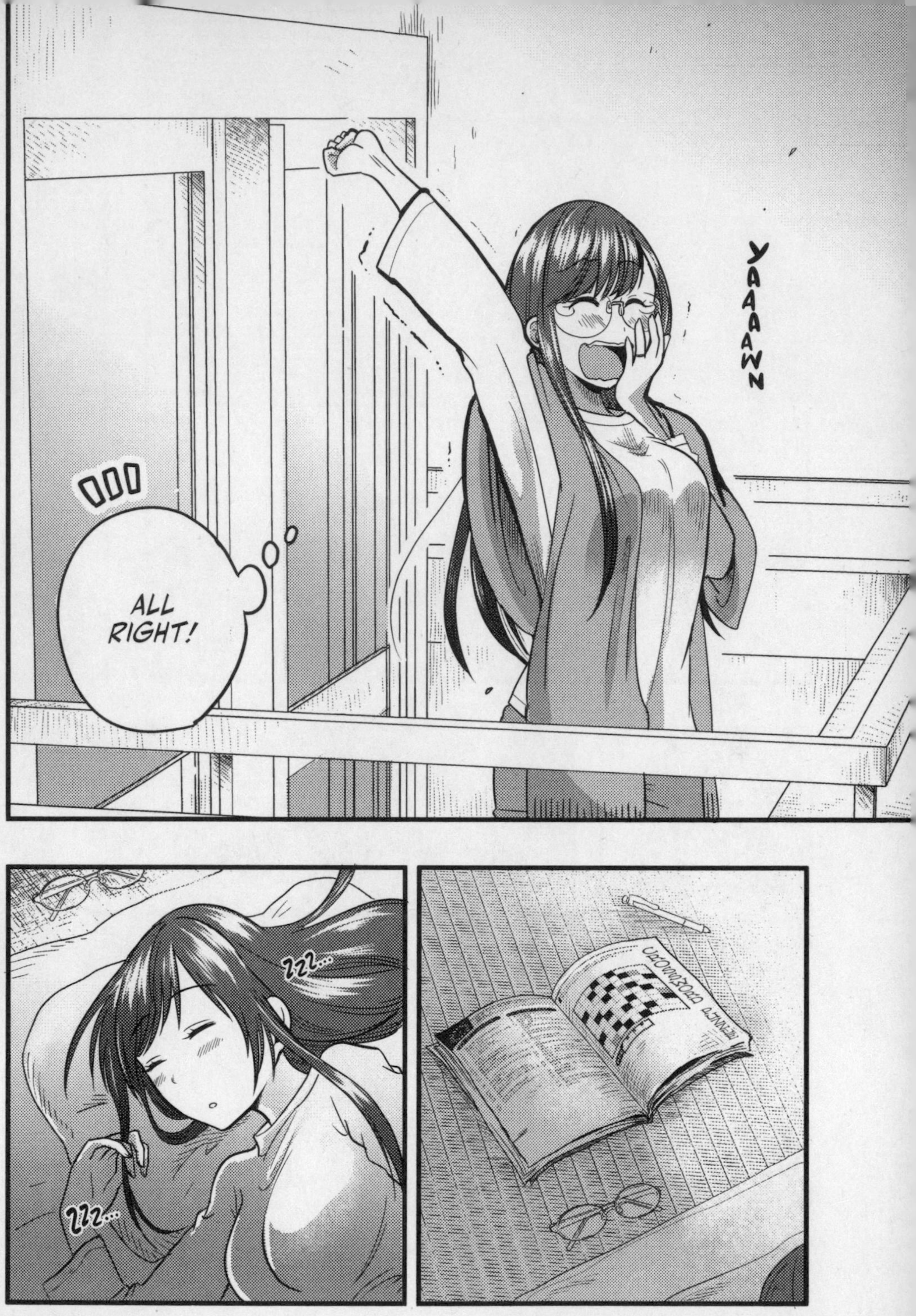
YAAAAWN
DDD
ALL RIGHT!
ZZZ...
ZZZ...

Beauty and the FEAST.

Beauty and the FEAST.

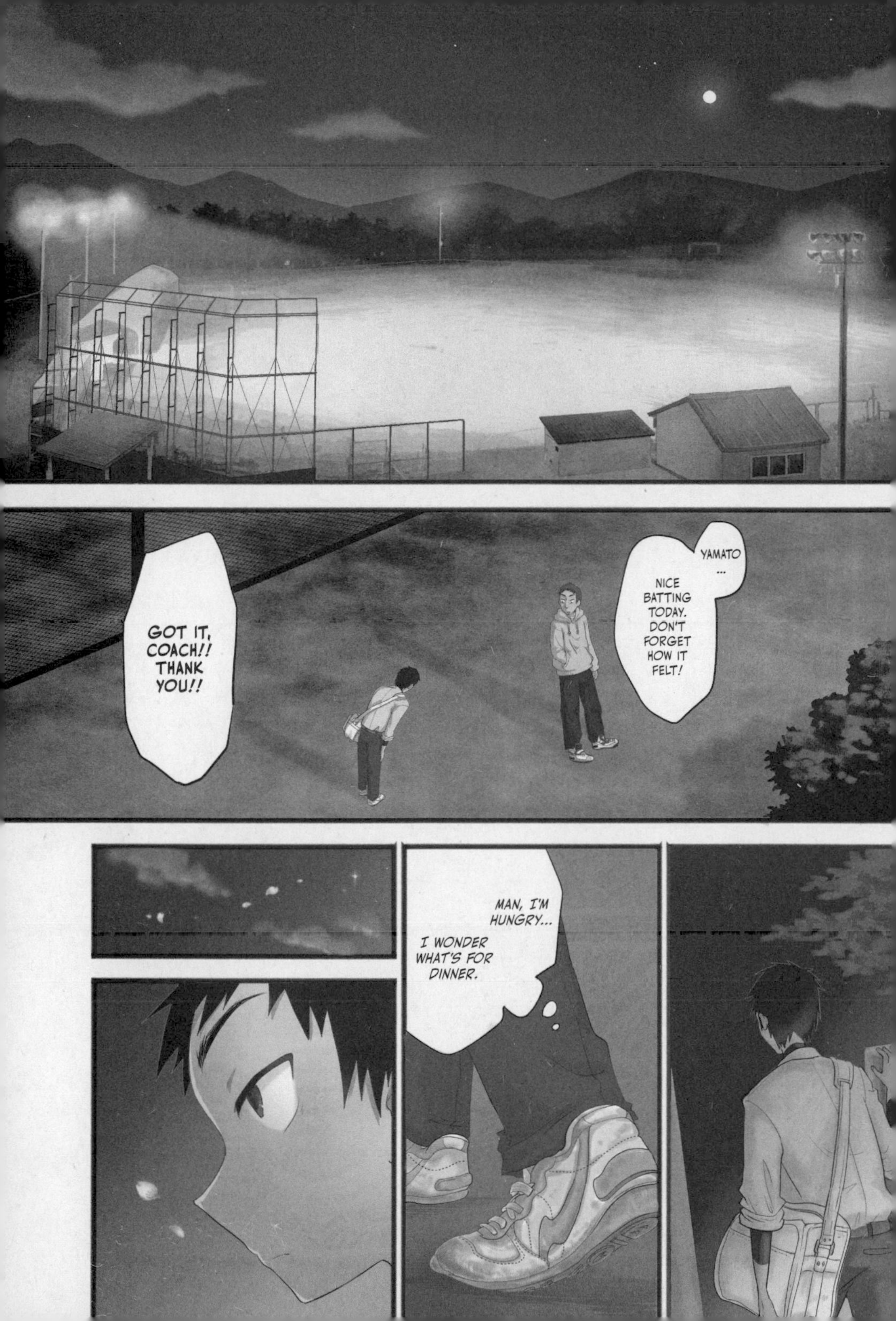
YAMATO ...
NICE BATTING TODAY. DON'T FORGET HOW IT FELT!
GOT IT, COACH!! THANK YOU!!
MAN, I'M HUNGRY...
I WONDER WHAT'S FOR DINNER.

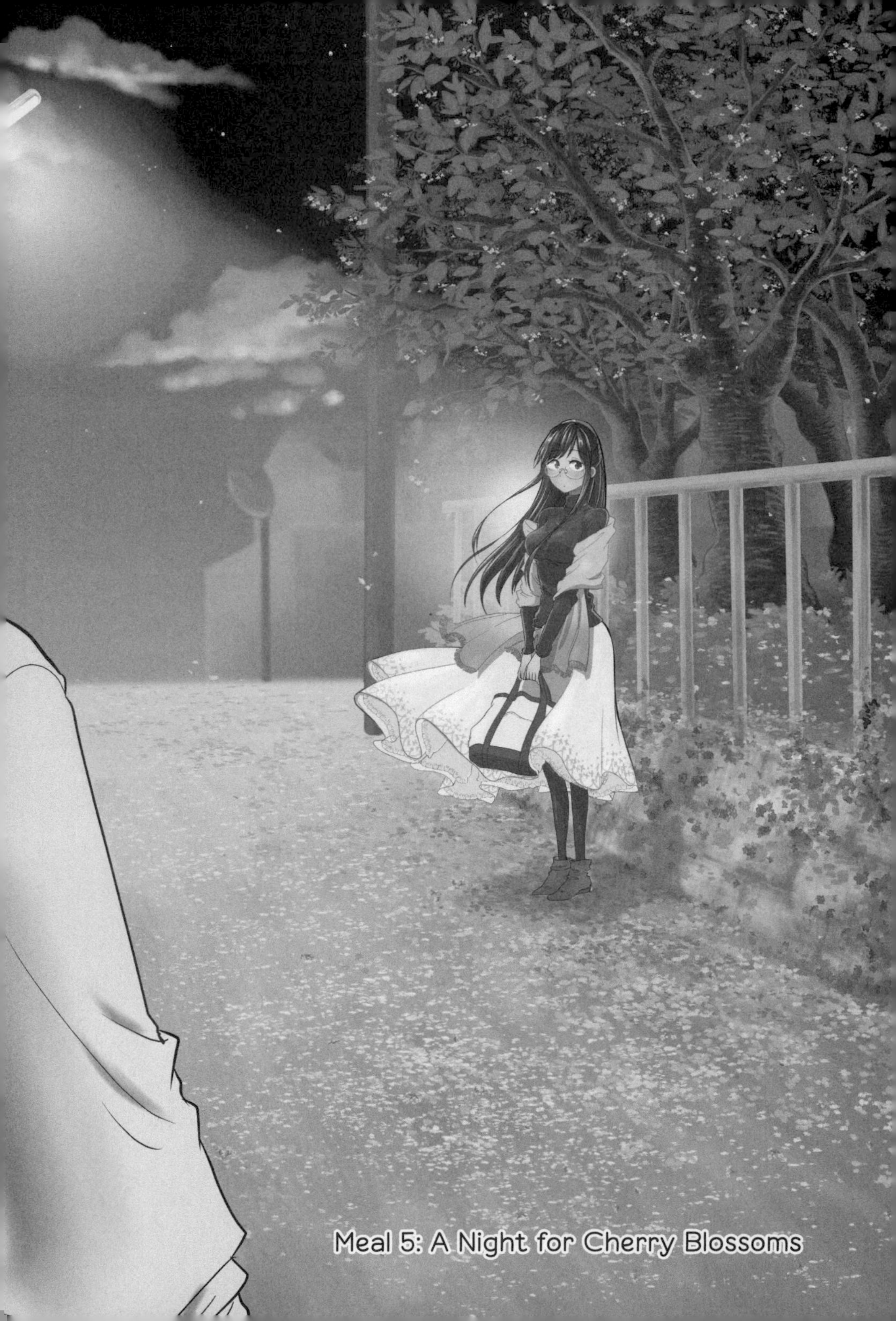

Meal 5: A Night for Cherry Blossoms

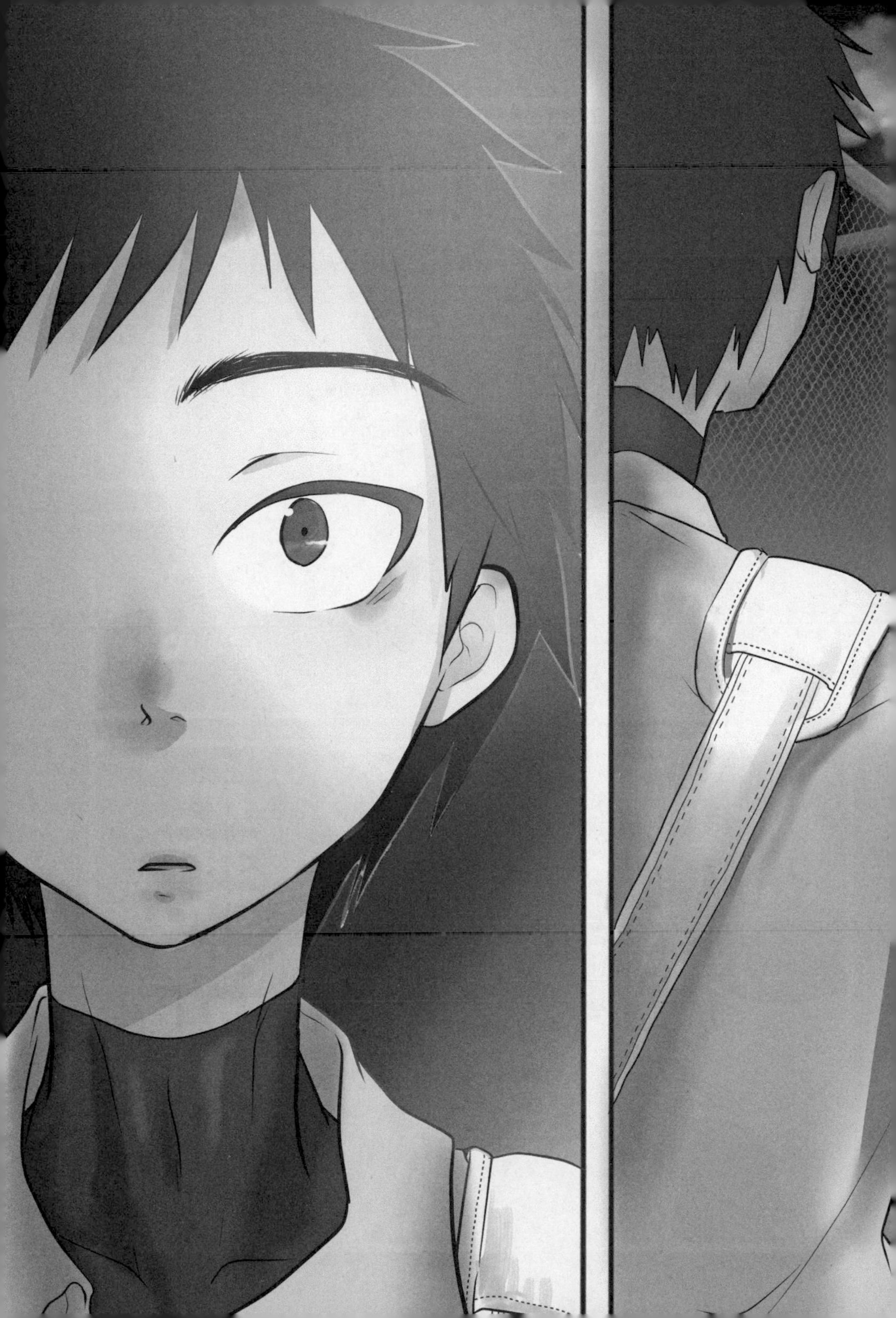

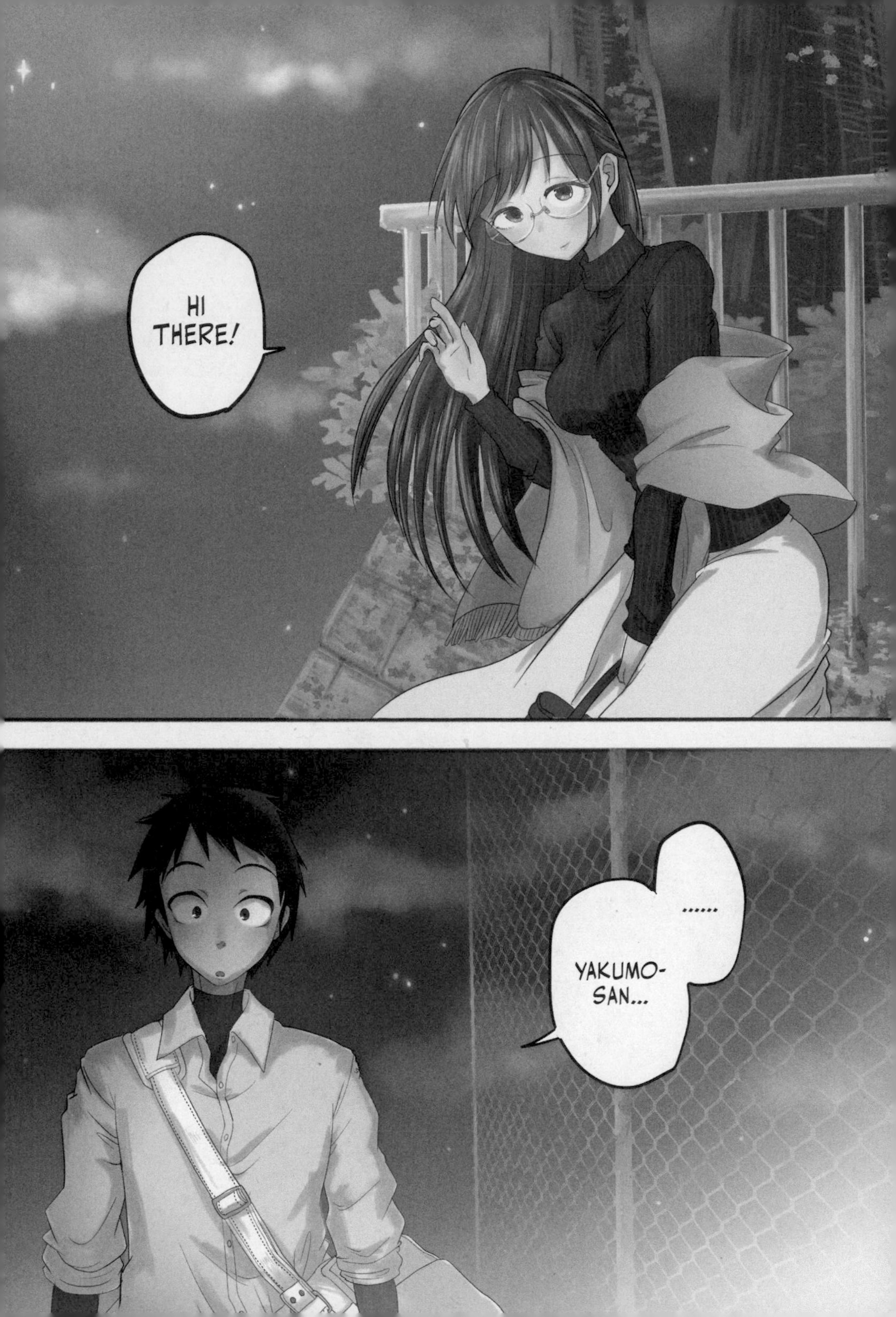
HI THERE!
......
YAKUMO-SAN...

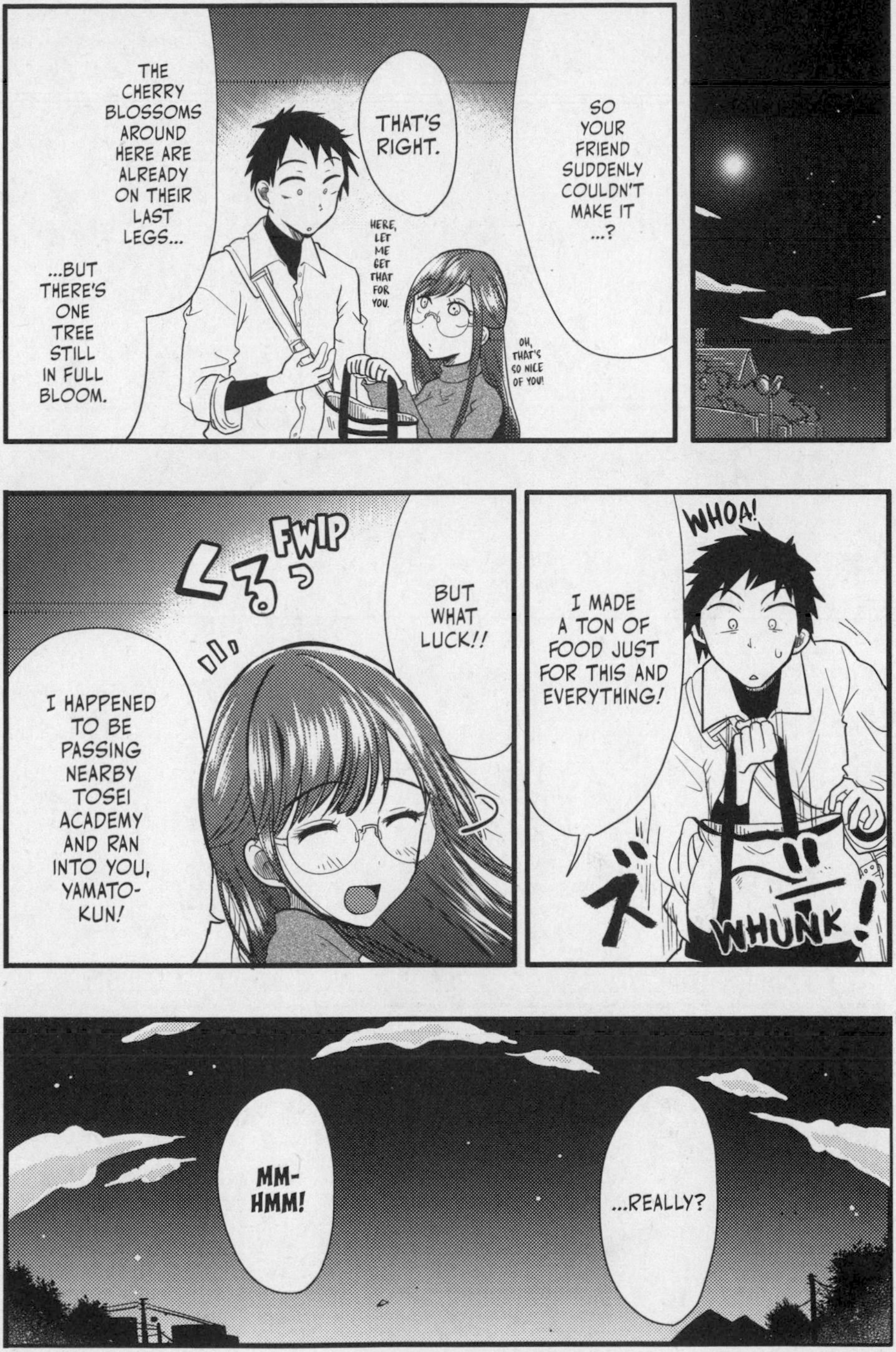
SO YOUR FRIEND SUDDENLY COULDN'T MAKE IT ...?
THAT'S RIGHT.
HERE, LET ME GET THAT FOR YOU.
OH, THAT'S SO NICE OF YOU!
THE CHERRY BLOSSOMS AROUND HERE ARE ALREADY ON THEIR LAST LEGS...
...BUT THERE'S ONE TREE STILL IN FULL BLOOM.
WHOA!
I MADE A TON OF FOOD JUST FOR THIS AND EVERYTHING!
WHUNK!
FWIP
BUT WHAT LUCK!!
I HAPPENED TO BE PASSING NEARBY TOSEI ACADEMY AND RAN INTO YOU, YAMATO-KUN!
...REALLY?
MM-HMM!

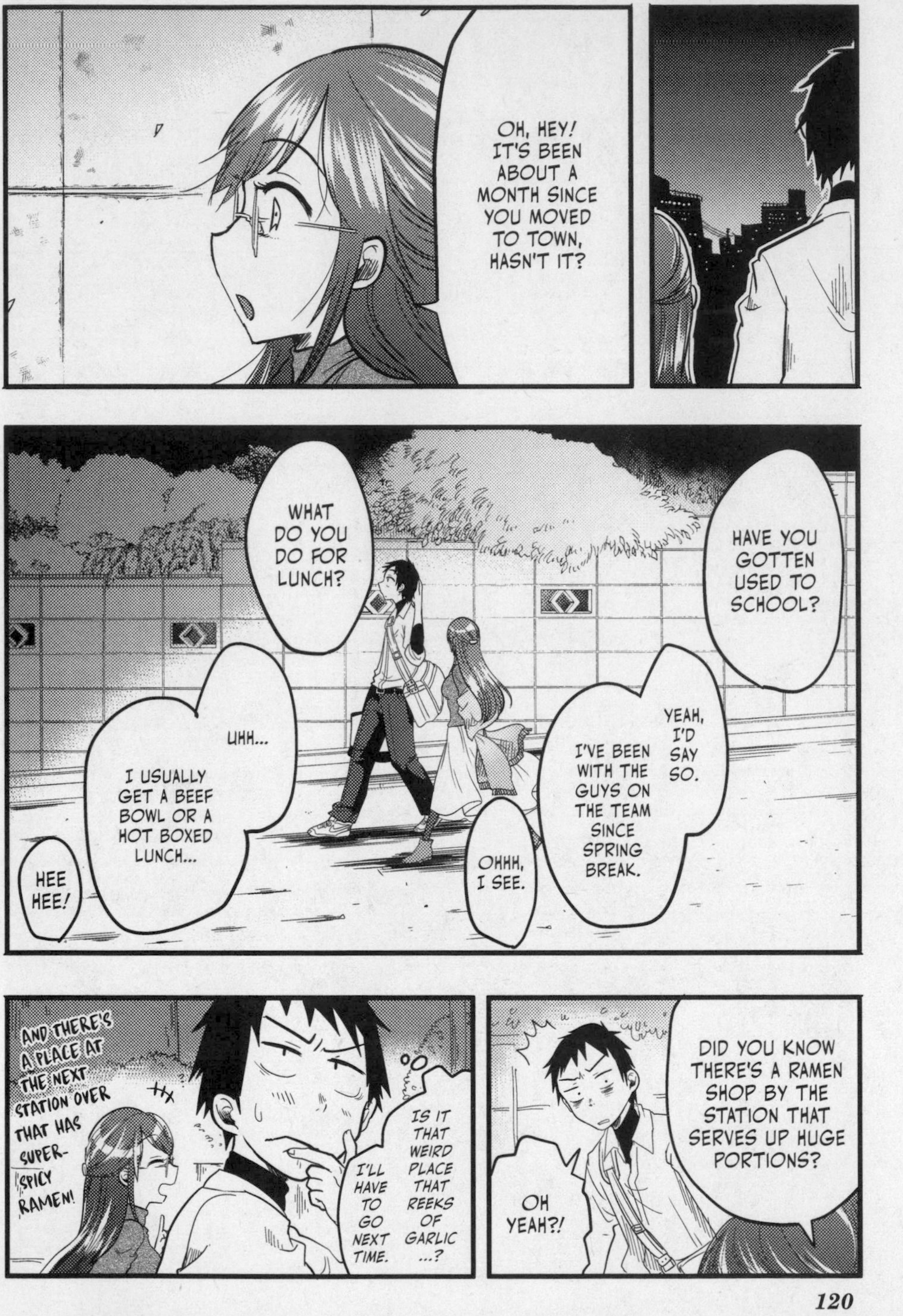
OH, HEY! IT'S BEEN ABOUT A MONTH SINCE YOU MOVED TO TOWN, HASN'T IT?
HAVE YOU GOTTEN USED TO SCHOOL?
YEAH, I'D SAY SO.
I'VE BEEN WITH THE GUYS ON THE TEAM SINCE SPRING BREAK.
OHHH, I SEE.
WHAT DO YOU DO FOR LUNCH?
UHH...
I USUALLY GET A BEEF BOWL OR A HOT BOXED LUNCH...
HEE HEE!
DID YOU KNOW THERE'S A RAMEN SHOP BY THE STATION THAT SERVES UP HUGE PORTIONS?
OH YEAH?!
IS IT THAT WEIRD PLACE THAT REEKS OF GARLIC ...?
AND THERE'S A PLACE AT THE NEXT STATION OVER THAT HAS SUPER-SPICY RAMEN!
I'LL HAVE TO GO NEXT TIME.

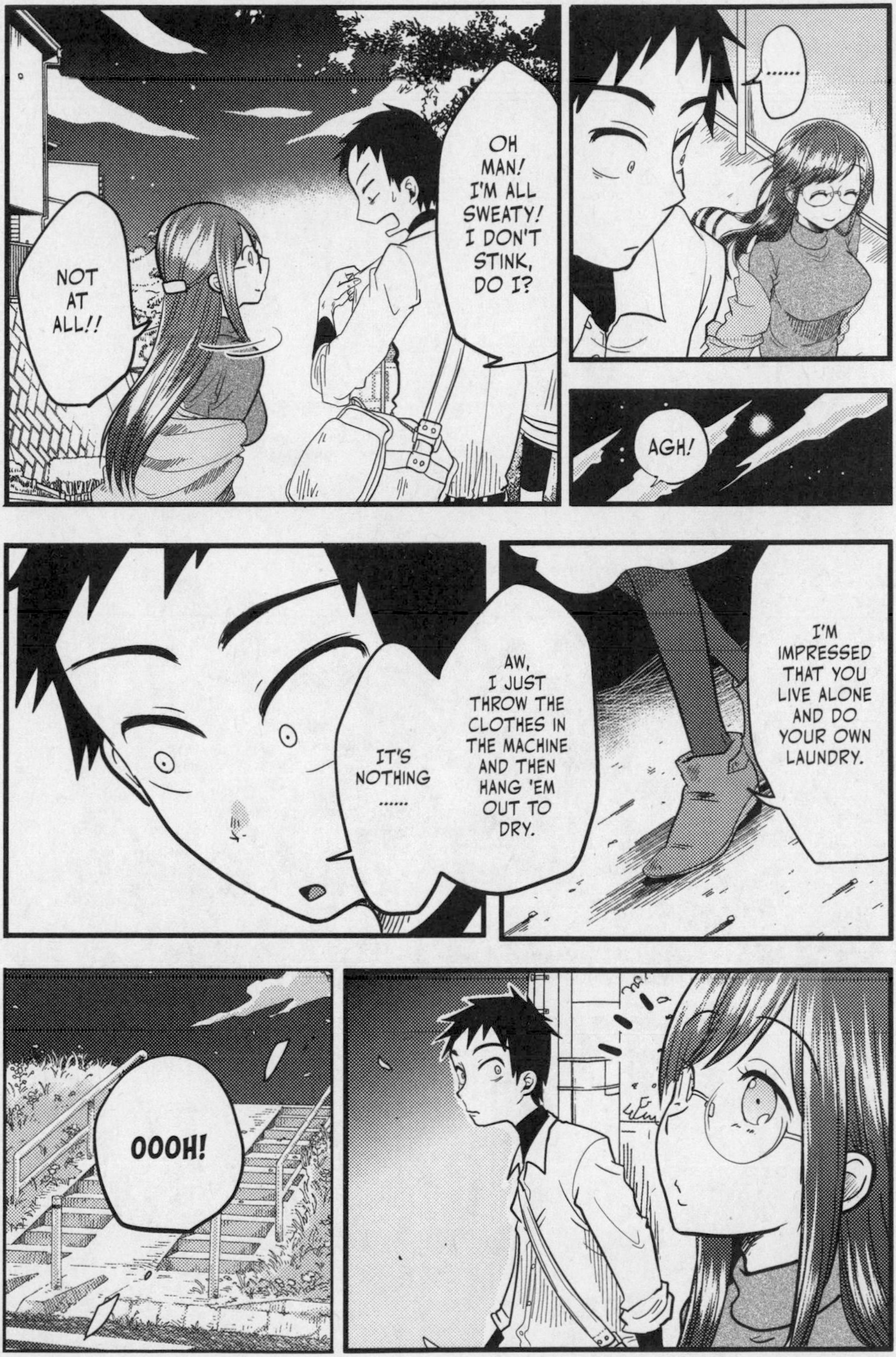
……
AGH!
OH MAN! I'M ALL SWEATY! I DON'T STINK, DO I?
NOT AT ALL!!
I'M IMPRESSED THAT YOU LIVE ALONE AND DO YOUR OWN LAUNDRY.
AW, I JUST THROW THE CLOTHES IN THE MACHINE AND THEN HANG 'EM OUT TO DRY.
IT'S NOTHING ……
OOOH!

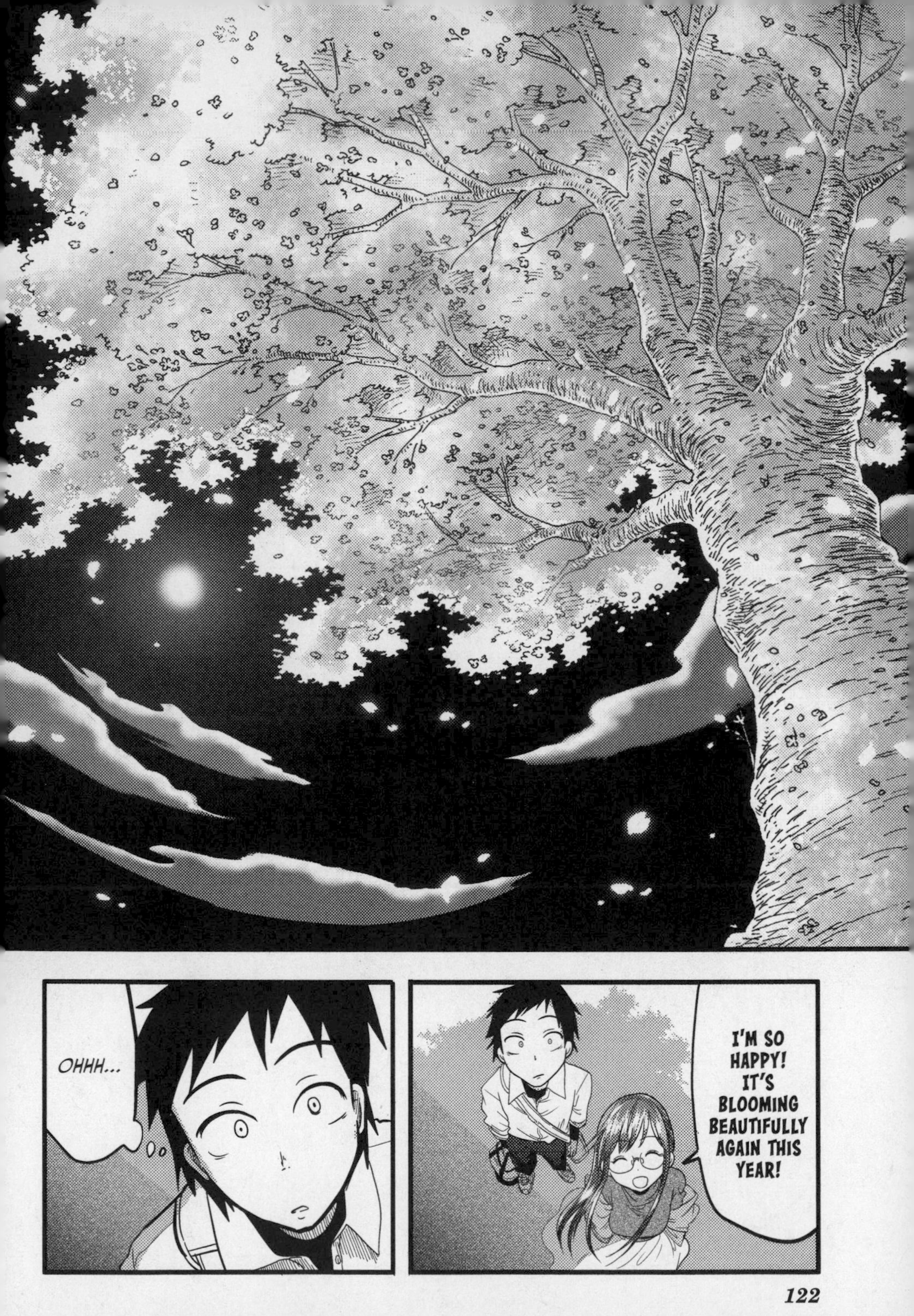
I'M SO HAPPY! IT'S BLOOMING BEAUTIFULLY AGAIN THIS YEAR!
OHHH...

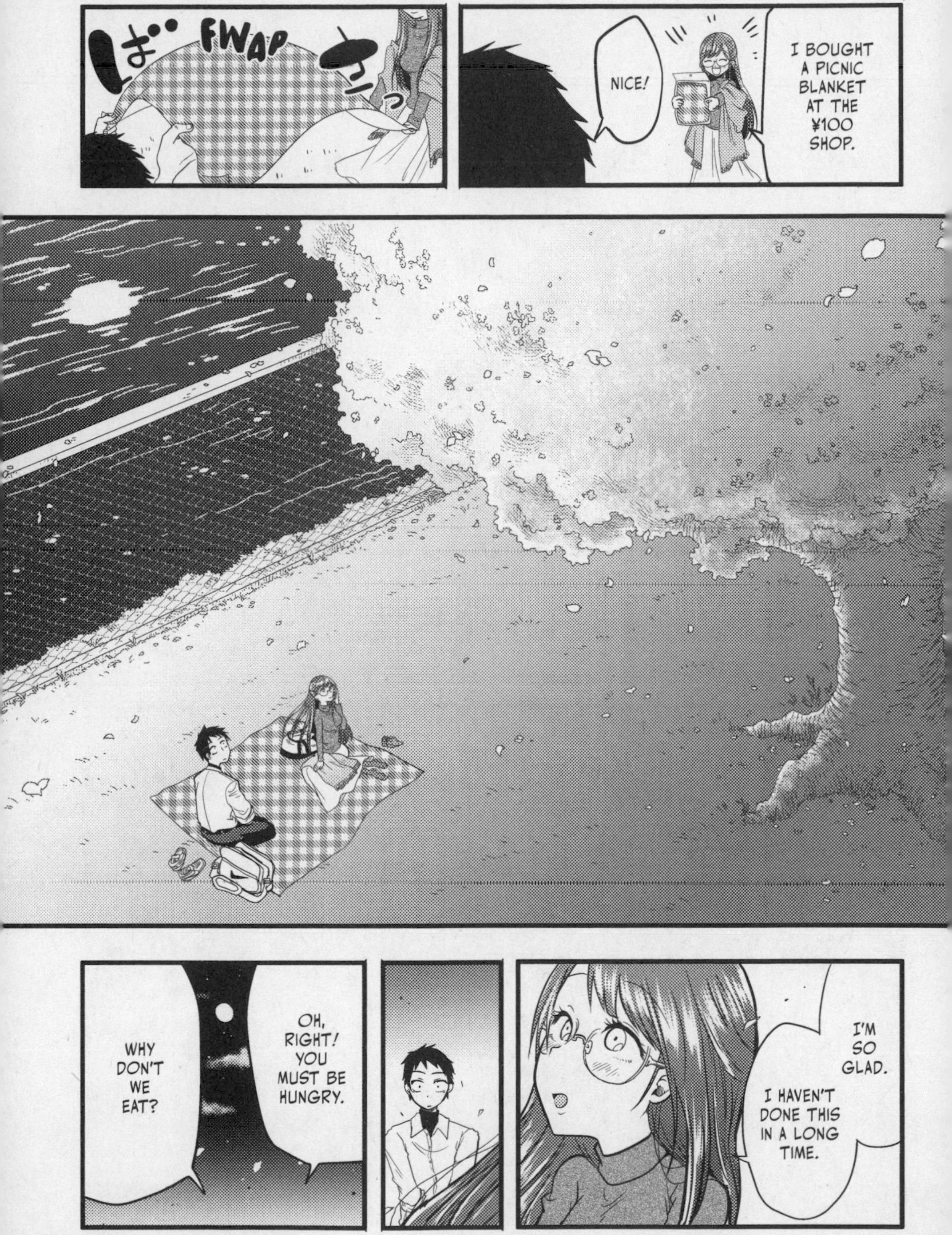
I BOUGHT A PICNIC BLANKET AT THE ¥100 SHOP.
NICE!
FWAP
I'M SO GLAD.
I HAVEN'T DONE THIS IN A LONG TIME.
OH, RIGHT! YOU MUST BE HUNGRY.
WHY DON'T WE EAT?

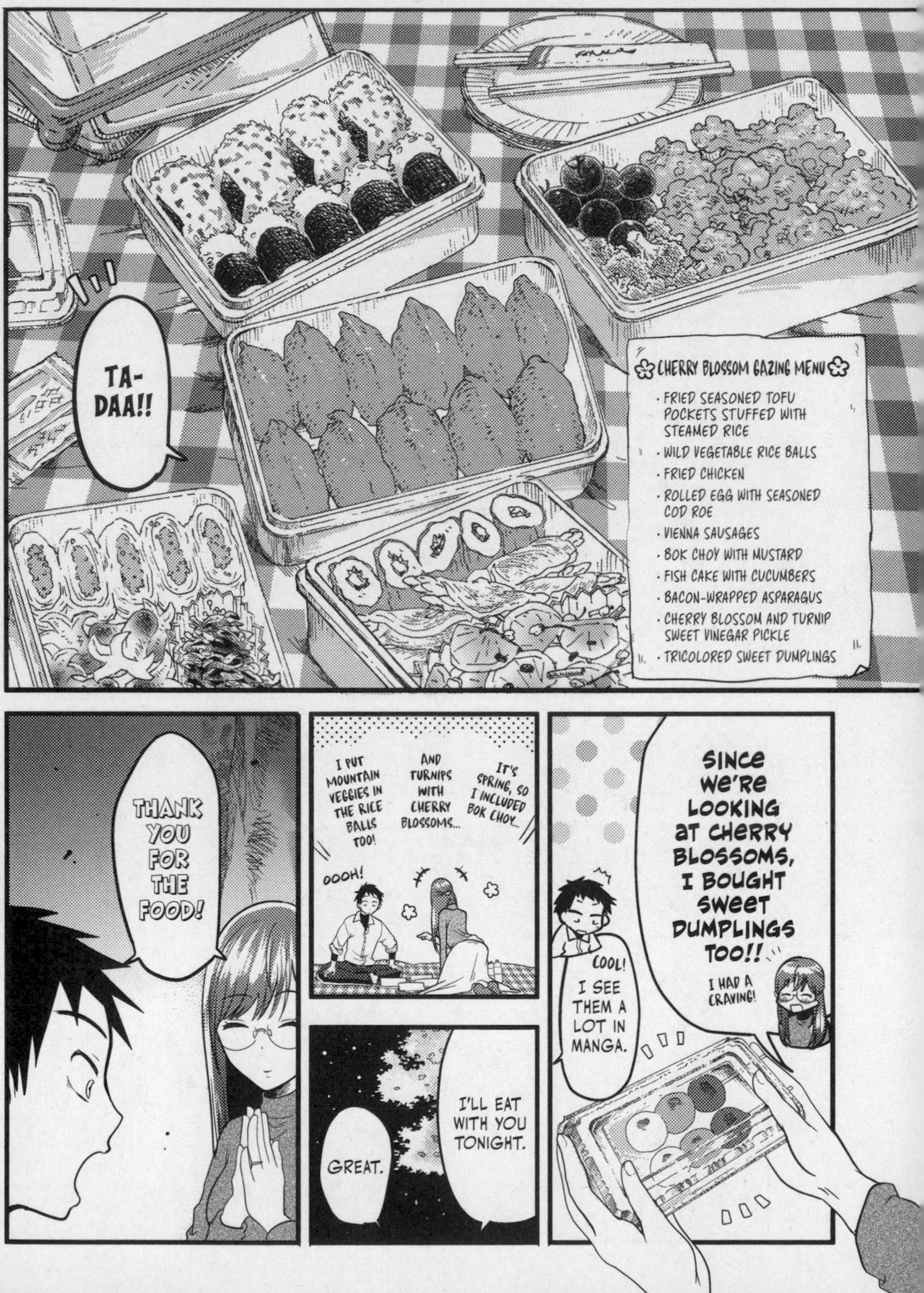
TA-DAA!!
CHERRY BLOSSOM GAZING MENU
· FRIED SEASONED TOFU POCKETS STUFFED WITH STEAMED RICE
· WILD VEGETABLE RICE BALLS
· FRIED CHICKEN
· ROLLED EGG WITH SEASONED COD ROE
· VIENNA SAUSAGES
· BOK CHOY WITH MUSTARD
· FISH CAKE WITH CUCUMBERS
· BACON-WRAPPED ASPARAGUS
· CHERRY BLOSSOM AND TURNIP SWEET VINEGAR PICKLE
· TRICOLORED SWEET DUMPLINGS
SINCE WE'RE LOOKING AT CHERRY BLOSSOMS, I BOUGHT SWEET DUMPLINGS TOO!!
I HAD A CRAVING!
COOL! I SEE THEM A LOT IN MANGA.
IT'S SPRING, SO I INCLUDED BOK CHOY...
AND TURNIPS WITH CHERRY BLOSSOMS...
I PUT MOUNTAIN VEGGIES IN THE RICE BALLS TOO!
OOOH!
I'LL EAT WITH YOU TONIGHT.
GREAT.
THANK YOU FOR THE FOOD!

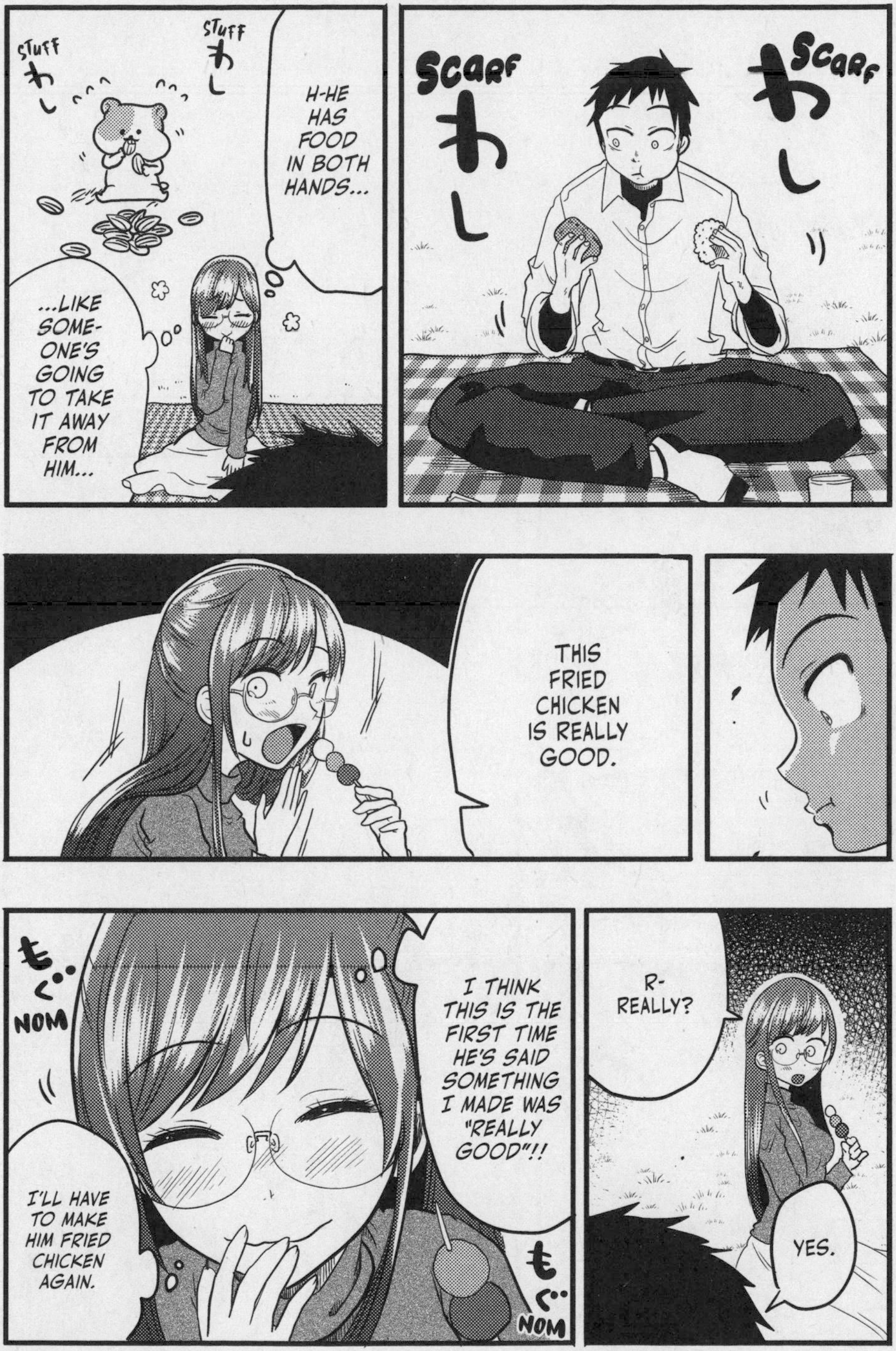

SCARF
わし
SCARF
わし
H-HE HAS FOOD IN BOTH HANDS...
STUFF
わし
STUFF
わし
...LIKE SOME-ONE'S GOING TO TAKE IT AWAY FROM HIM...
THIS FRIED CHICKEN IS REALLY GOOD.
R-REALLY?
YES.
I THINK THIS IS THE FIRST TIME HE'S SAID SOMETHING I MADE WAS "REALLY GOOD"!!
もぐ
NOM
もぐ
NOM
I'LL HAVE TO MAKE HIM FRIED CHICKEN AGAIN.

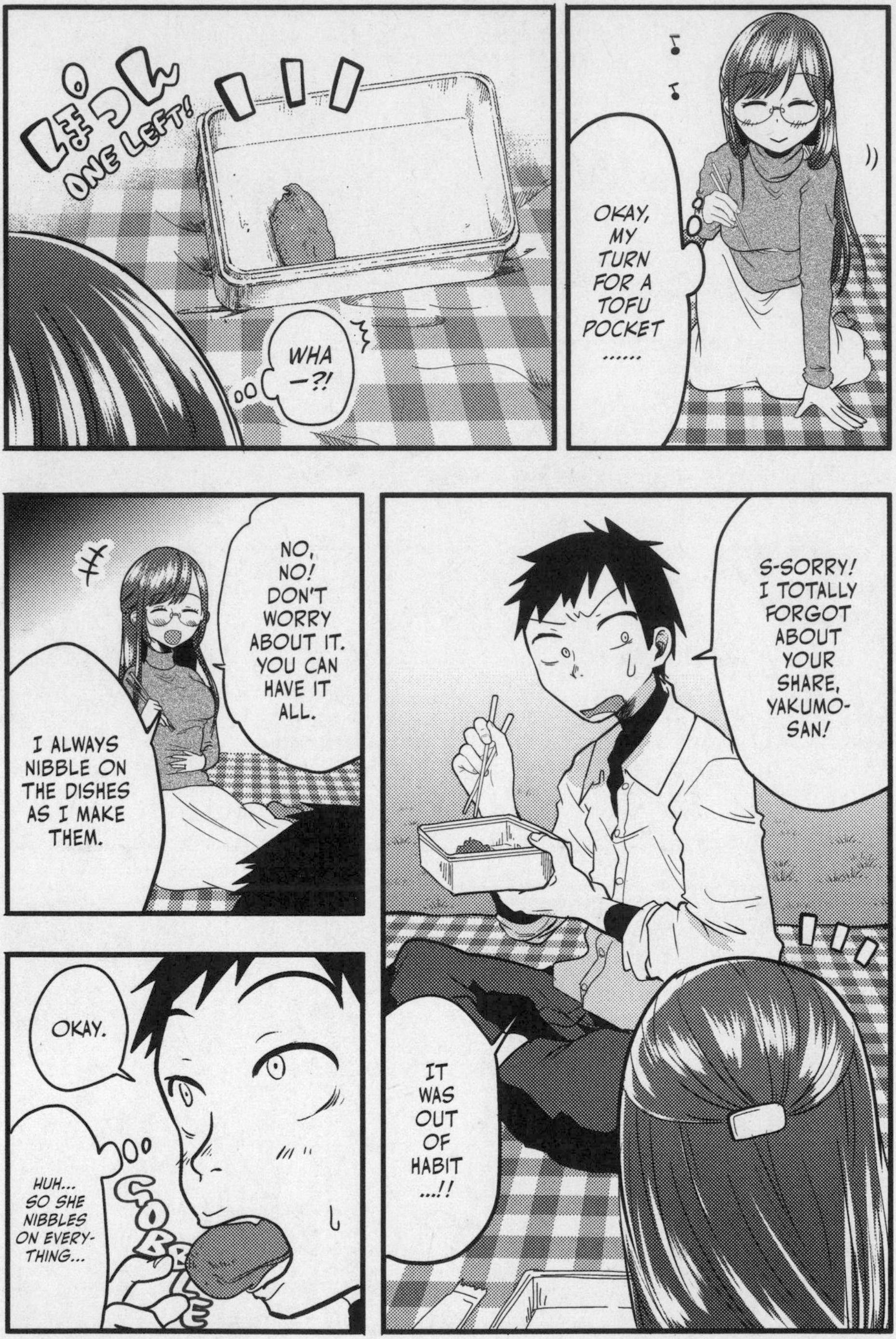
OKAY, MY TURN FOR A TOFU POCKET ......
ぽつん
ONE LEFT!
WHA—?!
S-SORRY! I TOTALLY FORGOT ABOUT YOUR SHARE, YAKUMO-SAN!
IT WAS OUT OF HABIT ...!!
NO, NO! DON'T WORRY ABOUT IT. YOU CAN HAVE IT ALL.
I ALWAYS NIBBLE ON THE DISHES AS I MAKE THEM.
OKAY.
HUH... SO SHE NIBBLES ON EVERY-THING...
GOBBLE

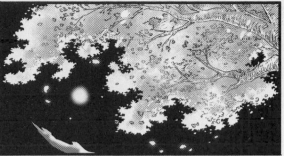

THE CHERRY BLOSSOMS ARE TRULY BEAUTIFUL, AREN'T THEY?

SOME PEOPLE EVEN COME FROM FAR AWAY TO SEE THEM...

THE CHERRY BLOSSOM TREES AROUND HERE ARE FAMOUS.

NOD

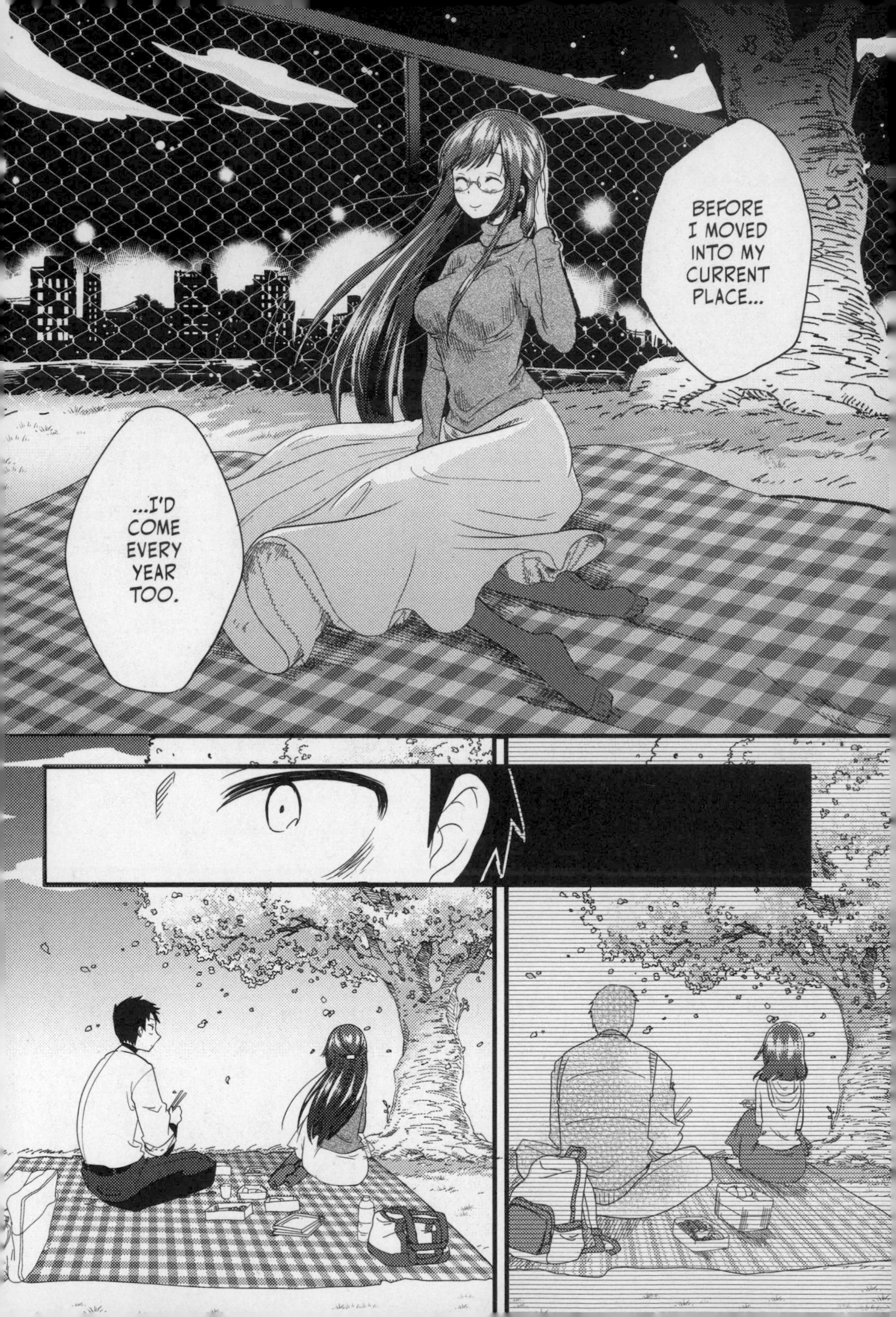
BEFORE I MOVED INTO MY CURRENT PLACE...
...I'D COME EVERY YEAR TOO.

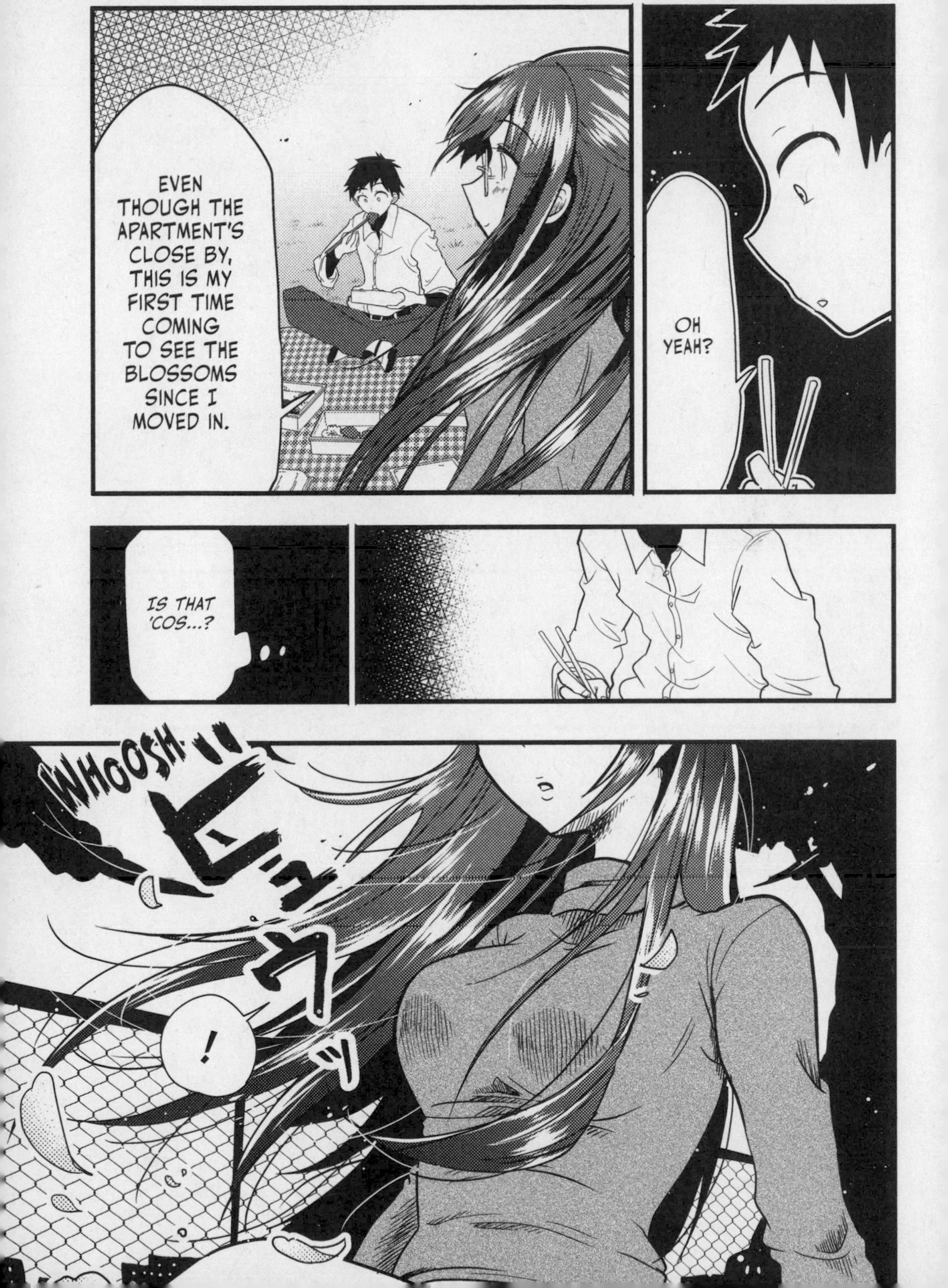
OH YEAH?
EVEN THOUGH THE APARTMENT'S CLOSE BY, THIS IS MY FIRST TIME COMING TO SEE THE BLOSSOMS SINCE I MOVED IN.
IS THAT 'COS...?
WHOOSH!!
!

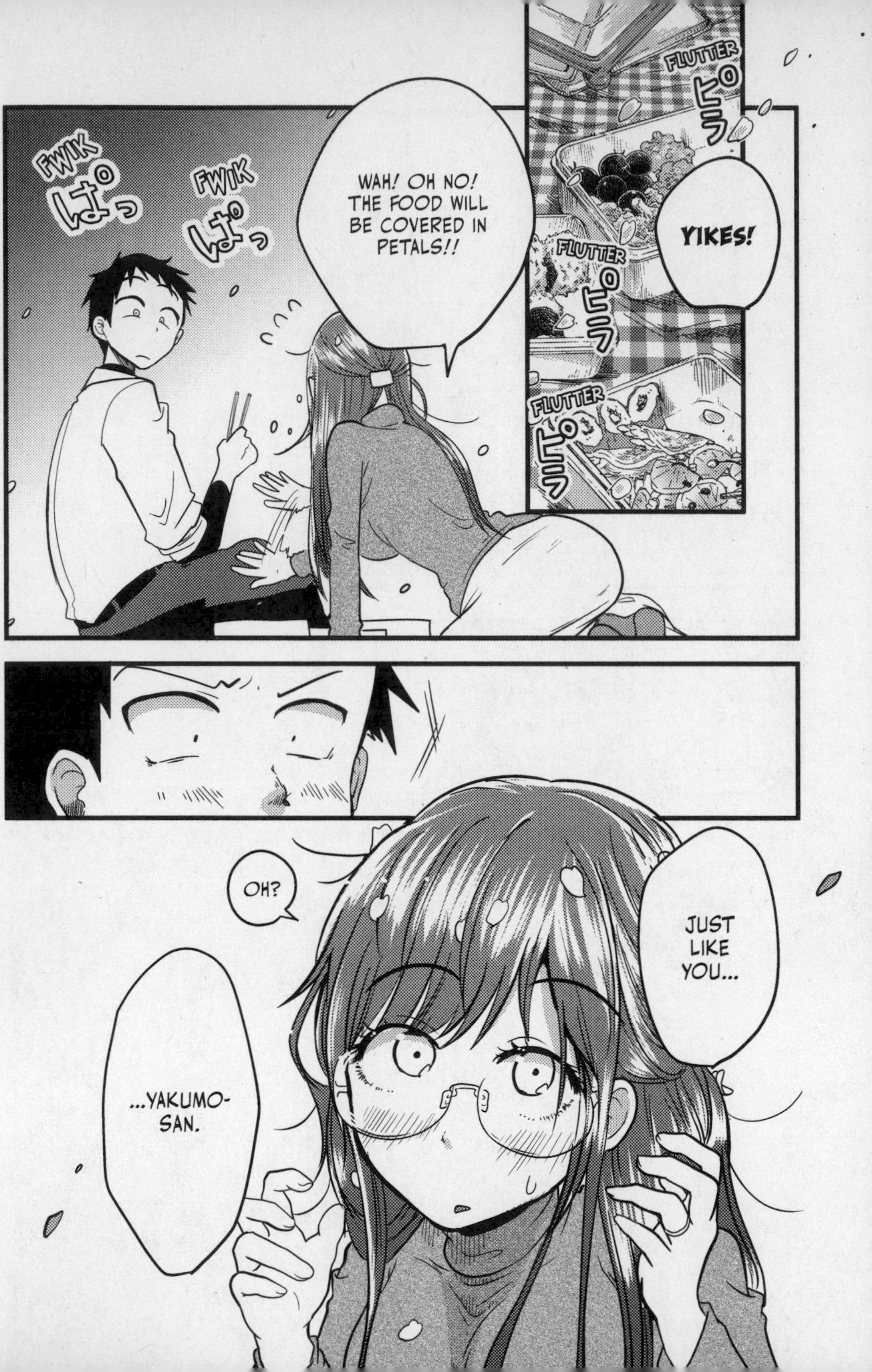
FLUTTER
ピラ
YIKES!
FLUTTER
ピラ
FLUTTER
ピラ
WAH! OH NO! THE FOOD WILL BE COVERED IN PETALS!!
FWIK
ぱっ
FWIK
ぱっ
JUST LIKE YOU...
OH?
...YAKUMO-SAN.

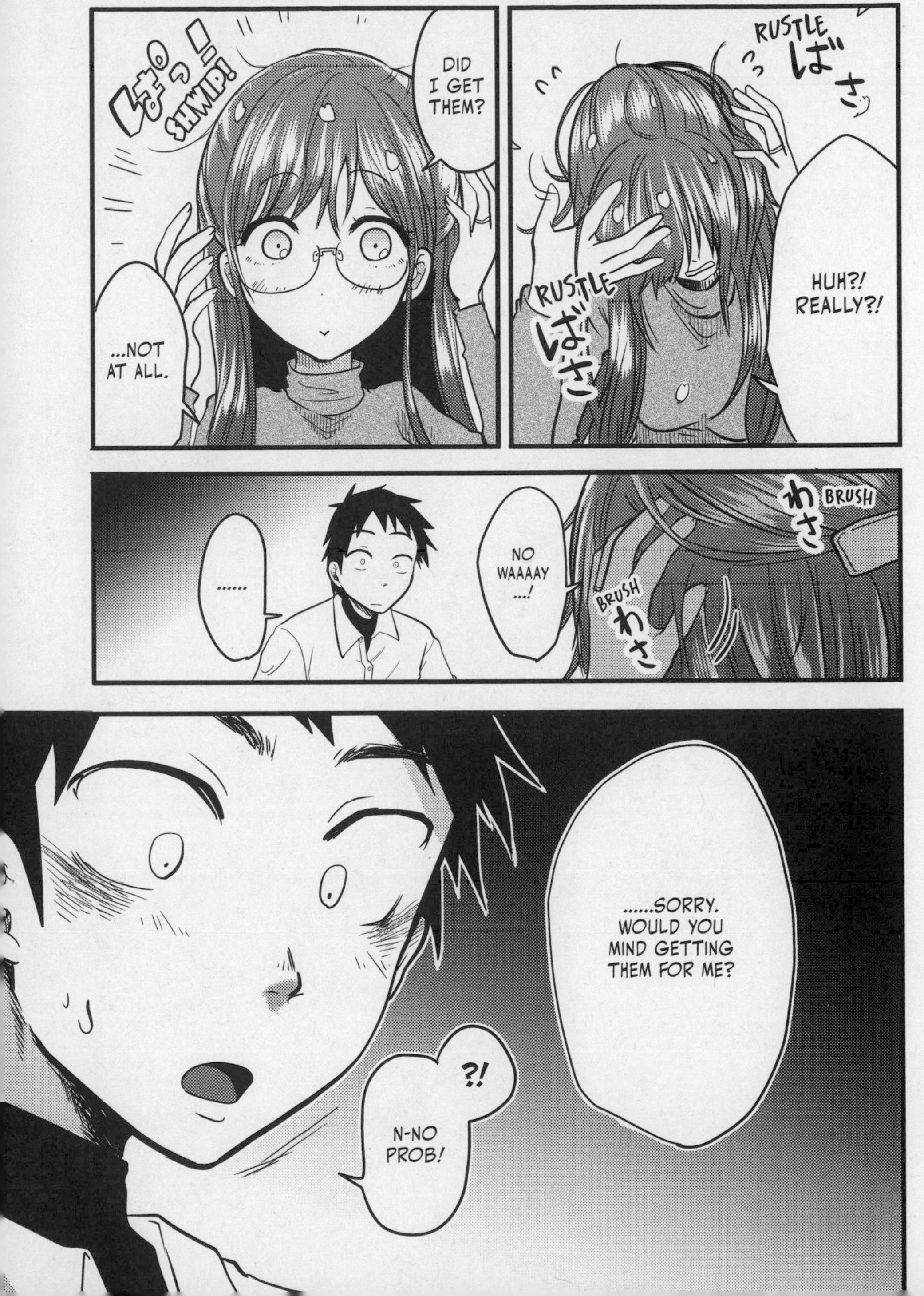
RUSTLE ばさ
HUH?! REALLY?!
RUSTLE ばさ
DID I GET THEM?
SHWIP!
...NOT AT ALL.
わさ BRUSH
BRUSH わさ
NO WAAAAY ...!
......
......SORRY. WOULD YOU MIND GETTING THEM FOR ME?
?!
N-NO PROB!

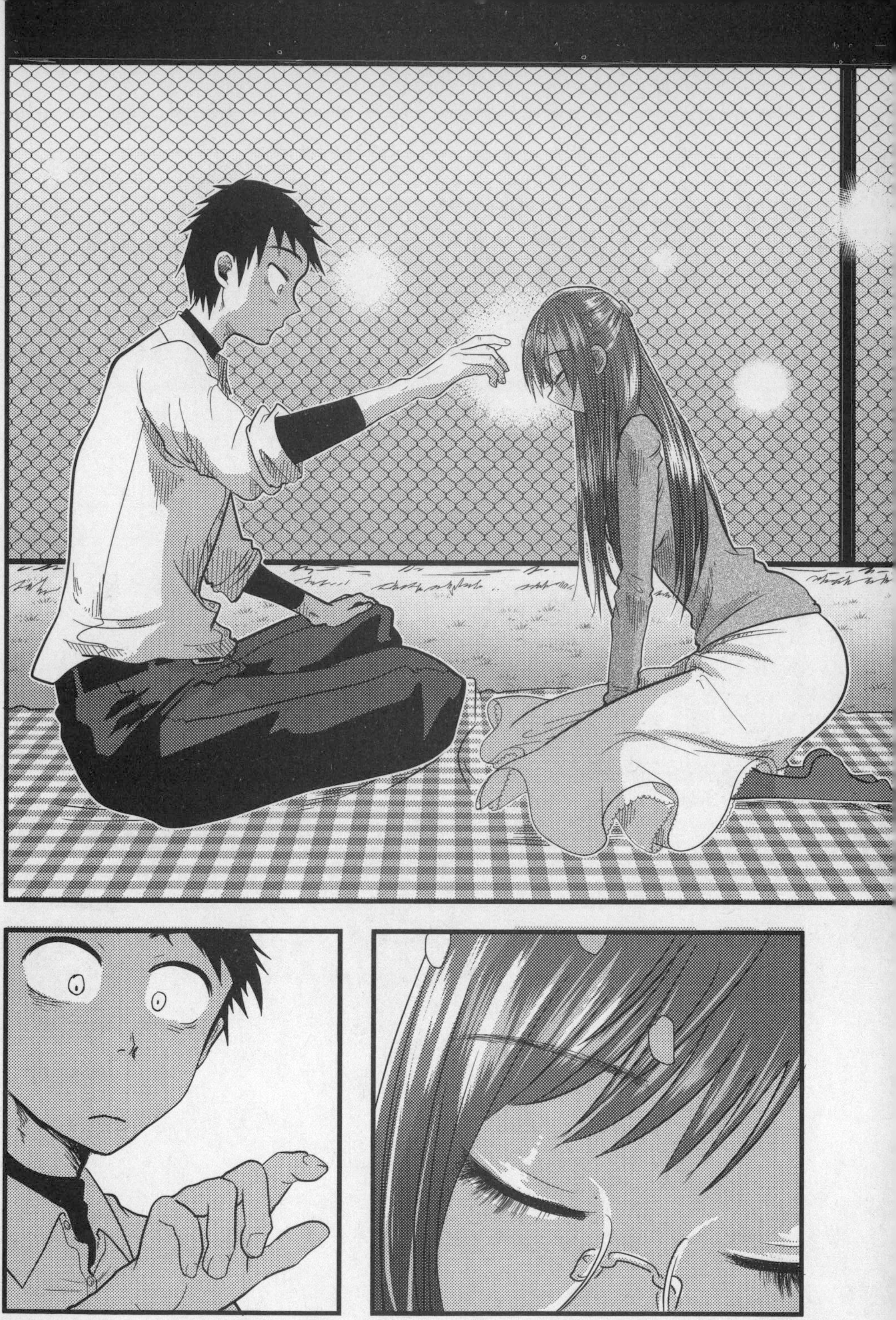

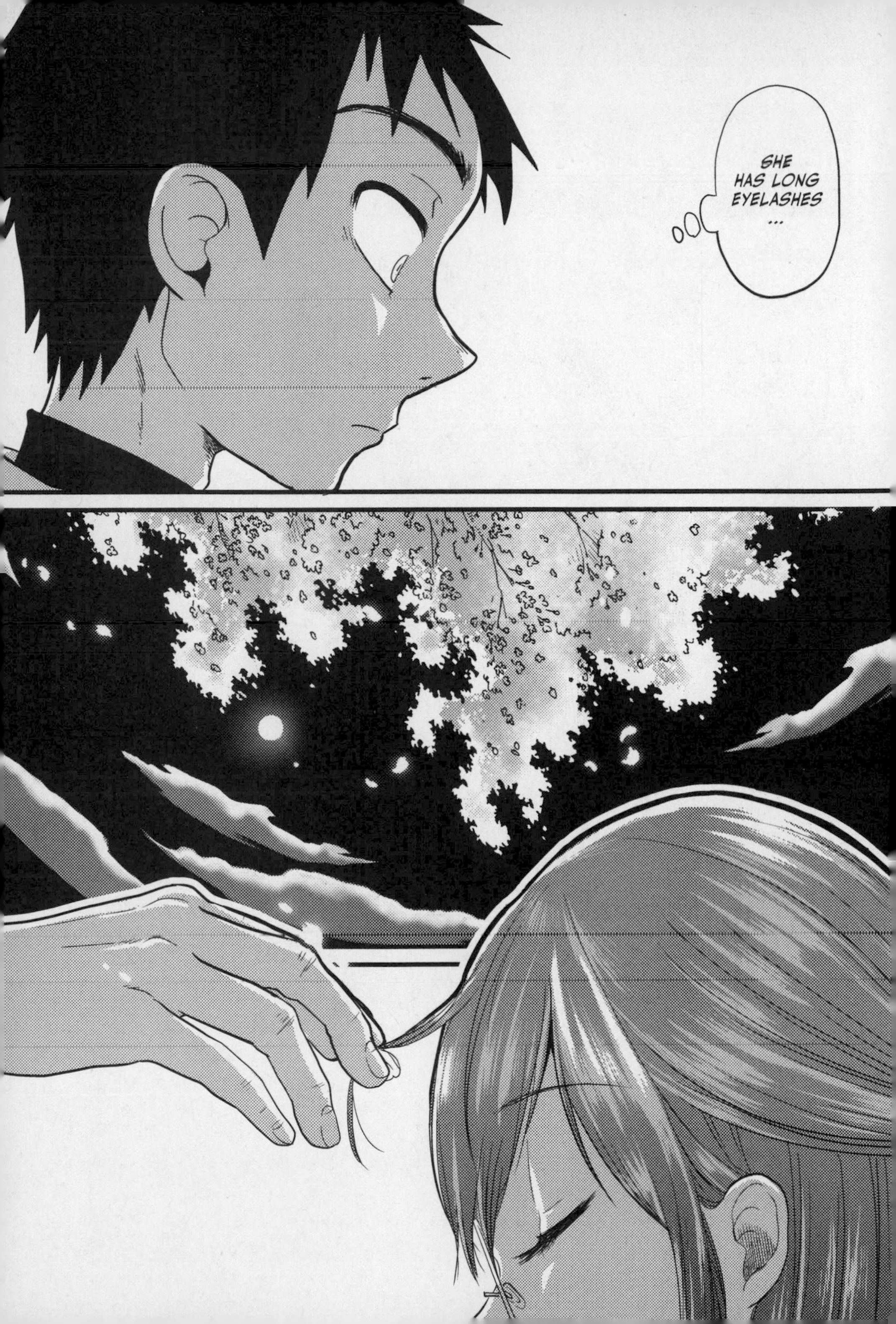
SHE HAS LONG EYELASHES ...

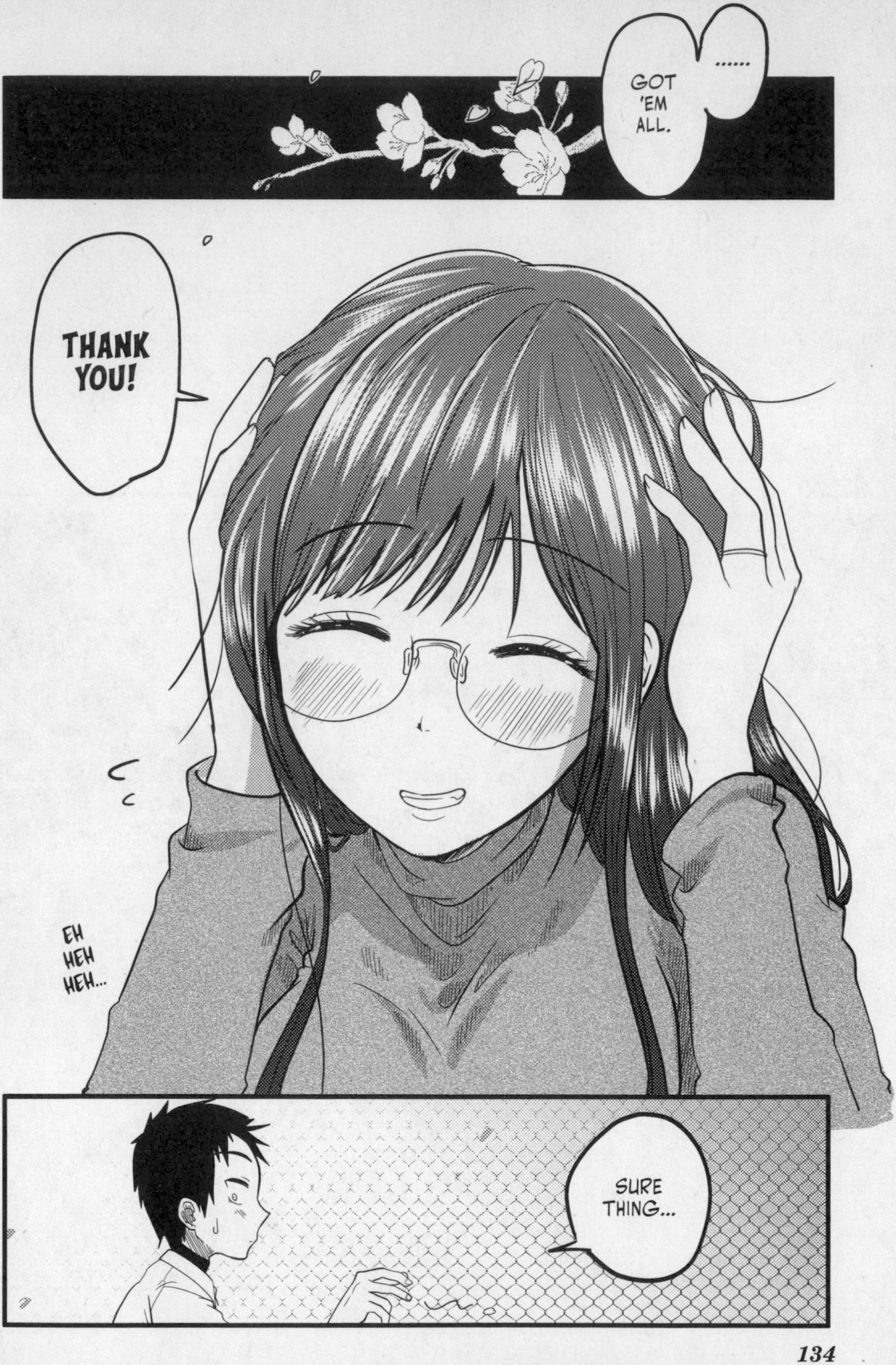
......
GOT 'EM ALL.
THANK YOU!
EH HEH HEH...
SURE THING...

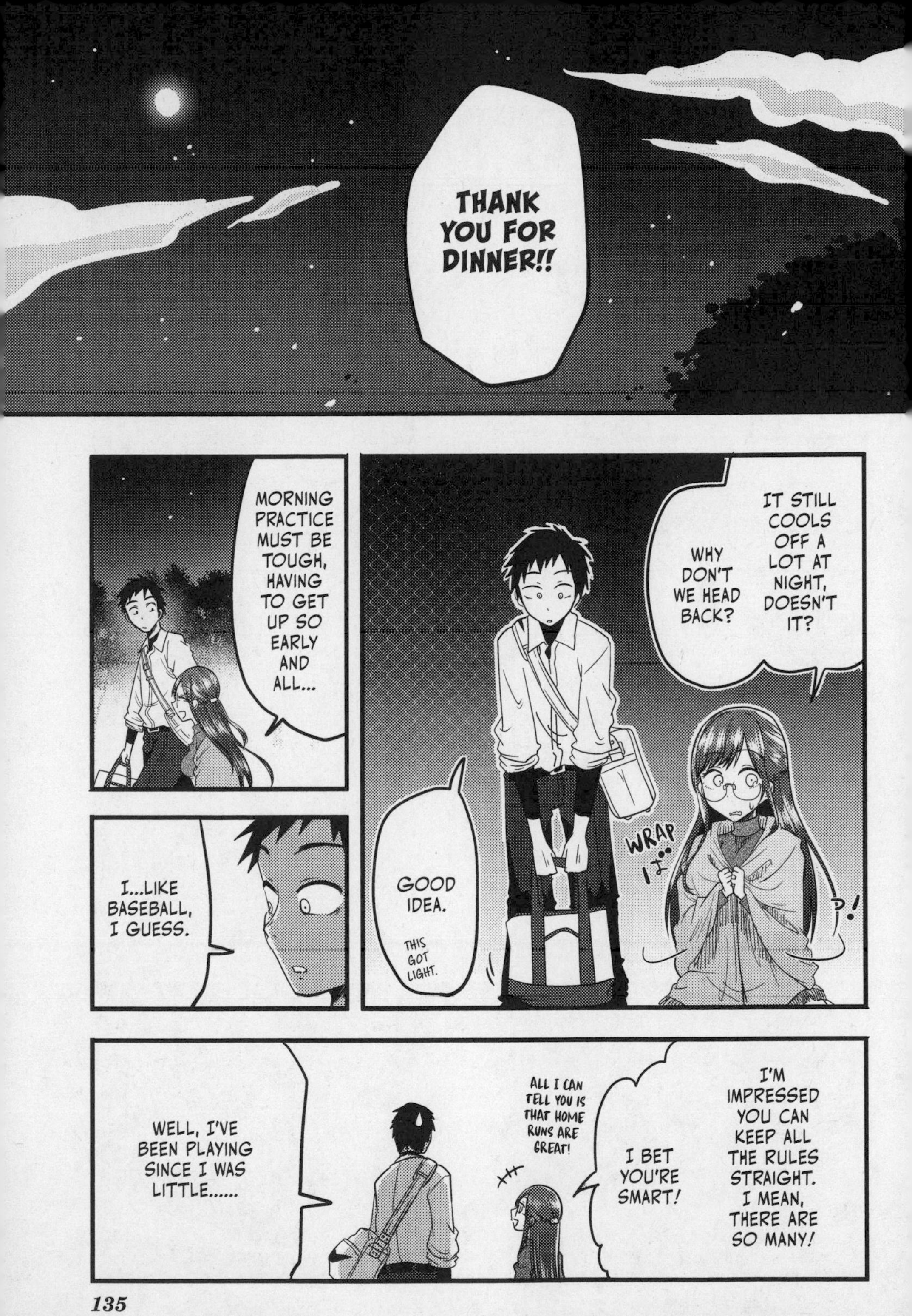
THANK YOU FOR DINNER!!
IT STILL COOLS OFF A LOT AT NIGHT, DOESN'T IT?
WHY DON'T WE HEAD BACK?
WRAP
GOOD IDEA.
THIS GOT LIGHT.
MORNING PRACTICE MUST BE TOUGH, HAVING TO GET UP SO EARLY AND ALL...
I...LIKE BASEBALL, I GUESS.
I'M IMPRESSED YOU CAN KEEP ALL THE RULES STRAIGHT. I MEAN, THERE ARE SO MANY!
I BET YOU'RE SMART!
ALL I CAN TELL YOU IS THAT HOME RUNS ARE GREAT!
WELL, I'VE BEEN PLAYING SINCE I WAS LITTLE......

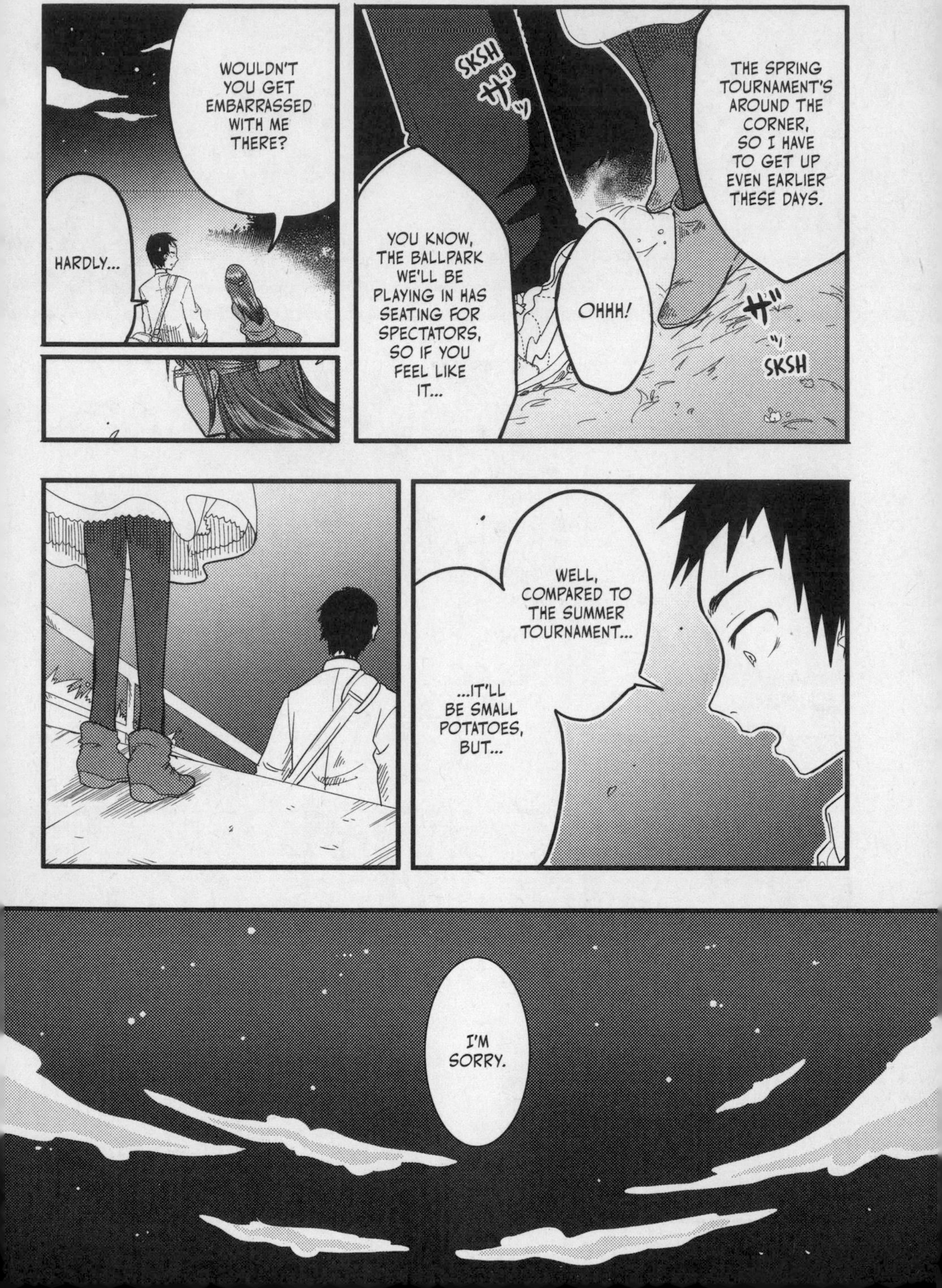
THE SPRING TOURNAMENT'S AROUND THE CORNER, SO I HAVE TO GET UP EVEN EARLIER THESE DAYS.
ザッ
SKSH
OHHH!
SKSH
ザッ
YOU KNOW, THE BALLPARK WE'LL BE PLAYING IN HAS SEATING FOR SPECTATORS, SO IF YOU FEEL LIKE IT...
WOULDN'T YOU GET EMBARRASSED WITH ME THERE?
HARDLY...
WELL, COMPARED TO THE SUMMER TOURNAMENT...
...IT'LL BE SMALL POTATOES, BUT...
I'M SORRY.

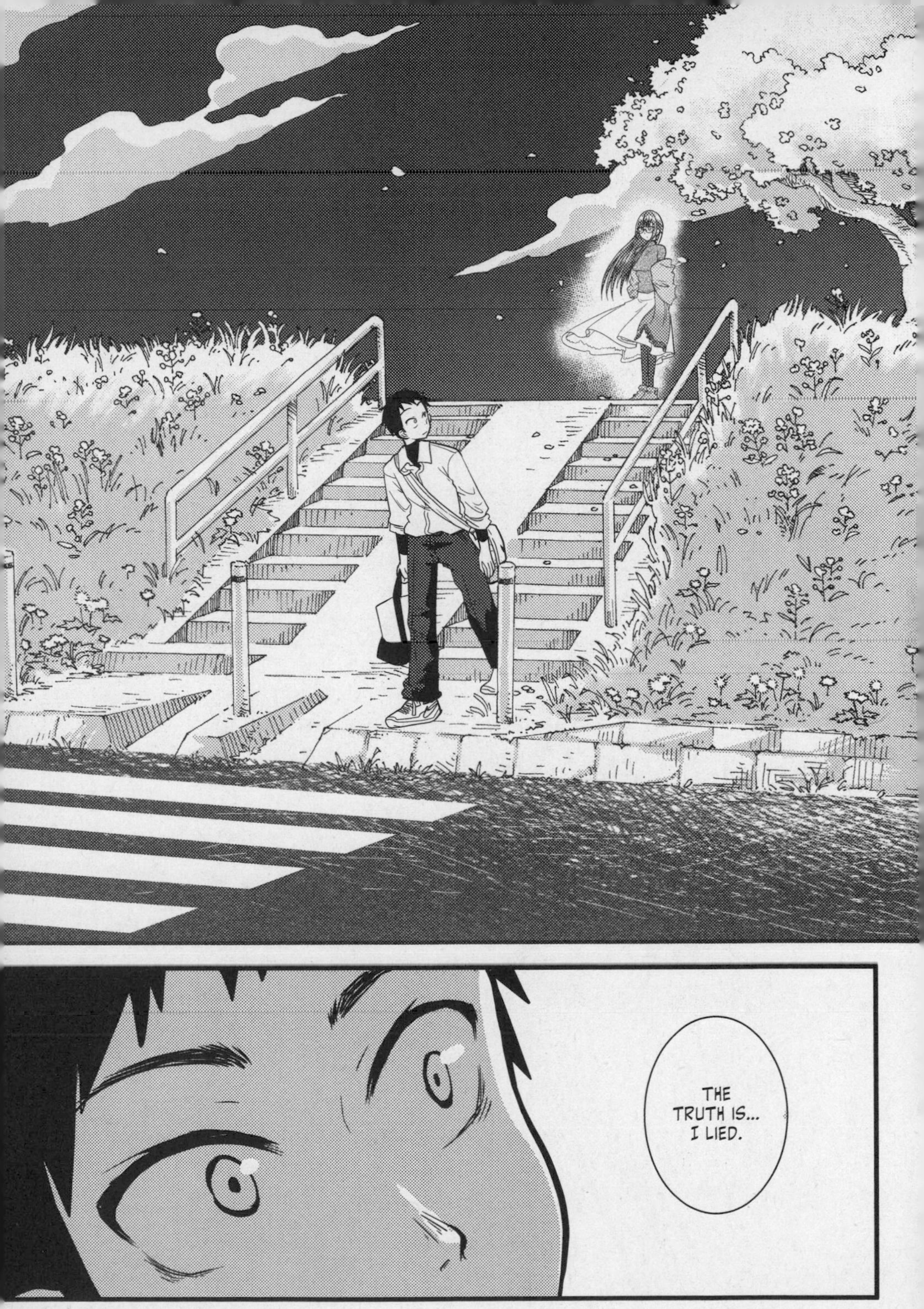
THE TRUTH IS... I LIED.

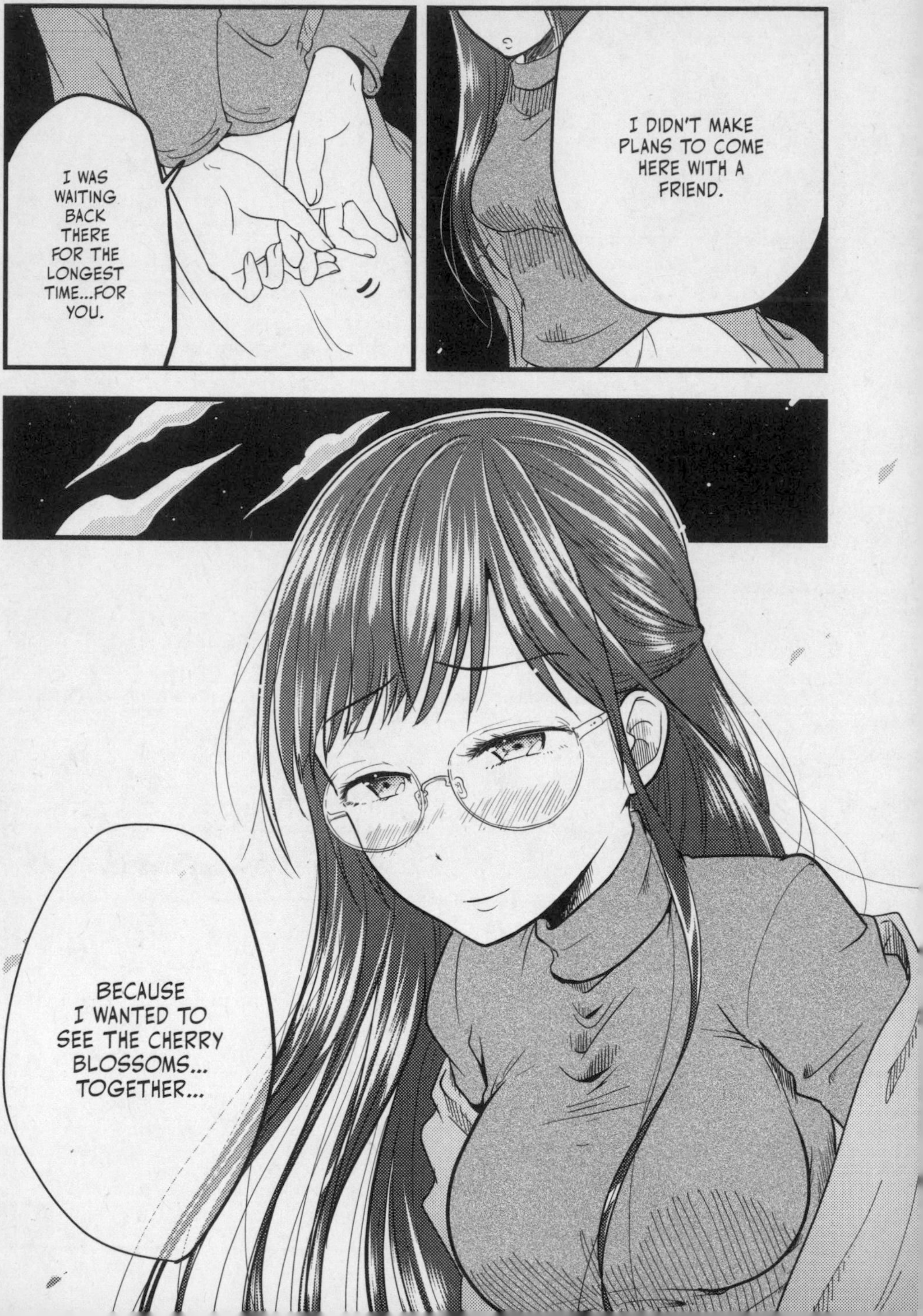
I DIDN'T MAKE PLANS TO COME HERE WITH A FRIEND.
I WAS WAITING BACK THERE FOR THE LONGEST TIME...FOR YOU.
BECAUSE I WANTED TO SEE THE CHERRY BLOSSOMS... TOGETHER...

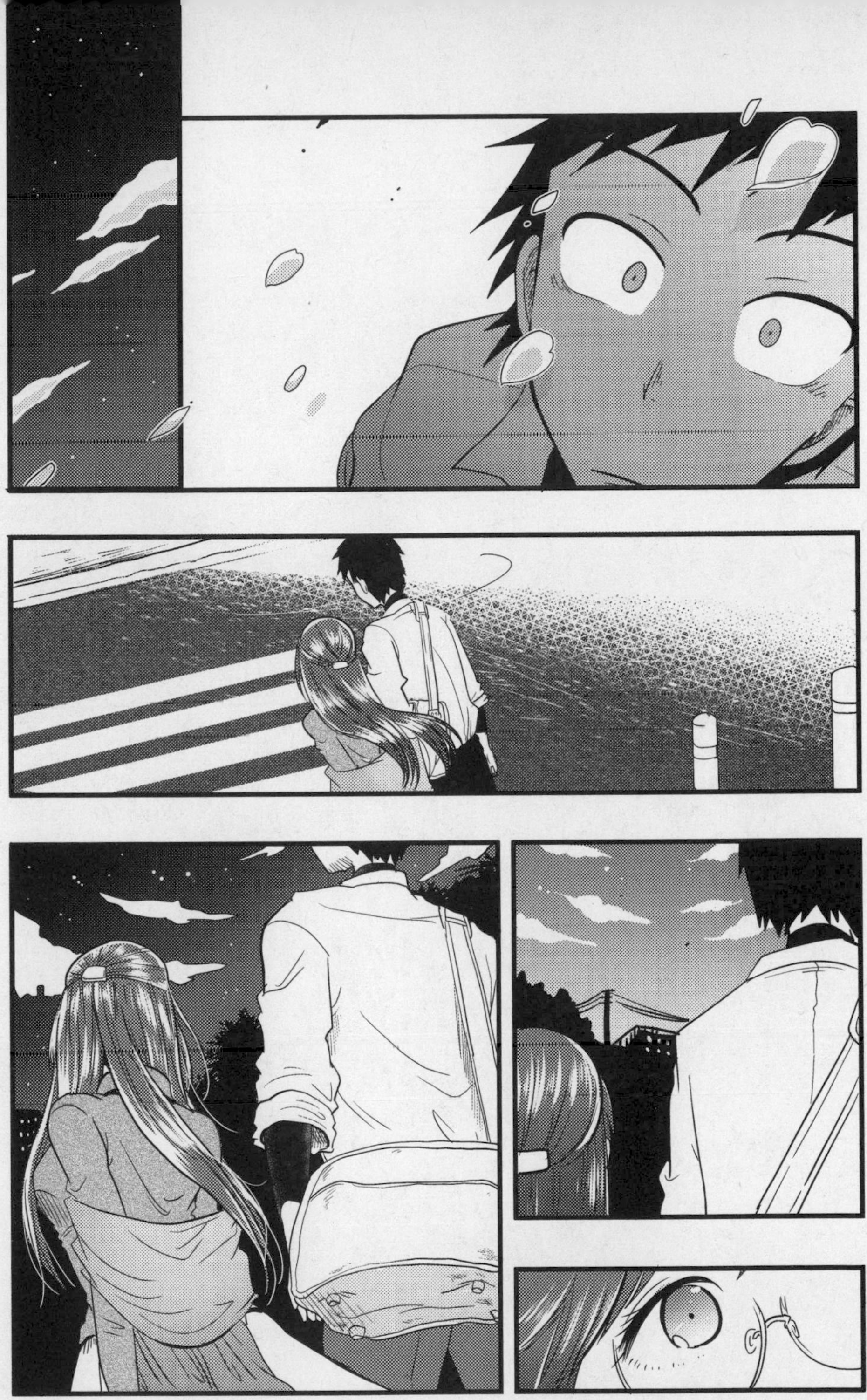

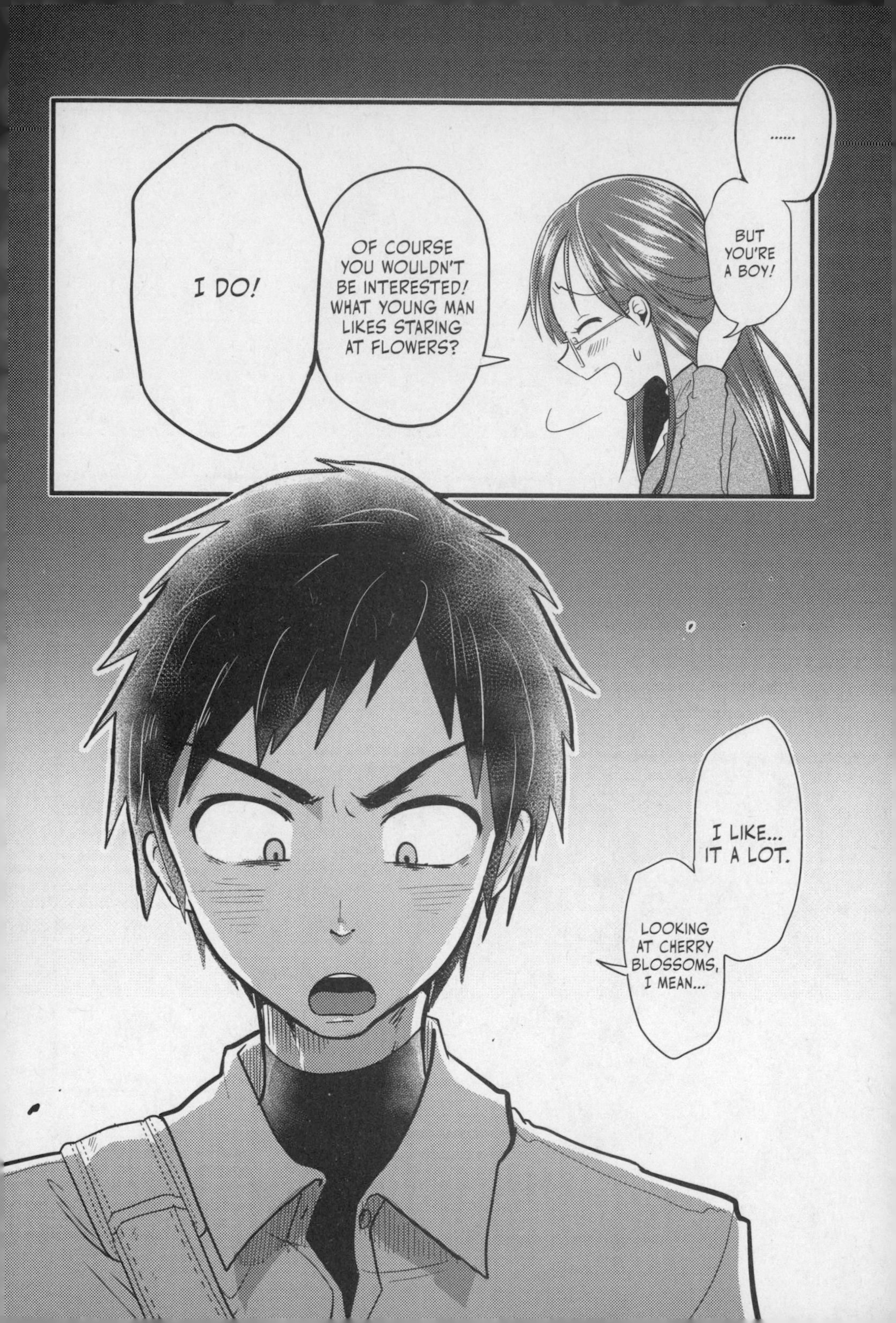
......
BUT YOU'RE A BOY!
OF COURSE YOU WOULDN'T BE INTERESTED! WHAT YOUNG MAN LIKES STARING AT FLOWERS?
I DO!
I LIKE... IT A LOT.
LOOKING AT CHERRY BLOSSOMS, I MEAN...

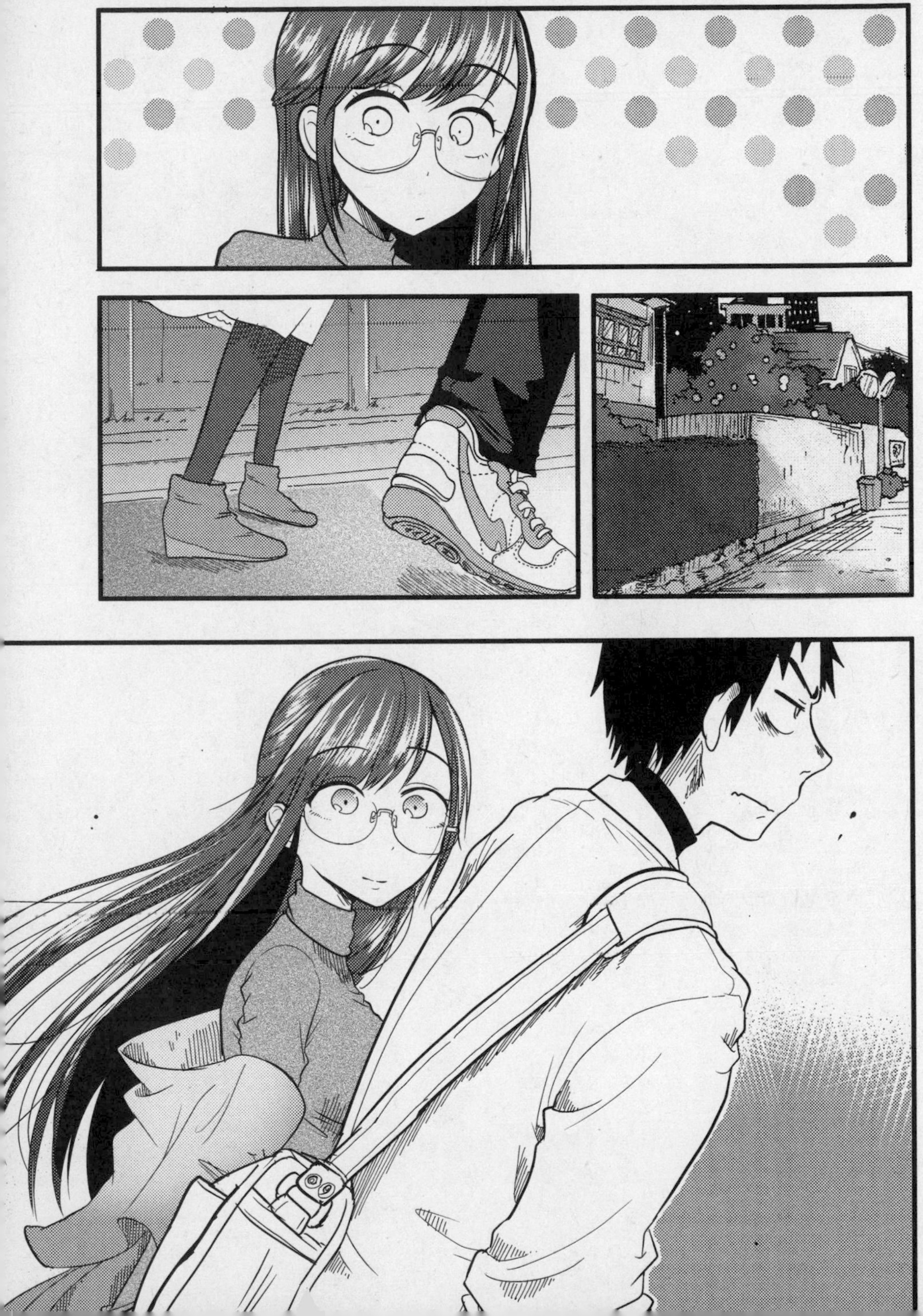

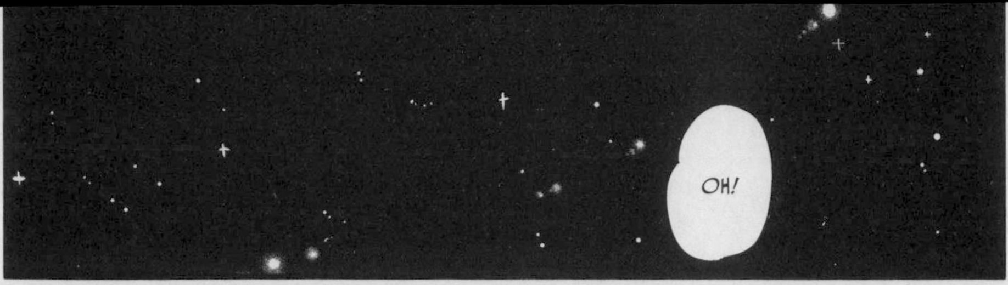
OH!
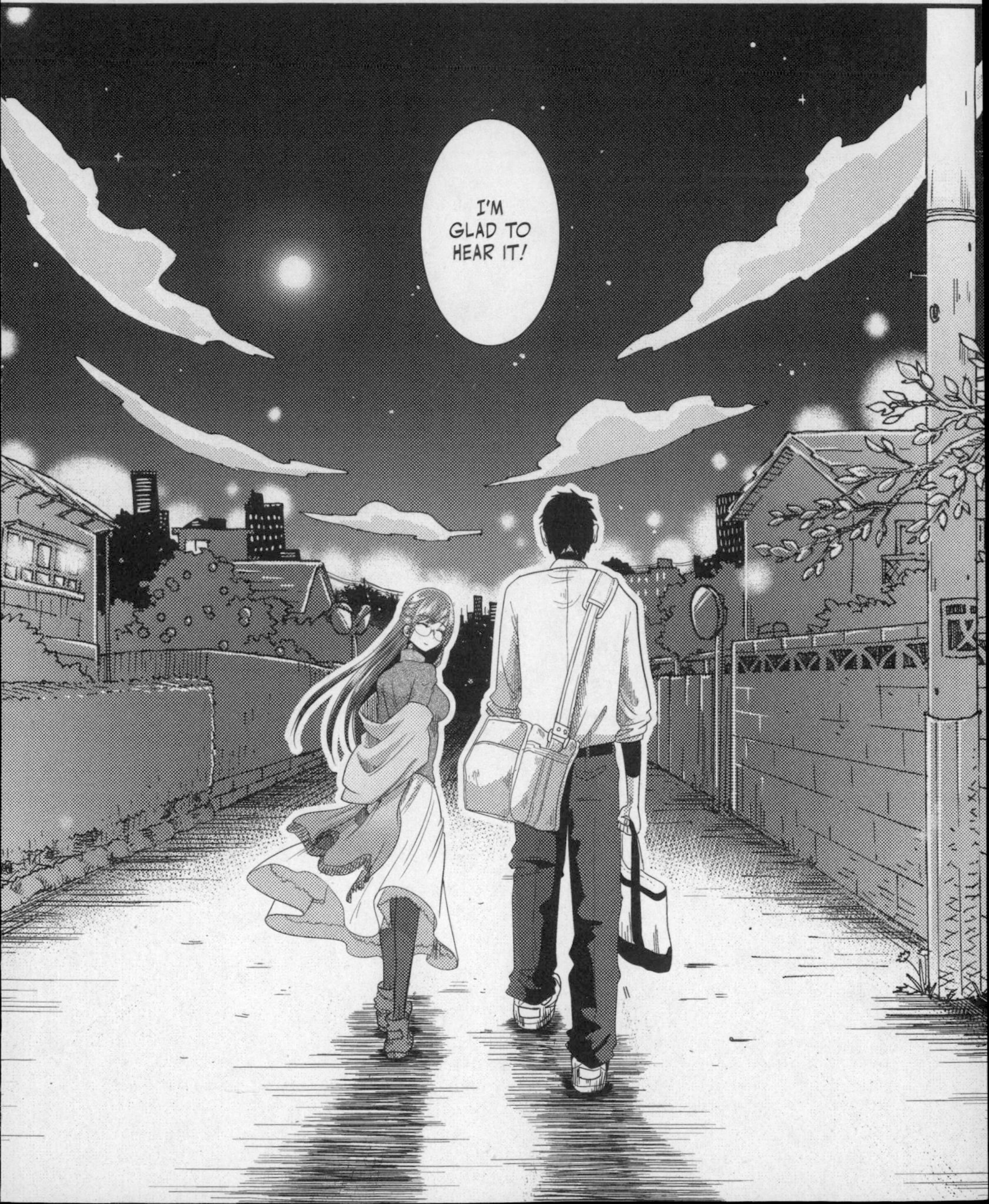
I'M GLAD TO HEAR IT!

Beauty and the FEAST

Beauty and the FEAST

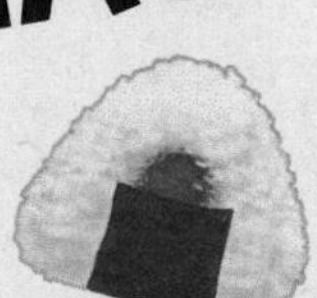

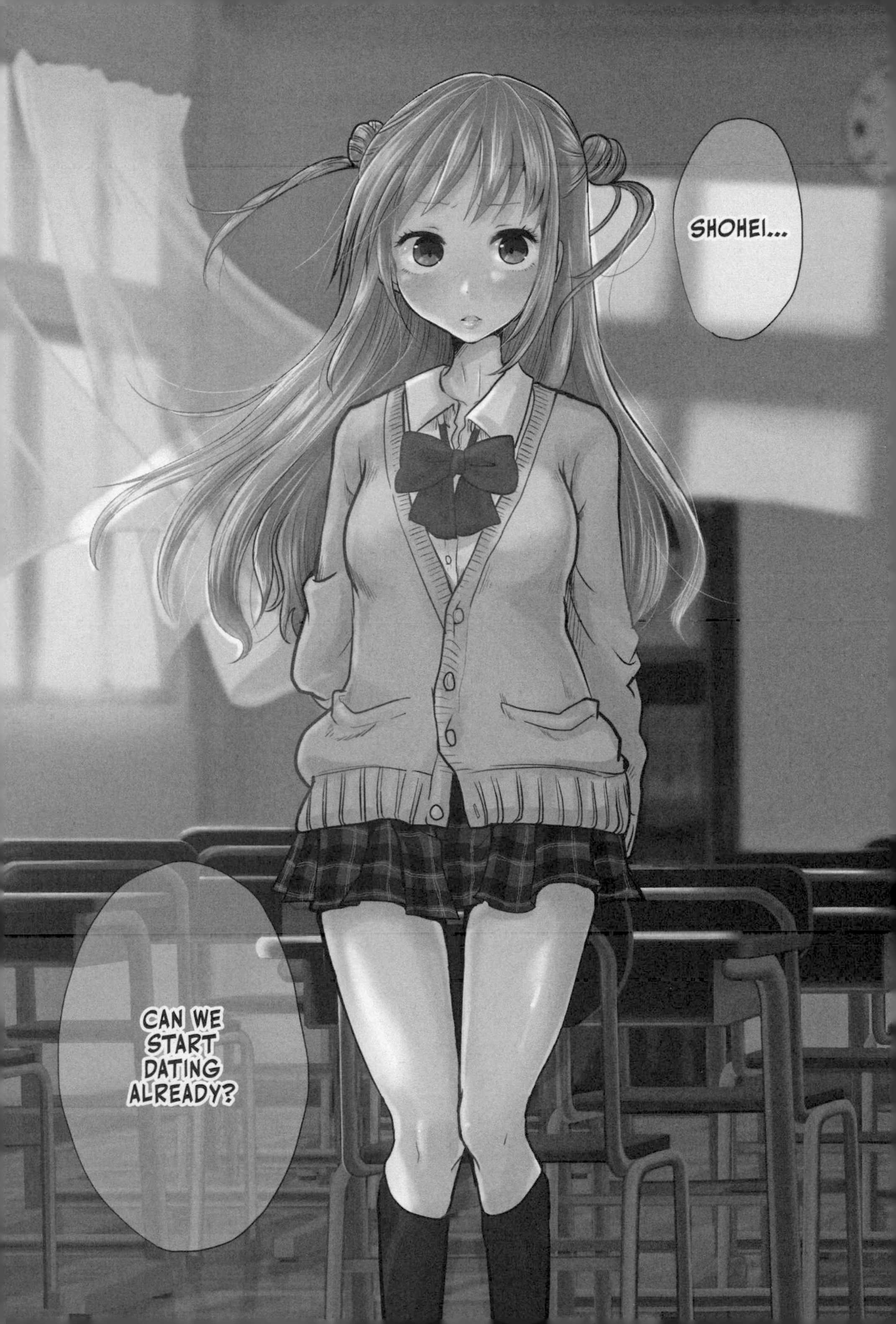
SHOHEI...
CAN WE START DATING ALREADY?

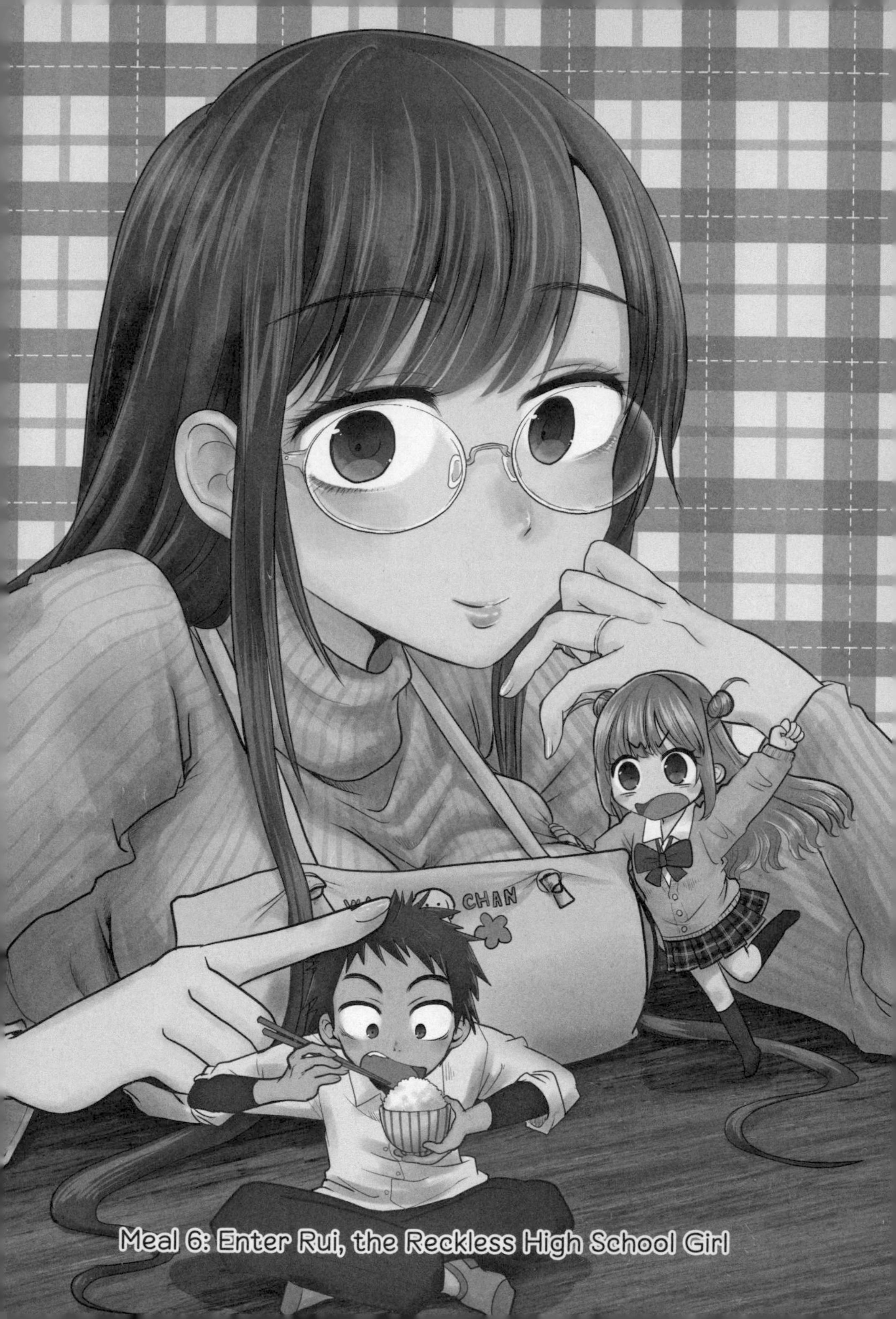
CHAN

Meal 6: Enter Rui, the Reckless High School Girl

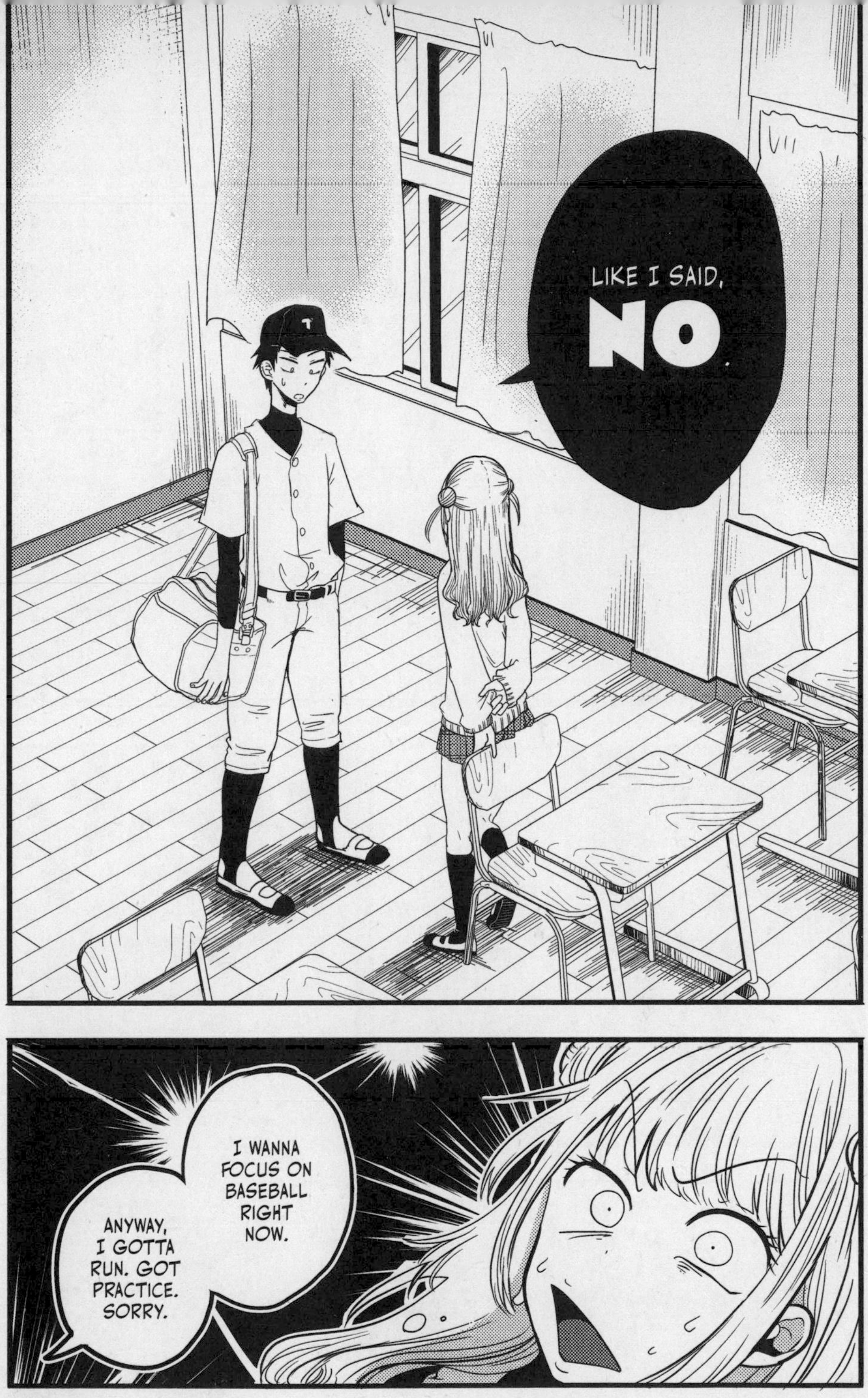
LIKE I SAID, NO.
I WANNA FOCUS ON BASEBALL RIGHT NOW.
ANYWAY, I GOTTA RUN. GOT PRACTICE. SORRY.

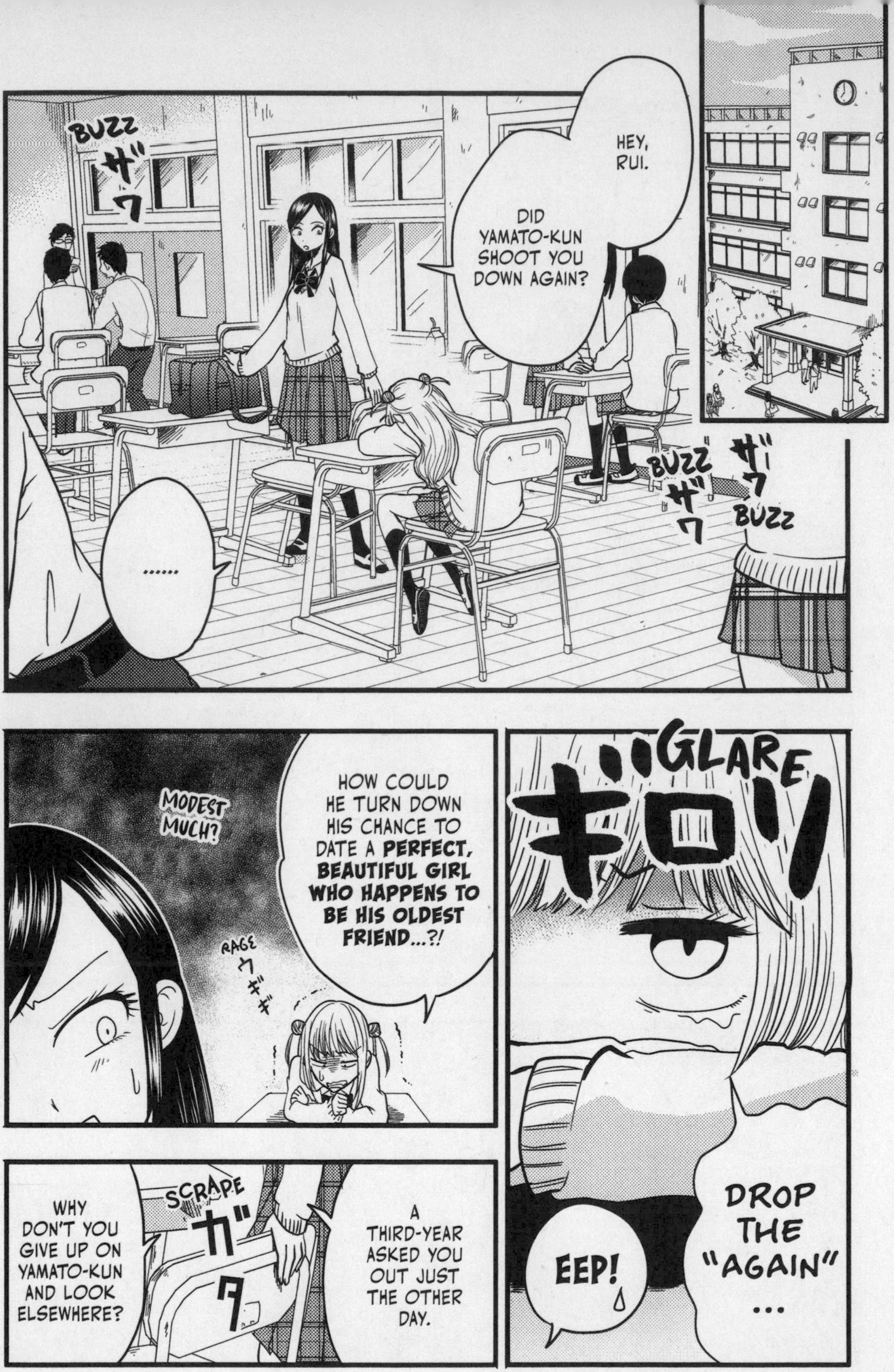

HEY, RUI.
DID YAMATO-KUN SHOOT YOU DOWN AGAIN?
BUZZ ザワ
BUZZ ザワ
BUZZ ザワ
......
GLARE
ギロッ
DROP THE "AGAIN" ...
EEP!
HOW COULD HE TURN DOWN HIS CHANCE TO DATE A **PERFECT, BEAUTIFUL GIRL WHO HAPPENS TO BE HIS OLDEST FRIEND...?!**
MODEST MUCH?
RAGE ウギギ
A THIRD-YEAR ASKED YOU OUT JUST THE OTHER DAY.
SCRAPE ガタ
WHY DON'T YOU GIVE UP ON YAMATO-KUN AND LOOK ELSEWHERE?

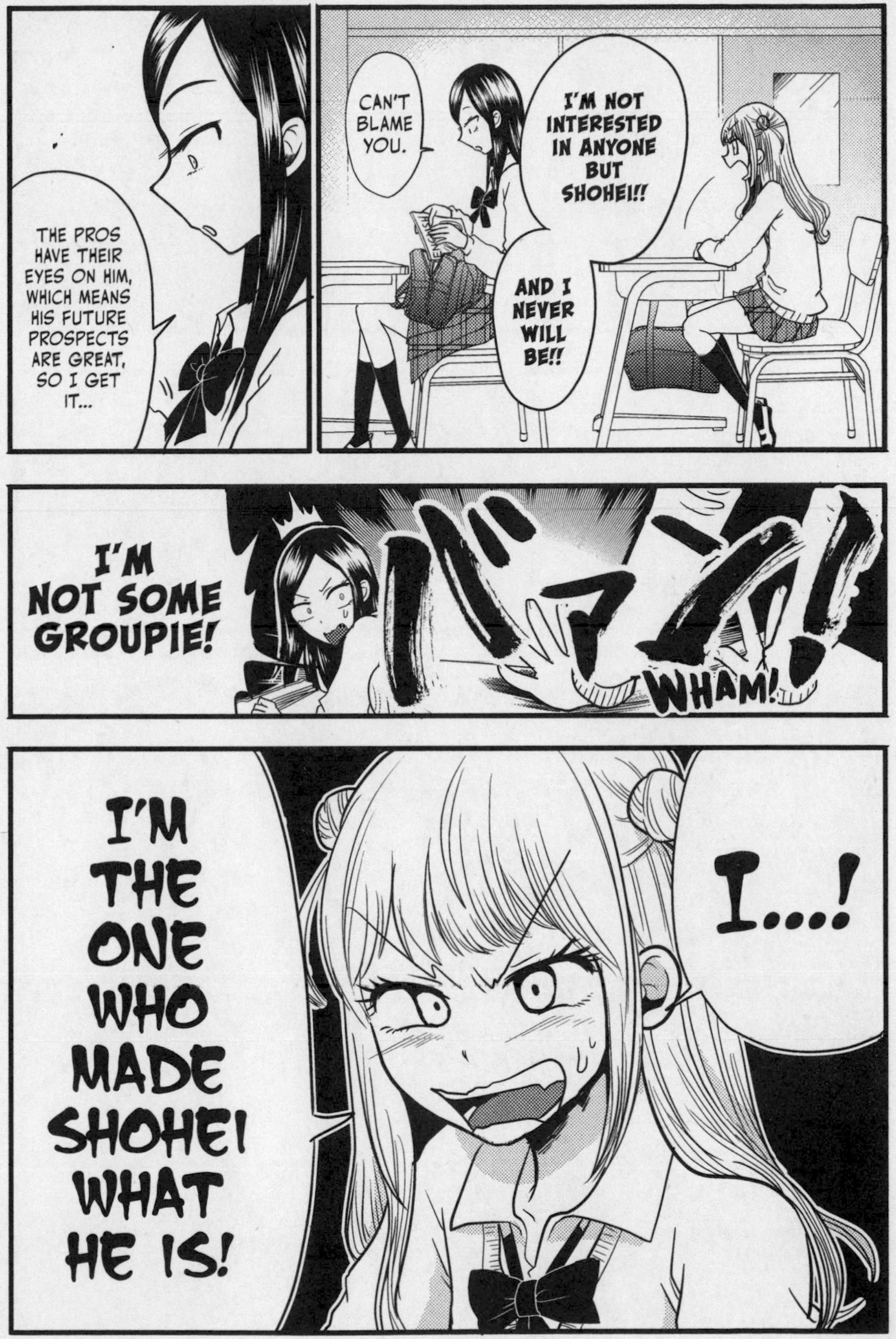
I'M NOT INTERESTED IN ANYONE BUT SHOHEI!!
AND I NEVER WILL BE!!
CAN'T BLAME YOU.
THE PROS HAVE THEIR EYES ON HIM, WHICH MEANS HIS FUTURE PROSPECTS ARE GREAT, SO I GET IT...
バァン!
WHAM!
I'M NOT SOME GROUPIE!
I...!
I'M THE ONE WHO MADE SHOHEI WHAT HE IS!

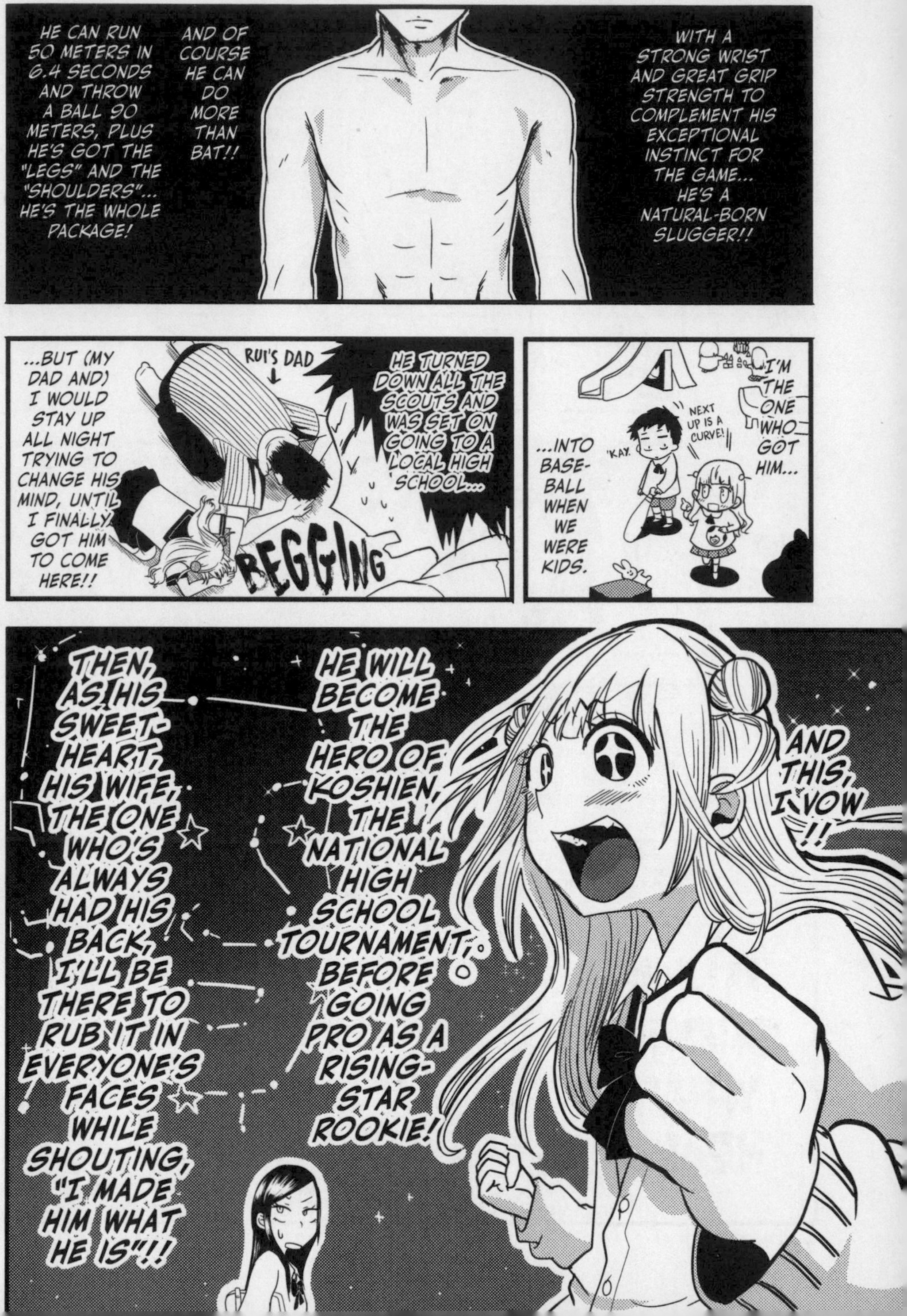
WITH A STRONG WRIST AND GREAT GRIP STRENGTH TO COMPLEMENT HIS EXCEPTIONAL INSTINCT FOR THE GAME... HE'S A NATURAL-BORN SLUGGER!!
AND OF COURSE HE CAN DO MORE THAN BAT!!
HE CAN RUN 50 METERS IN 6.4 SECONDS AND THROW A BALL 90 METERS, PLUS HE'S GOT THE "LEGS" AND THE "SHOULDERS"... HE'S THE WHOLE PACKAGE!
I'M THE ONE WHO GOT HIM...
NEXT UP IS A CURVE!
'KAY.
...INTO BASE-BALL WHEN WE WERE KIDS.
HE TURNED DOWN ALL THE SCOUTS AND WAS SET ON GOING TO A LOCAL HIGH SCHOOL...
RUI'S DAD
...BUT (MY DAD AND) I WOULD STAY UP ALL NIGHT TRYING TO CHANGE HIS MIND, UNTIL I FINALLY GOT HIM TO COME HERE!!
BEGGING
AND THIS, I VOW!!
HE WILL BECOME THE HERO OF KOSHIEN, THE NATIONAL HIGH SCHOOL TOURNAMENT, BEFORE GOING PRO AS A RISING-STAR ROOKIE!
THEN, AS HIS SWEET-HEART, HIS WIFE, THE ONE WHO'S ALWAYS HAD HIS BACK, I'LL BE THERE TO RUB IT IN EVERYONE'S FACES WHILE SHOUTING, "I MADE HIM WHAT HE IS"!!

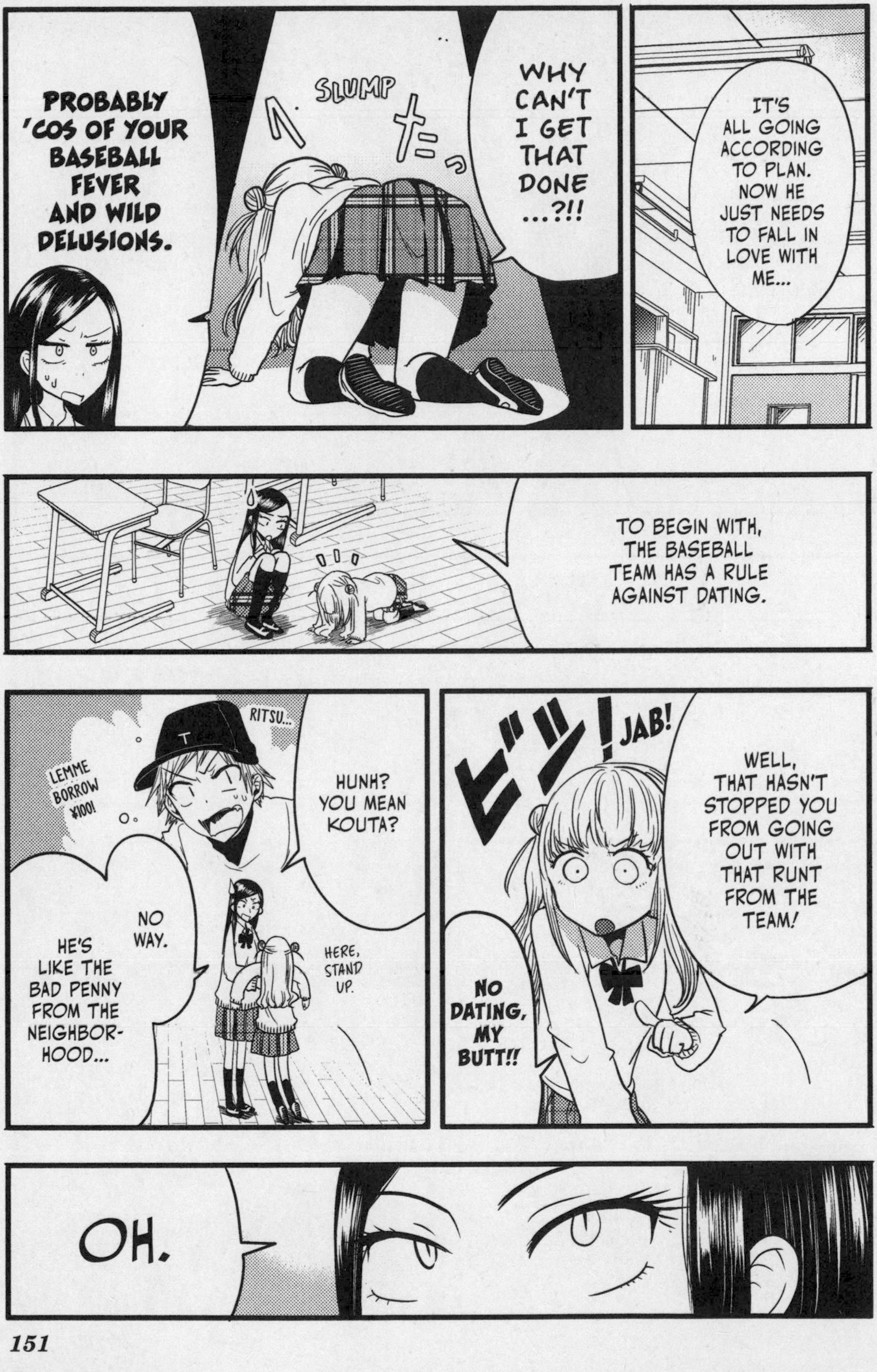
IT'S ALL GOING ACCORDING TO PLAN. NOW HE JUST NEEDS TO FALL IN LOVE WITH ME...
WHY CAN'T I GET THAT DONE ...?!!
SLUMP
PROBABLY 'COS OF YOUR BASEBALL FEVER AND WILD DELUSIONS.
TO BEGIN WITH, THE BASEBALL TEAM HAS A RULE AGAINST DATING.
JAB!
WELL, THAT HASN'T STOPPED YOU FROM GOING OUT WITH THAT RUNT FROM THE TEAM!
NO DATING, MY BUTT!!
HUNH? YOU MEAN KOUTA?
RITSU...
LEMME BORROW ¥100!
HERE, STAND UP.
NO WAY.
HE'S LIKE THE BAD PENNY FROM THE NEIGHBOR-HOOD...
OH.

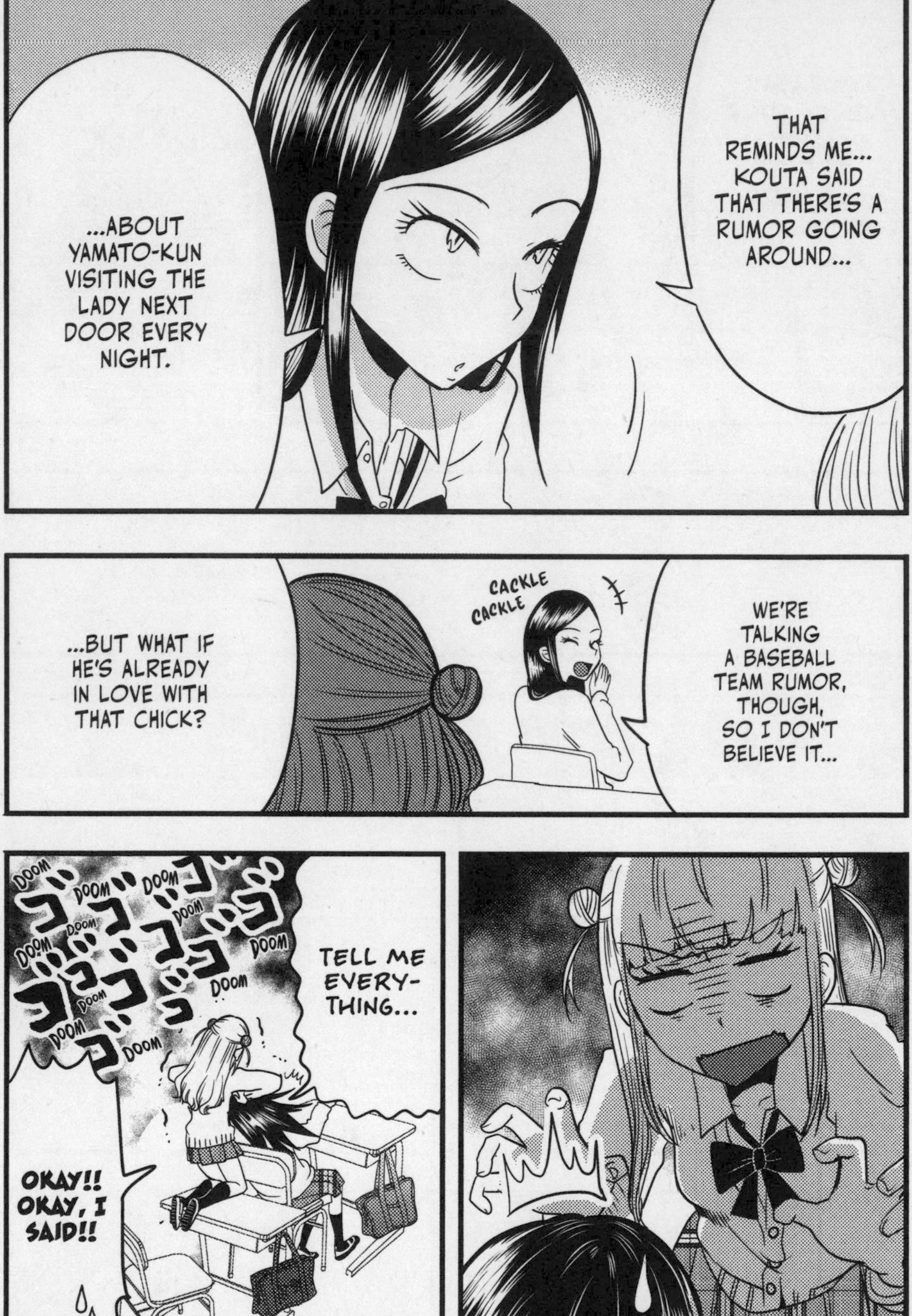
THAT REMINDS ME... KOUTA SAID THAT THERE'S A RUMOR GOING AROUND...
...ABOUT YAMATO-KUN VISITING THE LADY NEXT DOOR EVERY NIGHT.
WE'RE TALKING A BASEBALL TEAM RUMOR, THOUGH, SO I DON'T BELIEVE IT...
CACKLE CACKLE
...BUT WHAT IF HE'S ALREADY IN LOVE WITH THAT CHICK?
TELL ME EVERY-THING...
DOOM DOOM DOOM DOOM DOOM DOOM DOOM DOOM DOOM DOOM DOOM
OKAY!! OKAY, I SAID!!

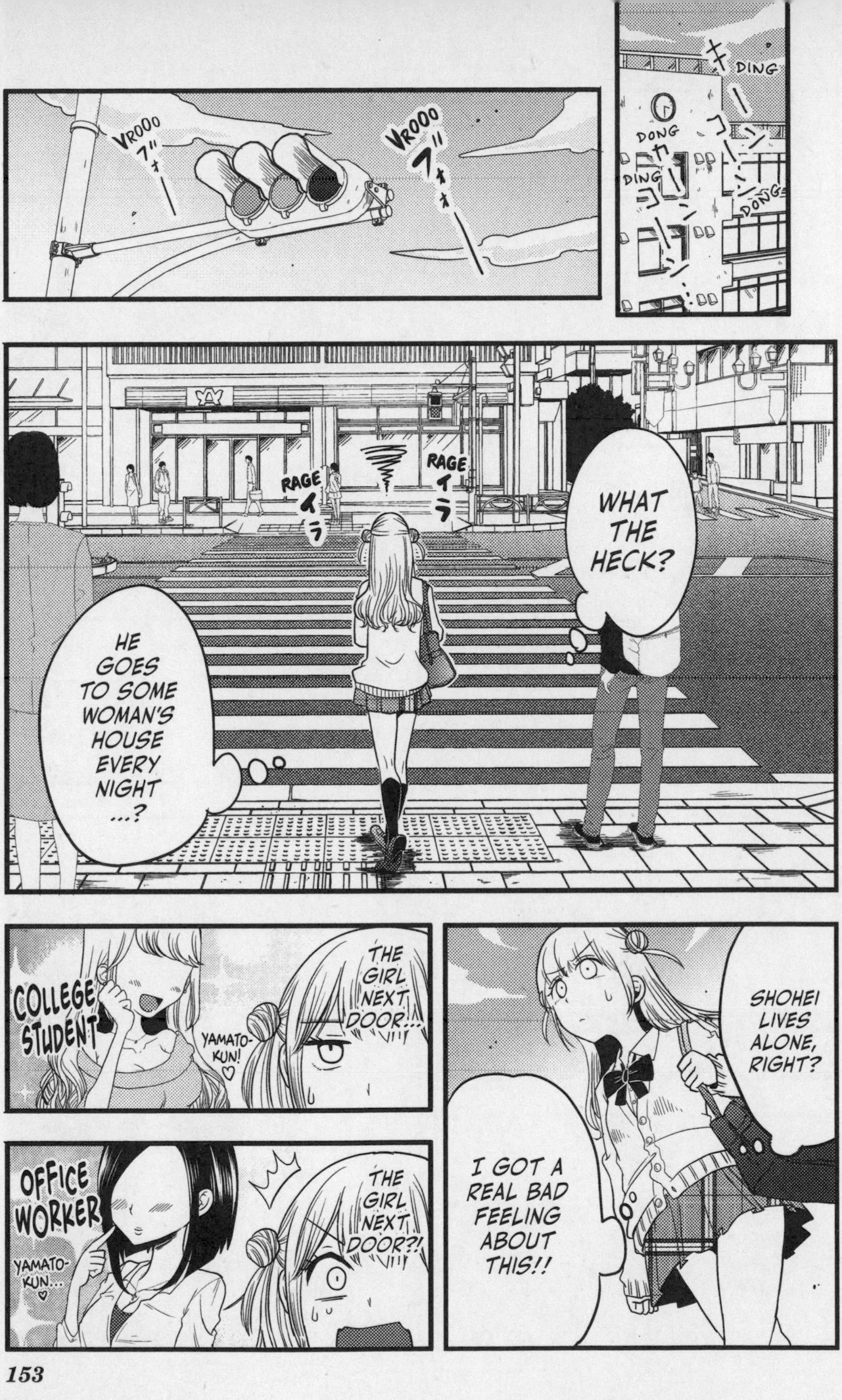

DING
DONG
DING
DONG
VROOO
VROOO
RAGE
RAGE
WHAT THE HECK?
HE GOES TO SOME WOMAN'S HOUSE EVERY NIGHT ...?
SHOHEI LIVES ALONE, RIGHT?
I GOT A REAL BAD FEELING ABOUT THIS!!
THE GIRL NEXT DOOR...
YAMATO-KUN! ♡
COLLEGE STUDENT
THE GIRL NEXT DOOR?!
YAMATO-KUN... ♡
OFFICE WORKER

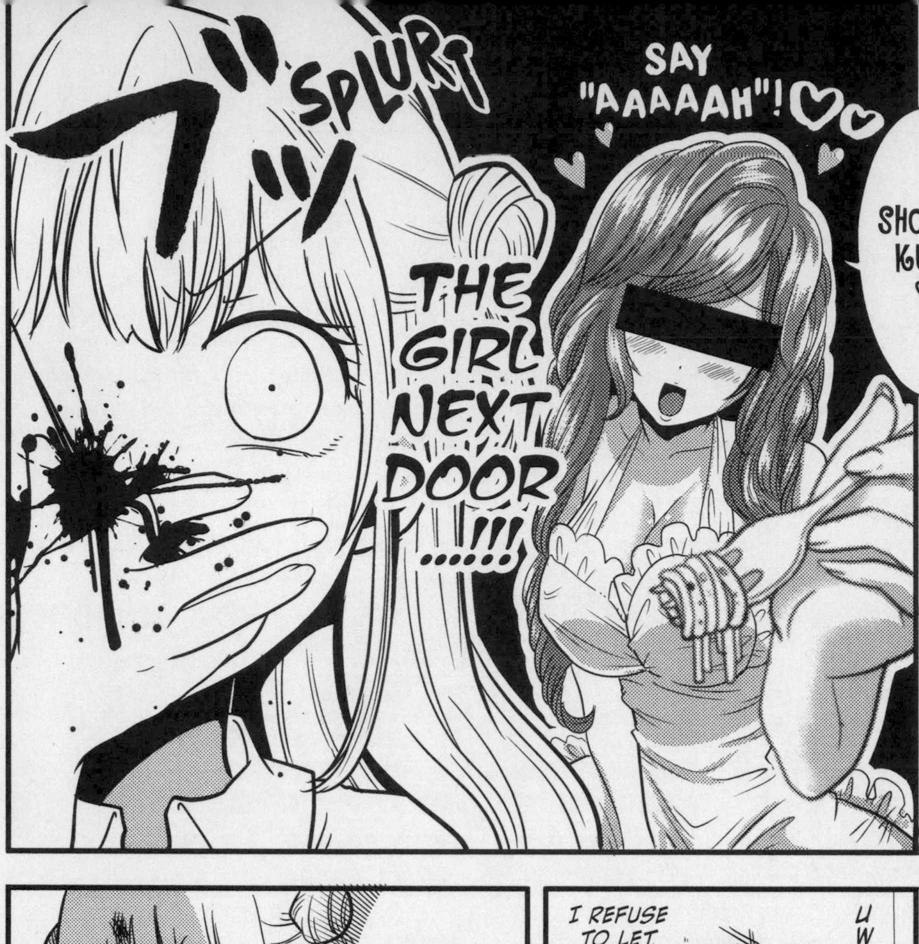
SAY "AAAAAH"! ♡
SHOHEI-KUN! ♡
SPLURT
THE GIRL NEXT DOOR ......!!!
I REFUSE TO LET SOMETHING OUT OF A TABLOID OR DIRTY NOVEL HAPPEN ON MY WATCH!!
UWOOOOOAH!!
BAM
ガン
BAM
UNTIL SHOHEI REALIZES WHAT A CATCH I AM...
HFF! HFF!
...I'LL EXTERMINATE ANY AND ALL WOMEN WHO COZY UP TO HIM!!

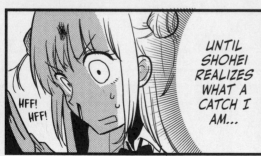

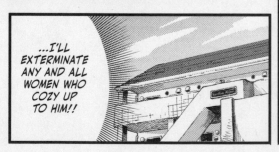

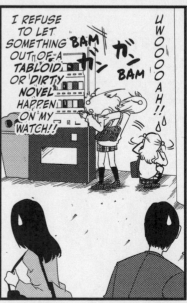

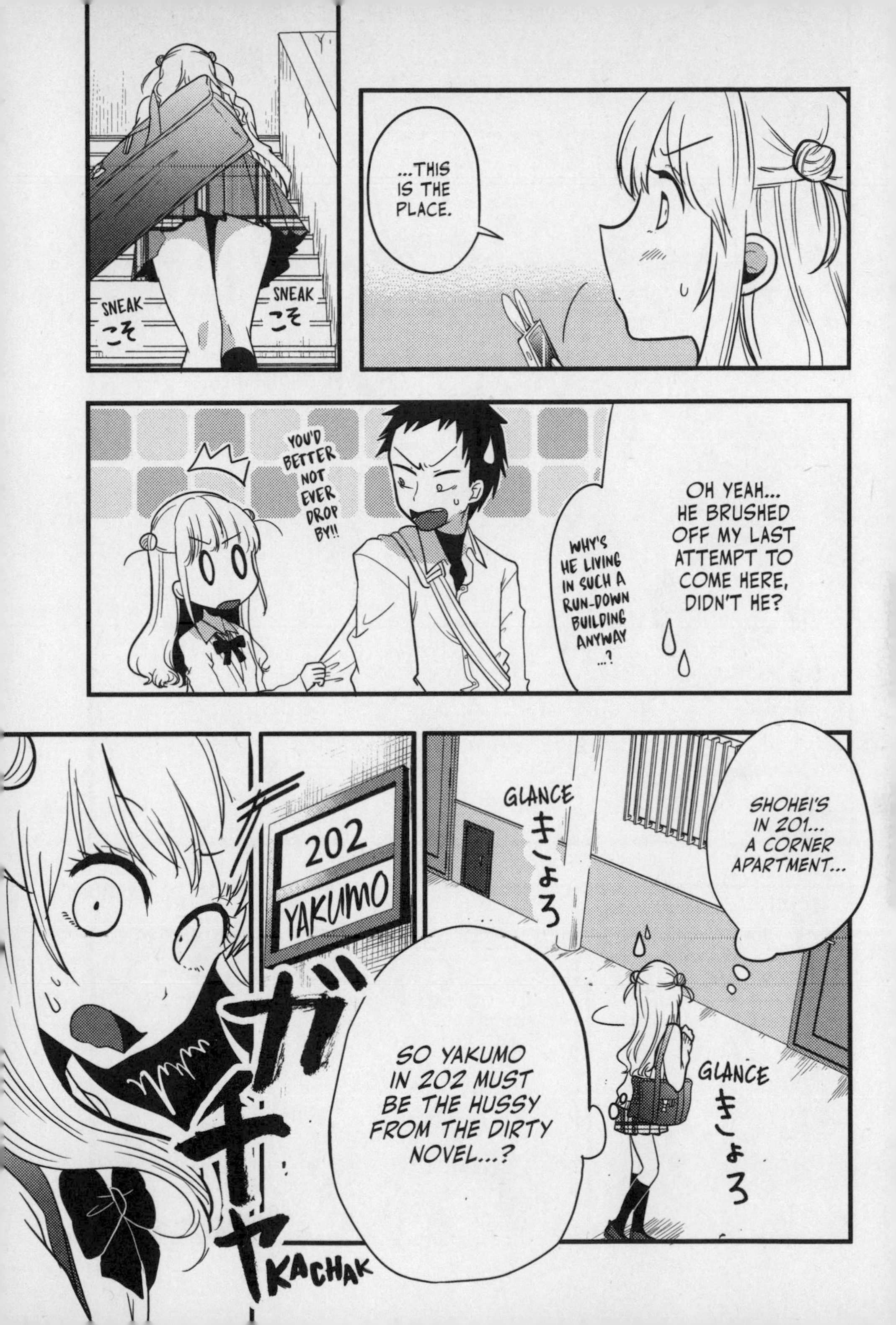
...THIS IS THE PLACE.
SNEAK こそ
SNEAK こそ
OH YEAH... HE BRUSHED OFF MY LAST ATTEMPT TO COME HERE, DIDN'T HE?
WHY'S HE LIVING IN SUCH A RUN-DOWN BUILDING ANYWAY ...?
YOU'D BETTER NOT EVER DROP BY!!
SHOHEI'S IN 201... A CORNER APARTMENT...
GLANCE きょろ
GLANCE きょろ
SO YAKUMO IN 202 MUST BE THE HUSSY FROM THE DIRTY NOVEL...?
202
YAKUMO
ガチャ
KACHAK

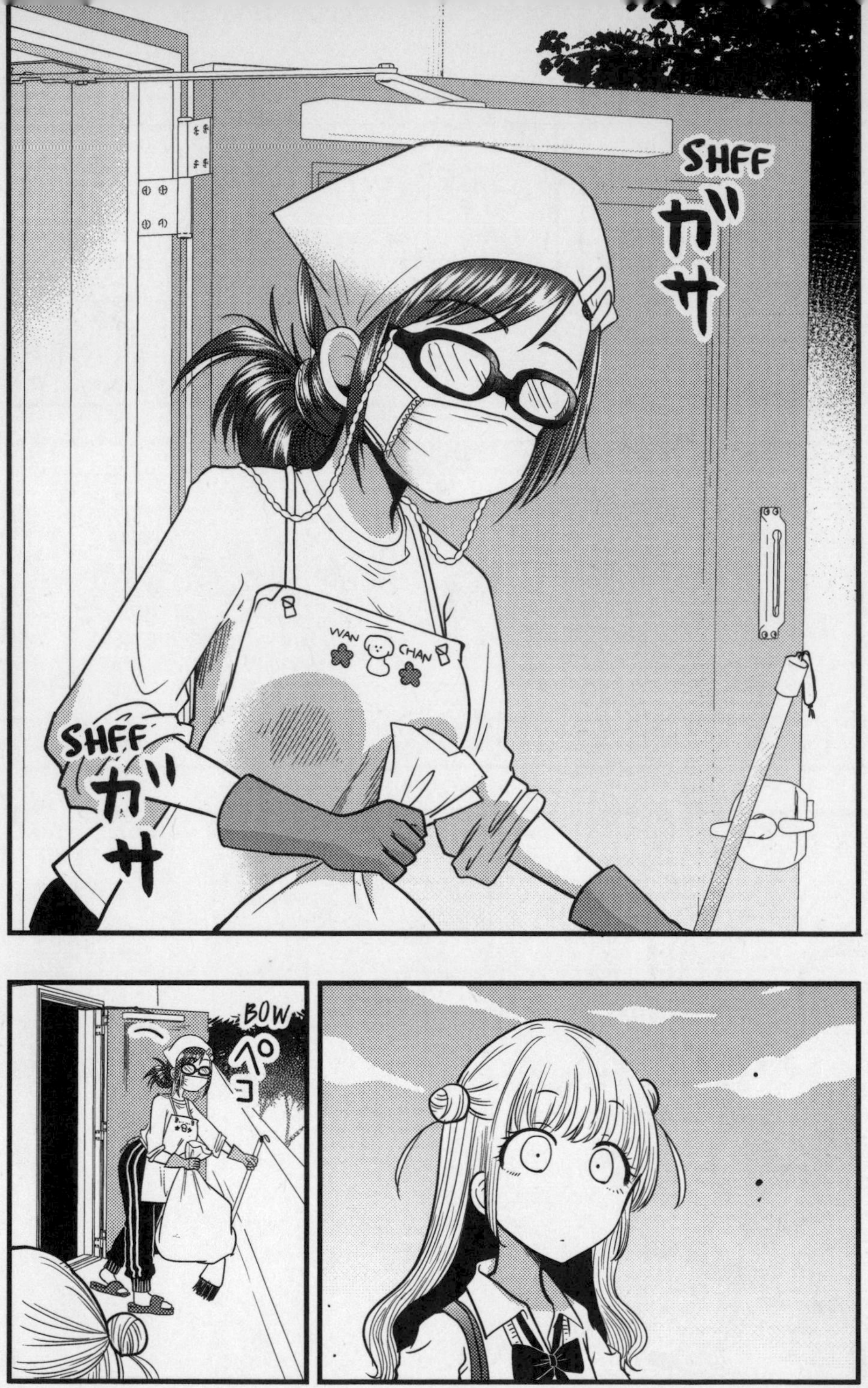
SHFF
ガサ
SHFF
ガサ
BOW
ペコ

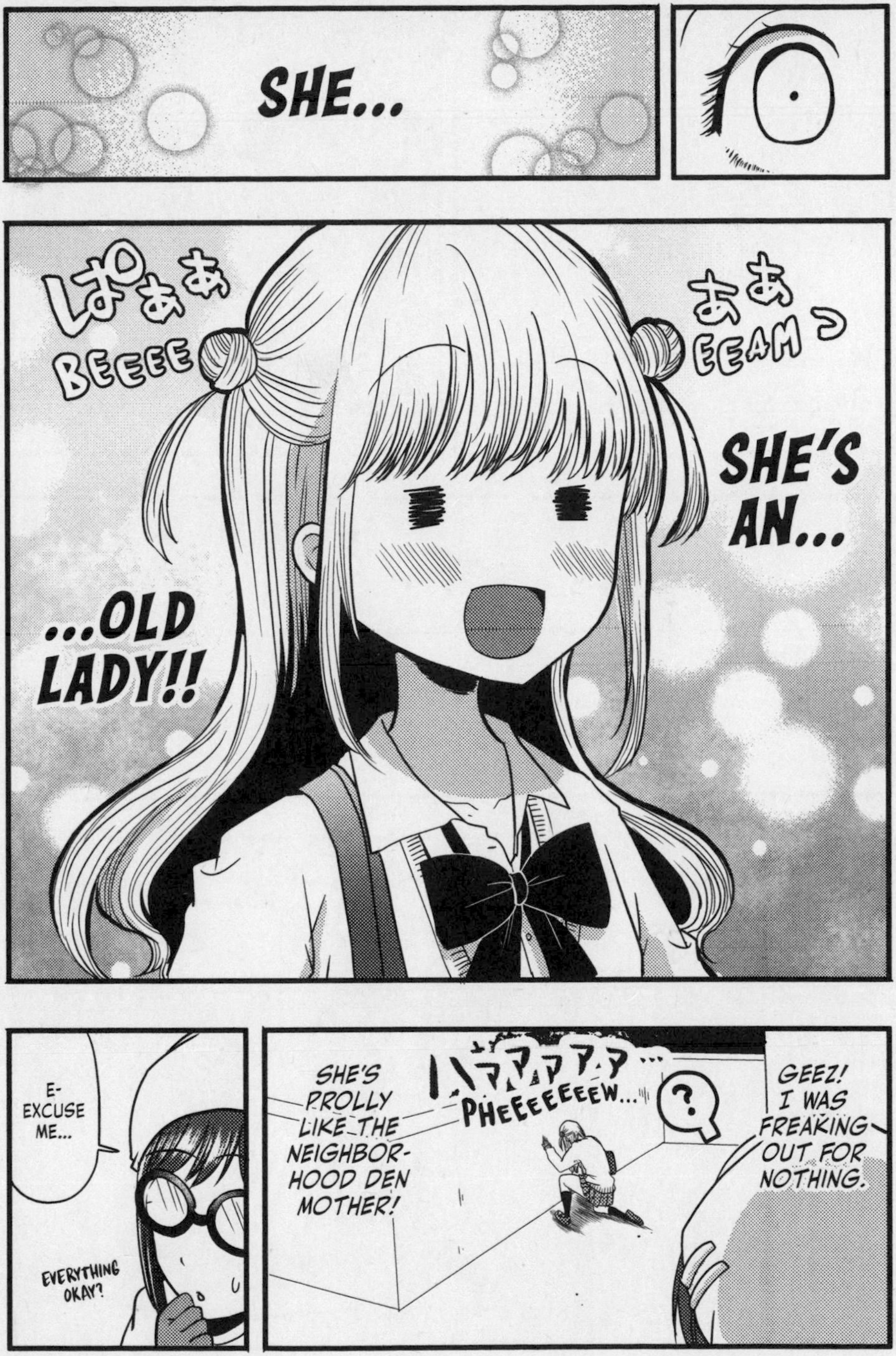
SHE...
ぱぁぁ BEEEE
ああっ EEAM
SHE'S AN...
...OLD LADY!!
GEEZ! I WAS FREAKING OUT FOR NOTHING.
?
ハァァァァァ... PHEEEEEEW...
SHE'S PROLLY LIKE THE NEIGHBOR-HOOD DEN MOTHER!
E-EXCUSE ME...
EVERYTHING OKAY?

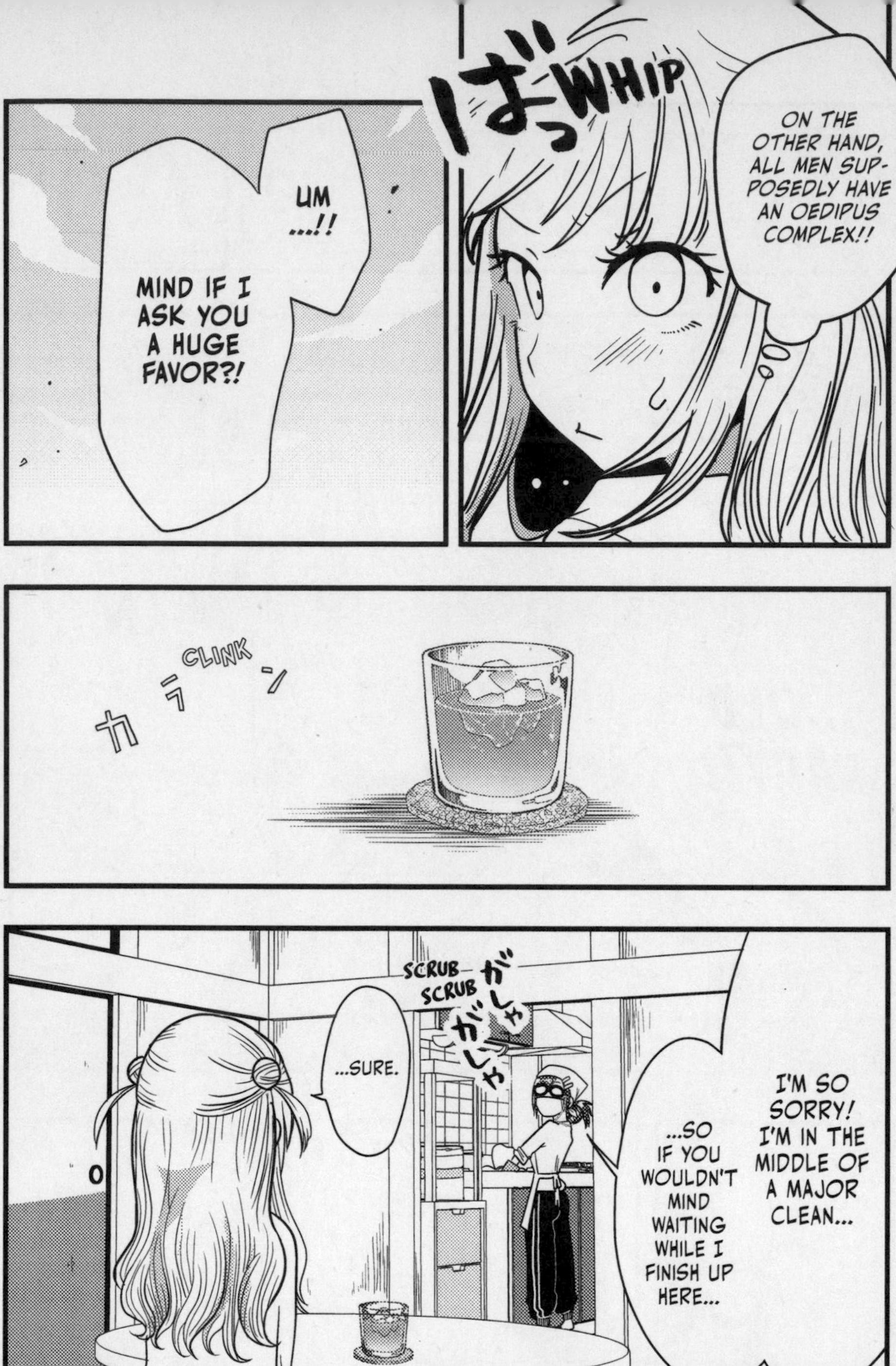
ばっ WHIP
ON THE OTHER HAND, ALL MEN SUPPOSEDLY HAVE AN OEDIPUS COMPLEX!!
UM ...!!
MIND IF I ASK YOU A HUGE FAVOR?!
CLINK
カラン
I'M SO SORRY! I'M IN THE MIDDLE OF A MAJOR CLEAN...
...SO IF YOU WOULDN'T MIND WAITING WHILE I FINISH UP HERE...
SCRUB SCRUB
がしゃがしゃ
...SURE.

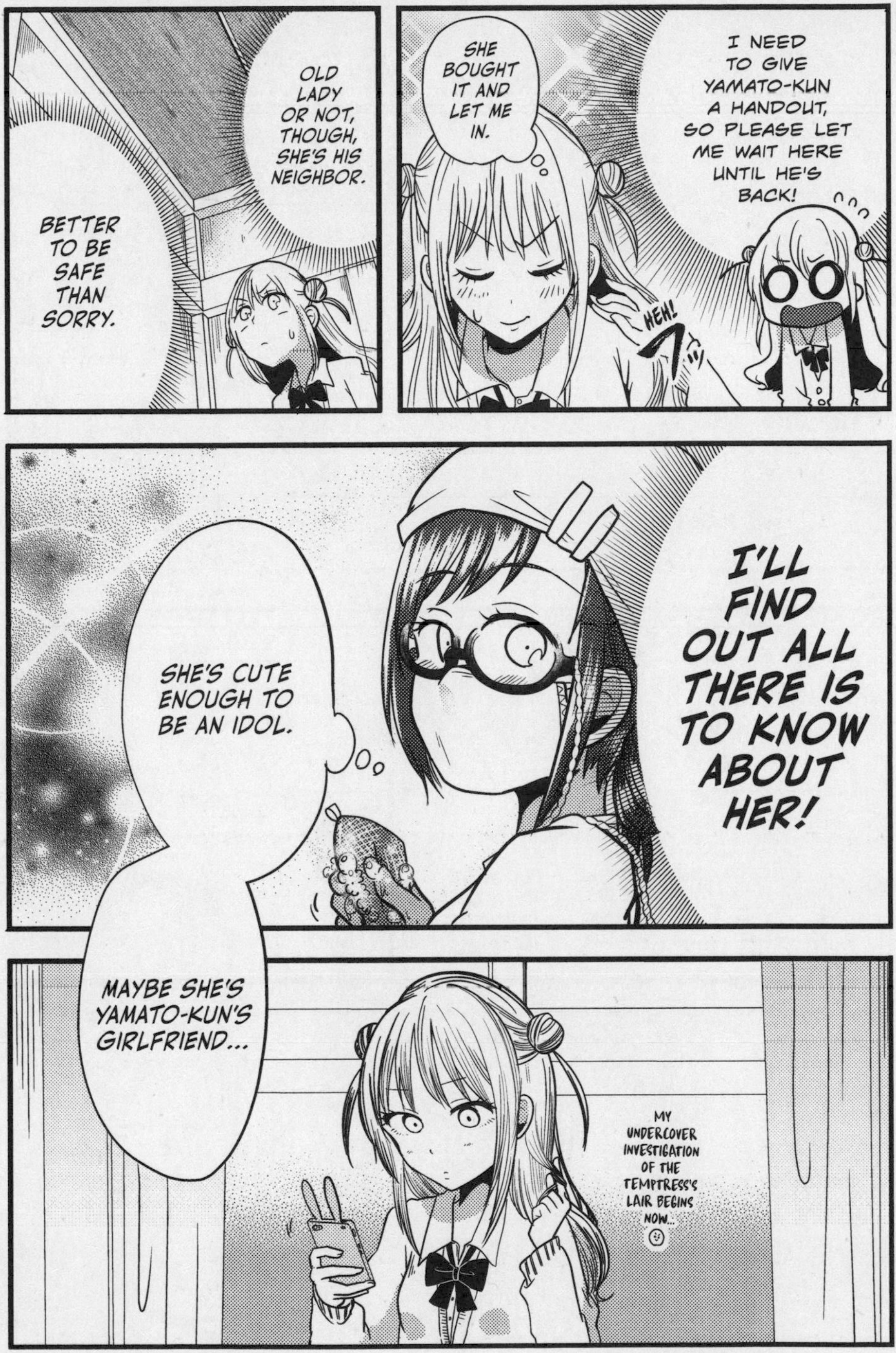
I NEED TO GIVE YAMATO-KUN A HANDOUT, SO PLEASE LET ME WAIT HERE UNTIL HE'S BACK!
SHE BOUGHT IT AND LET ME IN.
HEH!
OLD LADY OR NOT, THOUGH, SHE'S HIS NEIGHBOR.
BETTER TO BE SAFE THAN SORRY.
I'LL FIND OUT ALL THERE IS TO KNOW ABOUT HER!
SHE'S CUTE ENOUGH TO BE AN IDOL.
MAYBE SHE'S YAMATO-KUN'S GIRLFRIEND...
MY UNDERCOVER INVESTIGATION OF THE TEMPTRESS'S LAIR BEGINS NOW...

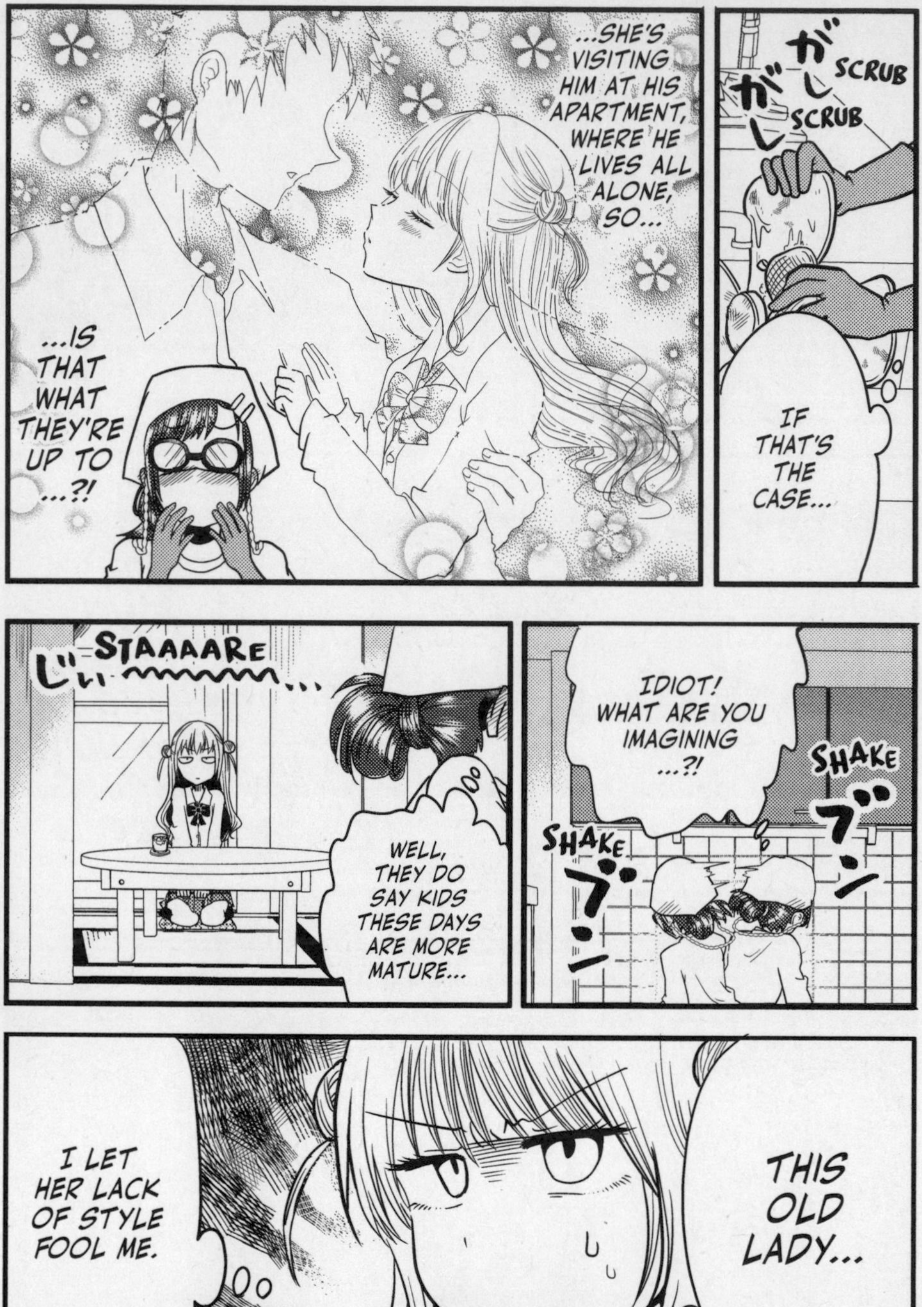
がし がし
SCRUB
SCRUB
IF THAT'S THE CASE...
...SHE'S VISITING HIM AT HIS APARTMENT, WHERE HE LIVES ALL ALONE, SO...
...IS THAT WHAT THEY'RE UP TO ...?!
IDIOT! WHAT ARE YOU IMAGINING ...?!
SHAKE
ブン
SHAKE
ブン
じぃ〜…
STAAAARE
WELL, THEY DO SAY KIDS THESE DAYS ARE MORE MATURE...
THIS OLD LADY...
I LET HER LACK OF STYLE FOOL ME.

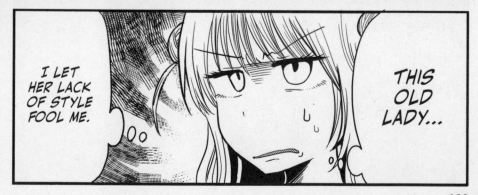

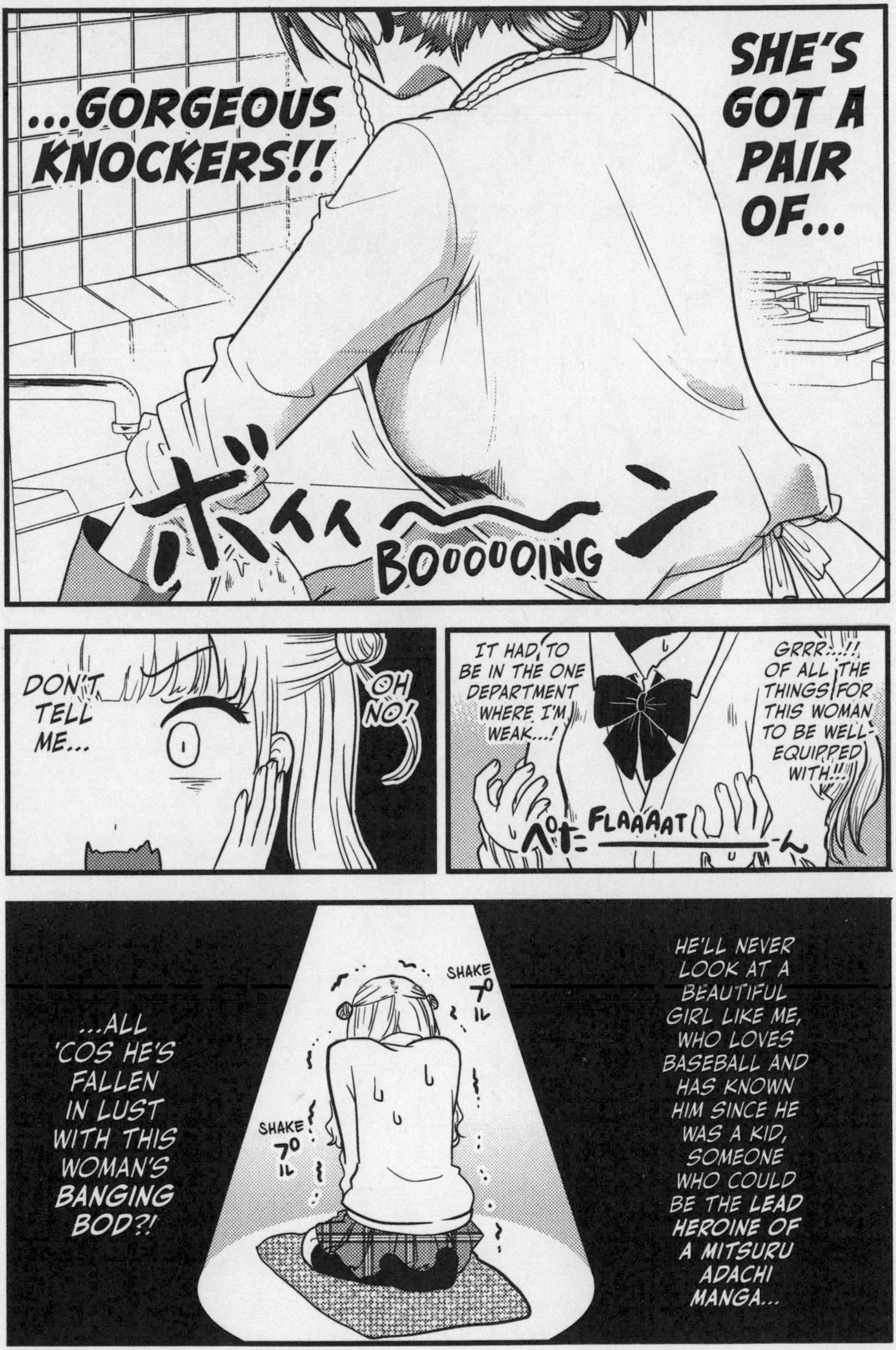

SHE'S GOT A PAIR OF...
...GORGEOUS KNOCKERS!!
BOOOOOING
GRRR...!! OF ALL THE THINGS FOR THIS WOMAN TO BE WELL-EQUIPPED WITH!!
IT HAD TO BE IN THE ONE DEPARTMENT WHERE I'M WEAK...!
FLAAAAT
OH NO!
DON'T TELL ME...
HE'LL NEVER LOOK AT A BEAUTIFUL GIRL LIKE ME, WHO LOVES BASEBALL AND HAS KNOWN HIM SINCE HE WAS A KID, SOMEONE WHO COULD BE THE LEAD HEROINE OF A MITSURU ADACHI MANGA...
SHAKE
SHAKE
...ALL 'COS HE'S FALLEN IN LUST WITH THIS WOMAN'S BANGING BOD?!

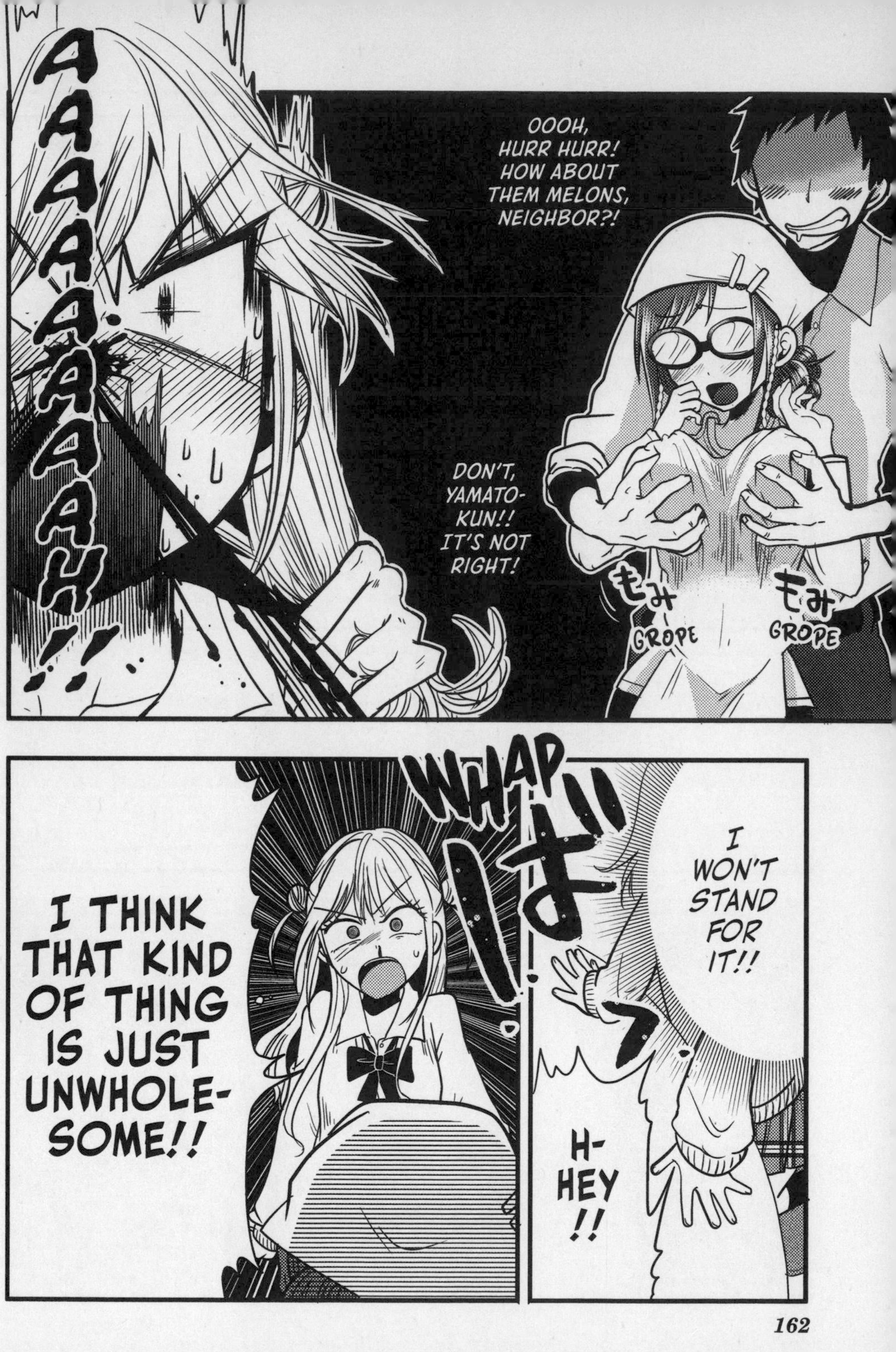
OOOH, HURR HURR! HOW ABOUT THEM MELONS, NEIGHBOR?!
DON'T, YAMATO-KUN!! IT'S NOT RIGHT!
もみ GROPE
もみ GROPE
AAAAAAAAAAAH!!!
I WON'T STAND FOR IT!!
H-HEY!!
WHAP
ば
I THINK THAT KIND OF THING IS JUST UNWHOLE-SOME!!

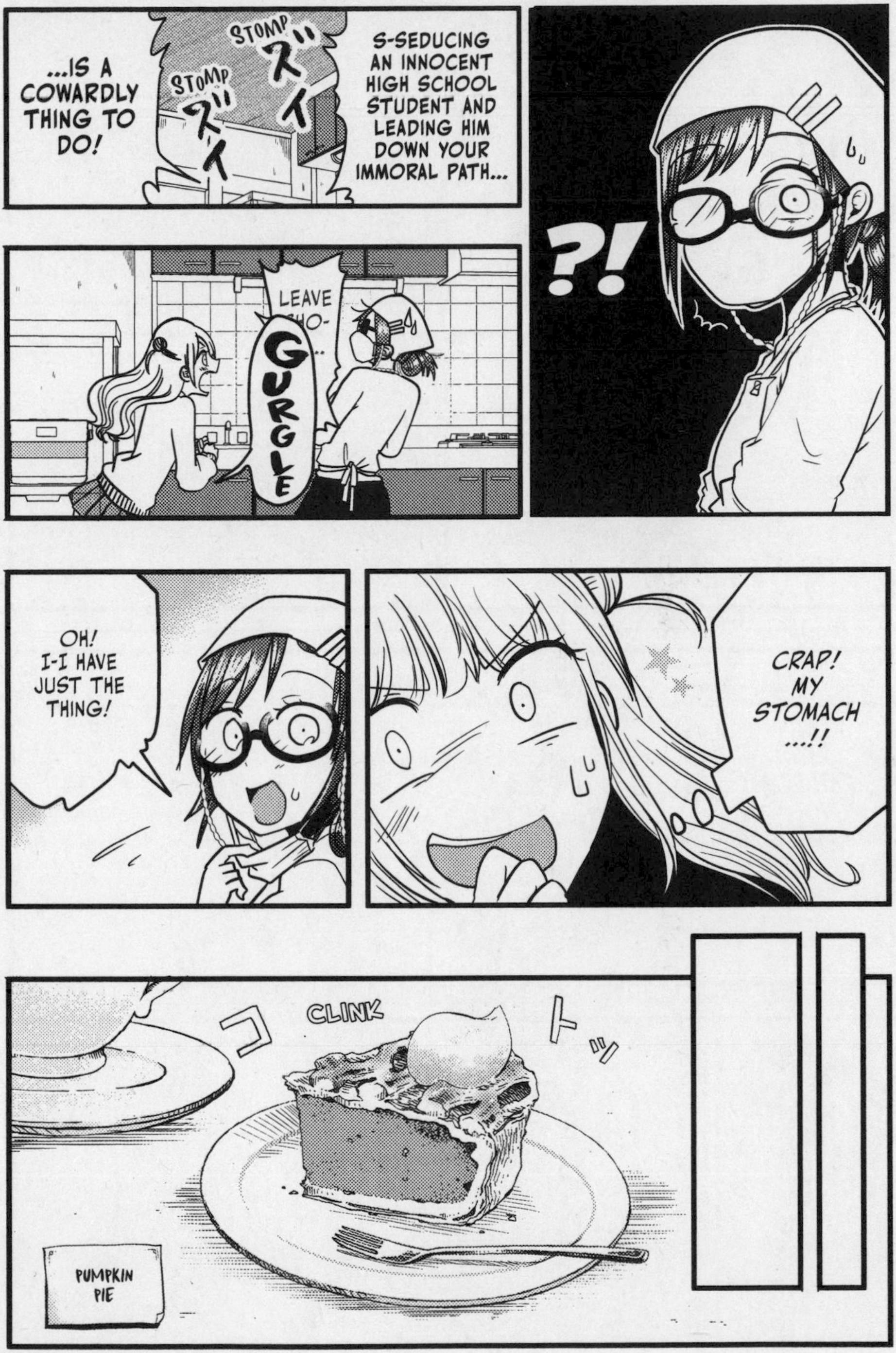
?!
S-SEDUCING AN INNOCENT HIGH SCHOOL STUDENT AND LEADING HIM DOWN YOUR IMMORAL PATH...
STOMP ズイ
STOMP ズイ
...IS A COWARDLY THING TO DO!
LEAVE SHO-...
GURGLE
CRAP! MY STOMACH ...!!
OH! I-I HAVE JUST THE THING!
CLINK
コトッ
PUMPKIN PIE

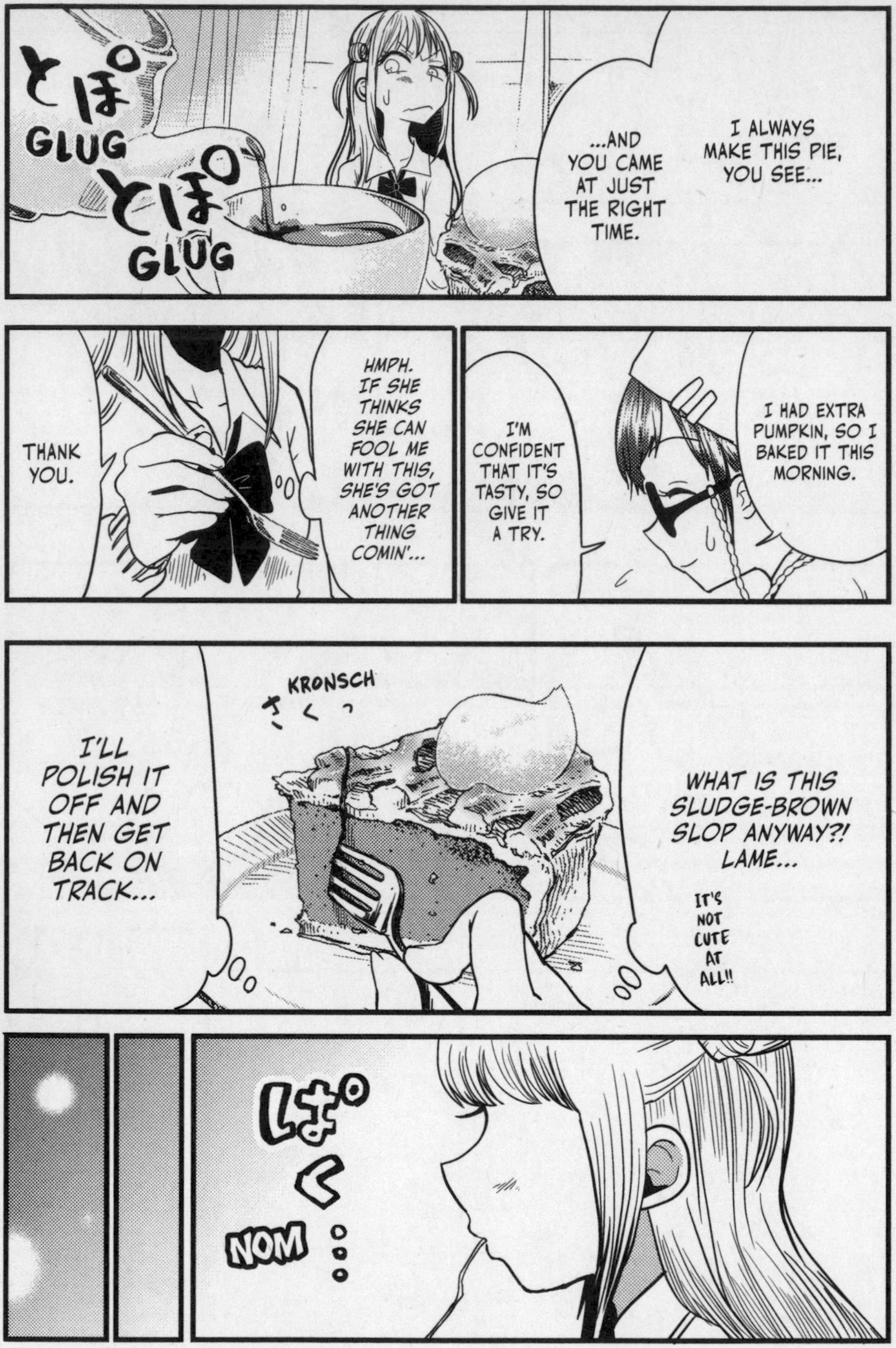
I ALWAYS MAKE THIS PIE, YOU SEE...
...AND YOU CAME AT JUST THE RIGHT TIME.
とぽ
GLUG
とぽ
GLUG
I HAD EXTRA PUMPKIN, SO I BAKED IT THIS MORNING.
I'M CONFIDENT THAT IT'S TASTY, SO GIVE IT A TRY.
HMPH. IF SHE THINKS SHE CAN FOOL ME WITH THIS, SHE'S GOT ANOTHER THING COMIN'...
THANK YOU.
WHAT IS THIS SLUDGE-BROWN SLOP ANYWAY?! LAME...
IT'S NOT CUTE AT ALL!!
さくっ
KRONSCH
I'LL POLISH IT OFF AND THEN GET BACK ON TRACK...
ぱく
NOM

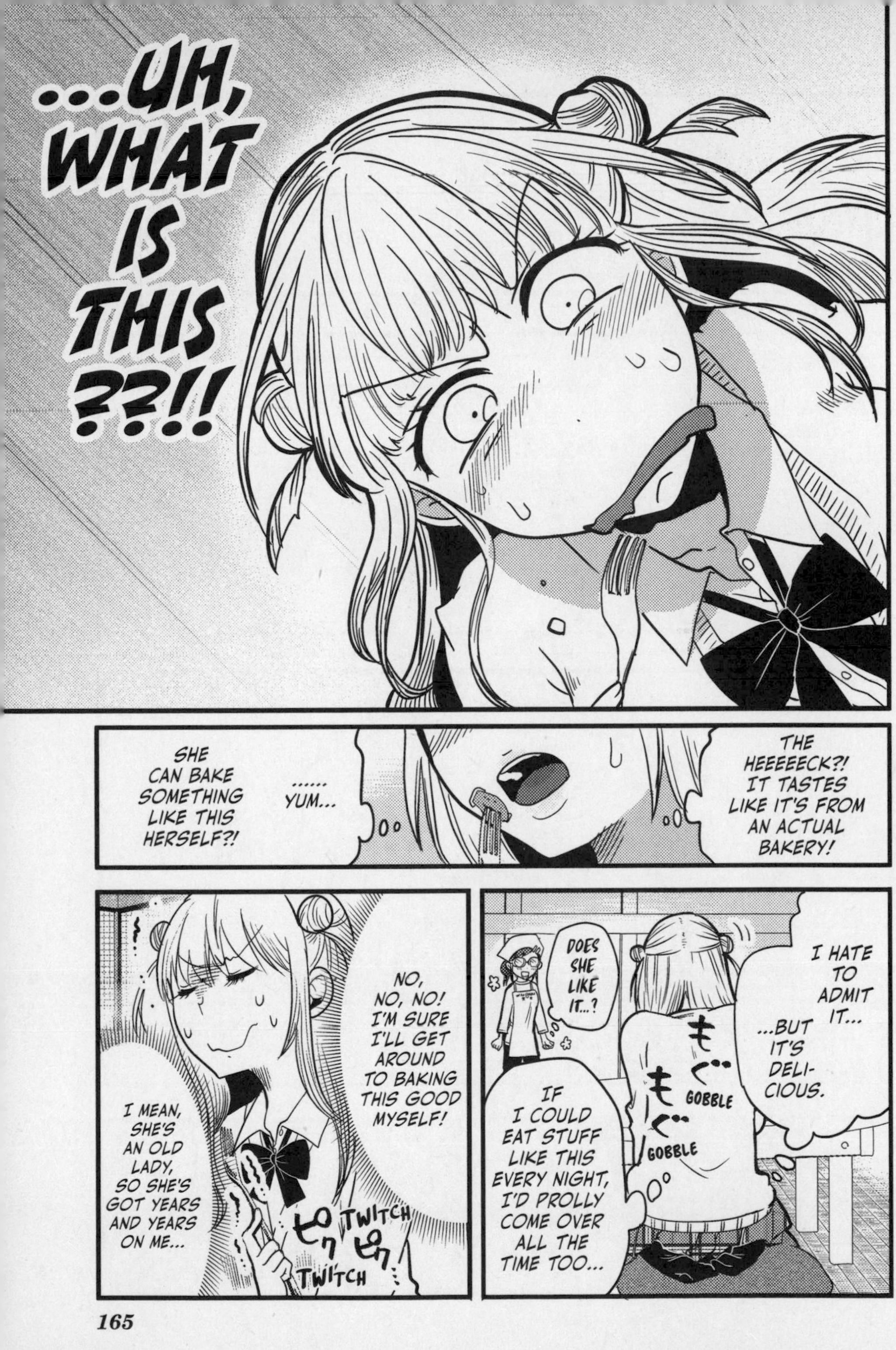
...UH, WHAT IS THIS ??!!
THE HEEEEECK?! IT TASTES LIKE IT'S FROM AN ACTUAL BAKERY!
...... YUM...
SHE CAN BAKE SOMETHING LIKE THIS HERSELF?!
I HATE TO ADMIT IT...
...BUT IT'S DELICIOUS.
DOES SHE LIKE IT...?
もぐもぐ GOBBLE GOBBLE
IF I COULD EAT STUFF LIKE THIS EVERY NIGHT, I'D PROLLY COME OVER ALL THE TIME TOO...
NO, NO, NO! I'M SURE I'LL GET AROUND TO BAKING THIS GOOD MYSELF!
I MEAN, SHE'S AN OLD LADY, SO SHE'S GOT YEARS AND YEARS ON ME...
ピクピク TWITCH TWITCH

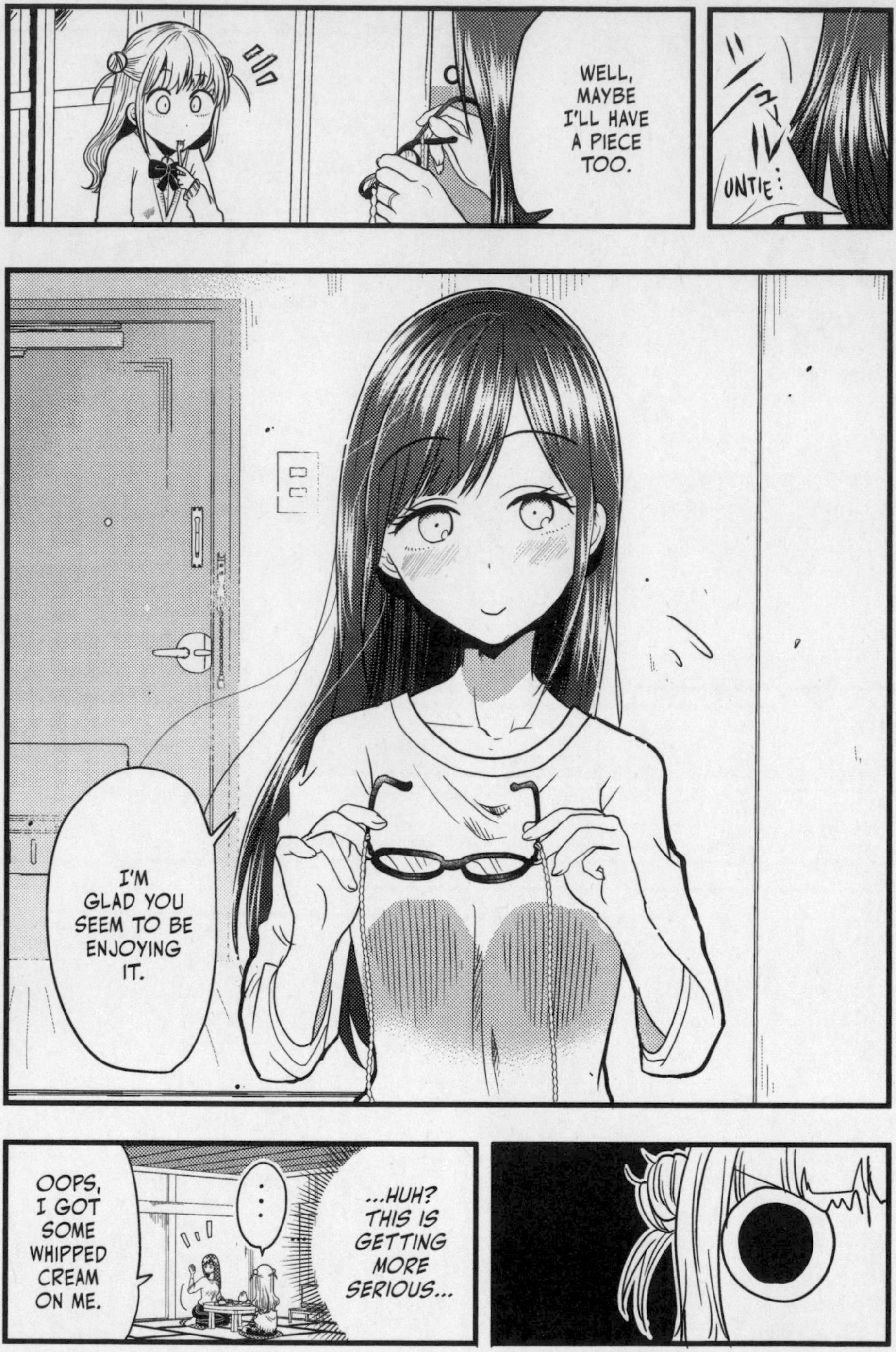
UNTIE
WELL, MAYBE I'LL HAVE A PIECE TOO.
I'M GLAD YOU SEEM TO BE ENJOYING IT.
...HUH? THIS IS GETTING MORE SERIOUS...
...
OOPS, I GOT SOME WHIPPED CREAM ON ME.

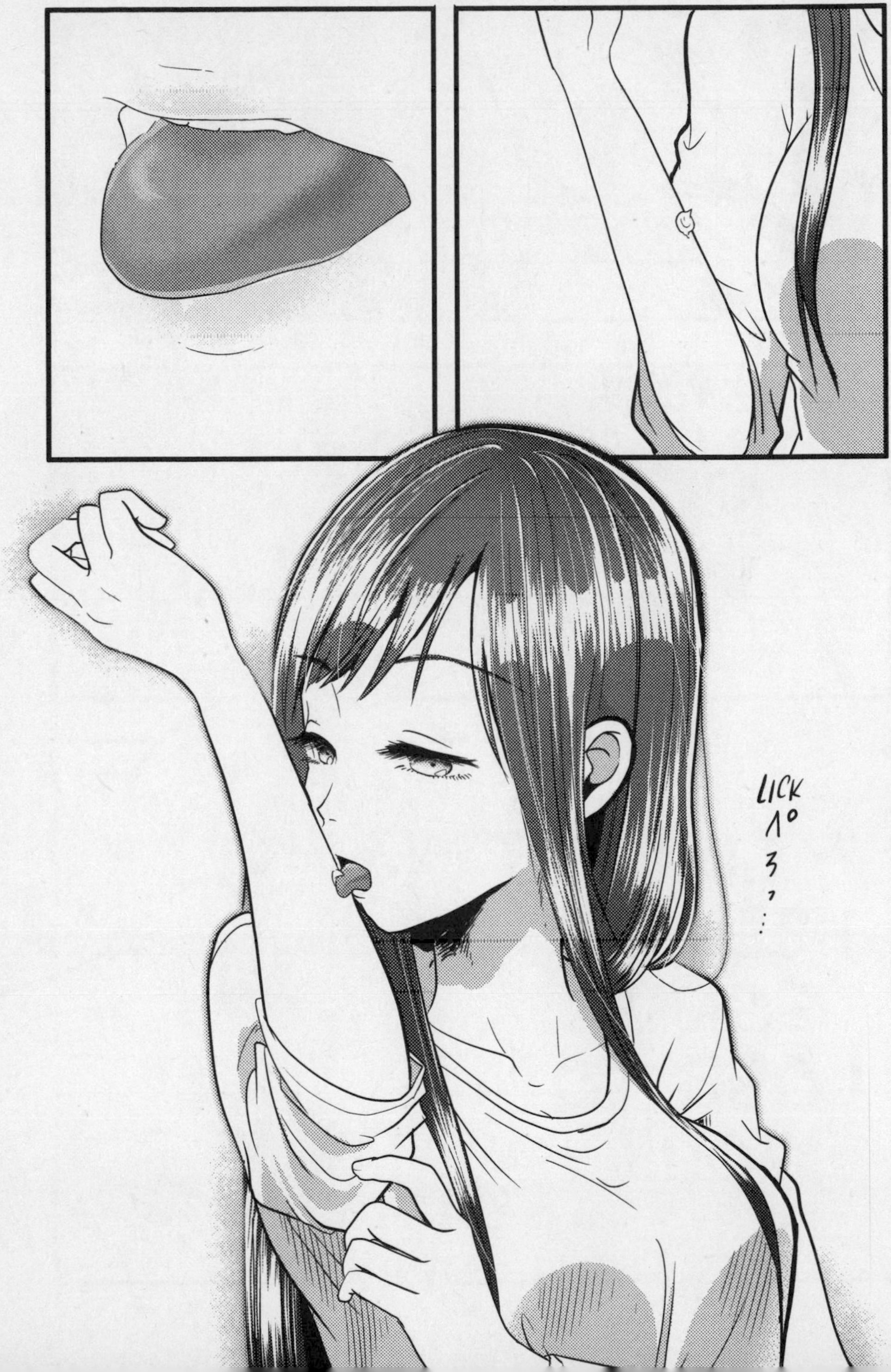
LICK
ぺろっ…

SPURT 11

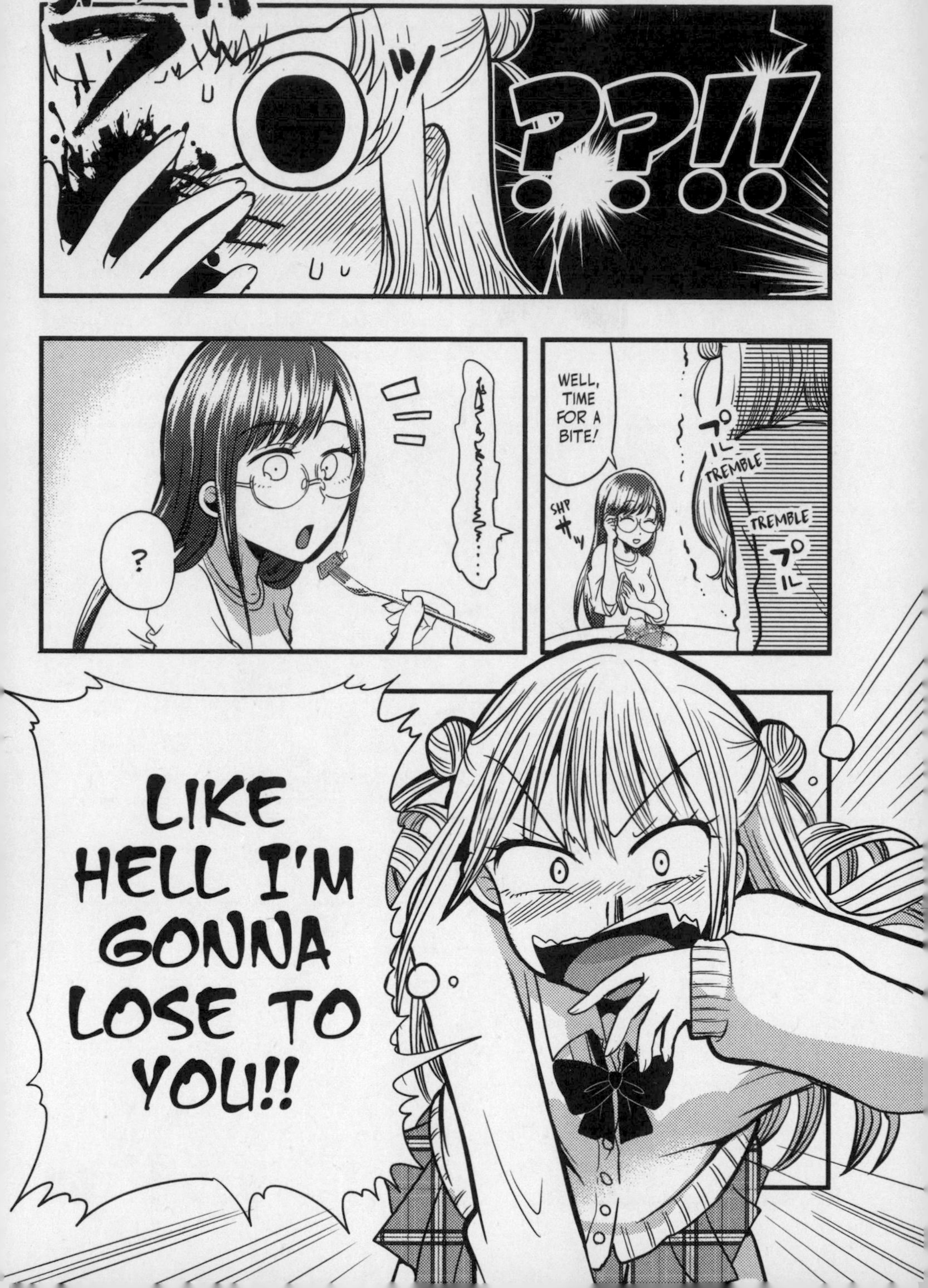
??!!
WELL, TIME FOR A BITE!
TREMBLE
SHP
TREMBLE
?
LIKE HELL I'M GONNA LOSE TO YOU!!

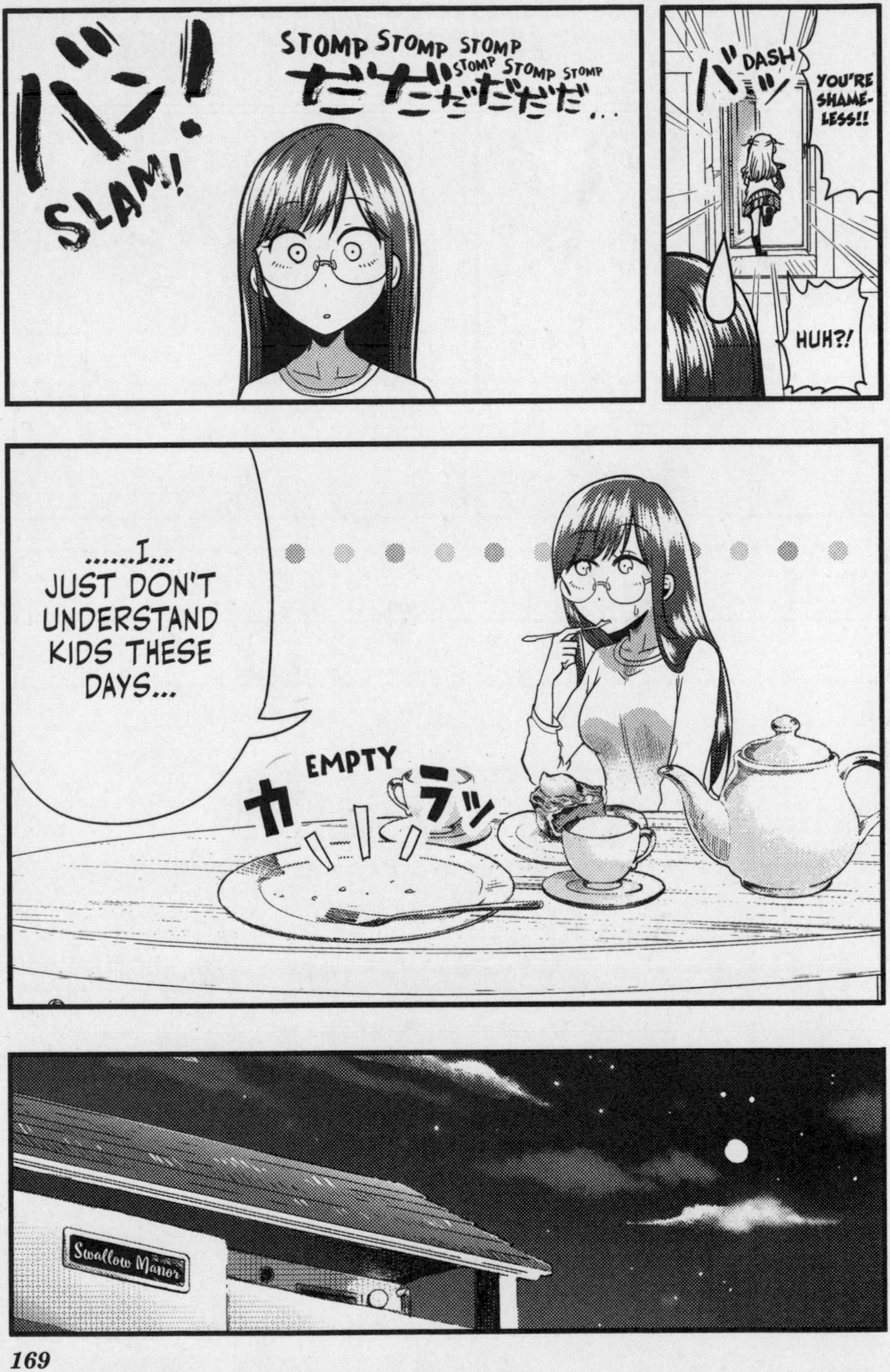
バッ
DASH
YOU'RE SHAMELESS!!
HUH?!
バン!
SLAM!
STOMP STOMP STOMP STOMP STOMP STOMP
だだだだだだ...
......I... JUST DON'T UNDERSTAND KIDS THESE DAYS...
EMPTY
カラッ
Swallow Manor

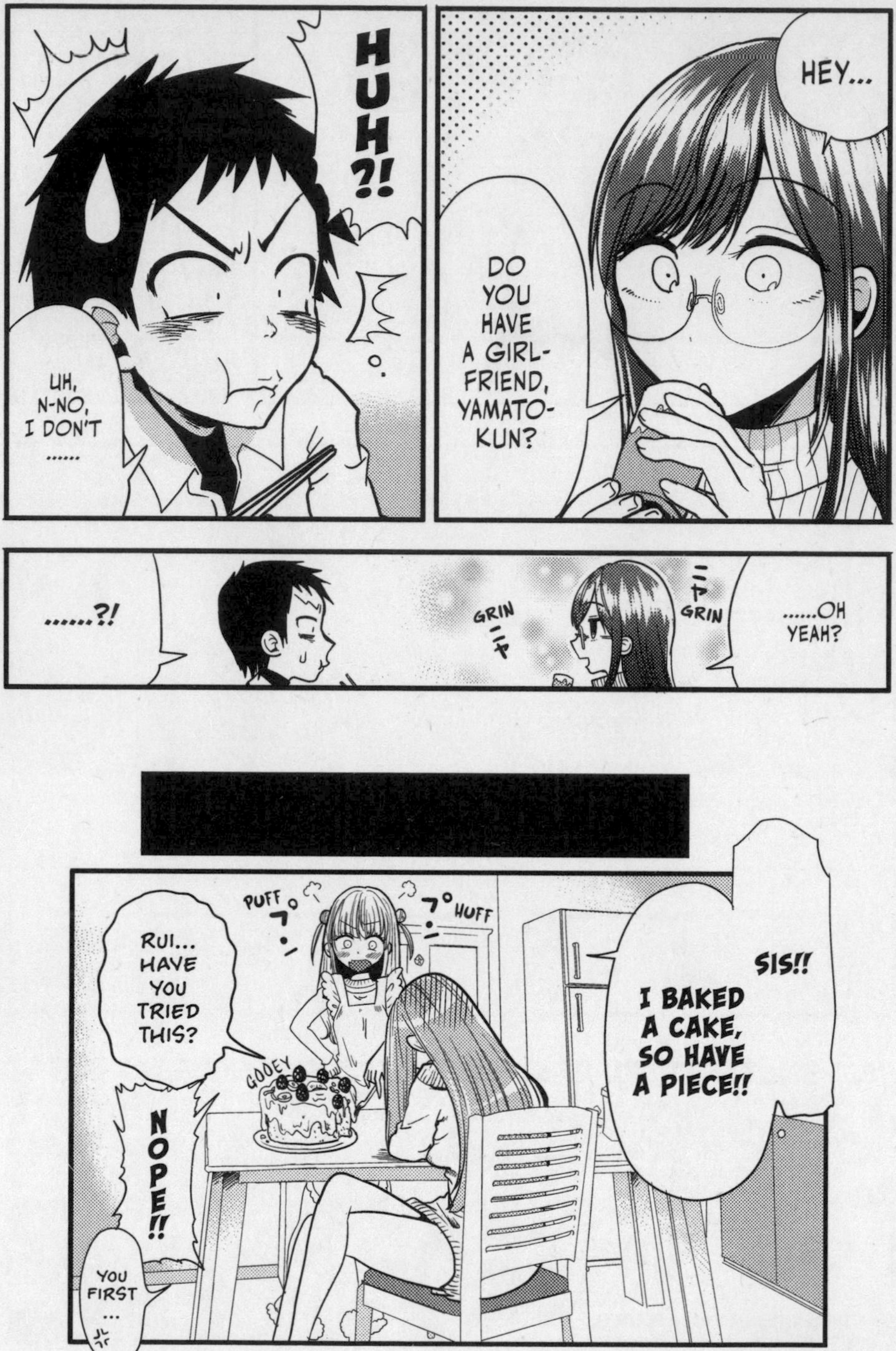
HEY...
DO YOU HAVE A GIRL-FRIEND, YAMATO-KUN?
HUH?!
UH, N-NO, I DON'T ......
......OH YEAH?
GRIN
GRIN
......?!
[redacted]
SIS!! I BAKED A CAKE, SO HAVE A PIECE!!
HUFF
PUFF
RUI... HAVE YOU TRIED THIS?
GOOEY
NOPE!!
YOU FIRST ...

Beauty and the FEAST.

Beauty and the FEAST

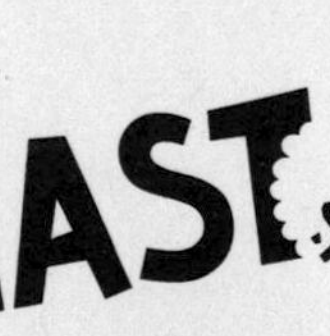

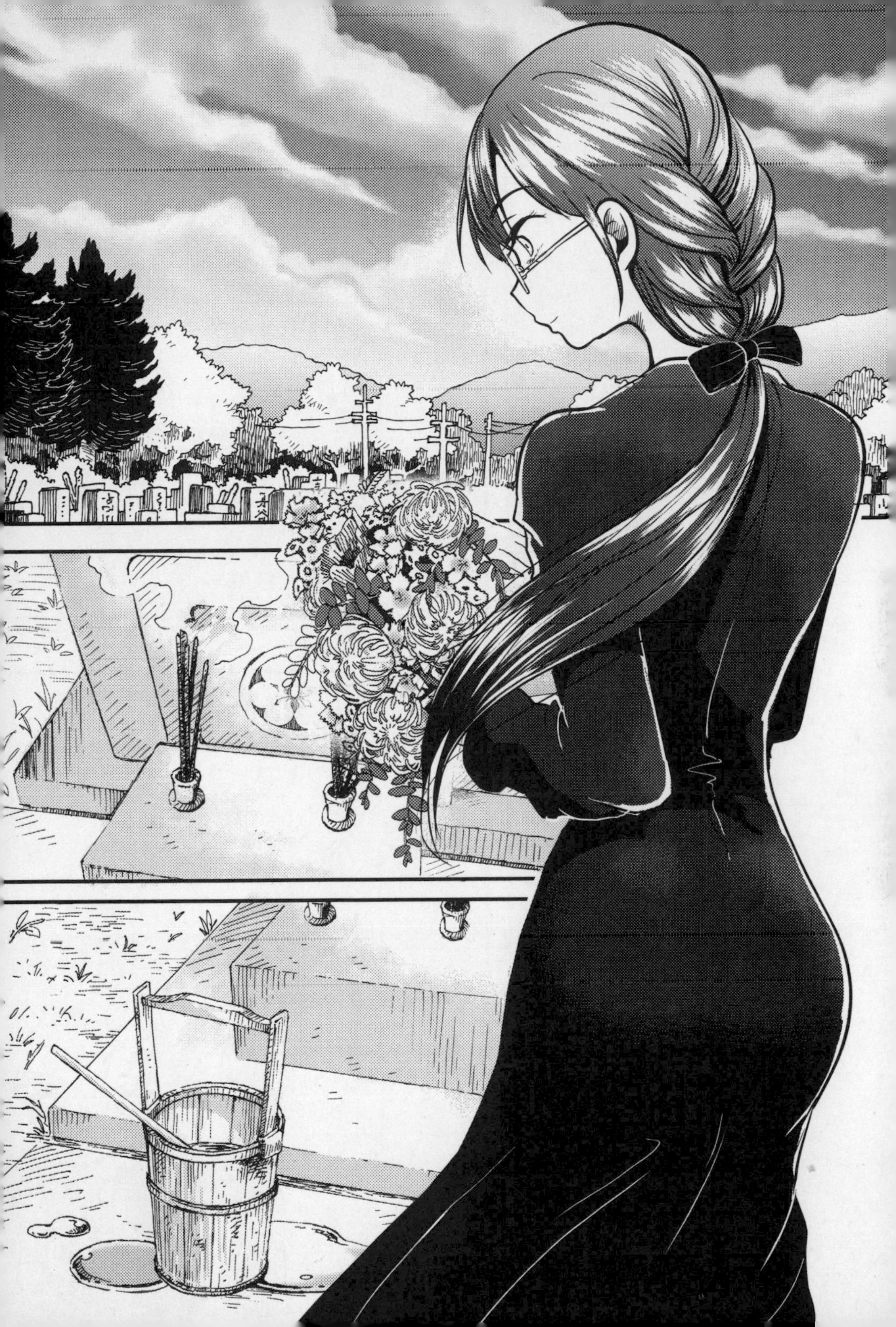

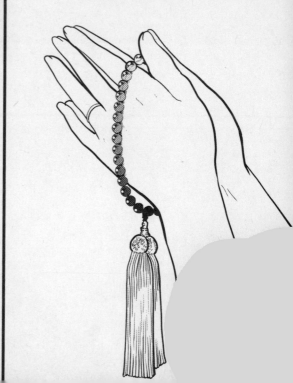

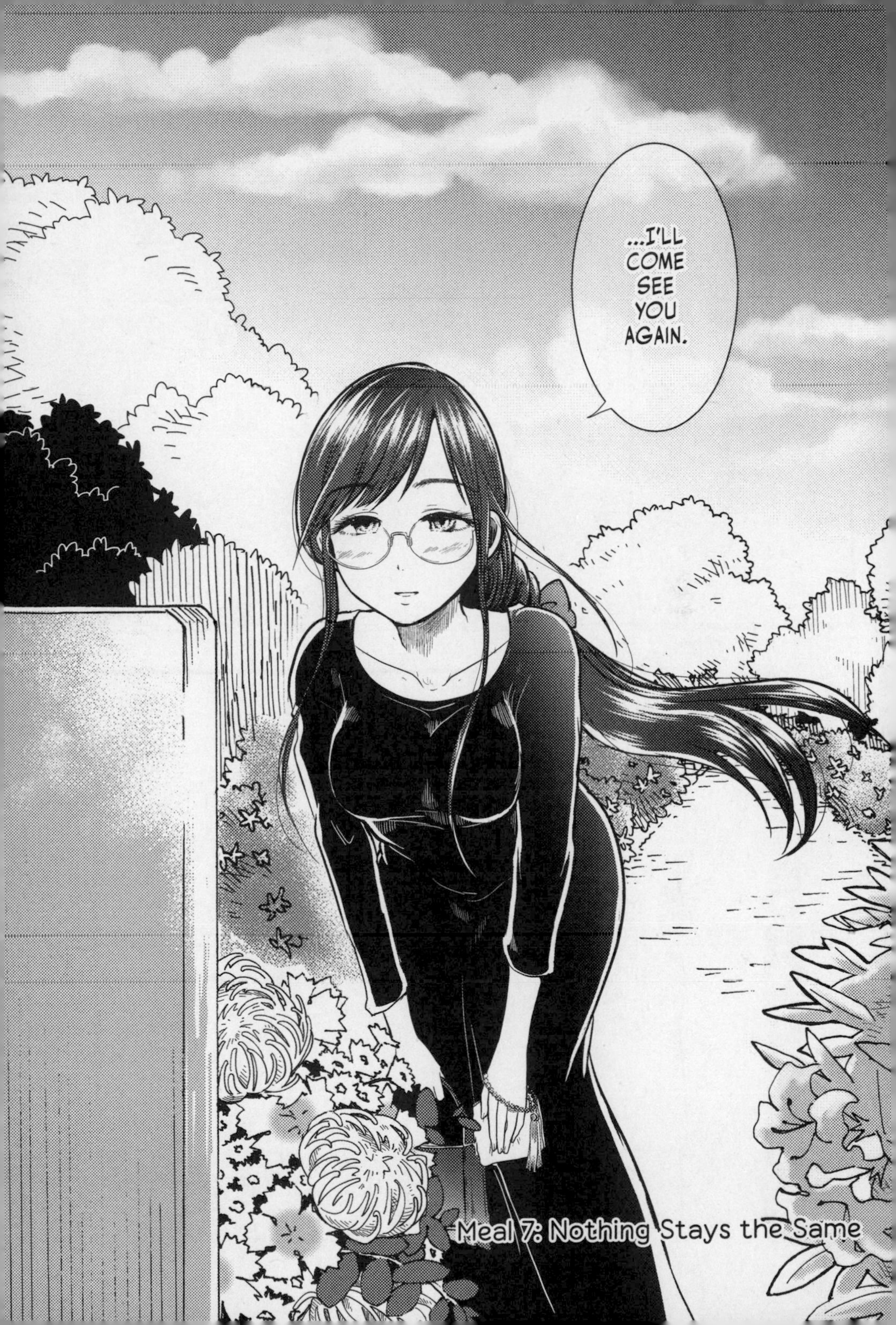
...I'LL COME SEE YOU AGAIN.
Meal 7: Nothing Stays the Same

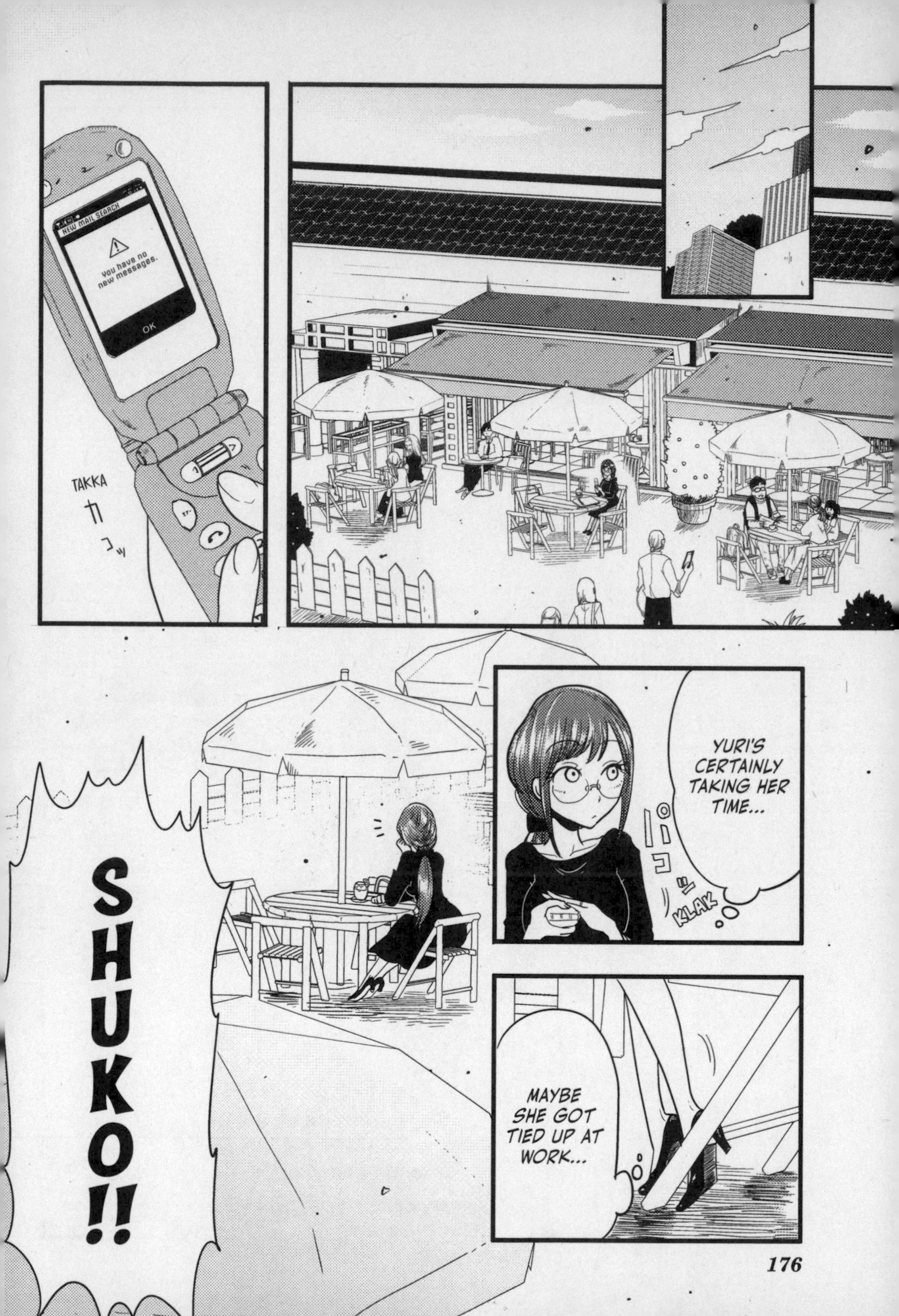
NEW MAIL SEARCH
You have no new messages.
OK
TAKKA
YURI'S CERTAINLY TAKING HER TIME...
KLAK
MAYBE SHE GOT TIED UP AT WORK...
SHUKO!!

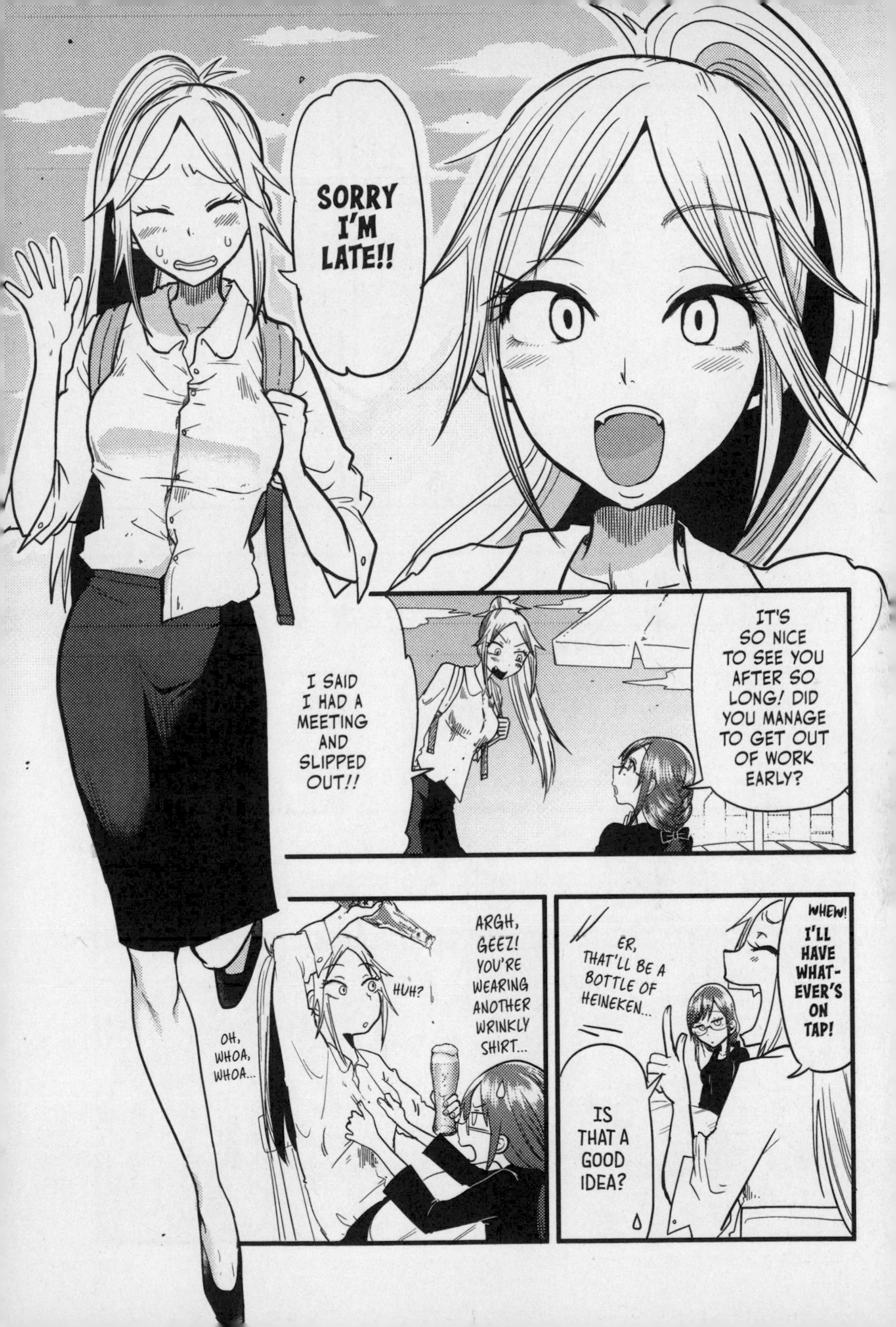
IT'S SO NICE TO SEE YOU AFTER SO LONG! DID YOU MANAGE TO GET OUT OF WORK EARLY?
I SAID I HAD A MEETING AND SLIPPED OUT!!
WHEW! I'LL HAVE WHAT-EVER'S ON TAP!
ER, THAT'LL BE A BOTTLE OF HEINEKEN...
IS THAT A GOOD IDEA?
ARGH, GEEZ! YOU'RE WEARING ANOTHER WRINKLY SHIRT...
HUH?
OH, WHOA, WHOA...
SORRY I'M LATE!!

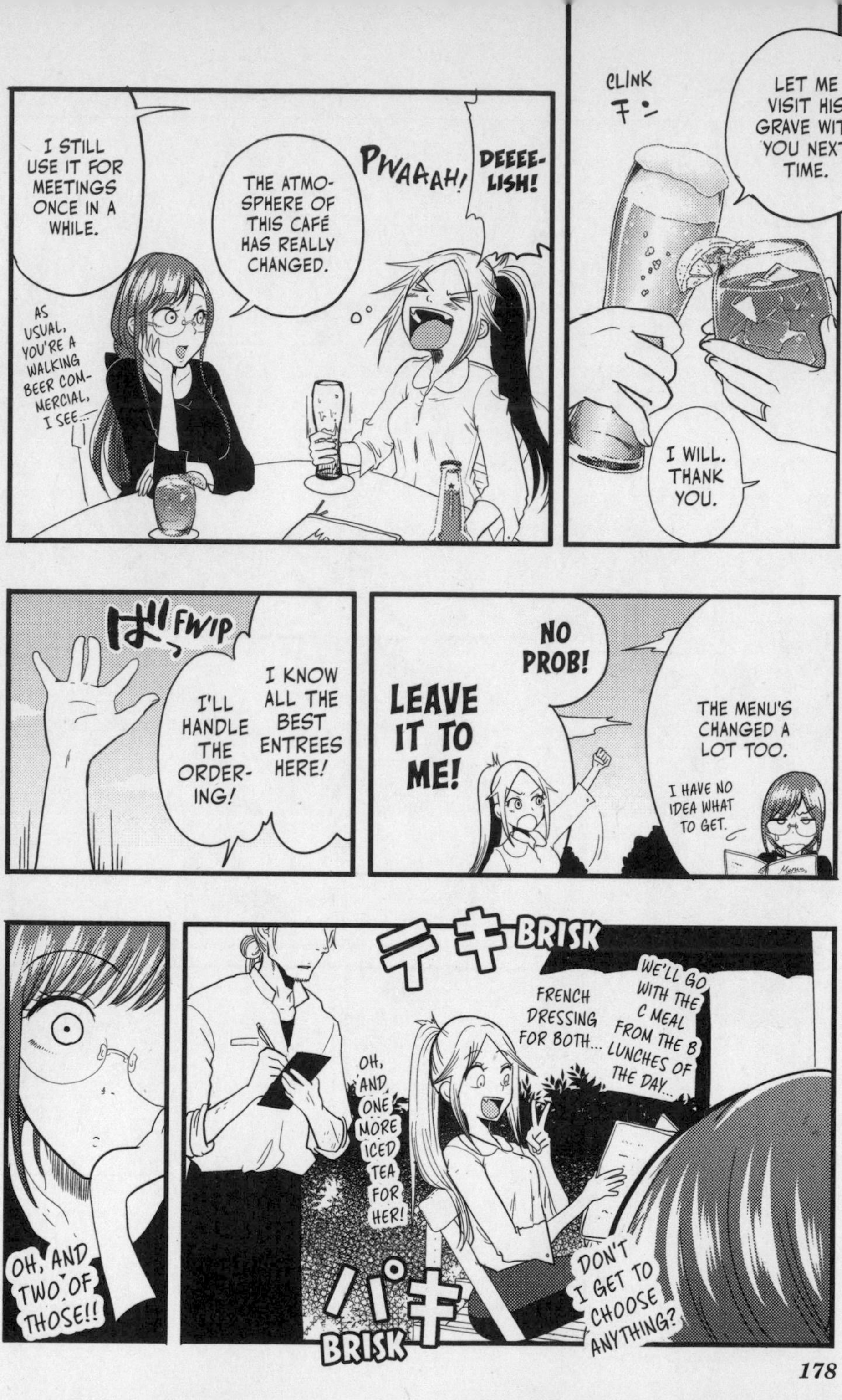
LET ME VISIT HIS GRAVE WITH YOU NEXT TIME.
CLINK
チン
I WILL. THANK YOU.
DEEEE-LISH!
PWAAAH!
THE ATMO-SPHERE OF THIS CAFÉ HAS REALLY CHANGED.
I STILL USE IT FOR MEETINGS ONCE IN A WHILE.
AS USUAL, YOU'RE A WALKING BEER COM-MERCIAL, I SEE...
THE MENU'S CHANGED A LOT TOO.
I HAVE NO IDEA WHAT TO GET.
NO PROB!
LEAVE IT TO ME!
ぱ! FWIP
I KNOW ALL THE BEST ENTREES HERE!
I'LL HANDLE THE ORDER-ING!
テキ BRISK
WE'LL GO WITH THE C MEAL FROM THE B LUNCHES OF THE DAY...
FRENCH DRESSING FOR BOTH...
OH, AND, ONE MORE ICED TEA FOR HER!
DON'T I GET TO CHOOSE ANYTHING?
パキ BRISK
OH, AND TWO OF THOSE!!

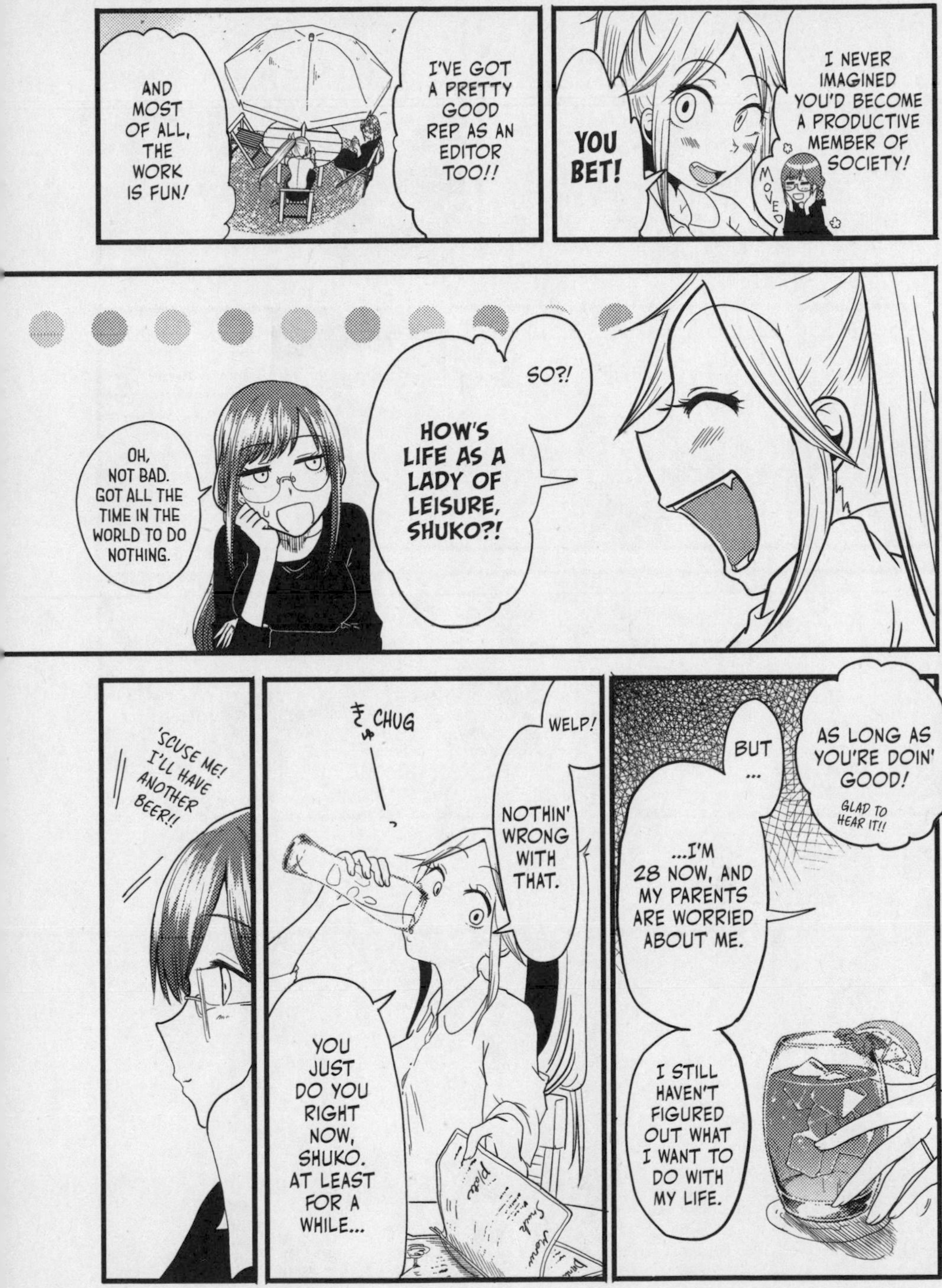
I NEVER IMAGINED YOU'D BECOME A PRODUCTIVE MEMBER OF SOCIETY!
MOVED
YOU BET!
I'VE GOT A PRETTY GOOD REP AS AN EDITOR TOO!!
AND MOST OF ALL, THE WORK IS FUN!
SO?!
HOW'S LIFE AS A LADY OF LEISURE, SHUKO?!
OH, NOT BAD. GOT ALL THE TIME IN THE WORLD TO DO NOTHING.
AS LONG AS YOU'RE DOIN' GOOD!
GLAD TO HEAR IT!!
BUT ...
...I'M 28 NOW, AND MY PARENTS ARE WORRIED ABOUT ME.
I STILL HAVEN'T FIGURED OUT WHAT I WANT TO DO WITH MY LIFE.
WELP!
NOTHIN' WRONG WITH THAT.
CHUG
YOU JUST DO YOU RIGHT NOW, SHUKO. AT LEAST FOR A WHILE...
'SCUSE ME! I'LL HAVE ANOTHER BEER!!

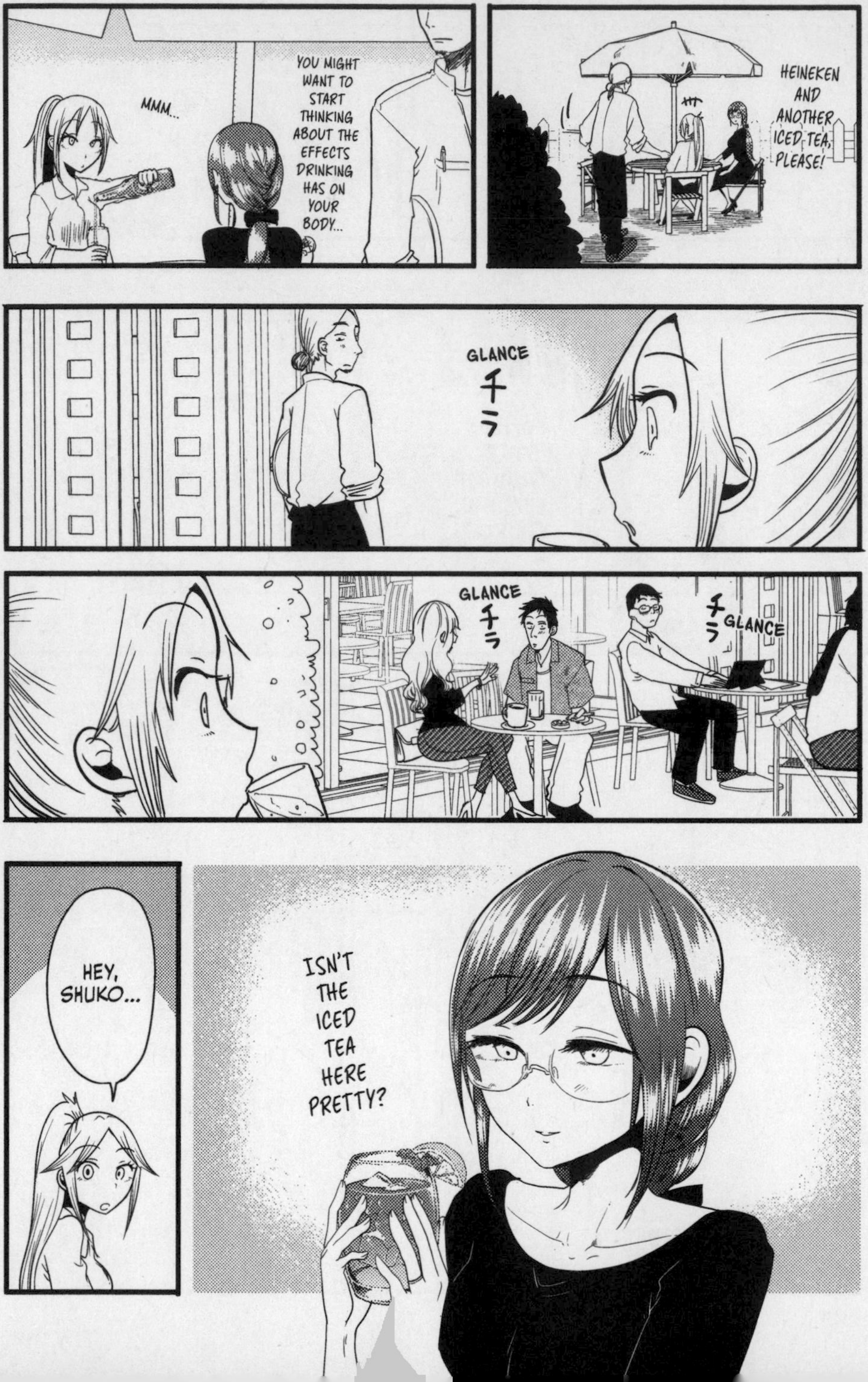
HEINEKEN AND ANOTHER ICED TEA, PLEASE!
YOU MIGHT WANT TO START THINKING ABOUT THE EFFECTS DRINKING HAS ON YOUR BODY...
MMM...
GLANCE
チラ
GLANCE
チラ
GLANCE
チラ
ISN'T THE ICED TEA HERE PRETTY?
HEY, SHUKO...

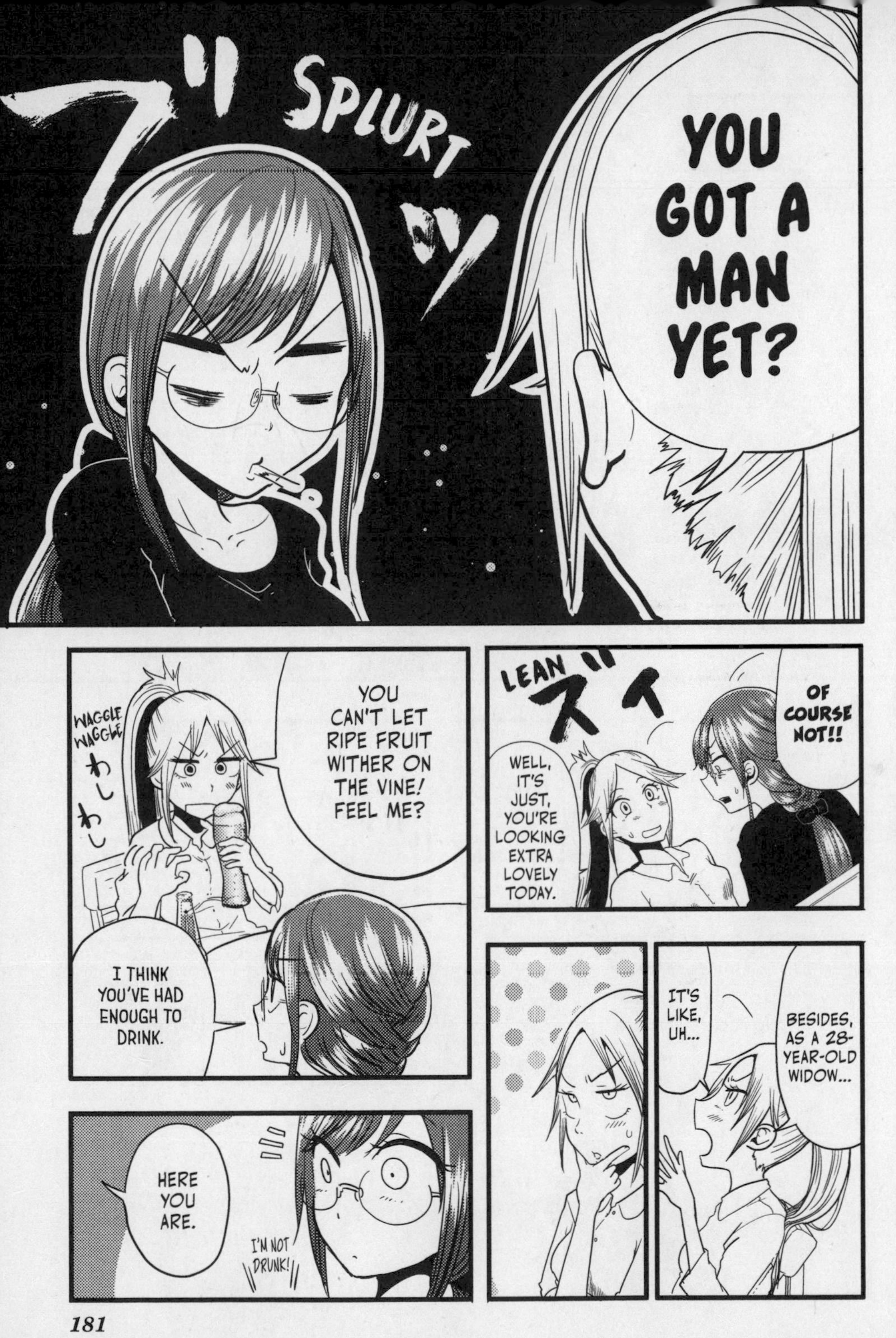
YOU GOT A MAN YET?
ズッ SPLURT
OF COURSE NOT!!
ズイ LEAN
WELL, IT'S JUST, YOU'RE LOOKING EXTRA LOVELY TODAY.
YOU CAN'T LET RIPE FRUIT WITHER ON THE VINE! FEEL ME?
わしわし WAGGLE WAGGLE
I THINK YOU'VE HAD ENOUGH TO DRINK.
BESIDES, AS A 28-YEAR-OLD WIDOW...
IT'S LIKE, UH...
HERE YOU ARE.
I'M NOT DRUNK!

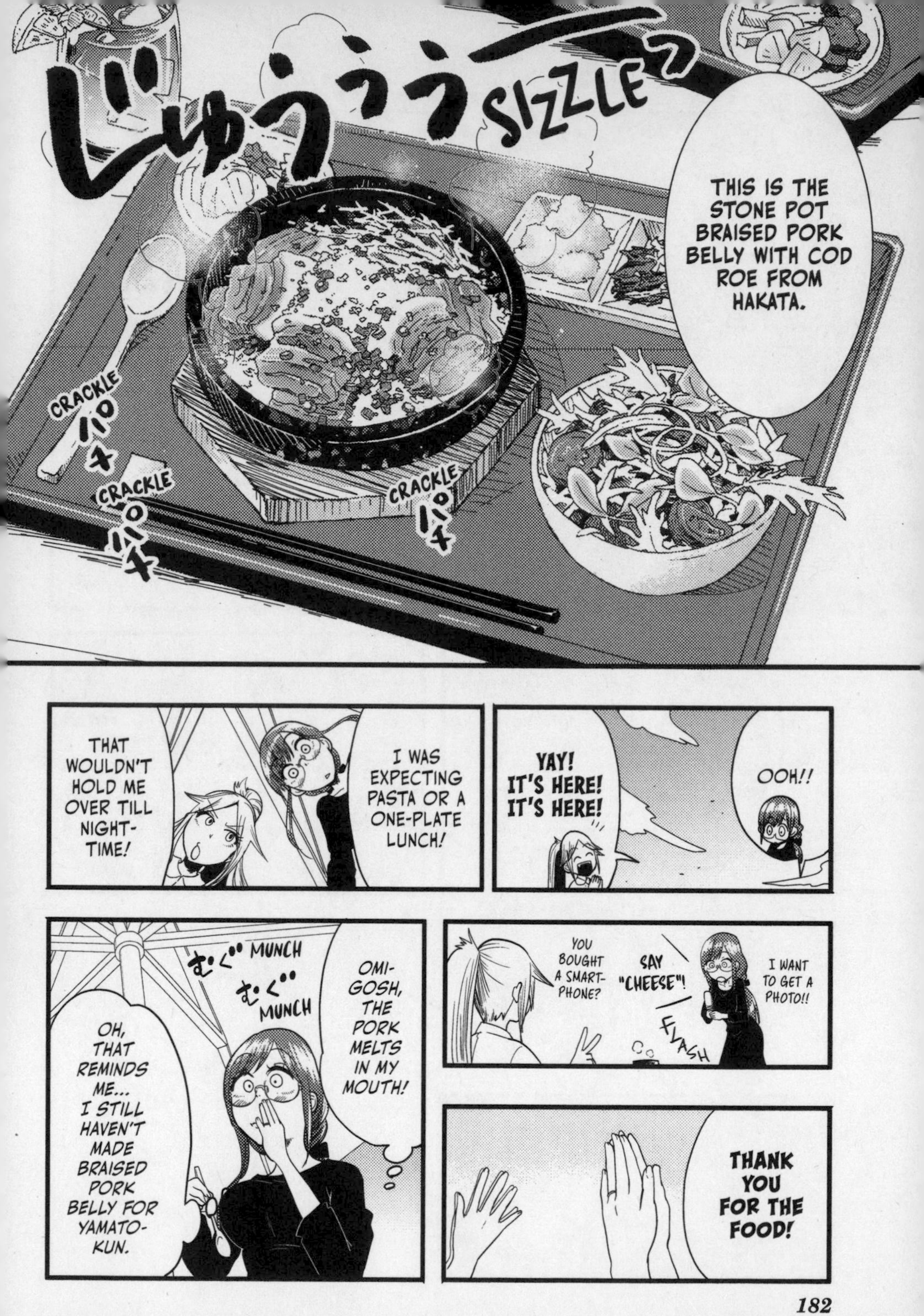

じゅううう SIZZLE
THIS IS THE STONE POT BRAISED PORK BELLY WITH COD ROE FROM HAKATA.
CRACKLE パキ
CRACKLE パキ
CRACKLE パキ
OOH!!
YAY! IT'S HERE! IT'S HERE!
I WAS EXPECTING PASTA OR A ONE-PLATE LUNCH!
THAT WOULDN'T HOLD ME OVER TILL NIGHT-TIME!
I WANT TO GET A PHOTO!!
SAY "CHEESE"!
YOU BOUGHT A SMART-PHONE?
FLASH
THANK YOU FOR THE FOOD!
むぐ MUNCH
むぐ MUNCH
OMI-GOSH, THE PORK MELTS IN MY MOUTH!
OH, THAT REMINDS ME... I STILL HAVEN'T MADE BRAISED PORK BELLY FOR YAMATO-KUN.

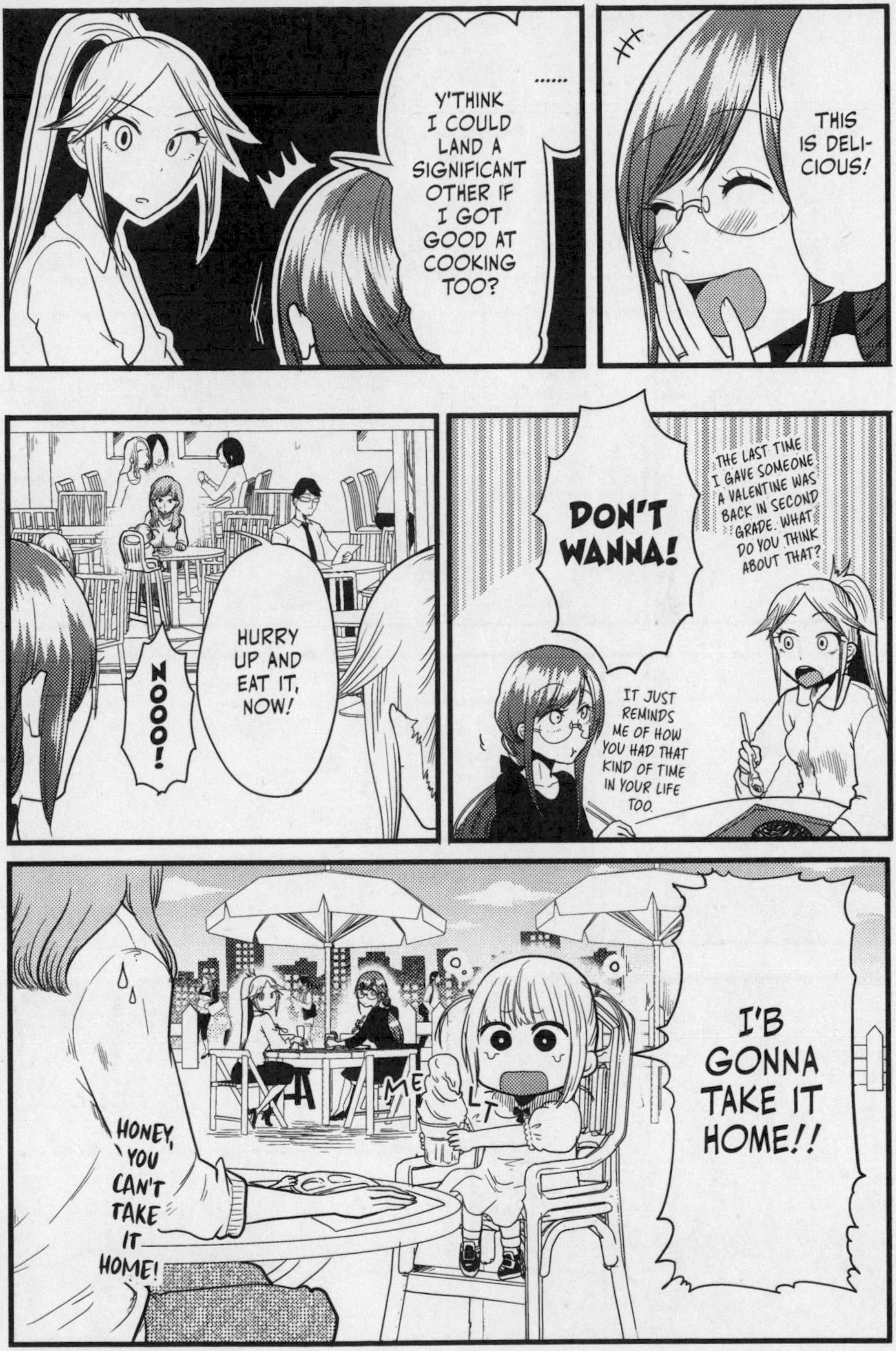
THIS IS DELICIOUS!
......
Y'THINK I COULD LAND A SIGNIFICANT OTHER IF I GOT GOOD AT COOKING TOO?
THE LAST TIME I GAVE SOMEONE A VALENTINE WAS BACK IN SECOND GRADE. WHAT DO YOU THINK ABOUT THAT?
DON'T WANNA!
IT JUST REMINDS ME OF HOW YOU HAD THAT KIND OF TIME IN YOUR LIFE TOO.
HURRY UP AND EAT IT, NOW!
NOOOO!
I'B GONNA TAKE IT HOME!!
MELT
HONEY, YOU CAN'T TAKE IT HOME!

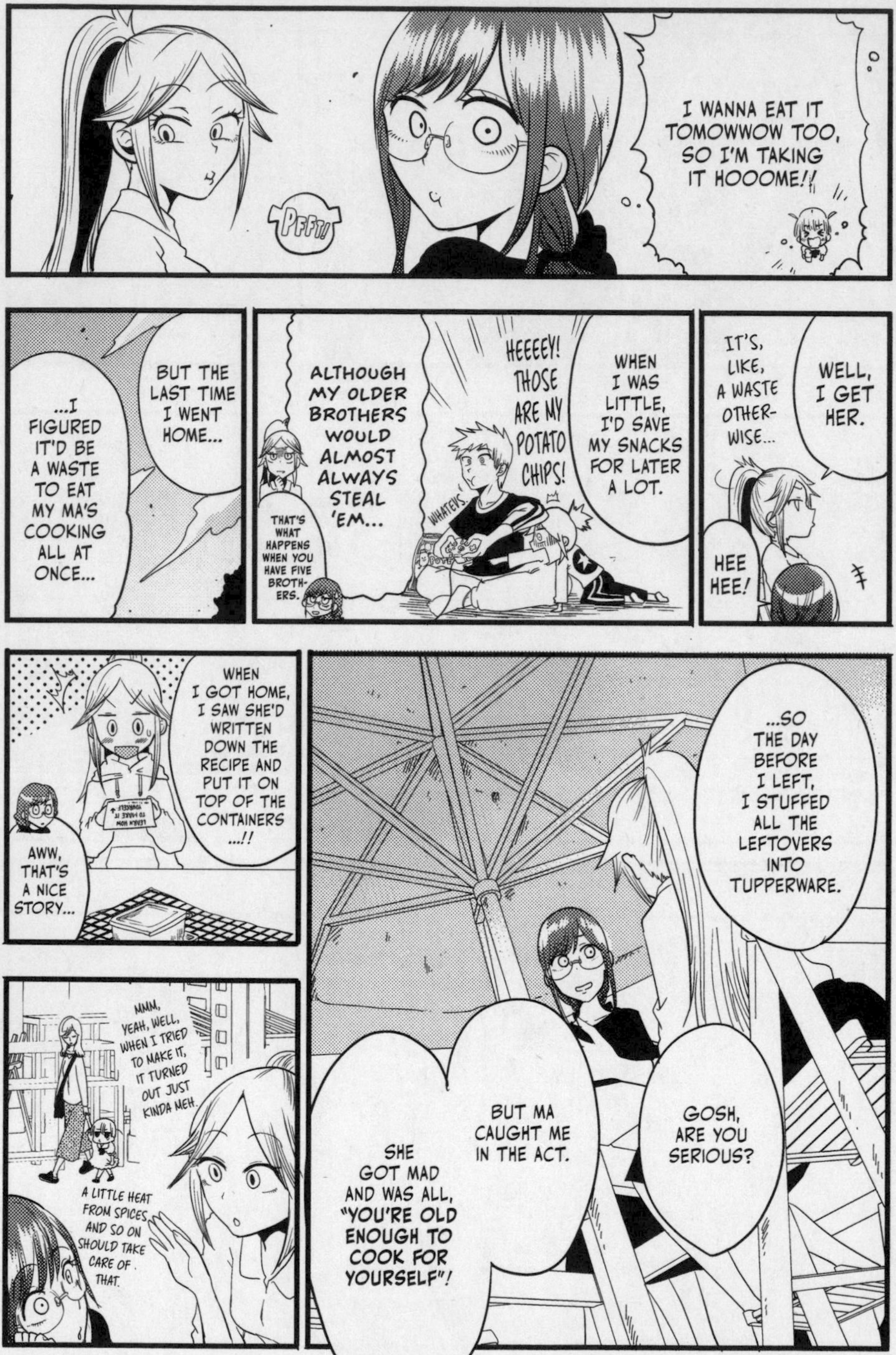
I WANNA EAT IT TOMOWWOW TOO, SO I'M TAKING IT HOOOME!!
PFFT!
WELL, I GET HER.
IT'S, LIKE, A WASTE OTHER-WISE...
HEE HEE!
WHEN I WAS LITTLE, I'D SAVE MY SNACKS FOR LATER A LOT.
HEEEEY! THOSE ARE MY POTATO CHIPS!
WHATEVS.
ALTHOUGH MY OLDER BROTHERS WOULD ALMOST ALWAYS STEAL 'EM...
THAT'S WHAT HAPPENS WHEN YOU HAVE FIVE BROTH-ERS.
BUT THE LAST TIME I WENT HOME...
...I FIGURED IT'D BE A WASTE TO EAT MY MA'S COOKING ALL AT ONCE...
...SO THE DAY BEFORE I LEFT, I STUFFED ALL THE LEFTOVERS INTO TUPPERWARE.
GOSH, ARE YOU SERIOUS?
BUT MA CAUGHT ME IN THE ACT.
SHE GOT MAD AND WAS ALL, "YOU'RE OLD ENOUGH TO COOK FOR YOURSELF"!
WHEN I GOT HOME, I SAW SHE'D WRITTEN DOWN THE RECIPE AND PUT IT ON TOP OF THE CONTAINERS ...!!
AWW, THAT'S A NICE STORY...
MMM, YEAH, WELL, WHEN I TRIED TO MAKE IT, IT TURNED OUT JUST KINDA MEH.
A LITTLE HEAT FROM SPICES AND SO ON SHOULD TAKE CARE OF THAT.

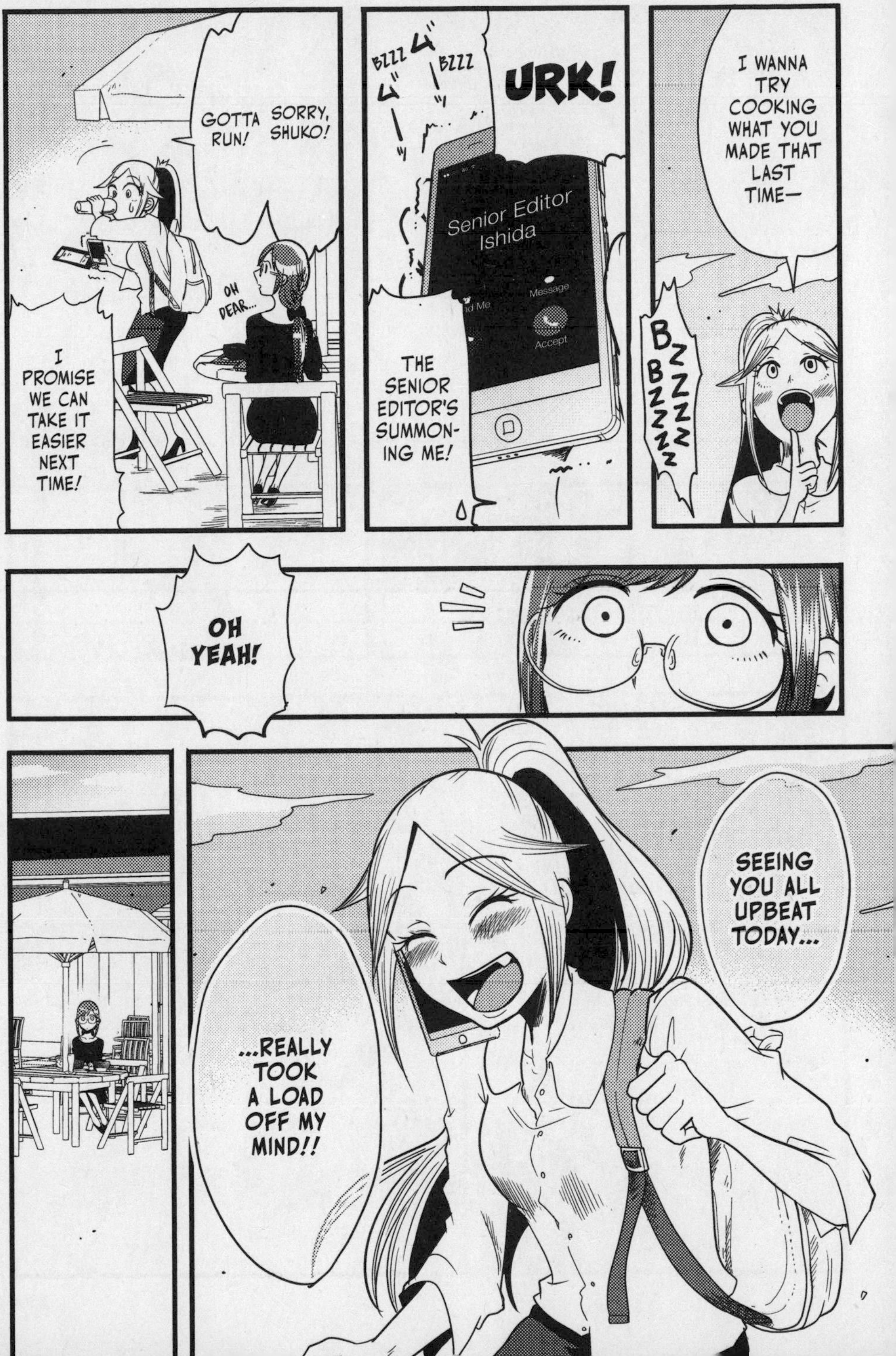
I WANNA TRY COOKING WHAT YOU MADE THAT LAST TIME—
BZZZZZZZZ
BZZZ BZZZ
URK!
Senior Editor Ishida
Message
Accept
THE SENIOR EDITOR'S SUMMONING ME!
SORRY, SHUKO!
GOTTA RUN!
OH DEAR...
I PROMISE WE CAN TAKE IT EASIER NEXT TIME!
OH YEAH!
SEEING YOU ALL UPBEAT TODAY...
...REALLY TOOK A LOAD OFF MY MIND!!

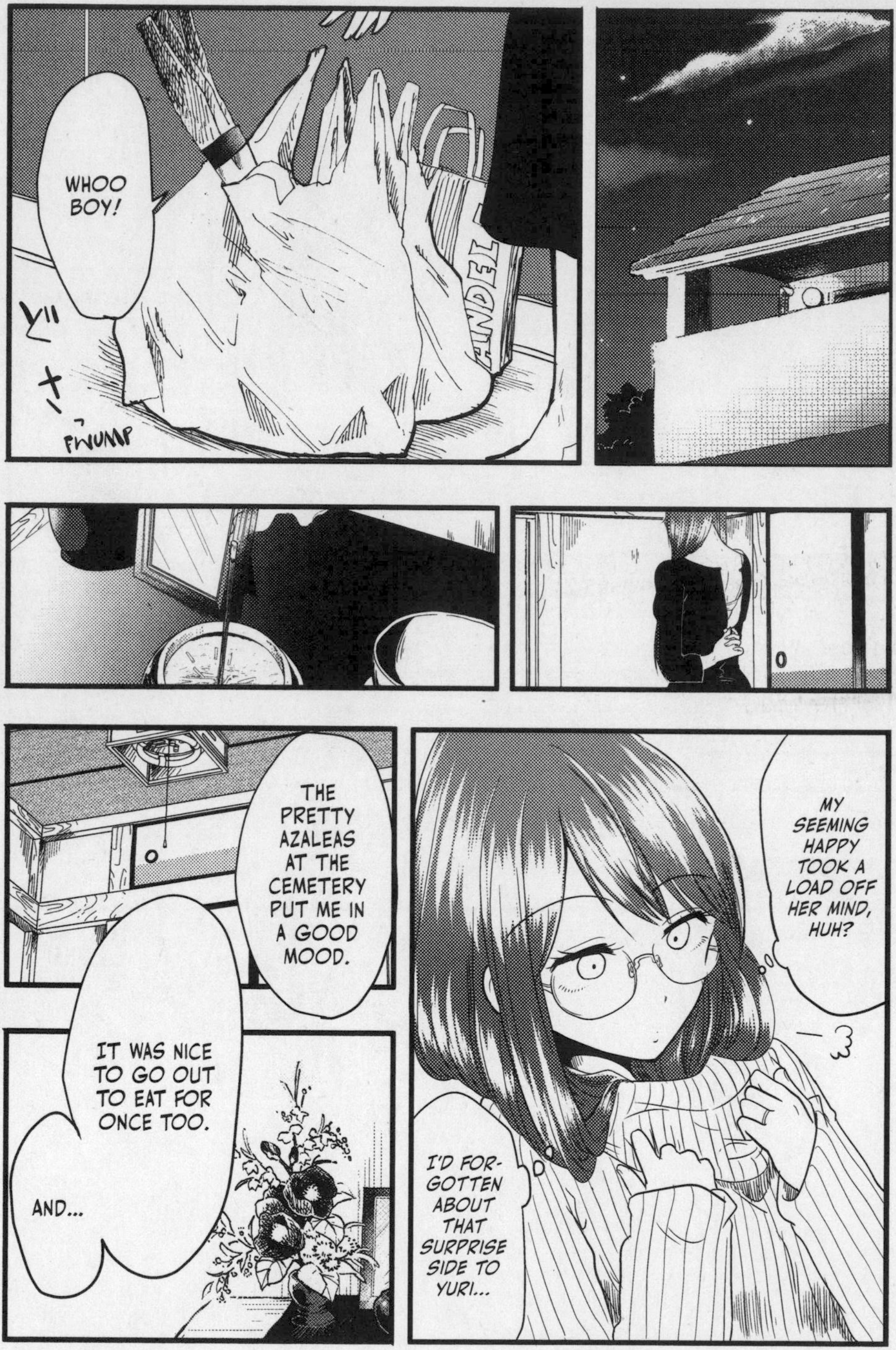
WHOO BOY!
どさ
FWUMP
MY SEEMING HAPPY TOOK A LOAD OFF HER MIND, HUH?
I'D FOR-GOTTEN ABOUT THAT SURPRISE SIDE TO YURI...
THE PRETTY AZALEAS AT THE CEMETERY PUT ME IN A GOOD MOOD.
IT WAS NICE TO GO OUT TO EAT FOR ONCE TOO.
AND...

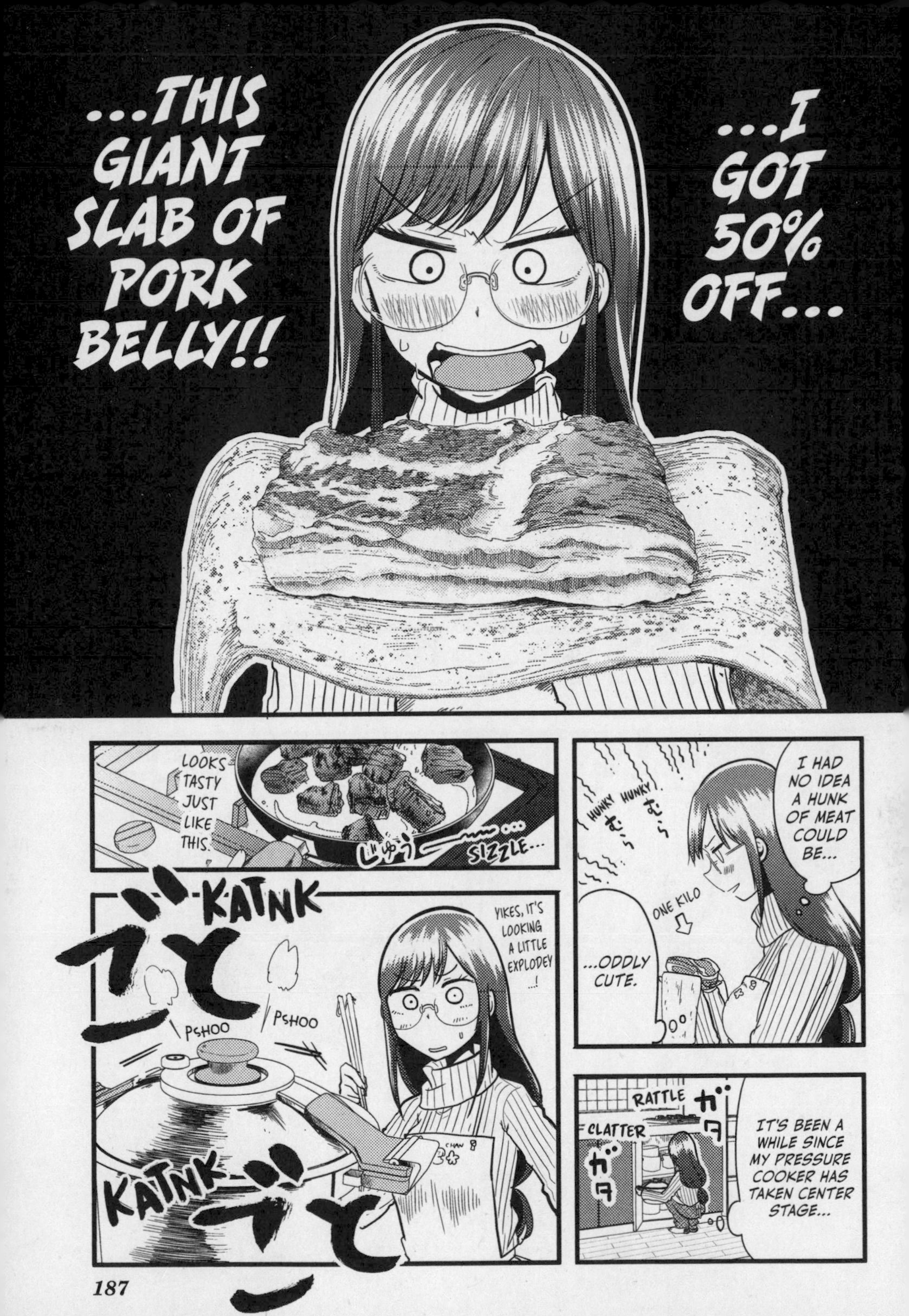
...I GOT 50% OFF...
...THIS GIANT SLAB OF PORK BELLY!!
I HAD NO IDEA A HUNK OF MEAT COULD BE...
HUNKY HUNKY
ONE KILO
...ODDLY CUTE.
RATTLE
CLATTER
IT'S BEEN A WHILE SINCE MY PRESSURE COOKER HAS TAKEN CENTER STAGE...
LOOKS TASTY JUST LIKE THIS.
SIZZLE...
KATNK
YIKES, IT'S LOOKING A LITTLE EXPLODEY...!
PSHOO
PSHOO
KATNK

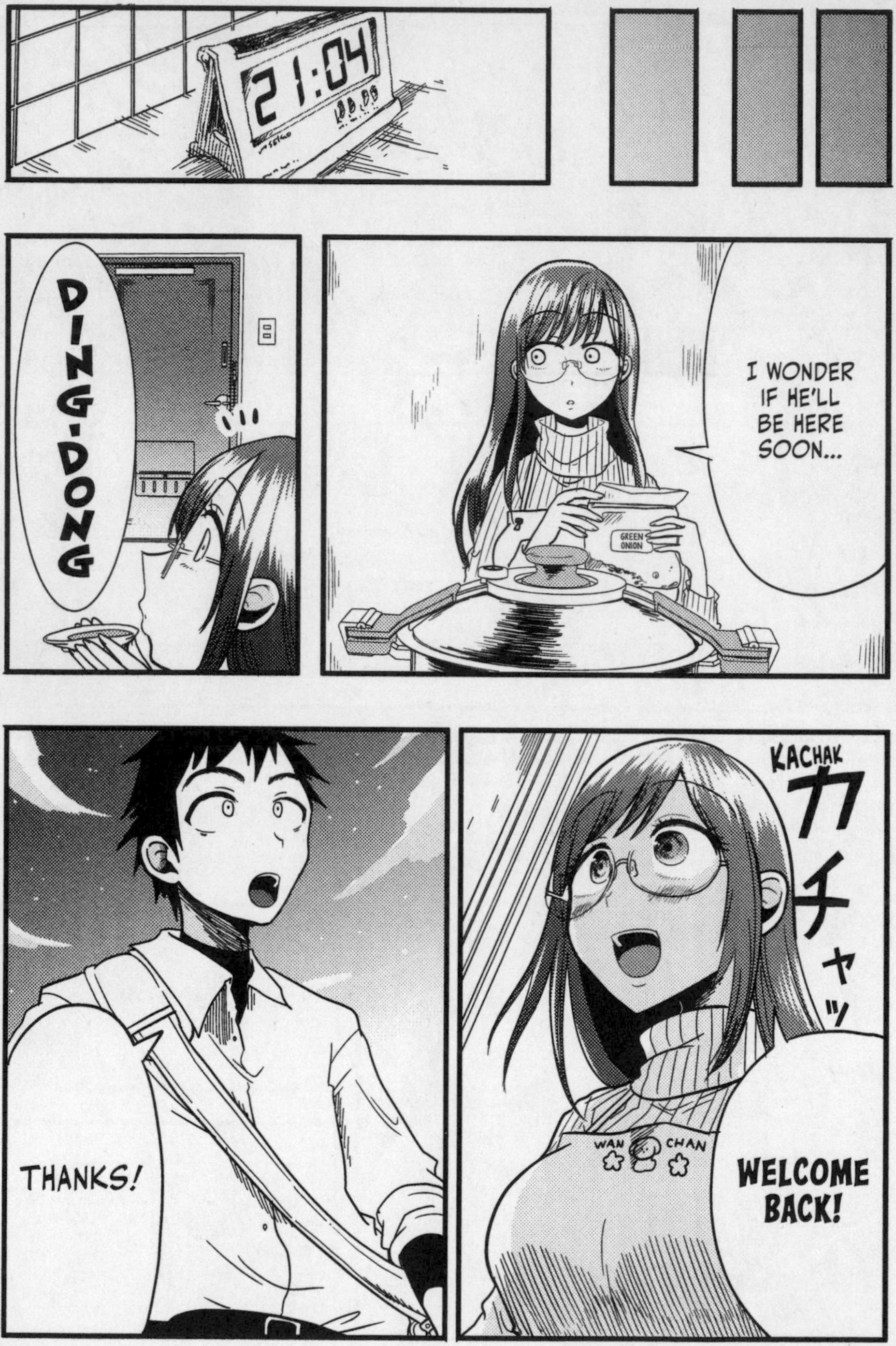
21:04
I WONDER IF HE'LL BE HERE SOON...
GREEN ONION
DING-DONG
KACHAK
カチャッ
WELCOME BACK!
WAN CHAN
THANKS!

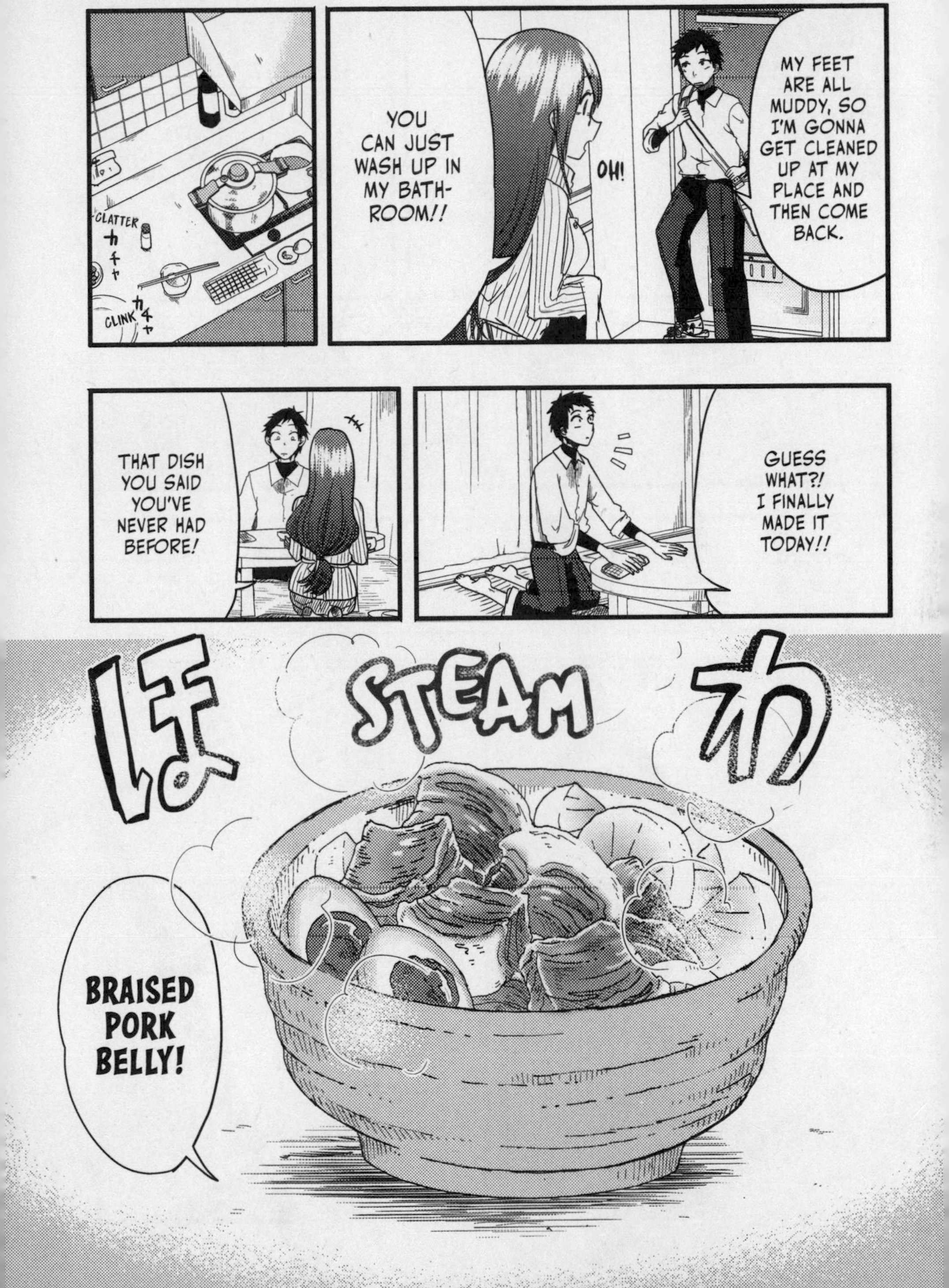
MY FEET ARE ALL MUDDY, SO I'M GONNA GET CLEANED UP AT MY PLACE AND THEN COME BACK.
OH!
YOU CAN JUST WASH UP IN MY BATH-ROOM!!
CLATTER
カチャ
カチャ
CLINK
GUESS WHAT?! I FINALLY MADE IT TODAY!!
THAT DISH YOU SAID YOU'VE NEVER HAD BEFORE!
ほ
STEAM
わ
BRAISED PORK BELLY!

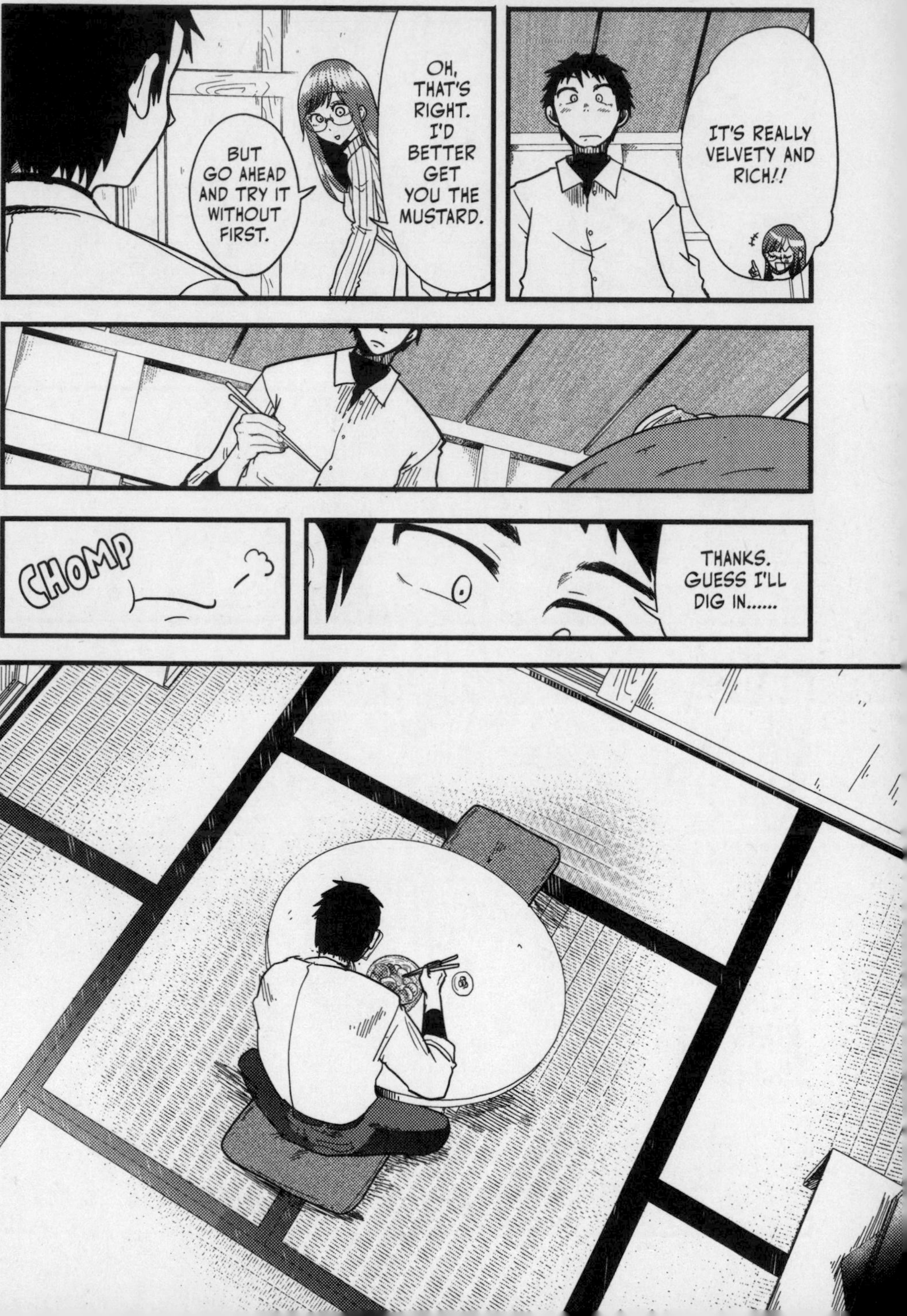
IT'S REALLY VELVETY AND RICH!!
OH, THAT'S RIGHT. I'D BETTER GET YOU THE MUSTARD.
BUT GO AHEAD AND TRY IT WITHOUT FIRST.
THANKS. GUESS I'LL DIG IN......
CHOMP

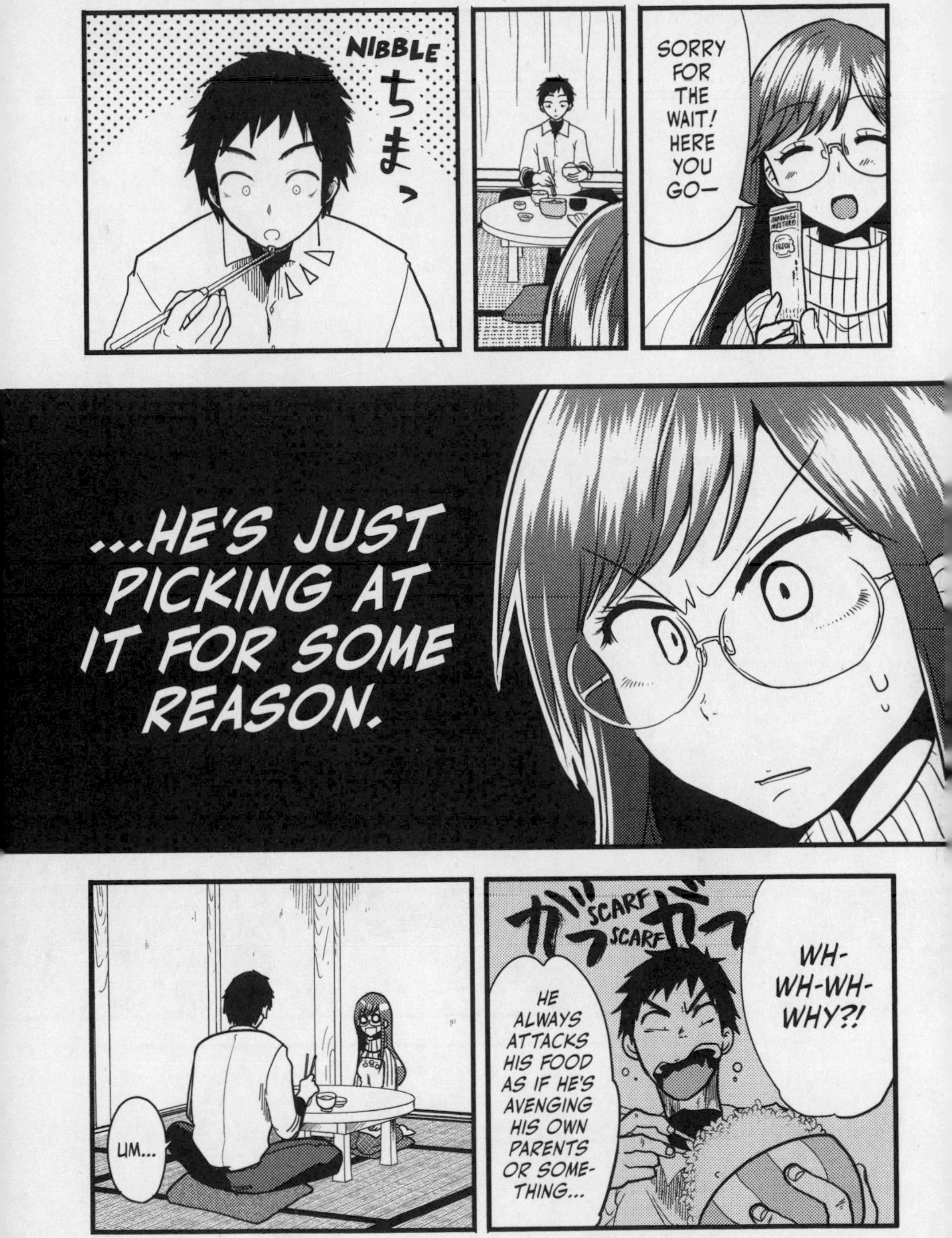
SORRY FOR THE WAIT! HERE YOU GO—
NIBBLE
ちまっ
...HE'S JUST PICKING AT IT FOR SOME REASON.
WH-WH-WH-WHY?!
ガツガツ
SCARF SCARF
HE ALWAYS ATTACKS HIS FOOD AS IF HE'S AVENGING HIS OWN PARENTS OR SOME-THING...
UM...

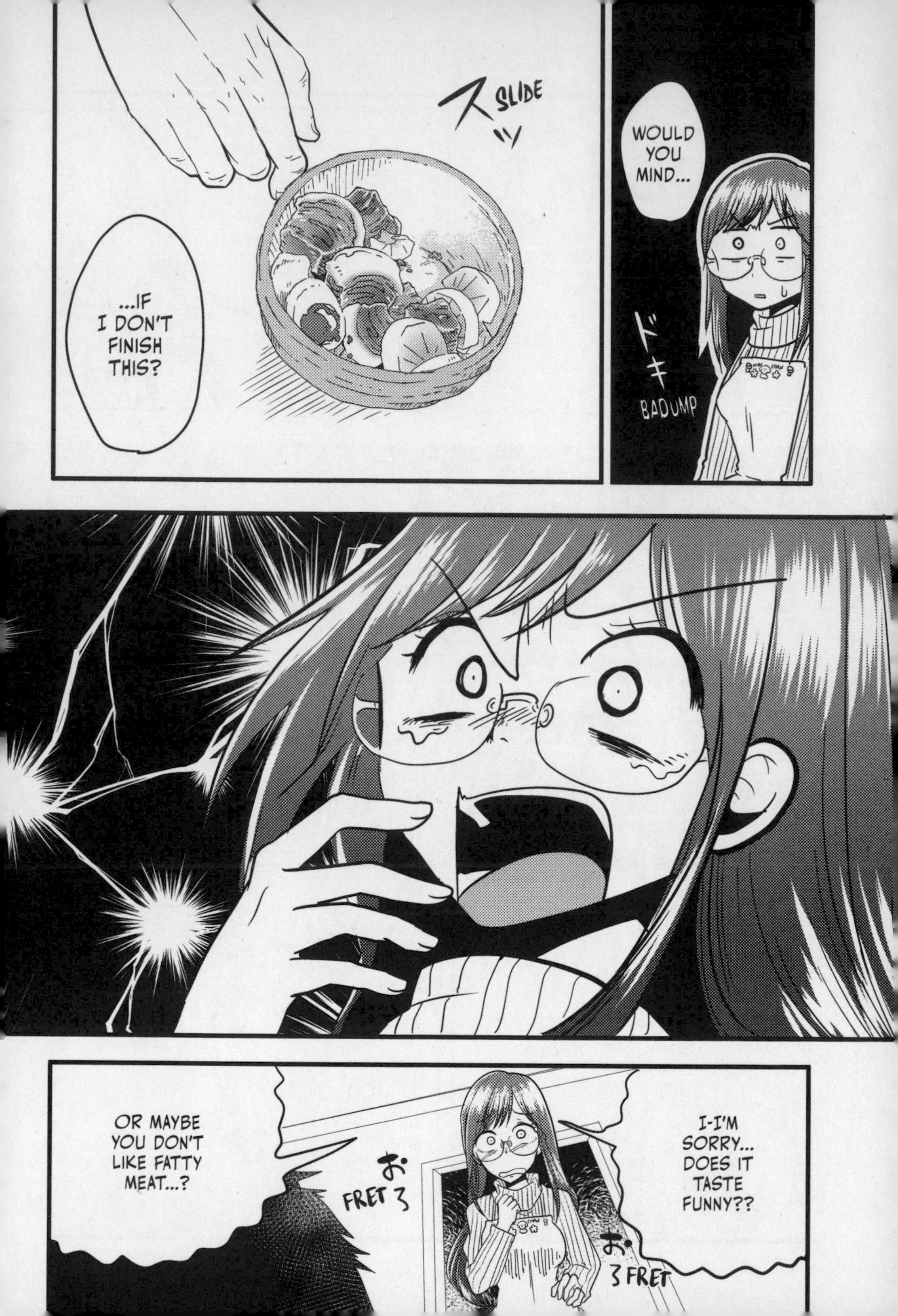
WOULD YOU MIND...
ドキ
BADUMP
スッ
SLIDE
...IF I DON'T FINISH THIS?
I-I'M SORRY... DOES IT TASTE FUNNY??
おろ
FRET
OR MAYBE YOU DON'T LIKE FATTY MEAT...?
おろ
FRET

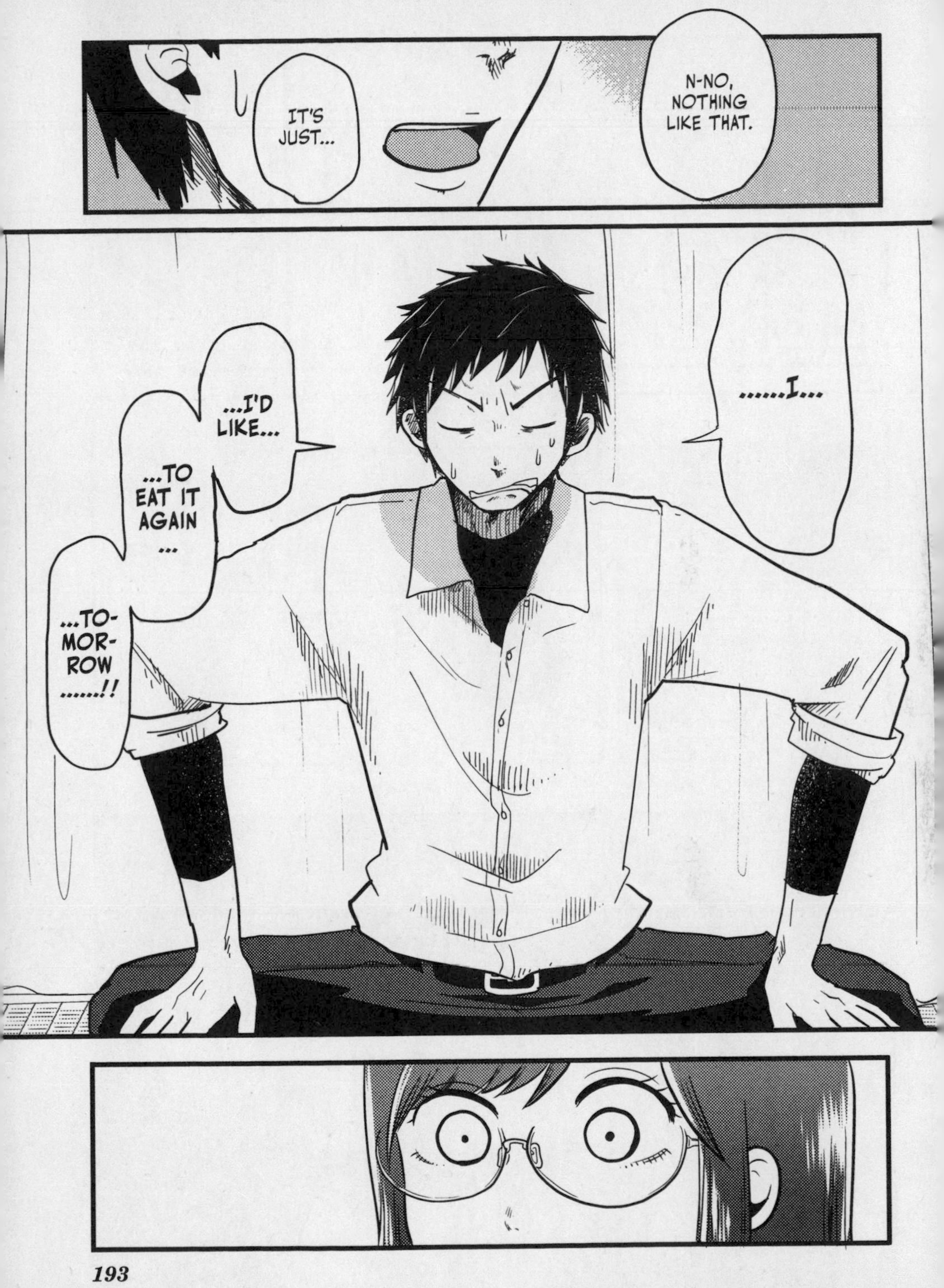
N-NO, NOTHING LIKE THAT.
IT'S JUST...
......I...
...I'D LIKE...
...TO EAT IT AGAIN ...
...TO-MORROW ......!!

AH HA HA HA HA HA HA HA!

W... WAS IT SOMETHING I SAID?!

AH HA HA HA HA HA HA HA!

PFFT!

THIS LOOKS LIKE IT TOOK A LOT OF WORK...

...AND IT'S DELICIOUS...

...SO IT SEEMS LIKE A WASTE TO JUST...

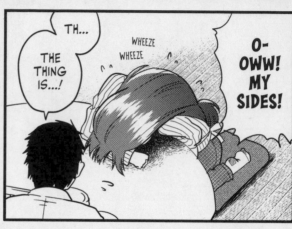

TH... THE THING IS...!

WHEEZE WHEEZE

O-OWW! MY SIDES!

WIPE

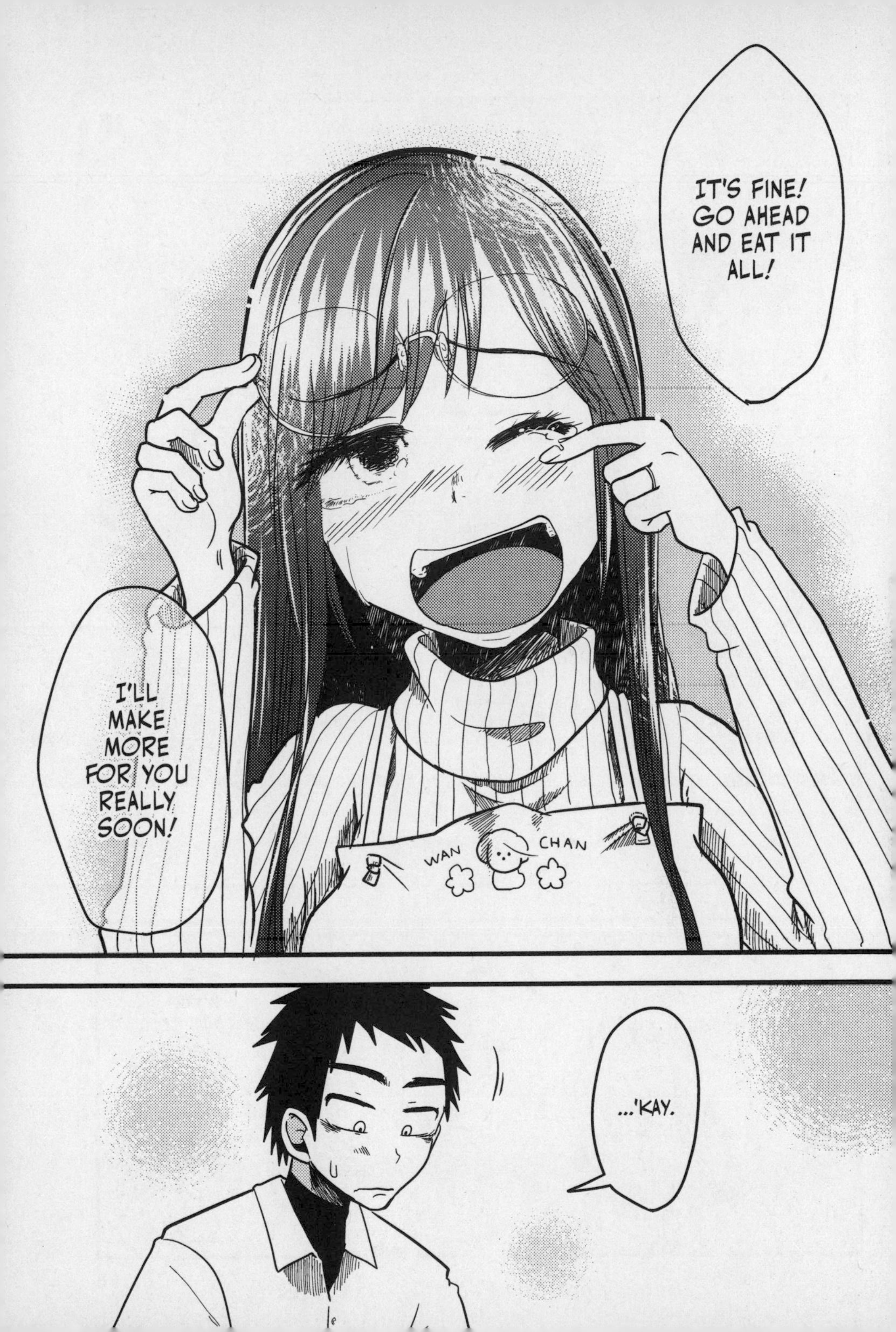
IT'S FINE! GO AHEAD AND EAT IT ALL!
I'LL MAKE MORE FOR YOU REALLY SOON!
WAN CHAN
...'KAY.

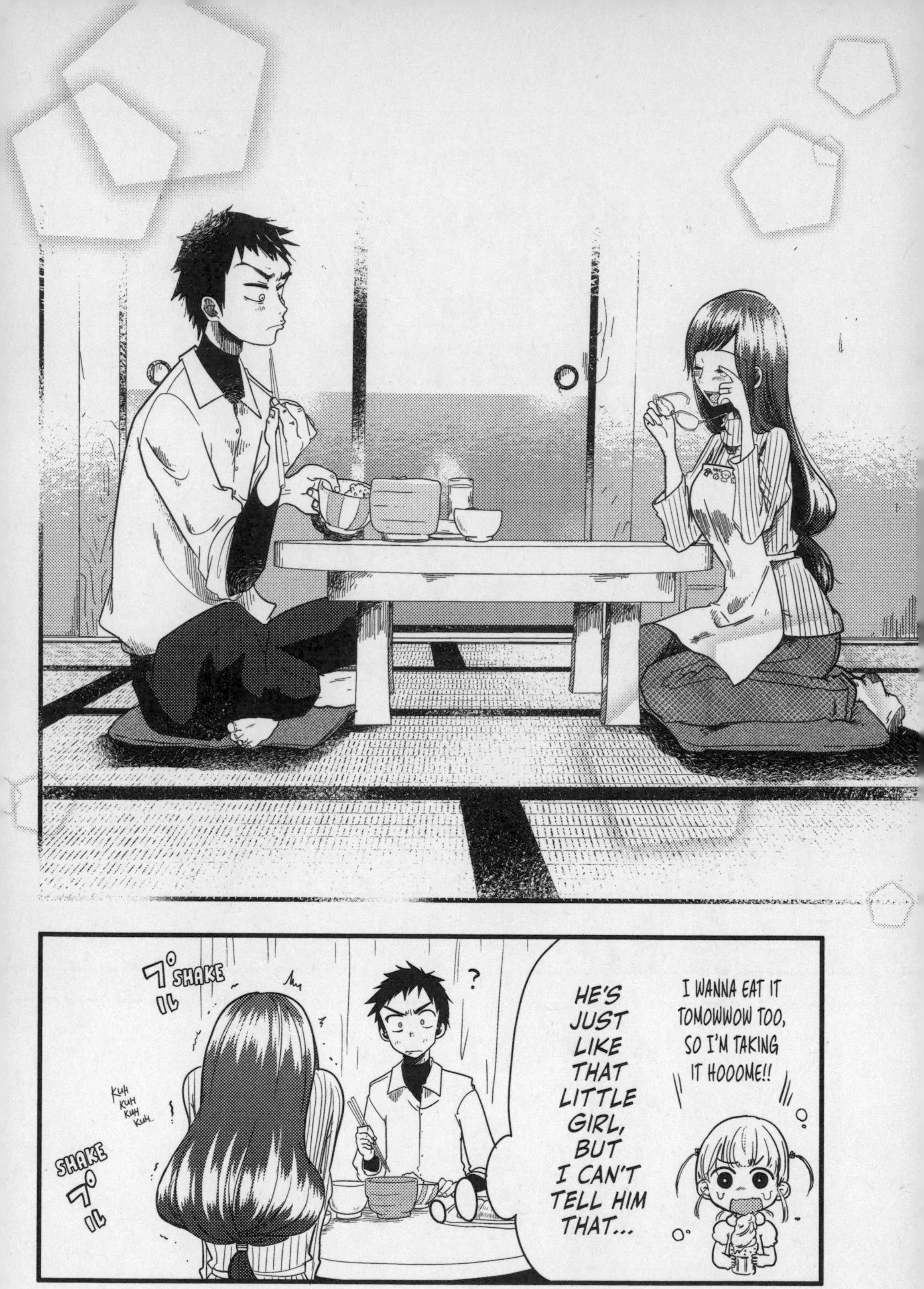
I WANNA EAT IT TOMOWWOW TOO, SO I'M TAKING IT HOOOME!!
HE'S JUST LIKE THAT LITTLE GIRL, BUT I CAN'T TELL HIM THAT...
?
SHAKE
KUH KUH KUH KUH...
SHAKE

Beauty and the **FEAST**.

Beauty and the **FEAST**

BONUS MANGA

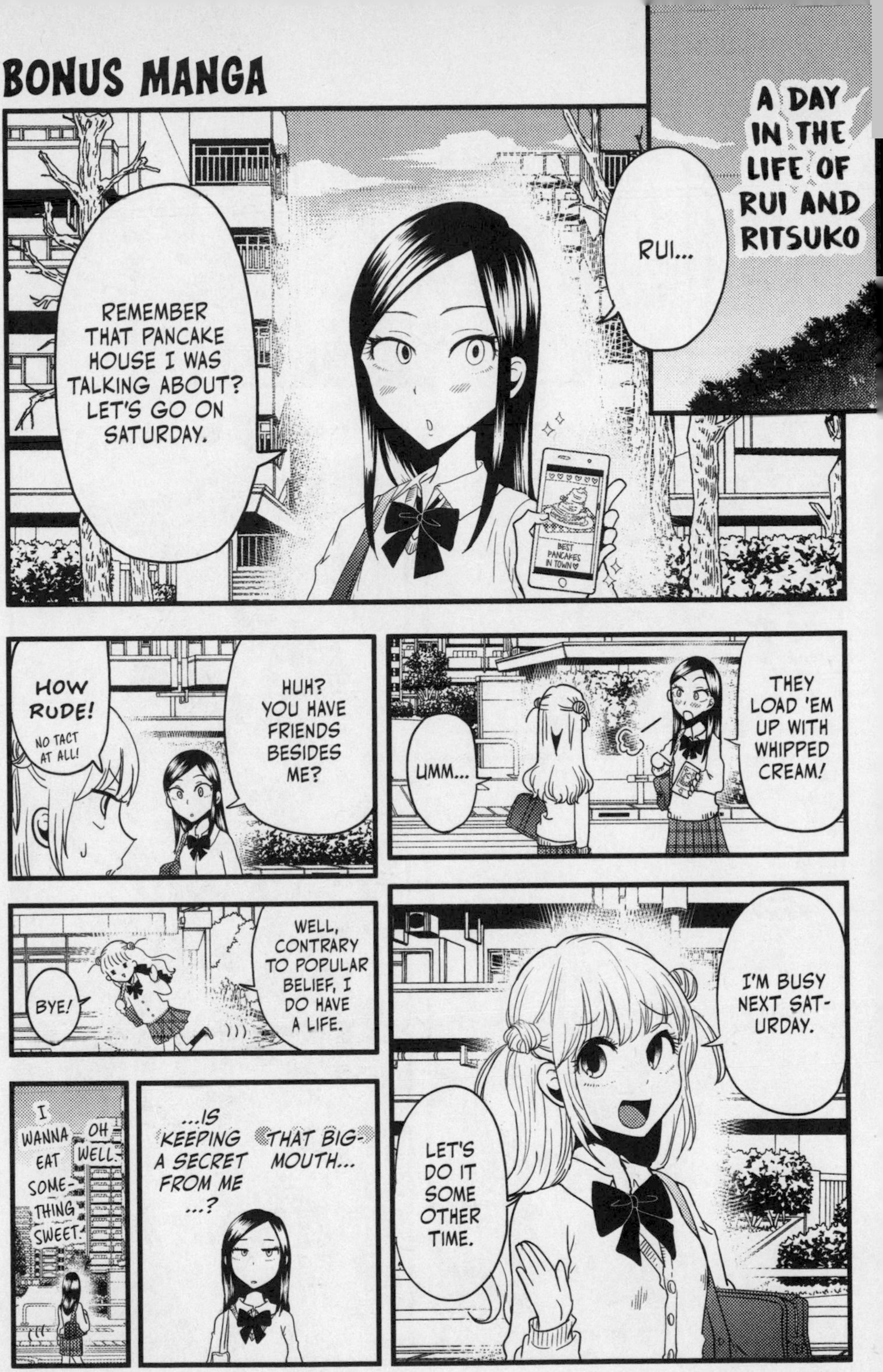
A DAY IN THE LIFE OF RUI AND RITSUKO
RUI...
REMEMBER THAT PANCAKE HOUSE I WAS TALKING ABOUT? LET'S GO ON SATURDAY.
BEST PANCAKES IN TOWN♥
THEY LOAD 'EM UP WITH WHIPPED CREAM!
UMM...
HUH? YOU HAVE FRIENDS BESIDES ME?
HOW RUDE!
NO TACT AT ALL!
I'M BUSY NEXT SAT-URDAY.
LET'S DO IT SOME OTHER TIME.
WELL, CONTRARY TO POPULAR BELIEF, I DO HAVE A LIFE.
BYE!
THAT BIG-MOUTH...
...IS KEEPING A SECRET FROM ME ...?
OH WELL.
I WANNA EAT SOME-THING SWEET.

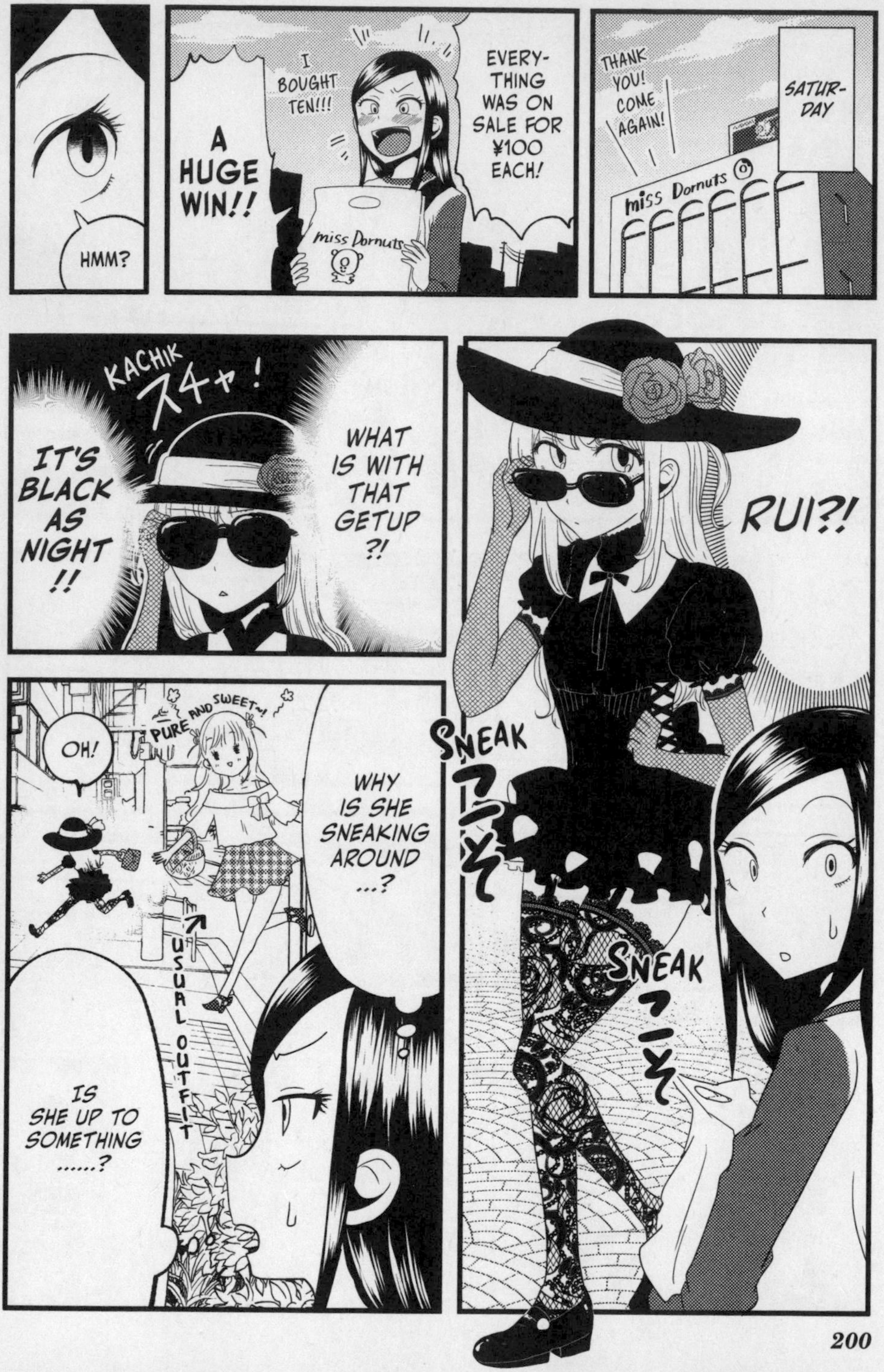
SATURDAY
THANK YOU! COME AGAIN!
miss Dornuts
EVERYTHING WAS ON SALE FOR ¥100 EACH!
I BOUGHT TEN!!!
A HUGE WIN!!
miss Dornuts
HMM?
RUI?!
SNEAK こそ
SNEAK こそ
KACHIK スチャ!
WHAT IS WITH THAT GETUP?!
IT'S BLACK AS NIGHT!!
OH!
PURE AND SWEET~!
USUAL OUTFIT
WHY IS SHE SNEAKING AROUND...?
IS SHE UP TO SOMETHING......?

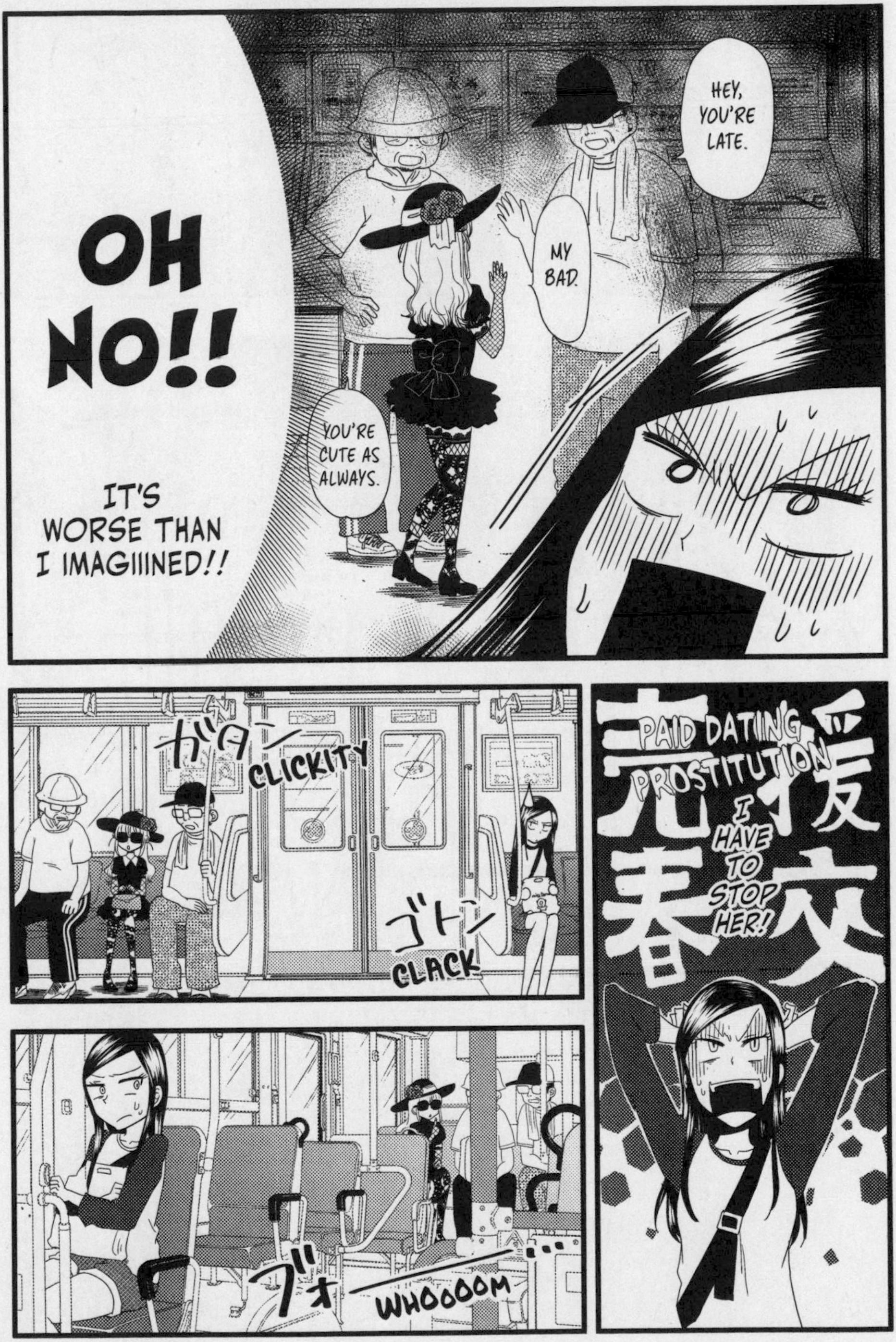

HEY, YOU'RE LATE.
MY BAD.
OH NO!!
YOU'RE CUTE AS ALWAYS.
IT'S WORSE THAN I IMAGIIINED!!
援交
PAID DATING
売春
PROSTITUTION
I HAVE TO STOP HER!
ガタン
CLICKITY
ゴトン
CLACK
ブオ
WHOOOOM

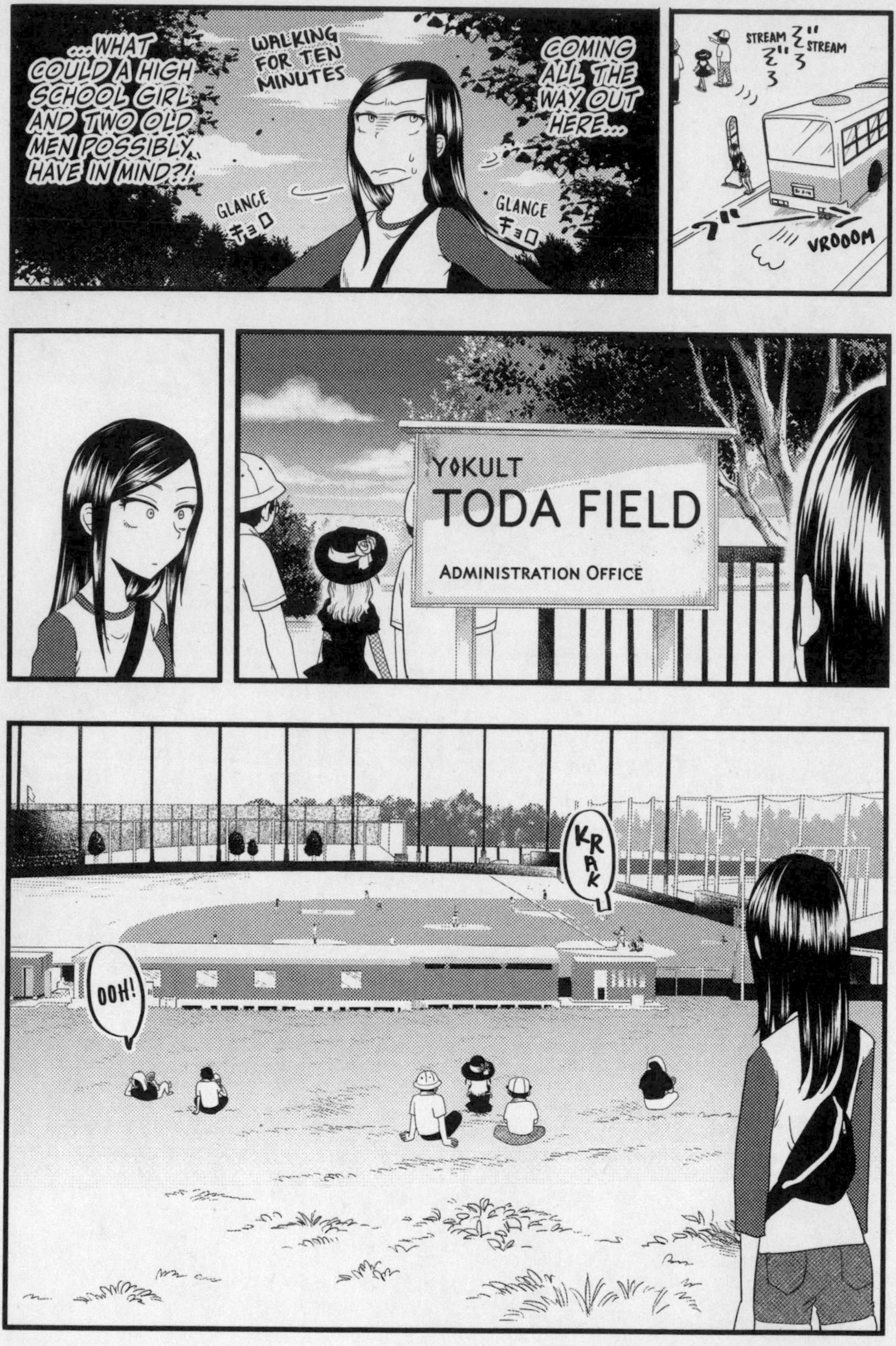
STREAM
STREAM
VROOOM
COMING ALL THE WAY OUT HERE...
WALKING FOR TEN MINUTES
...WHAT COULD A HIGH SCHOOL GIRL AND TWO OLD MEN POSSIBLY HAVE IN MIND?!
GLANCE
GLANCE
YOKULT
TODA FIELD
ADMINISTRATION OFFICE
KRAK
OOH!

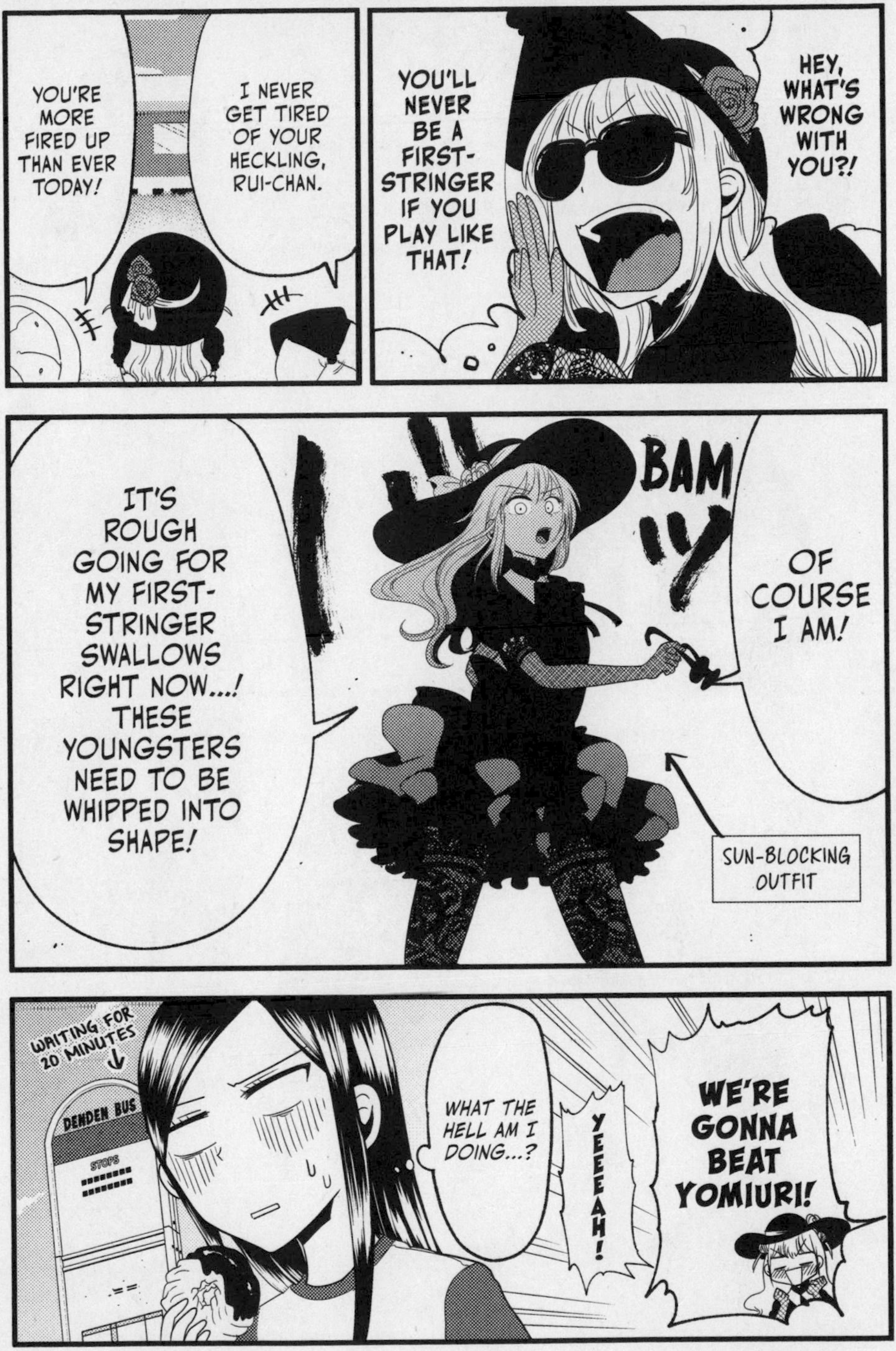
HEY, WHAT'S WRONG WITH YOU?!
YOU'LL NEVER BE A FIRST-STRINGER IF YOU PLAY LIKE THAT!
I NEVER GET TIRED OF YOUR HECKLING, RUI-CHAN.
YOU'RE MORE FIRED UP THAN EVER TODAY!
BAM
OF COURSE I AM!
IT'S ROUGH GOING FOR MY FIRST-STRINGER SWALLOWS RIGHT NOW...! THESE YOUNGSTERS NEED TO BE WHIPPED INTO SHAPE!
SUN-BLOCKING OUTFIT
WE'RE GONNA BEAT YOMIURI!
YEEEAAH!
WHAT THE HELL AM I DOING...?
WAITING FOR 20 MINUTES
DENDEN BUS
STOPS

THE END

~ THE INSIDE SCOOP: YAKUMO-SAN ~

SHUKO YAKUMO

28 YEARS OLD • 154cm • BLOOD TYPE O

THESE ILLUSTRATIONS ARE FROM THE ONE-SHOT MANGA. WHEN MY EDITOR AND I WERE LIKE, "LET'S DO A STORY ABOUT A WIDOW WHO FEEDS A BOY!", YAKUMO-SAN WAS AT FIRST SEXIER THAN SHE IS NOW. SHE WAS ALSO A CHARACTER WHO DIDN'T DISPLAY EMOTION, BUT THE MORE I DEVELOPED THE STORY, THE MORE SHE NATURALLY TURNED INTO THE EXPRESSIVE, CUTE, BIG-SISTER TYPE WE CURRENTLY KNOW. THE IMAGE I WAS GOING FOR WITH HER WAS "SOMEONE I'D LOVE TO HAVE AS A NEIGHBOR WHO WOULD SHARE HER FOOD WITH ME."

...I'M INTO VERTICALLY RIBBED OR STRIPED SWEATERS AND JEANS.

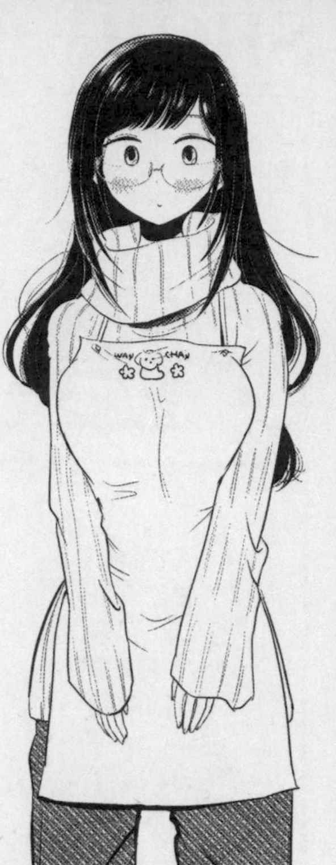

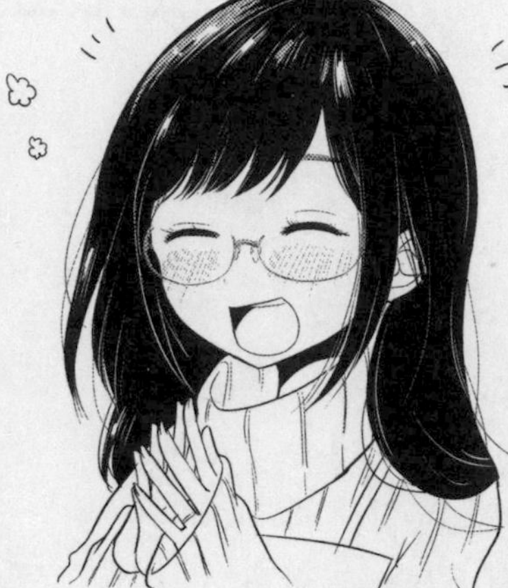

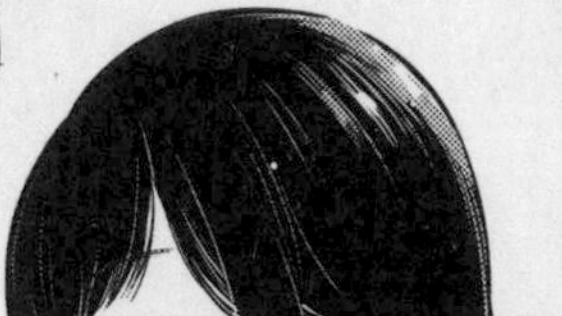

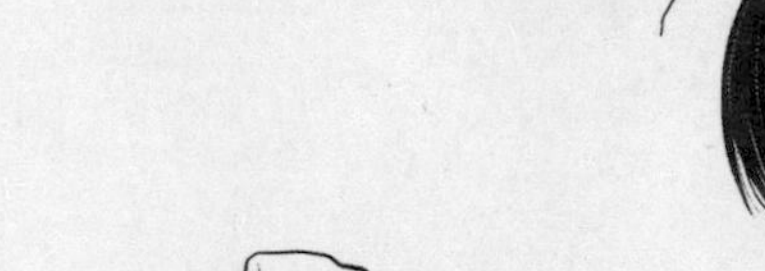

INSTEAD OF JUST LOVING TO COOK, YAKUMO-SAN IS THE TYPE WHO LOVES HAVING PEOPLE EAT HER COOKING. SHE MAJORED IN LITERATURE AT UNIVERSITY, AND SHE STILL FREQUENTLY GOES TO THE LIBRARY. HER INTEREST IN FASHION ONLY EXTENDS TO "THE BARE MINIMUM AND MOST DURABLE." SHE CUTS HER BANGS HERSELF. FOR THE PAST SEVERAL YEARS, SHE'S SAID TO HERSELF, "THIS IS THE YEAR I START A VEGETABLE GARDEN ON MY BALCONY..."

SHOHEI YAMATO
FIRST-YEAR HIGH SCHOOL STUDENT • 175CM • 63KG • BLOOD TYPE AB

THESE ILLUSTRATIONS ARE FROM WHEN THE ONE-SHOT WAS PUBLISHED. (YAMATO HAS
HARDLY CHANGED SINCE THEN...) THE IMAGE I WAS GOING FOR WAS "SOMEONE TO
WHOM I WISH I COULD FEED A LARGE QUANTITY OF FOOD"! AROUND THE TIME WHEN
THE SERIES WAS JUST A ONE-SHOT, HE HAD MORE OF A PRONOUNCED RESTING SCOWL
FACE... THE CURRENT YAMATO HAS A LITTLE MORE OF A SLEEPYHEAD VIBE.

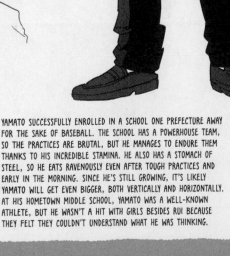

YAMATO SUCCESSFULLY ENROLLED IN A SCHOOL ONE PREFECTURE AWAY
FOR THE SAKE OF BASEBALL. THE SCHOOL HAS A POWERHOUSE TEAM,
SO THE PRACTICES ARE BRUTAL, BUT HE MANAGES TO ENDURE THEM
THANKS TO HIS INCREDIBLE STAMINA. HE ALSO HAS A STOMACH OF
STEEL, SO HE EATS RAVENOUSLY EVEN AFTER TOUGH PRACTICES AND
EARLY IN THE MORNING. SINCE HE'S STILL GROWING, IT'S LIKELY
YAMATO WILL GET EVEN BIGGER, BOTH VERTICALLY AND HORIZONTALLY.
AT HIS HOMETOWN MIDDLE SCHOOL, YAMATO WAS A WELL-KNOWN
ATHLETE, BUT HE WASN'T A HIT WITH GIRLS BESIDES RUI BECAUSE
THEY FELT THEY COULDN'T UNDERSTAND WHAT HE WAS THINKING.

RUI NISHIHARA

FIRST-YEAR HIGH SCHOOL STUDENT • 147CM • BLOOD TYPE B

ORIGINALLY, RUI WAS MEANT TO BE ON THE CHEERLEADING SQUAD BUT BECAME A BASEBALL FANATIC WHO ISN'T IN A CLUB OR ON A TEAM.

SHE AND YAMATO ARE FROM THE SAME NEIGHBORHOOD, SO THEIR PARENTS ARE FRIENDS TOO. HER DREAM FOR THE FUTURE IS TO MARRY YAMATO, BUT SHE'S BEEN TURNED DOWN BY HIM SEVERAL TIMES IN THE PAST. (YAMATO SAYS IT'S BECAUSE HE WANTS TO FOCUS ON BASEBALL.) YAMATO AND BASEBALL ARE PRETTY MUCH THE ONLY THINGS SHE THINKS ABOUT, AND SHE LETS HER IMAGINATION GET CARRIED AWAY WHEN IT COMES TO BOTH. RUI'S LOVE OF BASEBALL COMES FROM HER FATHER'S OWN BASEBALL OBSESSION. RUI'S NAME IS DERIVED FROM *RUI*, THE JAPANESE WORD FOR "BASE." LIKEWISE, HER OLDER SISTER, RAN, IS NAMED FOR "RUNS." RUI'S A PRETTY GIRL, SO IF SHE DIDN'T TALK SO MUCH, SHE'D BE POPULAR. IN ANY CASE, "BEING GOOD AT BASEBALL" IS THE TRAIT SHE FINDS MOST ATTRACTIVE IN THE OPPOSITE SEX, SO SHE'S FIXATED ON YAMATO. RUI HAS INHERITED HER FATHER'S OPINION THAT "A BASEBALL PLAYER'S WIFE SHOULD BE AN ANNOUNCER," SO RUI'S DOING HER BEST TO STUDY (ESPECIALLY ENGLISH) TO BECOME AN ANNOUNCER HERSELF.

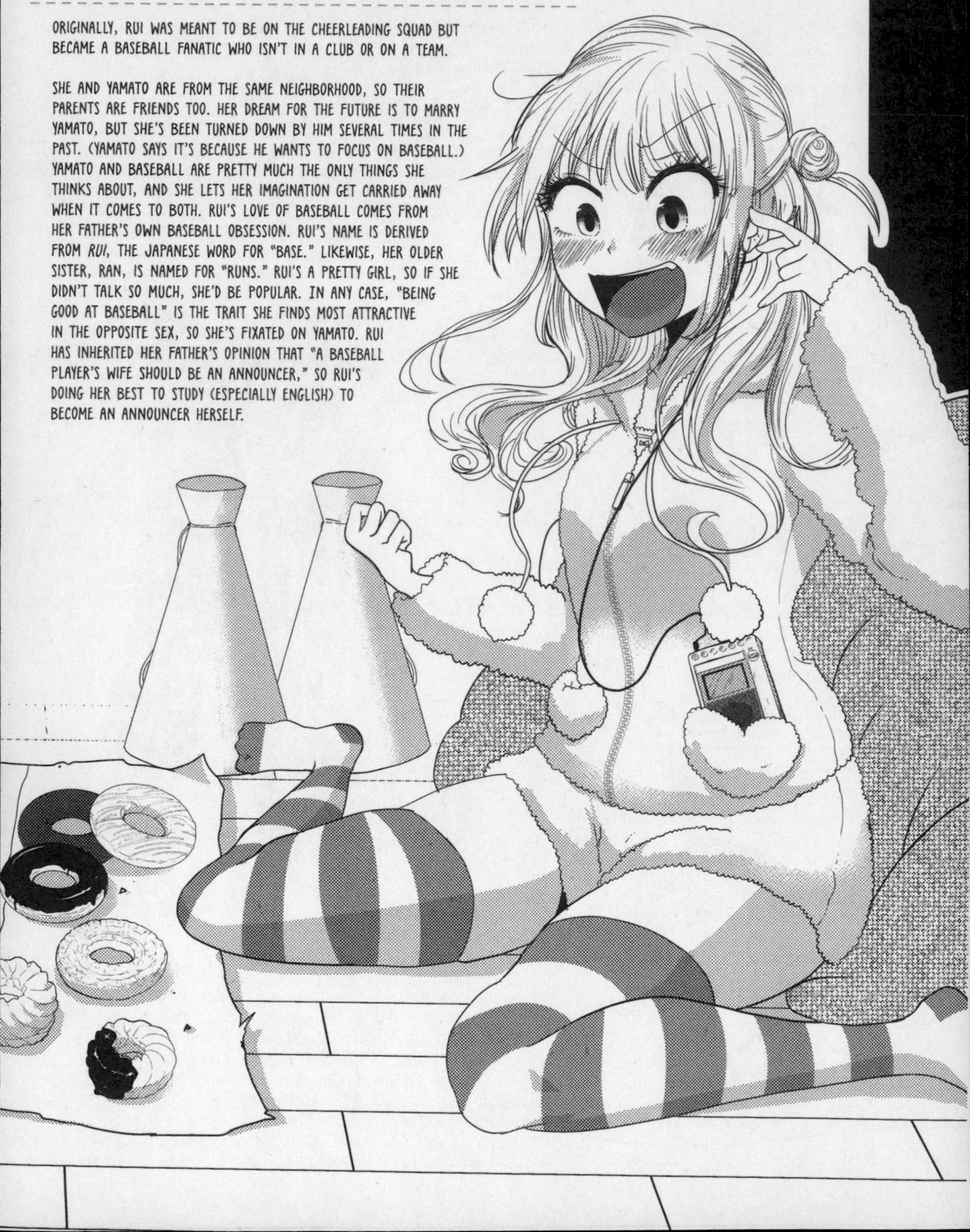

RITSUKO NAGAI

FIRST-YEAR HIGH SCHOOL STUDENT • 161CM • BLOOD TYPE A

A RARE GIRL WHO BEFRIENDED RUI (WHO DOESN'T SEEM TO HAVE MANY FEMALE FRIENDS). I PICTURED RITSUKO IN MY HEAD AS COOL, CALM, AND COLLECTED, BUT SHE MAY NOT HAVE TURNED OUT THAT WAY.

SHE INITIALLY BECAME FRIENDS WITH RUI BECAUSE THEIR STUDENT NUMBERS (ORDERED BY SURNAMES) IN CLASS WERE RIGHT NEXT TO EACH OTHER. RITSUKO DOESN'T EVEN KNOW THE RULES OF BASEBALL BUT LIKES IT BECAUSE "IT'S KIND OF INTERESTING," THANKS TO RUI'S PASSIONATE DISCOURSE ON THE SUBJECT. HER GRADES ARE TOP-NOTCH, AND SHE IS CURRENTLY AT THE HEAD OF HER CLASS. IN ADDITION TO ACADEMICS, RITSUKO ALSO DOES WELL IN ATHLETICS. SHE WAS ON THE TRACK AND FIELD TEAM IN MIDDLE SCHOOL AND EVEN PARTICIPATED IN A MEET AT THE CAPITAL. SHE APPEARS UNAPPROACHABLE AND SO ISN'T POPULAR, BUT THERE'S AT LEAST ONE BOY WHO SECRETLY HAS HIS EYE ON HER. RITSUKO HAS A SERIOUS SWEET TOOTH, AND SHE HAS A RITUAL OF EATING HOMEMADE WHIPPED CREAM RIGHT OUT OF THE BOWL AFTER EVERY EXAM. SHE'S CHILDHOOD FRIENDS WITH KOUTA, THE BOY WITH CATLIKE EYES WHO'S ON THE BASEBALL TEAM. THEIR RELATIONSHIP ISN'T GIRLFRIEND AND BOYFRIEND BUT MORE LIKE BIG SISTER AND KID BROTHER.

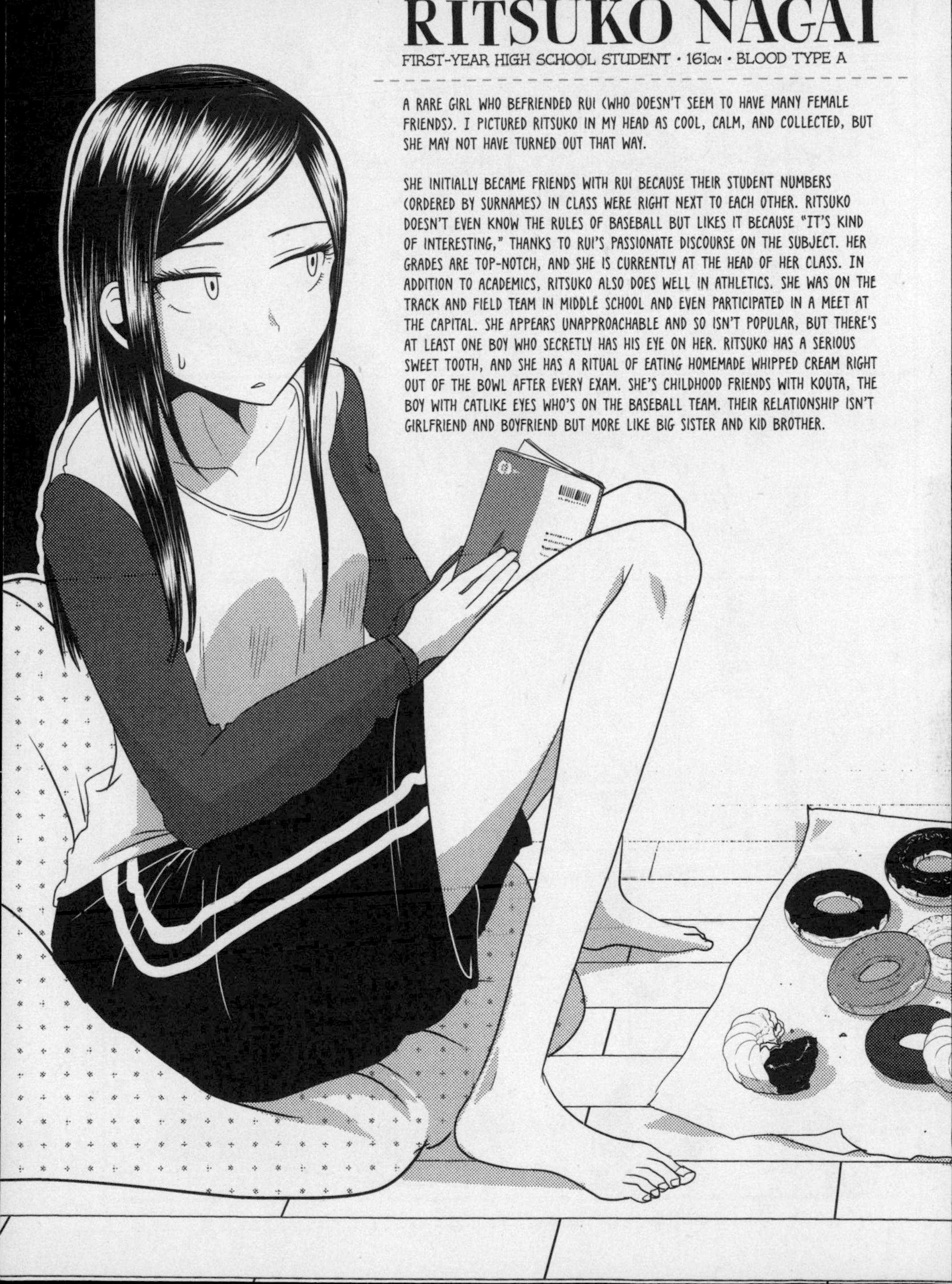

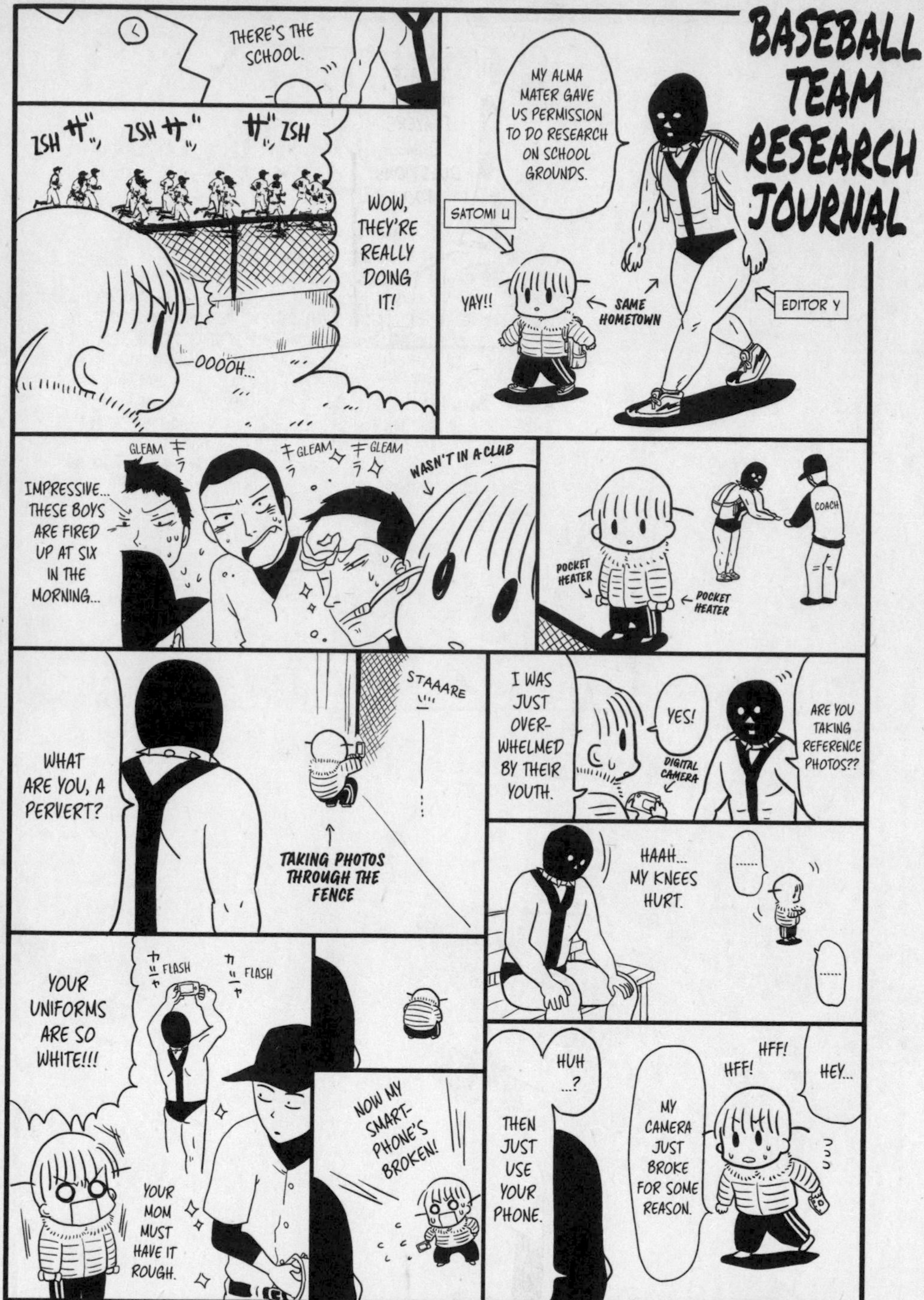
BASEBALL TEAM RESEARCH JOURNAL
MY ALMA MATER GAVE US PERMISSION TO DO RESEARCH ON SCHOOL GROUNDS.
SATOMI U
YAY!!
SAME HOMETOWN
EDITOR Y
THERE'S THE SCHOOL.
ザッ ZSH
ザッ ZSH
ザッ ZSH
WOW, THEY'RE REALLY DOING IT!
OOOOH...
COACH
POCKET HEATER
POCKET HEATER
WASN'T IN A CLUB
キラ GLEAM
キラ GLEAM
キラ GLEAM
IMPRESSIVE... THESE BOYS ARE FIRED UP AT SIX IN THE MORNING...
ARE YOU TAKING REFERENCE PHOTOS??
YES!
DIGITAL CAMERA
I WAS JUST OVER-WHELMED BY THEIR YOUTH.
STAAARE
TAKING PHOTOS THROUGH THE FENCE
WHAT ARE YOU, A PERVERT?
HAAH... MY KNEES HURT.
......
......
HEY...
HFF!
HFF!
MY CAMERA JUST BROKE FOR SOME REASON.
HUH ...?
THEN JUST USE YOUR PHONE.
NOW MY SMART-PHONE'S BROKEN!
カシャ FLASH
カシャ FLASH
YOUR UNIFORMS ARE SO WHITE!!!
YOUR MOM MUST HAVE IT ROUGH.

FLASH I BOUGHT A SELFIE STICK TO TAKE REFERENCE PHOTOS FROM UP HIGH. IT'S REALLY COOL.

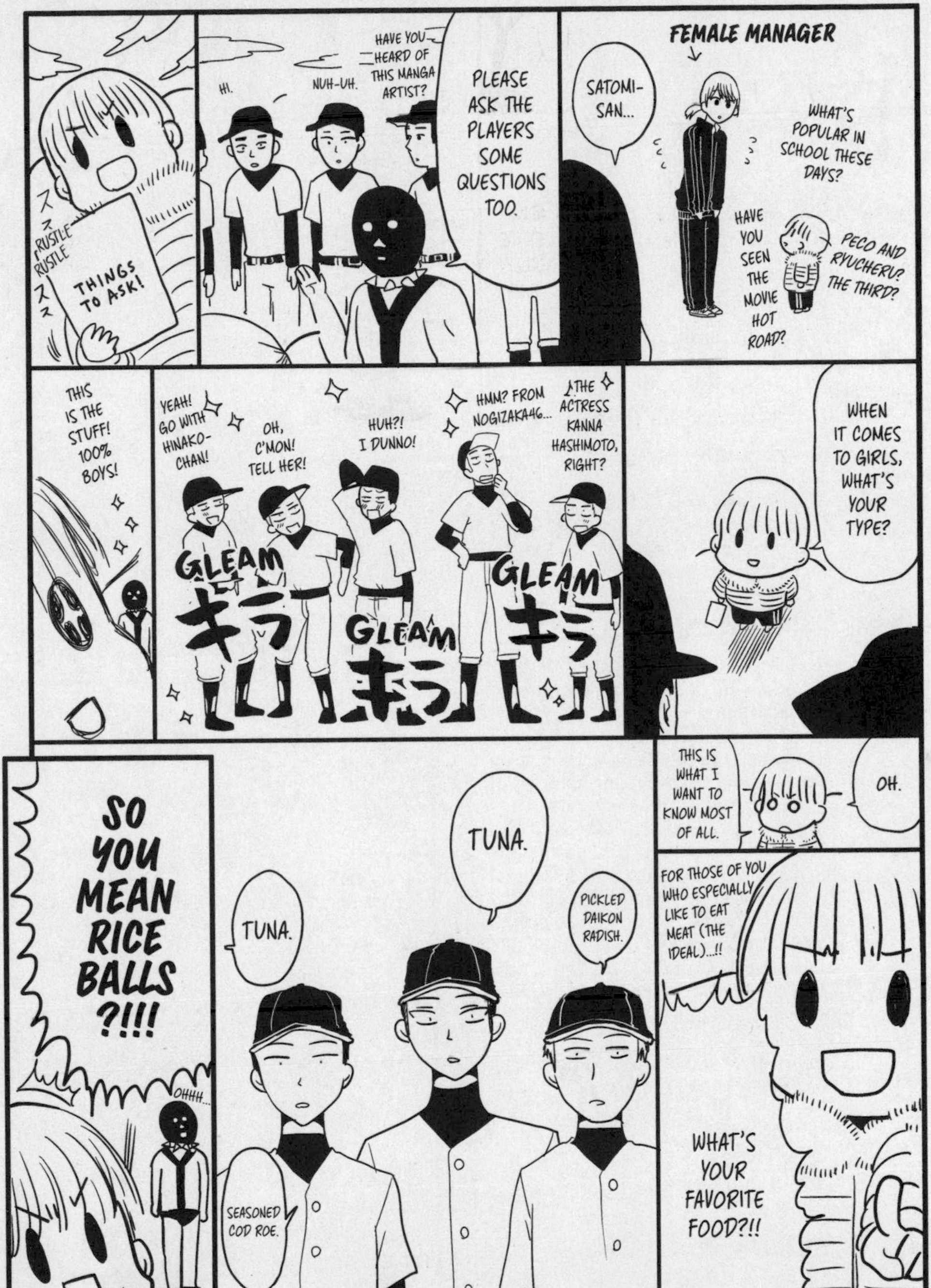
FEMALE MANAGER
SATOMI-SAN...
WHAT'S POPULAR IN SCHOOL THESE DAYS?
PECO AND RYUCHERU? THE THIRD?
HAVE YOU SEEN THE MOVIE HOT ROAD?
PLEASE ASK THE PLAYERS SOME QUESTIONS TOO.
HAVE YOU HEARD OF THIS MANGA ARTIST?
NUH-UH.
HI.
RUSTLE RUSTLE
THINGS TO ASK!
WHEN IT COMES TO GIRLS, WHAT'S YOUR TYPE?
THE ACTRESS KANNA HASHIMOTO, RIGHT?
HMM? FROM NOGIZAKA46...
HUH?! I DUNNO!
OH, C'MON! TELL HER!
YEAH! GO WITH HINAKO-CHAN!
GLEAM キラ
GLEAM キラ
GLEAM キラ
THIS IS THE STUFF! 100% BOYS!
OH.
THIS IS WHAT I WANT TO KNOW MOST OF ALL.
FOR THOSE OF YOU WHO ESPECIALLY LIKE TO EAT MEAT (THE IDEAL)...!!
WHAT'S YOUR FAVORITE FOOD?!!
PICKLED DAIKON RADISH.
TUNA.
TUNA.
SEASONED COD ROE.
SO YOU MEAN RICE BALLS?!!!
OHHH...
THE END

WELL, COME TO THINK OF IT, WHEN I WAS IN MIDDLE SCHOOL, I ATE A TON OF CANNED TUNA.

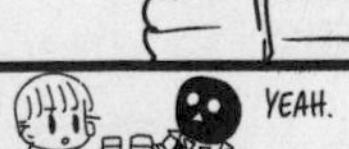
YEAH.

A BIG THANK-YOU TO THE BASEBALL TEAM!

Beauty and the FEAST

SATOMI U

(1)

Translation: **Sheldon Drzka**
Lettering: **Ken Kamura**
Cover Design: **Abigail Blackman**
Editor: **Tania Biswas**

BEAUTY AND THE FEAST Volume 1
© 2016 Satomi U/SQUARE ENIX CO., LTD.
First published in Japan in 2016 by SQUARE ENIX CO., LTD.
English translation rights arranged with SQUARE ENIX
CO., LTD. and SQUARE ENIX, INC.
English translation © 2021 by SQUARE ENIX CO., LTD.

ISBN: 978-1-64609-062-4

Library of Congress Cataloging-in-Publication Data
is on file with the publisher.

Printed in the U.S.A.
First printing, March 2021
10 9 8 7 6 5 4 3 2 1

SQUARE ENIX
MANGA & BOOKS
www.square-enix-books.com